Architects on Architecture

CREDITS

Art Direction and Design:
DeMartin, Marona & Associates, Inc./Ed deMartin, Margaret Bailey.

Printing:
Halliday Lithograph, West Hanover, Mass.

Binding:
Haddon Craftsmen, Scranton, Pa.

Paper:
Oxford Paper Mills' Sheerwhite Impregnated Smooth.

Cover:
Holliston Mills' Roxite DF.

Cover Screening:
Auto Screen Print, Inc., Pennsauken, N.J.

Endpapers:
Rhododendron Cover, Strathmore Paper Company.

*The type for this book was set by York Typesetting Company of
New York City. The body copy is set in 10/13 Palatino, the chapter
titles in 12 pt. Palatino Semi Bold, and the captions in 8 pt.
Palatino Italic. Helvetica and its variants are used on the title page.*

Architects on Architecture

New Directions in America

Paul Heyer

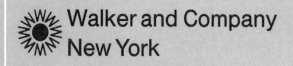 Walker and Company
New York

to my father and mother

The art of progress is to preserve order amid change and to preserve change amid order — *Alfred North Whitehead*

ACKNOWLEDGEMENTS

For their advice and suggestions about the architects I chose to include in this project I am thankful to: Arthur Drexler, John Entenza, Esther McCoy, Vincent Scully, Jr., Allan Temko, and my friend Jerzy Soltan. I remain disturbed at having had to exclude the work of many other talented architects.

I am deeply indebted to those who have helped develop my understanding and love of architecture: F. R. S. Yorke, Oskar Stonorov and Edward Stone, in whose offices I found opportunity and encouragement; and the many architects and friends in the other arts with whom I have studied and worked, and from whom I have benefited.

However short it must fall, I wish to express formal gratitude to the architects whose work is described in this book. Without their complete cooperation, confidence, patience in subjecting themselves to interview, suggestions for clarification in their respective texts, and generosity in making illustrative material available to me, this book would certainly not exist. I can never repay their kindness and, I hope, I will never forget their example of conviction. For making available essential additional photographs I am grateful to the Museum of Modern Art, New York. In addition, I would like to thank Saarinen Associates for providing photographs of Eero Saarinen's work.

For assistance in the preparation of the manuscript I am deeply indebted to the following: Roger Jellinek, whose encouragement, judgment, and editorial advice were a great help to me; Edward Burlingame, for his great interest and patient advice; and Juliet Attree, whose administrative skills, aid in transcribing the tapes of the interviews, and typing and checking of the entire manuscript gave the boundless support to this project for which any gratitude would be inadequate.

CONTENTS

PREFACE

This book presents the design approach, the ideas and the major work of some forty leading American architects or groups of architects. The architects were not selected to represent a preconceived point of view, but because their buildings, their statements and their concerns seem generally to represent the most positive and influential directions in American architecture today. Their approaches are diverse, ranging from the more rational, structural, to the more plastic, sculptural, while certain consistencies also indicate parallel ideas in general directions.

Although presented as a series of individual studies, I hope this book may offer its readers a comprehensive view of the problems and directions of modern American architecture generally. The project was conceived as an attempt to create a forum for the statement and discussion of various ideas, since a serious exchange of views remains the exception among architects.

The organization of the material in this book is loosely geographical, permitting an orderly yet flexible development of ideas and themes. A rigorous formal structure was avoided: form follows function and here the presentation of diverse ideas and approaches is the book's function. Major themes, usually suggested by the work or ideas of a particular architect, and limited historical commentary to provide the reader with a frame of reference, precede or are incorporated into individual presentations. Therefore, themes that are central to the convictions of many architects are often presented in a particular chapter. Consequently, it is not necessarily an architect's importance that determines the length and content of a chapter.

In the spring of 1964, extended interviews with the architects were tape recorded and these form the basis of this book. The architects also made lecture notes and written statements available to me for reference; where I found it to be advantageous I supplemented the tapes with limited extracts from these. For readability, I present what was initially a question-and-answer dialogue as a continuous statement by each architect. As far as possible I tried to preserve the architects' original words in order to retain the individual character of their expression and to lend immediacy to their statements. These statements are identified in the book by a slight separation from the rest of the text. Chapters were submitted to the architects for their clarifications, not censorship. Critical passages in the text, the frank expression of a given architect's personal convictions, are intended to be constructive, and it is appropriate to preface them by saying that while it is easy to criticize, it is extremely difficult to design architecture that is worthy of criticism.

Environment, education, the search for significance in architecture and the formulation of beliefs are central to each architect's approach. They also impose certain limitations. Where skepticism of a personal position has resulted in a reevaluation leading to a different approach, I have discussed these doubts and their outgrowth. Through this medium I have tried to trace the evolution of a personal design philosophy. Patterns of development and the exploration of ideas are evident in key buildings. Therefore, I have discussed each architect's philosophy in relation to his principal buildings, and I have attempted to define how an idea evolved and where it led, or is leading.

My purpose was to clarify and define those aspects of his work particular and pertinent to each architect, and these naturally provide the focus of the presentations.

However, before the interviews, I posed four broad questions to all of the architects to provide a context for their remarks.

First, that an architect must assume a dual responsibility: social and personal. Can these two responsibilities be compatible and complementary?

Second, that our burgeoning cities pose one of the most crucial issues of our time, and that it is the architect's responsibility, as a potential leader in his society, to help establish systems and principles for the growth and organization of our environment. Today there is no common understanding or method to allow diversity within order. How are we to regard Alfred North Whitehead's dictum, "The art of progress is to preserve order amid change and to preserve change amid order"?

Third, that unlike other artists, the architect cannot work alone. He must organize assistants and consultants, and over a period of time with the help of these he must preserve the integrity of his initial concept through the complete design process. As problems become larger and more complicated, are new methods of practice implied?

And fourth, that each generation assumes the responsibility for the education of its successors and that the values, directions and methods taught must have a significance and durability. What might these be?

INTRODUCTION

In the post-World War II years, leadership in the sphere of architecture is generally recognized as having centered in the United States. American architecture at its best remains a major force on the world scene. Scientific and technological advances, an expanding economy and a rising standard of living, the constant pressures of urbanization, a freedom of approach, and a pragmatic response to problems have all contributed to this circumstance. But, although many notable individual buildings have been constructed, the positive impact of American architects on urban America seems inconsequential. Unfortunately, too, work of quality is the exception. If one were to deduce standards from the buildings being constructed today, the inevitable conclusion would be that a sweeping and dramatic upgrading of those standards is one of the principal challenges to the profession.

When an architect talks of quality values in a building, he means many vital concerns. The building must enhance and dignify the lives of those who use it; to do this it must embrace its social purpose. It must develop a rapport with its site, be aware of its environment. It must have functional integrity and structural honesty, while making an expressive statement. It must be more than a slick facade and must avoid fads, to achieve a forthright statement of purpose without degenerating into depressing sterility or exhibitionistic vulgarity. Its appropriateness and relevance will come from a rational, common-sense disciplining that, coupled with the architect's sensitivity, will integrate and unify the whole. It must have a sense of timeliness and a sense of tradition: timeliness because it expresses its age—a century whose processes and techniques should usher in one of the great architectural epochs—and tradition because architecture, with its continuing concern for space, light and texture, is a great and enduring art.

But the complexities of architecture create formidable barriers to achieving the building of quality. The efforts of many are required to bring it about, including a client or committee who often have only a limited appreciation of the values that the architect seeks to create, and a building industry that is traditional in the worst sense—high costs for mediocre craftsmanship. If a building survives all this, from idea, to detail, to execution, it is usually an alien in surroundings more often than not shabby, sterile, or even vulgar—an environment utterly indifferent to the values the building seeks to demonstrate.

If, as is frequently said, we are not sure what we want as a society, we do seem sure that we want it at a bargain price. Our attitude towards office building, maximum rentable space with minimum aesthetic and social responsibility, has permeated our way of thinking like a cancer. Even the budget for some churches is established on a cost per pew basis. Concern for meaning and dignity, concern to elevate and celebrate life seem very remote. Unfortunately, this is the cultural climate within which the committed architect works.

Assuming that a building stands as a worthy or, in the case of the Seagram Building in New York, a noble statement, what then might its fate be? In 1963, the Appellate Court of the State of New York ruled against the owners to tax the Seagram Building on the initial cost of construction rather than on the rentable value of comparable New York office space. The Court stated that the extra expense of this building was "never satisfactorily explained, and does not do much credit to the sagacity of the corporate management."

Another reflection of our society's attitude towards its physical environment is in the preservation of what already exists, and is good. The wrecker's ball removed McKim, Mead and White's Pennsylvania Railroad Station in New York. The terminal space of travertine and granite, the space that *announced* arrival, is gone. Certainly it looked sad and gray before its demolition. Lack of care, attention and respect had been the cause.

Throughout the country, buildings of architectural and historic consequence are continually being razed to make way for parking lots and other so-called improvements. These acts of vandalism, these assaults on our heritage, evoke faint murmurs of protest, nearly always too late. Our bulldozer cult is a sad reflection upon the values of an affluent society. We are creating bleak, oppressive cityscapes, devoid of principles, a despair of mediocrity and ugliness.

Architecture is a social art. Consequently the architect must assume a vital role in shaping our physical environment. It seems especially fitting to remember today that a primary emphasis of the modern movement in architecture was the expression of a new and better way of life for the many: a social promise. Yet the architect's attitude towards what he can do to fulfill this promise is now one of resignation. In addition, our urban and suburban physical environment seems to accelerate our deteriorating condition: there are daily reports of increased poverty, crime, racial tension, drug addiction, and general anomie.

Suffocating subways, traffic jams, parking problems, foul air and polluted waters are now the facts of urban life. Our space explorations show that we have mastered a technology which could be applied to improving our physical world. However, the establishment of good planning in relation to our potential alone would not alter our basic values, values that compromise irrevocably the larger intentions of architects and planners.

Housing, for example, is the principal land consumer in our cities; in America today it is primarily the product of the investor, the contractor, the building codes and the tax structure. The consumer adapts. "Modern" and "functional" have become synonymous with "acceptable minimum." Anything not essential, anything that does not represent a viable investment, is discarded as useless luxury. Occasionally, capricious design elements are injected because they are considered good for public relations.

Suburban areas have developed a stupefying sameness; identical boxes on identical-sized lots with a little something at the front door. Except for the occasional shopping center, community facilities are invariably lacking since there is no profit in their provision. In the city it is a similar story. Apartment buildings have become monontonous and dreary expanses of brickwork punctured by badly proportioned rectangles for windows. They contain Kafka-esque warrens of corridors and anonymous doors, flashily "decorated" lobbies and, sometimes, unimaginative minimal balconies and scant roof gardens. New concepts in housing are difficult to promote because they compete with conventional, profitable developments, and because the people who advocate them have no political muscle. Clearly, what is needed to house our society are not unsympathetic apartment slabs or isolated minimal boxes, but complete neighborhoods that provide for and express the daily complexities of the life of the total community.

The magnitude of our challenge is inescapable and points inevitably towards new concepts. It is estimated that by the year 2000 the urban population of the United States will be around 370 million people—more than twice that of 1960. As urban concentration increases, it becomes clear that we must plan in order to preserve our rapidly vanishing, despoiled landscape. "In the next forty years we must rebuild the entire urban United States. . . . We must act to prevent an Ugly America . . . our society will never be great until our cities are great," said President Johnson in a speech made in 1964. "The city of man serves not only the needs of the body and the demands of commerce, but the desire for beauty and the hunger for community."

The ability to plan, order and discipline energies comprehensively is the mark of a mature society. Without good planning, without the pursuit of sound objectives, we fall victim—as our surroundings testify—to happenstance and accelerated chaos. The individual building makes an important contribution to a cityscape, but it must also be an element in harmony with a grander total vision. A building's influence extends beyond its property lines, and if our cities are to be great, our citizens must learn to recognize and demand great architecture. The solution to our urban problem requires a concerted effort, from the level of the Federal Government down, to undertake essential reforms and democratically establish the framework for order.

A good example of the positive influence of government initiative, in this instance an economic incentive that was something like an eleventh-hour transfusion for many cities, is the Urban Renewal Program, a direct result of the Housing Act of 1949. By this Act, the Federal Government was authorized to pay cities for at least two-thirds of the difference between the cost of acquiring and clearing blighted areas—often prohibitive for a private agency or government at a lower level to absorb—and the resale price to a private developer. Successive legislation, notably the 1954 Housing Act, has improved and expanded the program to finance commercial redevelopment, and the rehabilitation and conservation of existing buildings—in short, comprehensive urban planning. Previously, private property had been taken over by local governments for public use, now it could be taken for a direct public *purpose:* not only the removal of slums but also the planned reshaping and renewing of the city. The Federal Government now invests $700 million a year in the program. At the end of 1964, Urban Renewal Commissioner William L. Slayton reported that, excluding the cost of land, approximately $6.90 of private redevelopment investment is made for every $1.00 of Federal grants.

There are further hopeful signs. In 1965 a new Department of Housing and Urban Development was established, giving the cities an official representation in the Cabinet for the first time. Then, in January 1966, the President announced the "Demonstration Cities Program," which proposes a coordinated attack by Federal and local agencies—to be administered by the local community itself—on single blighted neighborhoods in 60 to 70 cities of varying size. Adding to existing urban and social programs, it proposes to allocate an additional $2-3 billion (probably an inadequate amount) over a five-year span, to improve the chosen communities and thereby set an example to others. Instead of clearance, it emphasizes rehabilitation, thereby minimizing relocation; it aims at low-rent housing and is formulated to allow neighborhood residents to participate in the plan. In these respects it differs from the usual urban renewal program and represents a refreshing new approach to these problems. The criticisms of "government interference" and "subsidies for uneconomic land use" are clearly refuted by the chaos that ensues from the principle that land is a commodity to be freely exploited. It is also patently obvious that many human needs are not going to be served by an entirely uncoordinated and undirected libertarianism. Land is a community to which man belongs and which, in turn, belongs to man.

Unfortunately, planning means many things to many people. It certainly need not constitute an imposition on individual freedom, but may rather be a process—enterprise within a rationale—to enable a natural, healthy evolution from where we are, to where we might ideally like to be. A very large segment of the urban population lives not where it wants to but where it has to. The result is a poor choice between bumper to bumper traffic snarls and bad mass-transit facilities.

Sullivan said that we built what we were and we were what we built. Somehow, soon, urban growth must provide benefits and opportunities to the majority. Architects and planners who can translate a society's needs into a meaningful vision, and the politicians and leaders in the community who can establish the necessary legislation, must collaborate to this end. Our cities need to be places of inspiration and stimulation that permit both privacy and community; centers of human thought and achievement that allow man to develop fully as an individual; even places of beauty.

The characteristic most expressive of the contemporary architectural scene is diversity. Unfortunately, according to those architects who regard significance in architecture as a corollary of order, this diversity of approaches to architectural problems is producing chaos in our cityscapes.

In view of the complexities of our restless, experimental society, it is hardly surprising that ours should be a time of diversity. This is an outgrowth of one of the most sweeping changes in the history of mankind, one that in the nineteenth century turned society from an agrarian into an essentially urban-industrial one: the Industrial Revolution. Revolution rather than evolution has produced an era of change amid search. It has also produced a time of opportunity, the implications of which, as we move into an era of almost inconceivable scientific and technological potential, we have still fully to realize.

Today, ours is a world that is increasingly questioning the intellectual and moral foundations of society, one that is probing the riches of science while remaining intrigued by the myths that underlie our civilization as though to seek out truths the rational mind has been unable to offer. The external world of our actions and the internal world of our thoughts have become divided, and the result has been a lack of unity in our lives, a fragmentation of collective and individual interests, of intellectual and emotional reactions.

Where pre-industrial society found its inspiration in the natural world, ours finds its stimulus in a scientific-mechanical one. In

America, a scarcity of skilled labor, a rapidly expanding consumer market, and the easy availability of natural resources within national boundaries have encouraged mechanization. With mechanization have come many forceful ideas that have changed our way of regarding and responding to things, for example, the economy of means principle, which is derived from the *idea* of mechanization. The restrained, no-more-no-less-than-is-correct-and-appropriate, has become a philosophy, a fundamental tenet of our time. To extend the economy of means principle to a moral level is to reaffirm the ageless idea that truth is beauty. This is a guide for the employment of the new materials and construction techniques that an age of advanced technology has given us.

There is an inseparable relationship between material and shape, structure and form. The architect, like the sculptor, naturally desires to express the intrinsic potential characteristic of the materials he employs and, conversely, to employ suitable materials to realize desired ends. In the past, structures had been essentially forms in compression, discontinuous structures of stone or brick where one element was placed upon another. With their slender constructions, the Gothic builders had tried to extend the limitation of this building technique to the extreme.

The problems of weight and mass that had limited architecture in the past were overcome when the industrial age provided us with two materials of great strength, both with the ability to be economically employed in tension and compression to form continuous structures: steel and reinforced concrete. It became possible to achieve greater structural efficiency with less visible effort, greater heights and spans, the enclosure of more space with less mass, and greater flexibility in the enclosure of that space.

The functional expression and drama of the suspension bridge could not have been achieved in anything but steel and steel cables; nor could the delicacy and transparency of Buckminster Fuller's geodesic domes; nor could Mies van der Rohe's elegant structural skeletons. The poetry of such structures is that of the immediately visible, correct and economic employment of a tremendously strong material.

In comparison with the linear nature of steel construction, reinforced concrete is a plastic material that can change in shape as it expresses the exact flow of stresses through a structure, a material that, with the exception of expansion joints, can be "endlessly" continuous; where the enclosure of space and structure can be one. Pre-cast concrete for precision and speed of assembly, systems of pre-tensioning and post-tensioning for greater strength, and improved methods of formwork for better finished surfaces, are among the refinements that have expanded the possibilities inherent in this responsive material. Steel and reinforced concrete, as well as new synthetic materials and advances in timber construction, have introduced methods of building with possibilities beyond those ever presented to architects before. Naturally this has led to great diversity of expression.

Then, too, new solutions to new problems were—and are being—sought. A roving, experimental inquiry followed the challenge. In America this search occurred in a country without really deep-rooted architectural traditions. This permitted a sense of freedom that has allowed American architects and artists in other creative fields to make important contributions to the development of new techniques and new ideas.

It is important, however, to distinguish between what is new and what is merely fashionable. New methods, new ideas concerning the relationship of form to content, pointing in turn towards new possibilities, have for the serious artist nothing to do with fashion. Rather, they represent the pursuit of significant directions of new growth.

The challenges of our scientific-mechanical world have often been interpreted with reference to a mode of thought that has had a profound influence on architectural developments: pragmatism. Resolving a problem pragmatically avoids abstract generalizations. Thus, general design determinants are modified by the precise circumstances and requirements of a particular problem. This does not mean that the architect starts afresh with each design— eventually even specific answers start to point towards general answers—but he does avoid *a priori* solutions in seeking to understand the individual laws that all buildings generate.

With increasing concern for the specific, there also has been a move away from an absolute aesthetic. Modern thought and particularly modern science have challenged the very idea of absolutes, of ideal or perfect states. Relativity and quantum physics ushered in, at the beginning of this century, what is known as the Second Scientific Revolution. The reign of determinism, of belief in absolutes, was thereby ended and the age of indeterminism began.

In architecture, an absolute aesthetic had produced an ideal: buildings designed for unified, supposedly known or predictable —and therefore essentially static—functions. Limited in its content, or awareness, and particularly in its interpretation of the world, this conception of architecture by the end of the nineteenth century had become one generally preoccupied with aesthetics. Consequently it was narrow in aim and tended to elicit narrow and limited responses from architects. However, architecture, paralleling developments in other disciplines, has in this century begun to abandon its faith in absolutes, in a finite design process and exclusive design concepts.

For instance, the move away from an absolute aesthetic is evident in buildings designed to respect the idea of growth and change, and to complement their environment. At an urban scale, for example, is the collective image of lower Manhattan. It is not the result of a finite design process, of one exclusive design concept, but the product of many random changing forces—an open viable process.

The magnitude of the problems and opportunities facing the architect today clearly requires him to be both cognizant of the interaction of the disciplines and the forces that act in his time, and responsive and sensitive to them. He needs to respect as a whole, a unity, what appears as divided and complex—but not by ignoring contrary factors or applying the few pat answers. Oversimplification is thus replaced by a synthesis in which even the determinants themselves cannot be considered as absolutes. Architecture must also look beyond contemporary forces and disciplines and must recognize that objects themselves are perceived and reacted to in different ways by different people.

Although the Greeks thought in terms of idealism, it was with a fundamental difference from those who, for example in the nineteenth century, relied upon classical patterns of thought. The Greeks were not atomistic in the application of their knowledge. They did not make specific judgments within one framework of reference—for example, art purely in aesthetic terms. The Greek writers were poets, philosophers and teachers, and while their intention was to create a thing of beauty, they also sought to go beyond this to show man's true moral and social nature.

To the Renaissance architect, believing in the idea of the "universal man," knowledge also appeared as homogeneous. Art and science appeared as one. Not surprisingly, architects facing the enormous technical challenges of the nineteenth century, which demanded a broader range of knowledge, forgot or ignored the importance of keeping architecture on a broad base. A great deal of our misplaced emphasis today, both in practice and in education, stems from this time.

For example, our system of architectural education has at its foundation the ideas of the nineteenth century. Principles of formal instruction owe much of their authority to the academic tradition established by the École des Beaux-Arts in Paris. The Bauhaus tried to change this and develop a new comprehensive set of principles appropriate to our epoch; however, it is largely the Beaux-Arts system that remains with us, instead of a more fundamental one, intellectually abreast of the complexity of our present problems and the resources available to solve them.

The Beaux-Arts avoided the realities of a problem by inventing a schedule of detailed requirements called the "program." This approach encouraged the architect to think in narrow terms. Today, our legacy from this is the architect who follows the practice of working from a client-formulated program. Clients presenting the architect with a program for a new building inevitably think of a familiar building that resembles what they think they will need. Invariably this is a myopic view of needs, and starts the architect over halfway along in the creative process, rather than at the beginning, when an imaginative and perceptive interpretation of real needs should occur.

Another dubious innovation of the Beaux-Arts was the *esquisse* or "sketch problem," a method of testing a student's ability which often produced results that were brilliant, but of a rather superficial nature. The student architect, isolated in a private cubicle that divorced him from all sense of reality, waiting for the detached moment of inspiration, was given a specific program which he then proceeded, usually during the course of a day, to resolve into a preliminary design presentation. This type of problem solving still persists in our schools. Students "survive" probably only because the process of problem resolving itself can be so absorbing. With the resources of knowledge at an architect's disposal today, his training obviously should be of a different nature. The student should be exposed to many aspects of his subject during his formative years. Design is of course vital. But an architect must also be taught to sense the forces in a structure, to understand the history of architecture not as one of appearances, but as form deriving from cultural forces and from methods of construction; to be aware that aspects of heating, lighting and acoustics can enrich an architectural solution when they are a part of the design process—considered later, they almost always detract; and to have a knowledge of the natural laws of the human environment and of the individual's response to them.

The need for a more viable design process, one that respects complexity and our scientific potential, is naturally related to the type of world we see in the future. In his presidential address to the British Association for the Advancement of Science in 1964, Lord Brain said: "The important division between people is not between the classical and scientific outlook on life, but between those who have been educated to see the world in terms of the rapidly changing environment which science is creating, with all its potentialities, and those who see it in terms of the static environment and frozen emotional attitudes of the past . . . we must prepare all our people for a new world which will be quite unlike the old.''

But architects have little more than the most fragile areas of agreement on what the physical nature of the new world might be, and without a central order or discipline architecture has become the domain of the individualist. This freedom implies that the architect has, in a sense, to educate himself, but what is gained by freedom, is lost by lack of order. The innovators are few: Most architects need a framework for action if their work is to have individual clarity and collective meaning.

Individual clarity takes on a special meaning today because the sense of liberation in architecture and other arts comes at a time when there is a new audience that imposes greater responsibility on the creative individual. Instead of a sensitive, cohesive audience —an educated elite—the artist faces many groups with many levels of receptivity. To the individual patron, on whom the artist has always relied, is now added a mass patronage created by the impact of mass education. As a result, indiscriminate recognition seems more of a danger in our permissive age than was the neglect of the creative individual in the past. We are only too familiar with the frequent ridiculous forms that are reared up as buildings today, forms decked out in nonsensical paraphernalia that is a travesty of all that is noble in the art of architecture.

The idea of collective meaning also has a new importance. With the pressures brought by the Industrial Revolution came as well the means to shape our physical environment. Architects struggled to understand how to employ those means. Since there was no agreement on how to determine and direct change, random forces began to create the uncontrolled fabric of cities. In a time of maximum change, there was a minimum of predetermination. In employing new building methods and materials and in responding to social changes, the architects of this century have produced numerous brilliant individual structures, but this has been at the expense of the unity, harmony and scale that are fundamental to a civilized and healthy enviroment. In the search for the new, it is easy to overlook the limited role that isolated buildings play in the city.

The architect, like the artist, must attempt to bring diversity into a harmonious and viable unity to preserve diversity while not allowing it to freewheel into chaos. It is a delicate, yet vital, balance.

Order and unity are not a mold, a constraint tantamount to dictatorship. Instead they reflect the understanding of a hierarchy of values, a recognition of objectives, and an agreement on principles. These establish a framework not for uniformity, but for purposeful action. Chaos comes from uncertainty and indecision; convictions are the prelude to order and unity. Convictions, that is, in significant directions.

Paul Heyer
New York City, Spring 1966

THE DEVELOPMENT OF MODERN ARCHITECTURE

It seems incomprehensible to us today that the unadorned structures that have become symbols of our age and stir our imagination with their scale and daring should have been considered unacceptable at the turn of the century. Ideas that have now been assimilated and become synonymous with our culture had to be vigorously defended and pursued.

Faced in the latter half of the nineteenth century with the unprecedented implications of urbanization and the challenge of using an unknown science and technology inventively, architects retreated to a preference for the known, to the styles of classic architecture. This gave rise to eclecticism; an architecture of borrowing and of free selection. Beaux-Arts was the education; the academy was the spirit. The resulting approach had two particularly skillful practitioners: Henry Hobson Richardson and the office of McKim, Mead and White.

Richardson's was a love of Romanesque forms, which he used in broad, simple flat surfaces. He gained strength and drew analogies from history, rather than directly imitating it. His romantic, robust architecture and his imaginative use of stone in arched structures was not unknown to, or unappreciated by, Louis Sullivan. In the Marshall Field Warehouse, built in 1885-1887, and one of his and Chicago's finest structures, Richardson was moving towards simpler forms and their expression.

McKim, Mead and White's was a love of the elegance of the early Italian Renaissance. They carefully reproduced buildings and details that they admired, and their craftsmanship was usually superb. Often it was superior to and more eloquent than the original itself, and of a quality too rarely seen today. Their well-mannered, grandiose architecture reflected a cultivated taste, and was seductive to those desiring dignified, prestigious buildings.

But eclecticism produced an architecture detached from the reality of the pressures of the Industrial Revolution. Art and science were pursuing diverse paths and architecture was adrift; the result was a period of reaction from the most important facts of the time. What architecture needed was not nostalgia for the past, however beautifully executed, but the utilization of industry's new potential in order to tackle its own particular problems. In the early impulse to utilize the latent potential of the new technology, the seeds of modern architecture were sown by many who were not even architects, and who were in different parts of the world.

The Crystal Palace for London's great exhibition in 1851 was an early Victorian concept without precedent. Joseph Paxton employed contemporary industrial techniques to produce a completely prefabricated structure of cast iron and glass, the first of its type on such a grand scale. With its lightness, transparency, machined elegance and speed of erection, it majestically expressed the potential horizons of the new technology. Although for many it was a realized dream of the future, its extreme break with tradition offended the sensitivities of some "cultured gentlemen." Faced with "the machine," England in the 1860's found emotional security in a craft movement that was something of an anachronistic rejection of it. William Morris stated that the "root and basis of all art lies in the handicrafts." Although many interesting buildings resulted from this movement, the English had essentially turned their backs on an industrial technology that was the most advanced in the world, an age that they themselves had created.

In the United States, as early as 1848, a five-story factory of iron skeleton facade construction erected in New York by James Bogardus had floors that were supported on iron columns rather than by exterior masonry walls. Employing the same principle and using prefabricated parts, Bogardus erected many buildings in several American cities; the St. Louis river front district had several among its more than 500 iron structures. This system of construction is one of the principal influences on the development of an American architectural style.

However, the most significant developments in the United States took place in Chicago in the last two decades of the nineteenth century, after the Great Fire of 1871 had created the opportunity to rebuild the central area. The rapid growth of this burgeoning economic center for the entire Middle West and West resulted in congestion and in the escalation of land values; the only antidote was to build upwards. In New York, Elisha Graves Otis had developed in 1857 the world's first safe passenger elevator, thereby solving the problem of vertical transportation. In addition, the development of techniques for manufacturing rolled steel enabled architects to build safe, economical high-rise structures. The subsequent interaction led to the birth of a new architectural form: the skyscraper.

The weight of solid masonry construction had imposed limits on the height of a building. Daniel Burnham and John Root had extended this to the extreme in 1881, when they erected the Monadnock Building, a seventeen-story structure with walls twelve feet thick at the building's base. More modest in vertical aspirations but equally forceful and excellent was the Auditorium Building in 1889, one of the last masonry structures by Dankmar Adler and Louis Sullivan. A challenge of great functional complexity—it housed a business block, a hotel and an auditorium—it was Sullivan's first great opportunity for a powerful statement. The auditorium is acknowledged to be one of the finest acoustic chambers built; a shambles today, it is being restored by Skidmore, Owings and Merrill. Although the massive masonry of both of these Chicago buildings demonstrated a spirit of clear and simple structure, they represented a grand close to a chapter that had endured for centuries; in the new age of technology, dawn was already breaking on the idea of a slender, structural steel skeleton.

In 1883, William Le Baron Jenney was responsible for the first skyscraper free of the limitations of masonry—a ten-story, fireproof, well-lit office building for the Home Insurance Company of Chicago. Whereas this building found the inspiration for its expression in history, his Leiter Building, constructed the same year as the Auditorium Building, moves towards a much more

The Crystal Palace, London, England.

Marshall Field Wholesale Store, Chicago, Illinois.

unadorned contemporary expression. Here Jenney hung the external sheathing walls to a pure structural steel skeleton, the base of which was the length of a Chicago city block.

But it was Louis Sullivan who clarified the implications of designing for height: "It must be tall, every inch of it tall. The force and power of altitude must be in it, the glory and pride of exaltation must be in it. It must be every inch a proud and soaring thing, rising in sheer exaltation that from bottom to top it is a unit without a single dissenting line."

The Wainwright Building, St. Louis, in 1890, and a subsequent development from it that resulted in his best skyscraper, the Guaranty Building, Buffalo, in 1894, showed that Sullivan immediately recognized that a tall structure needed a base related to human scale, vertical continuity in an uninterrupted shaft, and special articulation or capping as a termination against the sky. Another excellent example of the work of the Chicago School was the Reliance Building, Chicago, in 1894, by Burnham and Root. In such early structures the curtain-wall vernacular of glass reached a level of accomplishment only to be surpassed at a much later date by Mies van der Rohe, utilizing a more advanced technology.

The desirability of natural light for commercial office buildings gave architects incentive to reduce the structure as much as possible, filling the voids of the slender structural cage with large horizontal expanses of glass—the "Chicago window."

Louis Sullivan, a major force in the Chicago School, was born in Boston in 1856 and studied at the Massachusetts Institute of Technology for a year before working for six-month periods in Philadelphia and in the Chicago office of Jenney. After a further six months of study at the École des Beaux-Arts in Paris, he returned to Chicago just after the Great Fire. He worked in several offices, and in 1881 became Dankmar Adler's partner, after a year in his office.

Sullivan's chief draftsman during those eventful years was a man destined to surpass even the achievements of his *Lieber Meister* and become a legend in American architecture: Frank Lloyd Wright. It is difficult to discern a strong influence of the one upon the other. Sullivan's architecture was urban, restrained in character and *classic* in organization; in contrast, Wright's architecture soon developed into the expression of asymmetrically composed masses and subtly interpenetrating spaces more suited to stand alone, preferably in a natural rather than an urban context.

In the Carson, Pirie Scott department store in 1900, Sullivan's last important commission, an unadorned structural grid of clearly expressed verticals and horizontals resulted in a beautifully proportioned facade of quiet repose and noble simplicity. Whereas his skyscrapers usually expressed verticality, here an emphasis on the horizontal was derived from the uninterrupted floor space of the building. Sullivan's love of delicate ornament shows in the display windows at the ground level, where it is appropriately related to a person's range of vision, and where a greater richness and intricacy is used to emphasize the principal entrance.

Sullivan thought of ornament as deriving from or expressing the spirit of the mass—an organic system of ornamentation. The virtues of a clean structural expression and the later anathema against ornament may have been anticipated by Sullivan when he said: "A building quite devoid of ornament may convey a noble

Auditorium Building, Chicago, Illinois.

and dignified sentiment by virtue of mass and proportion." There is nothing archaeological in the spirit of Sullivan's use of ornament, employed repetitively to accentuate aspects of his buildings and to develop continuity in their surfaces.

Sullivan reasoned that in a tall structure, where function remained constant, the form should not change: "Form follows function." His meaning has often been too literally interpreted and used to justify the type of austere architecture that he himself would have deplored. It was often seen, said Wright ". . . as a physical raw materialism instead of the spiritual thing it really is: the idea of life itself—bodily and spiritually—intrinsic organism. Form and function as one." Sullivan wrote: "That which exists in spirit ever seeks and finds its visible counterpart in form, its visible image . . . a living thought, a living form." Sullivan articulated another pillar of architectural philosophy when he said: "It is of the very essence of every problem that it contains and suggests its own solutions." Sullivan hoped that the Chicago Exposition of 1893 would provide the catalyst modern architecture needed to establish it and give it impetus. This was not to be. The grandiose Classical theme eventually selected prompted a massive demonstration of academic classicism that was to prove seductive to architects and public alike. The Exposition provided an ominous twilight to an era that had defied the shifting soil of Chicago and soared skywards with irrepressible optimism. With a few notable exceptions—for example, Wright and individual architects in areas such as California—American architecture relapsed into a period of Classical revival, cloaking buildings in period trappings and producing an architecture of effect rather than principle. Although the spirit of the Chicago School was obscured, it had inspired some great buildings, and it is worth noting today that there was a diversity of approach in its architecture. The Chicago Exposition was a complete reversal of direction.

With Adler and Root dead and Burnham following the pattern set by the Exposition, Sullivan became disillusioned. After the Carson, Pirie Scott department store in 1900, he had hardly any commissions. He wrote:

So, must I seek my way alone—if way there be.
So, must my soul abide its wintertime.
So, must the tiny, hidden seed of hope await the day.
For Sullivan there was not to be another day. He died in 1924, a lonely, neglected figure. He had written: " . . . the architect who combines in his being the powers of vision, of imagination, of intellect, of sympathy with human need and the power to interpret them in a language vernacular and true—is he who shall create poems in stone . . ." Sullivan sought to bring to his use of the machine the poetry of the artist—a synthesis that architecture is still searching for.

In Europe in the last decade of the nineteenth century, Otto Wagner, a Viennese architect, began eliminating Renaissance trappings from his buildings and pursuing a more "essential" architecture. At that time, there was a growing excitement among a small European group for the simple, functional products of American industry. Adolf Loos, also from Vienna, had worked as a mason for three years in America and, as Le Corbusier later said, was one of the first to realize the splendor of industry and its close connection with aesthetics. America was the land of technology and opportunity for Loos—an attitude shared by many other pioneers of modern architecture, as is shown by

Home Insurance Building, Chicago, Illinois.

their subsequent domicile here. Reacting against the decorative excesses of the Art Nouveau, in 1908 Loos published an essay entitled *Ornament und Verbrechen*. Taking the view that ornament is a crime, Loos wrote: "The evolution of culture marches with the elimination of ornament from useful objects." In the same year, Matisse wrote: "All that is not useful in a picture is detrimental. A work of art must be harmonious in its entirety; for superfluous details would, in the mind of the spectator, encroach upon the essential elements." In that same year, H. P. Berlage, a Dutch architect who did much to publicize Wright's work in Europe (Wright's work was also known through two portfolios that were published in Germany in 1910 and 1911), clearly pointed the direction when he wrote: "And thus in architecture, decoration and ornament are quite inessential while space-creation and the relationships of masses are its true essentials."

Just as the office of Jenney was a gathering place for many of the later important architects of the Chicago School, so, in Berlin, the office of Peter Behrens was a center of search and expression for new principles. It was here, in 1908, that Mies spent three years and here that he met Gropius, who was Behrens's chief designer; it was also here that Le Corbusier came for five months in 1910. The edict "Less is More," implying the elimination of the irrelevant, and the disciplined simplicity of the essential—later to be particularly associated with Mies's architecture—came from Behrens's office.

Both Americans and Europeans had been moving towards a more rational and structural approach to architecture. But the philosophical point of departure that radically affected both art and architecture came from two revolutionary movements that formulated a whole new space-time concept: Cubism, for the interpenetration of space; Futurism, for the simultaneity of movement.

On the charred walls of the burnt-out shell of Frank Lloyd Wright's theater in Taliesin West, Arizona, is the following quotation from Lao-tze: "The reality of the building does not consist in the roof and walls, but in the space within to be lived in." The Chinese philosopher expresses here the eternal concern of architecture: the creation of space. This concern became intensified at the turn of the nineteenth century.

Space has gone through three stages of architectural development: outer space, or the interplay and visual tension created in the relationship of static volumes; inner space, or emphasis on the hollowed-out interior volume and the continuity of interior space, where the exterior form was the result of the defined space within; and the interpenetration of space, where the two former phases were intermingled when a new period was initiated by the discovery that sight is an organic process, one in which motion initiates a way of seeing and recording phenomena that is more than a passive transfer of images. The single viewpoint of perspective, which had dominated art and architecture since the start of the fifteenth century, was superseded upon the recognition of the implications of a three-dimensional comprehension of space. This was particularly evident in the Cubist paintings of Braque and Picasso between 1909 and 1914. Solid objects were painted transparently, overlapping and fragmented to represent simultaneously both their external and internal appearance. By separating an object or scene into its component parts and showing these from several viewpoints on the one canvas, time, the fourth dimension, was introduced. This led architects to explore the relationship of volume, space and transparency instead of mass and solidity.

Wainwright Building, St. Louis, Missouri.

The Futurists found in the schematic orderliness of the Cubist's paintings the vocabulary with which to represent their ideas. However, their leading painter, Umberto Boccioni, was principally influenced by Marcel Duchamp, a Parisian who, although he used Cubist forms, was closer in spirit to their own ideas. But where the Cubists had essentially led an optical revolution from within art, the Futurists responded directly to the idea of representing the drama of the forces of motion. In 1909, the galvanizing rhetoric of the first Futurist Manifesto, written by their youthful leader, Filippo Marinetti, was something of a clarion call for that time. It rejected tradition and the past and evoked the splendors of the machine age. For the visual arts it was a prevision—one which, before it became an adjunct of Fascism, inspired the prophetic urban projects of Antonio Sant' Elia.

It has been a tradition in architecture to design for permanence. Marinetti attacked eternal, permanent values when he wrote: " . . . against the conception of the immortal and imperishable we set up the art of the becoming, the perishable, the transitory and the expendable." Today, the idea of the expendable building is further from anarchy than it was then, although some architects still regard obsolescence not as a positive factor, but as an avoidance of the real problem. Actually, the idea of obsolescence has become increasingly pervasive in industry and all the arts. In architecture it has led to the recognition that by their nature and function some structures should be designed for obsolescence. Mies, in a way, has given this idea a most sophisticated compromise in which the shell of a building is conceived as a permanent predetermined frame enclosing a flexible universal space in which areas can be variously defined to accommodate a variety of changing functions at different times.

Reliance Building, Chicago, Illinois.

In the early 1920's, the Dutch de Stijl group brought art and architecture together within a universal aesthetic principle. They further emphasized the dynamic fluency of space that the Cubists had explored, and gave it architectonic expression. And departing from the Futurist's individual, romanticized view of the machine, they "saw machinery as the agent of collective discipline and an order that drew nearer and nearer to the canons of Classical aesthetics, "writes Reyner Banham. In other words, an instrument, not an objective, of human existence.

The transparent drawings of Theo van Doesburg destroyed mass and rigidly defined volumes by intersecting planes that often delineated space—seemingly without a conscious effort to form spaces—and made architects more acutely aware of the significance of interpenetrating space. With elemental simplicity, Piet Mondrian, another member of the group, explored the new space concept in his geometric canvases. His style had evolved to a nonfigurative expression when, in the first issue of the magazine *De Stijl* in 1917, he wrote: "The life of contemporary cultivated man is turning away from nature; it becomes more and more an a-b-s-t-r-a-c-t life." Abstract painting was moving art away from a representation of nature, as experiments were made in the interaction of form and the relationship of colors. Just as Impressionism had first indicated a new method of perception, so abstract art moved towards more intellectual and scientific engagements. Architecturally, the movement towards abstraction was evident in Mies's 1923 project for a country house employing a structure of brick walls that, through simple planes, subtly suggested a rich sequence of "unending space," extending outwards into the landscape.

Guaranty Building, Buffalo, New York.

Germany in the 1920's became the center for developments and study, with the Bauhaus School as the galvanizing force. It was directed by Walter Gropius, and its slogan, "Art and technology, the new unity," expressed the new spirit. The Bauhaus buildings at Dessau by Gropius in 1926 have been described as the first compelling masterpiece of the modern movement. They are a large, free-plan composition in which separate volumes are derived from specific functions and related so that the total complex cannot be appreciated without moving around it. Since there is no one dominant facade or view, the complex is important from all views. The design approach in the buildings was essentially that of a clearly expressed, regular structure within which an informal distribution of spaces was organized. What in classic architecture had been solid and rigidly space-defining external walls became white, light, stuccoed skins with generous glass areas. Later this came to be called the International Style.

The emphasis on the practical resolution of a building's needs, or fitness for purpose as an expressed objective, was labeled as Functionalism. Although Functionalism was the verbalized architectural determinant of the period, the two most outstanding buildings, Le Corbusier's Villa Savoye at Poissy in 1928-1930, and Mies's Barcelona Pavilion in 1929, both clearly went a tremendous step beyond functional considerations per se. In any event, since Mies's building was essentially symbolic, form could hardly have been derived from function.

By the late 1920's Wright in America, Mies and Gropius in Germany, and Le Corbusier in France were established as the polarizing forces of the new architecture. In the political and social upheavals of the 1930's, Mies and Gropius came to America. The heroic early period of the modern movement had ended.

In America, eclecticism was still the dominant approach. The problem remained one of winning the revolution: of taking architects and public alike away from the past styles to an acceptance of an architecture based on technology, one in which a building's design is initially approached from a resolution of needs. A reaction of great strength and lofty principles was needed—the International Style was just that. It was publicized in this country by an important exhibition mounted at the Museum of Modern Art, New York, in 1932.

The doctrine of this revolution was one of integrity. A concept was arrived at after responding to functional necessities. Ethics forbade any suggestion of decorative treatment; obviously, there were also economic reasons for eliminating decoration. Much of the richness in earlier periods was a result of inherited decorative treatments, and the familiarity and manipulation of a vocabulary that had been refined over the decades; it was too soon for familiarity with the vocabulary, and, anyway, the sparse lines and crystalline simplicity of the International Style looked convincing in contrast with a rich existing fabric.

But, as in all revolutionary movements, the stimulus provided by new factors often leads to the neglect of some durable ones. In the more relaxed period that follows, this inevitably results in certain reassessments. As architecture moved into a transitional period, ours became such a time of reassessment. There was the recognition that some of the beguiling qualities of earlier periods were absent; that shadow, texture, durability, and scale belong to all periods and that human consciousness is continuous; that practicality must be balanced by psychological factors, and that these are not in conflict with functionalism, but expand its meaning. The directions of the search were centrifugal. Validity was found in certain precedents in history as well as in the great force of technology, and the approaches of Wright, Mies and Le Corbusier suggested directions. The search was for a viable approach.

Diversity was evident, for example, in the way in which the elements or functional groupings of a building were related. The architects of the 1920's moved from the tight forms of the Chicago period of the 1880's—as Wright had also done in his Oak Park houses—to looser, open forms, free of the demands of symmetry, forms that responded to and expressed the functional disparate elements of a building within articulated, separate volumes. However, this approach among lesser architects often led to amorphous, straggling buildings: the result of a cluttered, ill-considered approach to a problem or the absence of a clear directive, an absence that disguised itself behind the label of free-planning.

Parallel variations on these two basic approaches, tight forms as opposed to loose forms, can be identified in what has been referred to as Mies's universalism and Wright's personalism. Mies's is a more classical, formal architectural expression, one in which functions are resolved within a minimum of larger elements—if possible one overall envelope within which space divisions appear almost as a diagram—and in which the consequent expression is one of quiet unity. Function is subject to an external order or discipline. Wright, however, used the functional complexities of a building as the integral means of form and expression. Variations in space were fundamental to his architecture, and his interior volumes were almost sculptured by their containers.

In the 1950's there was a swing back to tighter forms and a move towards a more integrated architecture. At present, the general search among good architects is for a relaxed distillation of earlier principles, a search to produce a more unified and coherent architecture while also not forcing functional needs into a formal straitjacket. Technology is employed as the means, and the end is seen in terms of space for human use—varying spaces which depend on one another to constitute a rich sequence of space. Materials are used for their own inherent qualities, without over-refinement or trickery of detail. Recognition is given to the fact that at least a quarter to a third of the cost of a building is absorbed by mechanical equipment, and a move made to design buildings that integrate such equipment and make it a positive part of the architecture. Finally, there must be a spatial idea that in its phrasing governs the concept of a building, an idea that can be assimilated and evaluated as the motivating architectural force.

Though all of the above relates to the building per se, good architects have not forgotten the environment. In general they seem to feel a great frustration at not being able to meet what they increasingly recognize as their great challenge: a framework for life, at our new urban scale, one in which needs are answered and life itself is heightened. This seems the catalyst for a period now embryonic.

Carson, Pirie Scott Department Store, Chicago, Illinois.

LUDWIG MIES VAN DER ROHE

Mies van der Rohe came to Chicago and became director of the School of Architecture at Illinois Institute of Technology in 1938. By then, he had already ensured his reputation as one of the great pioneers in the evolution of modern architecture. Today he is without peer in the architecture of steel.

That Mies came to Chicago is probably only coincidence. He takes taxis from his apartment to his office, says that he rarely sees the city, and claims not really to know the work of the "Chicago School." Mies had established his own direction in his early work, and in an important period of research in the 1920's, when his thoughts crystallized in a series of perceptive magazine articles.

If Chicago did not affect Mies's approach, he certainly influenced its architects, and American architecture in general. The United States, an essentially steel-building country as Gordon Bunshaft has pointed out, afforded him the opportunity to continue his work and teaching, while advanced technology and resources enabled him to execute many of his earlier concepts. In Chicago he entered a relatively no-nonsense, unprejudiced society accustomed to innovation; a society content to see the "bones" of a building and the marks that revealed how a concept was realized. In this atmosphere Mies ignored the incongruities of fashion and pursued his own beliefs with singular conviction. He still does. His dedication to objectivity and refinement, as against change, in architecture is Olympian. He is a perfectionist.

Mies tries to preserve his insularity and formulate his own intellectual course. His reading—almost exclusively in philosophy and science (and sociology when he was young, although he now believes this a waste of time since he feels it does not have much to do with building)—is directed toward the search for truth and eventually towards the clarity of honest construction. Mies quotes Thomas Aquinas: "Truth is the significance of facts," and this has been his guide. He believes that architecture is neither a fashion nor something eternal but is a part of an epoch; not everything, but the essence of an epoch, an expression of its energy. He believes that this essence is the evolving form that is not invented, but which we are working on without being aware of it: "And when this great form is fully understood, then the

27

epoch is over—then there is something new."

In teaching, Mies encouraged his students to analyze the intellectual and cultural aspects of other periods and the significance of their buildings to their epoch, with relation to their similarities and differences to ours. The passage of time often clarifies the real significance of facts. And to understand the galvanizing facts of the present and to react positively and rationally to them, to have a sense of continuity to test these facts and place them in perspective, is to be objective and significant. The answers we find to significant facts, believes Mies, will be our contribution to architectural development. To Mies there is already one undeniable fact: our epoch is under the influence of science and technology.

Mies's conviction and rigor have made him the conscience of American architecture, a measure of architectural morality. He has said: "All individualism is a left-over from the time of Luther —when he said, 'Here I stand.' I would look for more profound principles. . . . Since the authentic approach to architecture should always be the objective, we find the only valid solutions of that time to be in those cases where objective limits were imposed and there was no opportunity for subjective licence." Mies believes that the great architectural periods in history restricted themselves to clear principle, and that this is the only way to create important architecture.

Mies was born in the German city of Aachen in 1886. The town's ancient medieval buildings, particularly the ninth-century chapel founded by Charlemagne, stimulated his early interest in building: "I was impressed by the strength of these buildings because they did not belong to any epoch. . . . All the great styles had passed, but they were still there . . . they were really built." Mies appreciates Romanesque and Gothic cathedrals, Roman aqueducts, and modern suspension bridges—so, to "built," we can add "with structural clarity." Mies, himself, is a master at putting the elements of a building together. His concern for the nature and precision of building is not surprising, since his father, whom he often helped in the stonecutting shop, was a master mason. Mies still likes to say, "Architecture begins when you place two bricks *carefully* together." In place of architecture, Mies prefers to use the German word *Baukunst; bau* meaning construction, and *kunst* simply its refinement.

In 1905 Mies moved to Berlin, working first for an architect and furniture designer, Bruno Paul, and then for Peter Behrens (to whose office also came Le Corbusier and Walter Gropius) whom Mies described as having "a great sense of form." Behrens's enthusiasm for the neoclassic, monumental public building of Carl Friedrich Schinkel was soon shared—and never forgotten—by Mies. In a similar classic manner, he invariably places his buildings on a podium, giving them a sense of containment and detachment from their environment. When asked if it was possible to use a design elsewhere, (he was referring to his proposal for a convention hall in Chicago, but it is obviously a general statement) he replied: "Of course. I don't feel site is *that* important. I am first interested in a good building; then I place it in the best possible spot." Also in the classic manner, his buildings tend towards symmetry and a balanced composition, although he does not pursue this to the point that it becomes formalistic: "We refuse to recognize problems of form, but only problems of building. Form is not the aim of our work, but only the result. Form, by itself, does not exist."

Project for a brick country house.

Project for a glass skyscraper.

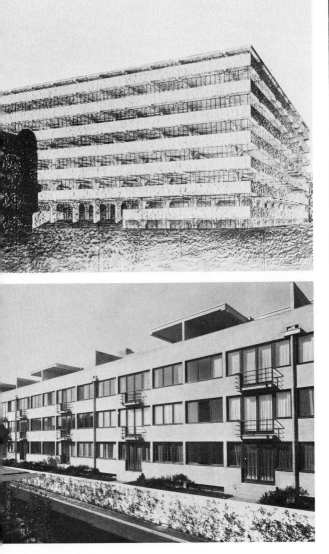

Project for a glass and concrete office building.

Apartment house, Werkbund Exposition, Stuttgart, Germany.

Mies considers the envelope of a building as more than a facade: "Sullivan still believed in the facade. He did not consider that just the structure could be enough. Now we would go on for our own time, and we would make architecture with the structure only. . . . There is an aphorism by Goethe—'It is neither core nor shell—it is all one.' The interior and exterior of my buildings are one—you cannot divorce them. The outside takes care of the inside."

On a visit to Holland in 1912 Mies saw the work of Hendrik Berlage which impressed upon him the importance of structure and confirmed him in the idea of developing a structural approach to architecture. Mies believed that this would at least be a reasonable and safe approach. By structure he means a philosophical idea: "The structure is the whole, from top to bottom, to the last detail—with the same ideas."

After the First World War Mies designed three projects that were to be significant in his subsequent work. First, he made studies for an uncompromising statement of the new technology—an all-glass skyscraper where the non-structural glass skin was separated from the structural bones behind. Studying a model made from narrow, vertical strips of glass placed at slight angles to each other to produce a multifaceted skin, he became convinced that it was not light and shadow that were important, but reflections. A large photograph of the drawing for this building still hangs in his office. Second, emphasizing horizontal rather than vertical character, he designed a rectangular concrete office building—its clearly-expressed structural system of regularly-spaced columns with cantilevered floor slabs, turned up to form a continuous parapet, above which was a continuous perimeter ribbon window. Finally, the Brick Country House in 1923 (very much a part of the interest in spatial relationships at that time) had brick walls that supported the roof, while the overlapping planes articulated a subtle sequence of flowing space. The vernacular of these projects is now familiar; what remains today is Mies's perception and the evidence of an unerring ability to state a premise with the utmost simplicity and clarity.

Mies was appointed First Vice-President of the Deutscher Werkbund Exhibition at Stuttgart in 1927. It was to demonstrate new ideas in residential building, and among the foremost modern European architects he invited to design buildings were Le Corbusier, Gropius, Oud, Stam, Behrens, Hilberseimer, Poelzig and the Tauts. It produced the first en masse showing of what is known now as the "International Style," and it had far-reaching architectural implications. For it, Mies himself designed a four story apartment building with a regular steel skeleton structure.

For the German Pavilion at the 1929 Barcelona International Exposition, Mies designed an architectural milestone which the critic Henry Russell Hitchcock described as ". . . one of the few buildings by which the twentieth century might wish to be measured against the great ages of the past." Its disciplined restraint had a close spiritual affinity to the paintings of Piet Mondrian. The de Stijl aesthetic, of continuous flowing and channeled space, had here been given its most masterly and poetic expression. Elegant materials that were beautifully detailed created an unostentatious nobility and showed that opulence and simplicity could be synonymous in modern architecture. Mies believes that one of the reasons for its wide acclaim was its rich materials of marble, onyx, travertine, tinted glass and chrome, at a time when

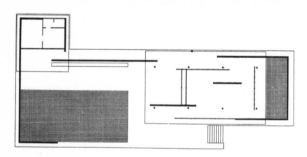

Barcelona Pavilion.

Project for a group of court-houses.

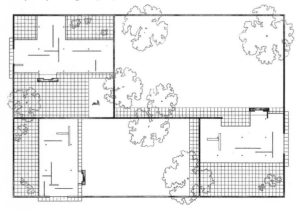

modern architecture was austerely functional.

The Pavilion was set on a raised podium that created a monumental sense of dignity, and preserved a detachment from the surroundings. Eight columns supported a flat roof slab beneath which non-structural walls, at points placed close to columns and continuing out beyond the roof slab to accentuate this fundamental difference, created a rich and dramatic space sequence. Two reflecting pools, a sculpture, and Mies's furniture—the Barcelona group that Mies designed for this Pavilion is a furniture classic—completed the composition. The clarity of Mies's statement was probably overwhelming in a Europe aggravated by war and inflation. Regrettably its life-span was only that of the Exposition. Without a specific functional purpose to fulfill, Mies had exercised his usual discipline, taste and reason; such projects usually allow the architect the most license to raise absurdities, as evidenced in the recent New York World's Fair.

The Tugendhat House, built in 1930 at Brno, Czechoslovakia, continued Mies's preoccupation with elegant materials and flowing space, here related to the functional complexities of a house. The principal area, a generous, open 50 feet by 80 feet, is articulated by a straight wall of onyx and a curved wall of macassar ebony, defining the four functional areas of living, dining, library and entrance hall. Mies himself designed every visible element, ensuring total unity. He has often said: "God is in the details."

In an interesting series of studies for "court houses," Mies developed a roofed, living space related through a glass screen wall to an open garden space, where each is private within a peripheral wall. These studies were being made at the time of Mies's appointment as Director of the Bauhaus, in 1930, at the urging of Gropius who had resigned two years before. With increasing political interference, however, its activities were no longer free, and with the support of his faculty, Mies closed the school in 1933, so ending one of architecture's exciting periods.

Mies, like many of the other founders of the modern movement, came to America, where he remained as director of the School of Architecture at the Illinois Institute of Technology from 1938 until 1958, when he retired from teaching to devote all of his time to his architectural practice.

Mies's work made it possible for him to test the validity of ideas that teaching forced him to clarify. Both fields convinced him of the need for clarity and unity in thought and action as the means to achieve order in civilization. He said: "The function of education is to lead us from irresponsible opinion to truly responsible judgment." He believed that if there was nothing in the curriculum against reason, the student would tackle everything with reason; that the means and purpose must be clear to guide the total effort: what is possible in construction, necessary for use, and significant as art. He emphasized that a student must master the tools of his profession, learn to draw with exactness, understand the elements of a building and the implications of technology and construction as a preparation for design.

The Illinois Institute of Technology gave Mies the opportunity to work on a grand scale when he was commissioned to develop a master plan for its 110-acre campus in 1940. Since construction was to extend over a period of time Mies "had to decide on something that would not change, that would not be out of date by the time we had finished." He felt his concept would not become outmoded because: "It is radical and conservative at once. It is radical in accepting the scientific and technological driving and sustaining forces of our time. It uses technological means but it is not technology. It is conservative as it is not only concerned with a purpose, but also with a meaning, as it is not only concerned with a function, but also with an expression. It is conservative as it is based on the eternal laws of architecture: Order, Space, Proportion." Mies chose a clear, structural skeleton as a discipline that would last and provide maximum flexibility. The campus is planned on a 24-foot by 24-foot grid, with a similar structural bay and 12-foot ceilings in most of the buildings. The principal buildings relate symmetrically to a central axis running the short dimension of the site, and asymmetrically to the long axis. Individual building masses, partially overlapping, are grouped closely to form an interplay of defined, but not enclosed spaces that link sequentially throughout the plan. The two- and three-story buildings are constructed of black exposed steel frames, with precise buff-colored brick panels juxtaposed in subtle variations to large glass areas. This restrained vernacular creates great unity, consistent with Mies's idea that a building should be a simple, neutral frame leading to greater simplicity in the life of the building and the lives of those who use it.

When Mies designed Crown Hall in 1955, to house the Department of Architecture and Planning, it was the first building at I.I.T. to employ an exterior vernacular entirely of steel and glass. Although it is natural from his origins that Mies should have used infilling panels of brick, a traditional material with texture and durability that gives an immediately recognizable sense of scale, in some of the earlier buildings it was a somewhat incongruous choice of material in view of his interest in the industrialization of building methods.

Illinois Institute of Technology.

Crown Hall is a clear statement of Mies's philosophy. It is a meticulously refined exploitation of the aesthetic potential inherent in a steel structure. The main floor, a column-free space 220 feet by 120 feet, is raised 6 feet above the ground for natural ventilation and lighting of semi-basement workshop areas. Its 18-foot-high ceiling is suspended in an uninterrupted plane from four giant girders that span the full 120 feet and are exposed above the roof.

The Farnsworth House in 1950 preceded Crown Hall as Mies's first clear-span, open-space structure. This house has been de-

Tugendhat House, Brno, Czechoslovakia.

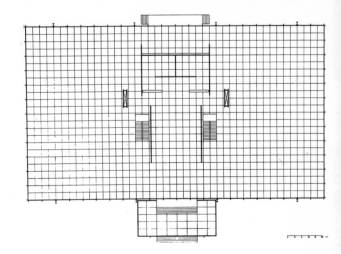

Crown Hall, Chicago, Illinois.

Farnsworth House, Plano, Illinois.

scribed as an architecture that manifests itself almost by its very absence—a poetic "obvious." The house consists of three "floating" planes; two supported between vertical columns, and the third providing a lower transition platform between the earth and floor levels. The solid service core, within the main volume of the glass enclosure, separates the living and sleeping areas. As in his earlier projects there is a total consistency and integration of concept, extending even to the placement of furniture. As Philip Johnson has written, "Mies gives as much thought to placing chairs in a room as other architects do to placing buildings around a square." If this approach to living requires a certain austerity and restraint of its occupants, perhaps it is a reasonable price to pay for such dignity. The detached quality of Farnsworth House is the very antithesis of Wright's principle that houses should seek a close harmony with nature. Mies's house establishes a harmony by receding, so that the landscape itself becomes the suggested space to be lived in. To Mies, the nature of house and landscape is different, and the differences are emphasized.

Crown Hall and Farnsworth House represented an idea of paramount importance that Mies had been developing since the early 1940's—the principle of Universal Space. It heralded a break with a singular concern for function. Contrary to Sullivan's idea that "form follows function," Mies says that while form cannot change, function does: "We do not let the function dictate the plan. Instead let us make room enough for *any* function." In not establishing a predetermined and contained allocation of space to accommodate the functional necessities of a building, but by providing a space adaptable to changing space requirements, Mies creates a flexible space capable of continual modification and thereby designs to counteract obsolescence. This idea indicates again the present polarity of approach to design. Mies believes that the scale of our society, with its technological and scientific forces, tends to negate the specific solution. Instead, these forces suggest the universal solution: a flexible response to the need for space at a vast scale; a more anonymous background giving maximum opportunity for individual liberty. To Wright this was an alien generalization, as his buildings demonstrate. To him, the universal approach was an abstraction synonymous with the anonymous man; he saw the personal space as the proper response to individual needs in a fixed time and place.

Mies's vision of an all-glass skyscraper was finally realized in

1951 when he built the twenty-six-story twin apartment towers on Lake Shore Drive in Chicago. The structural frame, 21 feet square by 10 feet high, is clearly expressed, with the service elements grouped around the central access corridor to keep the periphery of the building free for living spaces. The simple volume of the identical towers, placed at right angles to each other to create a varying joint silhouette, is emphasized by raising each shaft two stories above the travertine base and keeping the entrance lobbies back, thereby creating an all-around recessed colonnade within perimeter columns. Chicago building codes required that Mies fireproof his structural steel skeleton with 2 inches of concrete. Mies responded with a permanent formwork and facing of black steel plates for the columns and beams. This, of course, also expressed the nature of the structure. Glass was set on the outside edge of the column face and between the skeleton. To stress the vertical nature of his towers, and to relate skin and structure visually, Mies added steel "I" mullions, 8 inches deep, which divided the structural bays into four. The mullions create a subtle variation in the exterior. When an observer looks at them straight on, the exterior appears as glass and transparent. As the viewing angle becomes more acute, the elevation appears increasingly solid. By centering the mullions, the two central panes of glass are of equal width, while the two adjacent to columns are narrower. Although the mullions provide necessary separation and bracing for the windows, they certainly do not when attached to columns, and yet without them, "It did not look right," said Mies. An architect often comes to a point where a design needs a certain something, or problems indicate a certain direction. He is then guided by his experience and understanding of architecture as an art. This does not necessarily mean that he acts arbitrarily. The appropriateness of his direction at such a moment produces that something that elevates his work to the realm of art.

The ambiguity of the mullion condition of the Lake Shore Drive apartments may have prompted Mies's design, in association with Philip Johnson, for the Seagram Building in New York. Completed in 1958, it is one of the most elegant skyscrapers ever built. Set back from Park Avenue so that the purity of its 38-story shaft can be appreciated, it is approached formally across a granite plaza flanked by fountains. The plaza is actually a podium, elevated three steps above the level of the principal approach from Park Avenue, and up a short flight of steps beneath glass-roofed canopies on both side-street approaches. Here, Mies kept the structure within the skin of the building, but the structure is still clearly expressed as it forms a colonnaded entrance to a lobby that is an unusually noble 24 feet high. The structure is sheathed in brown-tinted glass, and with its bronze mullions and spandrels, it gives an impression of warm durability and quiet unity. It is particularly dramatic at night when its

Lake Shore Drive Apartments, Chicago, Illinois.

Project for a Convention Hall.

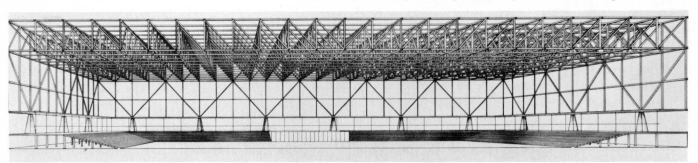

Seagram Building, New York, N. Y.

entrance lobbies and travertine-sheathed elevator shafts are bathed in a white light, contrasting with the deep black-brown tone of its "bones," while its windows emit a warm muted glow that emphasizes its elegant proportions. Mies was fortunate to have an appreciative client who was really willing to *build*. For this was not an inexpensive building; estimated at forty-five dollars per square foot, it cost some 43 million dollars. (It should be noted, however, that many of Mies's buildings are of a more competitive construction cost.) Like his Barcelona Pavilion, Mies's Seagram Building is a measure of modern architectural accomplishment. As Braque has written: "Nobility is produced by emotional restraint." Ironically, Mies's perfection seems to have marked an uneasy moment for some American architects who identify it with the "end of the road."

Mies's preoccupation has been with the high-rise skeleton structure, and the clear-span, open-space structure. One of Mies's current designs is for the Gallery of the Twentieth Century which will be part of Berlin's new cultural center. Again a clear-span structure, its genesis can be found in Mies's earlier studies. He had been interested for many years in the spatial possibilities of art galleries and museums. The Project for a Museum in a Small City, in 1942, one of Mies's first universal space studies, had various elements arranged under a single roof structure, producing a free-flowing space reminiscent of that of the Barcelona Pavilion. Mies commented that the first problem had been to establish the museum as a center for the enjoyment, not the interment, of art. He again employed the idea of a flexible open space in a painting and sculpture exhibition hall for Houston, Texas, in 1956. But it was in his proposals for the Chicago Convention Hall in 1954, and the Bacardi Office Building for Cuba in 1958, that the universal space concept was given its most forceful demonstration so far. The Convention Hall, monumental in scale, and a 700-foot-square plan, had no internal columns and was roofed by a space frame of steel trusses 30 feet in depth. The Bacardi Building was a 177-foot-square, its roof supported by only eight columns, placed peripherally.

The Gallery of the Twentieth Century will realize these spatial and structural concepts in terms of art exhibition, which Mies believes will provide a richness and variety not possible in the usual museum. The building is divided into two parts: a large hall for temporary exhibitions, and a museum for the gallery's permanent collection, which is, as in Crown Hall, a functional, yet clearly aesthetic, division. Mies said, "I finally decided upon a solution which located the exhibition hall on a terrace over the museum. This permitted the design of a clear and strong building which is in harmony with the Schinkel tradition in Berlin." A large foyer enables direct access to the exhibition area, with stairs to the permanent collection below. Low wood-paneled cores, housing the cloak rooms and ticket office, separate the foyer from the exhibition area. The only other fixed elements on this level are two mechanical shafts. Galleries for the permanent collection, in the podium below, connect directly with the museum's sculpture garden, and here also are found the administration and service areas. The granite-paved terraces and plaza space are to be used by all who attend the various activities of the cultural center. The exhibition area, walled in glass, is defined by a 216-foot-square roof that, similar to the Bacardi Building, is supported by eight peripheral steel columns.

In its order, clarity and discipline the Gallery of the Twentieth Century is as typical of Mies's handling of space and consideration of a building as the Guggenheim Museum in New York was of Wright's. The elegant, black structure will give to Berlin Mies's most poetic realization of the universal space concept. The motivating idea, the structural concept and the exacting details have a unity conditioned by the same general principles that express Mies's philosophical idea of structure. Quoting the physicist Schrodinger, Mies says: "The creative vigor of a general principle depends precisely on its generality." When Mies speaks of structure he refers not to a special solution but to a general idea. The very consistency of Mies's thinking has enabled him to achieve a range and scale of building types from a small house to the Gallery of the Twentieth Century, always evolving from his premise of universality, which Mies firmly believes is a principal characteristic of our epoch.

The apparent simplicity of Mies's architecture stems from a total rejection of the inessential. "Less is more," he says. His buildings are the fruits of long labor, the result of years of deep reflection. A lifetime's attainment is in their continuity. His office staff, of some twenty persons, is a homogeneous team aware of Mies's particular process of problem resolution. Refinement ensures a consistency of expression rather than the production of a new form for each new problem. His office is a large open space full of exquisitely executed study models of buildings and their detail, which are dismantled and reassembled countless times. Over all is Mies's masterly sure hand and his theme from Thomas Aquinas that "Reason is the first principle of all human work." Although his architecture may finally manifest itself as simple, this is certainly not synonymous with easy. His is a monumental effort that in the finished work may take no more than a few moments to declare itself.

Mies has been the recipient of many honors. In 1963 he became the first architect to be awarded the United States Medal of Freedom. Concluding his expression of gratitude on accepting the American Institute of Architects Gold Medal in 1960, he said: "Spinoza has taught us that great things are never easy. They are as difficult as they are rare."

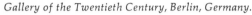

Gallery of the Twentieth Century, Berlin, Germany.

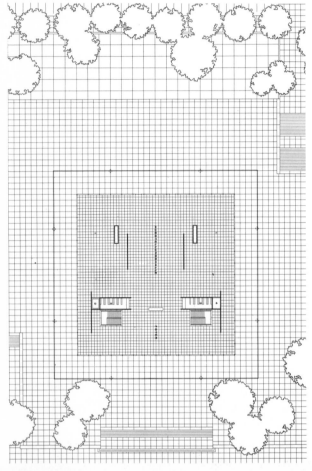

Geneva House, Geneva, Illinois.

JACQUES BROWNSON

The extraordinary clarity and discipline in Mies's architecture and his tremendous conviction in his ideas have had a telling influence on his students. Referring to the many who came to the Illinois Institute of Technology, Mies has said, "You only need ten to change the cultural climate if they are good." Among the good, Mies includes Jacques Brownson who was born in Aurora, Illinois, in 1923. Brownson studied at I.I.T. with Mies from 1946 to 1950, and taught there himself from 1948 until 1957.

In 1952 Brownson built his first independent building, a well-thought-through steel and glass house, in Geneva, Illinois. The interior of the house is a column-free, flexible space, 88 feet by 32 feet, where the plumbing and service equipment are the only fixed elements. The steel skeleton of eight columns and roof beams is constructed of rolled steel sections from which the exterior glass wall is hung.

In 1957 Brownson joined the busy Chicago office of C. F. Murphy Associates. He left the firm in 1966 to become Chairman of the Department of Architecture at the University of Michigan.

"I remember, when I was still in grade school, becoming aware that if you built things a certain way they held together, and if you did not follow certain principles they fell apart. At I.I.T. I came into contact with Mies and Hilberseimer; it was a question of how, through principles, buildings went together, and not trying to discover great building methods or some kind of self-expression. How do you put steel, wood or masonry together: what size do the members have to be: what are the principles of

37

Geneva House, Geneva, Illinois.

Continental Insurance Co., Chicago, Illinois.

building involved? This was their emphasis. Mies and Hilberseimer helped us build a vocabulary to work with and gave us an insight into the possibilities, an approach to understanding. They did not say that things had to be done a particular way, but they did say that when you are faced with a problem then what that problem really is has to be established. By clarifying it, finding out how it had been solved before, you had an opportunity—not the technique—and a method of solution. New possibilities were dependent upon you, and how clearly you saw the work to be done.

"The architect is given a problem to solve which usually falls into certain categories: a house, a school, a factory. He has the problem of constructing these buildings so that they make some kind of sense. The techniques of science and industry give him the tools and the materials. How he decides the proportions, the feeling for space, and what he wants to do with it, take the architect into the realm of architecture. There are many solutions, using the same basic materials and sections available to anybody. In building, an architect has to decide the best, most economical, and clearest way to put it together, getting the maximum use out of the space, and still achieve something besides mere building.

"There are three ways to design a glass wall: in front of the columns, between them, or behind them. One could look at the three possibilities and say it all looks the same—it is a glass building, but it is not. It is rather like looking at an oak or a maple tree—they have the same basic structure but each develops its own distinctive subtleties. Each has its own expression.

"It will be a long time before the skeleton system of building is invalid, although there will be different techniques of putting the bones together, and different expressions of it. Relatively few architects understand the principles involved in designing a clear structure; the curtain wall is only the outside of the building but it, too, must begin with a clear structure.

"The subjective in architecture does not exist any more than it does in science: When you are searching for an answer, if you are subjective you will not arrive at a clear solution. However, after working on a particular problem for a long period you may have an accumulation of objective thought behind you and then eventually arrive at a crossroads with none of the objective criteria pointing clearly in which direction to advance. Finally, your judgment leads you in one way; although you have nothing really to base it on, you make a decision. Then the intuitive, not the subjective, decides.

"Mies's buildings in steel and glass are only the beginning, not the end of the road. The possibilities are endless—he has opened up a horizon for us. I think the work to be done is in metals. In building, even in concrete structures, the work is done by metal—be it steel, aluminum or magnesium. I have yet to meet anybody who has worked or lived in a glass building who has not liked the spirit of being free in the landscape. Everybody wants to get out, to get away from the confining, enclosing mass; that is why we have more glass. A legitimate criticism is that we have not been able to solve the technical problems of glass buildings. Mechanical systems and climate control are not clearly understood even by engineers, and we are using the same glass discovered hundreds of years ago.

"Today, everything has to be a work of art or an expression of what is brand new, instead of working on a problem and finding out what needs to be solved. The extent of individual creation or personal solution—the 'Here I am'—usually ends up to be 'a little something' over the main entrance to the building.

"We are creating buildings today that were never thought of before in terms of use, and we are going to arrive at other new building types. Significantly, Mies was interested in analyzing how to develop different building types. One of his greatest proposals was the unconstructed Chicago Convention Center. His concern was with the use of such a building, an approach to building types rather than to each one as an individual solution.

"Working seriously you have to think of the problem and not worry whether it is going to be a work of art—that will naturally emerge. If the spirit of the building is there, it comes out in all the details. The dignity of the space, the force of the idea will come through. If you have an idea for the whole space of a building and cannot get all the little details, it will not defeat the initial idea. For instance, the forcefulness of the idea and the spirit of Chartres overpowers the later additions. A building is not an accumulation of details but is certainly enhanced by them. If the spirit is not there initially the details are not going to help.

"It has been said that a lot of the people at I.I.T. were under the influence of Mies—I cannot imagine a better influence. At least this gave them the opportunity of setting their sights a little higher. There has to be a high standard set; a teacher cannot make of somebody something that is not there, but he can give him the tools to work with, and open his eyes to the possibilities.

"It is not necessary for every architect to make something new, but simply give us good buildings. We need people who are general practitioners, who will take care of the everyday building problems and do a good workman-like job. Even more, we need people who can understand the relation of these buildings one to the other, and to the whole. To eliminate some of the chaos and unsightliness in our cities, we have to re-examine the structure and skeleton of the city, and discover the way, through principles, of putting the different parts together to make all the functions of the city work.

"There is an opportunity to work in Chicago that does not seem to exist in other places. Perhaps because everybody is so busy here, and wants to get into a new building so quickly, this in itself acts as a catalyst.

"Mies has brought to Chicago a rock-like determination that one should build clearly with the means and methods of our time. We have to think of the real meaning of our science and technology and not be swayed by the subjective approach. We can think of the future of architecture as standing on Mies's shoulders, and trying to carry it further."

Brownson has spoken of the need to persevere right through the many stages of a problem. Consequently, he involved himself with only one project at a time in the office of C. F. Murphy Associates. To him, the Farnsworth House, on which Mies spent five years, is the epitome of such endeavor; one is conscious of all the energy that has been exerted. His buildings, too, show the investment of much thought and the careful consideration and working-through of their many stages.

The Continental Center, a 23-story office building designed by Brownson and completed in 1964, is a disciplined architectural statement with a clear structure and long, horizontal glazed areas.

Chicago Civic Center, Chicago, Illinois.

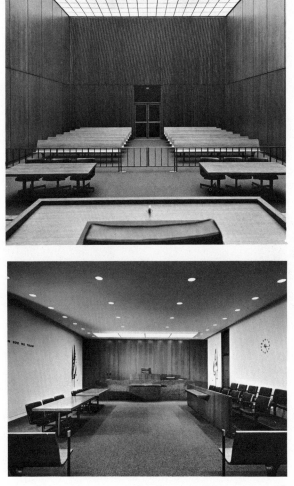

Chicago Civic Center, Chicago, Illinois.

It has its precedent in the broad, historic base of the whole Chicago school. The 42-foot-square structural bays and the 12-foot story height dominate the building's elevation. It is interesting to note that although Brownson's detailing shows the Miesian influence, he does not employ "I" beam mullions, a favorite device of Mies to emphasize the narrower window module as, for example, in the Lake Shore Apartments and the Seagram Building.

In the Chicago Civic Center, by C. F. Murphy Associates, with S.O.M. and Loebl, Schlossman and Bennett, Associated Architects, Brownson has been trying to extend the steel and glass vernacular beyond what has been done. It is a handsome, bold acquisition for Chicago, and a project that has required a four-and-a-half-year total involvement from Brownson. Its thirty-one floors, towering 630 feet, are supported by columns that decrease in dimension on the exterior as the building rises. The structural bays are the largest clear-spans yet constructed in a skyscraper: A monumental 87 feet by 48 feet, 4 inches, they provide a completely unobstructed floor space to accommodate the diverse court functions, their structural scale deriving from the special requirements of the problem.

One hundred and forty courtrooms and their supporting office activities are contained within the single tower that will have a heavy, daily traffic in excess of twelve thousand people. The typical floor-to-ceiling height is 12 feet, considerably more generous than the usual office tower; a ceiling depth of 6 feet at every floor level accommodates the depth of structural beams and provides space for the distribution of services. Smaller courtrooms, hearing rooms and offices have a 12-foot ceiling height, while the larger courtrooms, seating one hundred fifty, are of a nobler proportion, rising through two floors.

When a building has a permanent tenant, as the Civic Center does, it is not often well maintained since there is not the incentive to upgrade with each new tenant as in a typical office structure. To achieve a sense of permanence, durable materials of a natural finish were chosen for the interior. The exterior steel frame is clad in a special steel alloy; it contributes to the rigidity of the structure and requires no painting, since the protective coating is the oxidation of the alloy itself. Large panes of lightly-tinted glass will harmonize with the gradually oxidizing brown-black of the structure. Like the Seagram Building in New York, the shaft occupies only thirty percent of its site. The remainder, a granite-paved plaza, will create an open space for special civic functions and a dignified approach to the building.

The Law is one of the pillars of society and the building reflects this dignity and importance. Like Mies's buildings at I.I.T., it has a sense of permanence and subdued color that time will enhance rather than detract from. It is consistent with Brownson's belief that a building should have a positive value, and is not a fashion today to be changed tomorrow as casually as one changes a necktie.

Coming at a time when some architects are disenchanted with an expression they feel Mies has carried to the ultimate, this robust yet graceful building has special significance. It is a powerful, persuasive statement exploring the extensive possibilities of a now-familiar idiom. It shows that Brownson, too, is becoming a powerful architectural force.

HARRY WEESE

"If present day architecture is ever to mature, it needs to eschew the fashion of the hour and consider the realities of decades." It is particularly Weese's concern for his origins and the Chicago tradition that reflect in and distinguish his work. While many architects have looked to the pioneers of modern architecture for inspiration, Weese has found his in the museum of his urban environment. As he says, "We feel the whole gamut of architecture is our preserve, and we are not afraid to use forms that are outdated if they have any function. We are willing to risk seeming inconsistent. I get a great deal of pleasure in discovering old things that can be made new again as well as discovering new combinations." He often uses traditional materials to produce a modern and essentially urban robustness: "In some cases we find we must build along what seems to be nineteenth century standards. We cannot beat brick bearing walls and wood joists. It may be that the building industry is geared this way, but it may be for the reason that these materials are logical."

Harry Weese was born in a suburb of Chicago in 1915. After three years of study at the Massachusetts Institute of Technology and one at Yale, he returned to M.I.T. for a final year, graduating in 1938. He learned, and still believes, that the functionalist ethic is central to everything, and that the answer to every problem lies within it.

In 1938 he went to Cranbrook Academy, to study city planning under the direction of Eliel Saarinen, joining a number of outstanding talents that included: Eero Saarinen, Ralph Rapson, Philadelphia city-planner Edmund Bacon, sculptor Harry Bertoia, interior-designer Florence Knoll, and that most versatile designer, Charles Eames. After working for Skidmore, Owings and Merrill in Chicago for a year, he opened his own office. The war quickly terminated this venture and Weese went to sea as an engineering officer aboard destroyers. After the war he worked a further year with S.O.M. and then reopened his own office.

The influence of environment on his architecture can be seen in Weese's Walton Apartments built in 1952. Their precedent is Chicago's Reliance Building whose projecting bay windows al-

Eugenie Lane Apartments, Chicago, Illinois.

Walton Apartments, Chicago, Illinois.

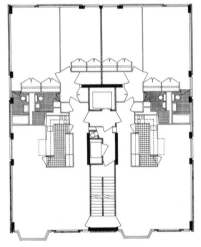

lowed occupants a clear view up and down the street, secured more daylight and caught passing breezes, while its undulating facade created a more plastic, exciting streetscape.

Completed in 1959, the American Embassy in Accra, Ghana, showed Weese's ability to look at a basic premise in an original way. He was asked to harmonize his design with the indigenous architectural tradition. He found that the Africans did not really want modern European office buildings and did not have the technology for total air-conditioning, and he sensed that they would regard a characteristically indigenous structure with pride. He discovered mahogany to be plentiful, and although told that in Ghana it was not possible to build in wood, he proceeded to ignore the advice: "If a rule can be made invalid you arrive at a new equation, and from the new equation you arrive on fresh ground instead of where everyone else is already standing. This is not being different for its own sake." Weese observed that the second-stories of old, wood buildings were intact, and only those whose first floors were in contact with the ground were infested with termites. He concluded that "if you built up in the air on stilts and used hardwood mahogany, which the white ants don't like, plus the insurance of preservatives, a new equation was quite possible." The Embassy building has a central court overlooked by a veranda which gives access to the offices. By using individual air conditioners in offices, Weese overcame major maintenance problems while ensuring that the diplomatic staff are not hermetically sealed in blissful, air-conditioned isolation.

"A personal philosophy is formulated from earliest experiences. This becomes a part of what you think architecture is. The environment I grew up in was tremendously eclectic. I did not realize this until a teacher showed us the basic architectural orders and asked us to see if we could spot them in buildings. That day my eyes were completely opened, as I saw houses that were just an accumulation of many motifs, with no reason behind them. I saw the advent of the ranch house, which was really an outgrowth of the Depression, when people could not afford two stories. Later it became the result of sheer laziness and cheap land, and sprawling cities made feasible by the automobile and the septic tank.

"When I started in architecture I was very much influenced by the Scandinavians. One of my favorites was and still is Aalto; the other is Le Corbusier. I have a tremendous respect for Mies but no emotional affinity, except for his cold and beautiful logic. The impact of Wright washed over me in my environment; I took him for granted and felt he took credit for the architecture of an entire era to which many others contributed. He ran away from the city, and to an extent, the great social dilemma of the Depression period. He designed Broadacre City (proto-suburbia), spawning the ranch house into the bargain, then later came back with the tongue-in-cheek proposal for a mile-high building in Chicago. I objected then, and still do, to this cavalier treatment of cities. But I admire his example of courage in the face of adversity, standing up for the prerogatives of his art, irresponsible though they may have been at many times. He gives every architect courage.

"Believing that architecture is simply a growing process, conditioned by the past, I am probably classed as an eclectic. But if we want to be civilized at all, we ought to know all that has gone before. This is the true measure of an architect. There are a lot of clever barbarians afoot—I do not know if they sprang out of test tubes—who celebrate nothing but contemporaneous conditions and ignore what has brought us to where we are. You never know where you are unless you know where you came from. Technologists who say that life would be simpler if houses did not weigh so much, oversimplify to a serious degree. Perhaps we need such shock treatment to prevent us from pursuing the same patterns, but I find most of it leads to dead ends. However, the age of plastics, glass and computers is very exciting. Engineering is equally as important as art in the forming of our environment. No artist could have thought of a suspension bridge, only someone motivated by a tremendous desire to span from here to there.

"In this age of increasing organization, man is losing touch with nature. Virtuoso performances receive acclaim. If an architect produces a tour de force defying gravity, it is bound to attract attention. But unless the work becomes part of the stream of development, it is meaningless. Civilization finds its own forms as it develops. My concern, and most action springs from protest against chaos, is helping to bring order from this chaos—an architect can only do so much.

"I would rather match a cornice line, or set one that could be matched, or establish a pattern that is good enough to be followed, than try to build yet another spectacular building that stands by itself. If vanity prompts one to break a cornice line then one should only be allowed to do so by setting back from the main street line. It would also be good to limit the materials used on the city street. The consistency of Paris results in part from this, but few living architects are prepared to pay more than lip service to this need to work within a context. We must respect the valid existing environment while building what is appropriate to present needs.

"Sometimes environments are so mixed that you have to seize on the essence of what they could become. Boston is not preserving its essential character very well with its current outcrop of new buildings, the largest of which is the Prudential Center. This is less an architectural decision than an economic one, as the Prudential Center was the "chosen instrument" to sustain the city's tax base. It looks more like an act of desperation, and this single building destroys the scale of Boston. Such permissiveness with the skyline destroys any sense that meaningful generating forces are at work. In the early 1930's Boston has a finely scaled, beautifully ordered brick skyline, punctuated by the gold dome of the State House, the Custom House tower, and numerous church spires. Now this skyline is becoming snaggle-toothed and haphazard with gross lumps of new buildings—I call it the rape of the sky. What will happen to historic Commonwealth Avenue? Are we going to allow tall buildings to so inflate land values that all existing buildings have to be destroyed? I think height limits are the only significant zoning controls.

"An architect must tackle the problems that come to him, but he can steer himself in certain directions by taking only commissions that allow him to follow his inclination. Le Corbusier was probably the best example of this. I do not suppose he accepted a commission that would not fit within his scheme of things, with the result that every building was a masterpiece, based on his previously-stated principles. I do not think there are many architectural ideas that he has not already stated.

"Le Corbusier was an artist who saw things not divorced from nature; he used natural forms, understood life, cities and how

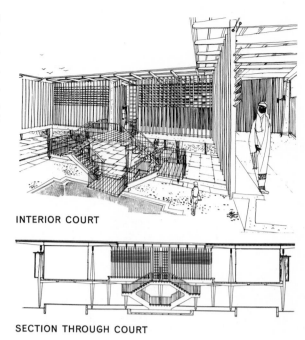

INTERIOR COURT

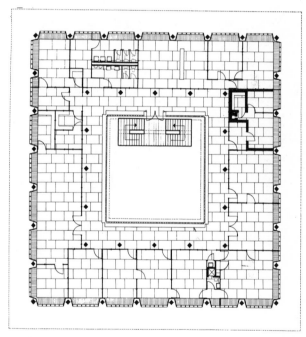

SECTION THROUGH COURT

MAIN FLOOR PLAN

American Embassy, Accra, Ghana.

43

Eugenie Lane Apartments, Chicago, Illinois.

La Salle redevelopment, Chicago, Illinois.

they grew. In the chapel at Ronchamp you find motifs and symbols of the Greek Islands, even to the boat in dry dock with the water line incised on it. Architecture is the form of everything in the external world, basic stimulation comes from nature. There are no new forms, they have all been found. Supersonic jets now look more and more like fish. Wright used the word organic for forms which were really most inorganic—crystalline and angular. The organic architects dare to follow something besides rigid geometry and venture off into truly plastic form. Eero Saarinen grasped this, and Le Corbusier was certainly the master of it, but architects who follow this path had better study sculpture and discipline themselves in three-dimensional composition, before rearing up permanent essays in pure form to public view.

"The minute the architect begins to study the human problem he is involved in, he writes a social program, which by his own prejudice and insight he can influence and advance. He aims high when he maintains that a given proposal is not only better from the point of view of land use but also of economics, health and privacy. We have designed buildings in which you have to walk up six stories, which comes rather hard to 'the bleeding-heart school of social welfare programmers'—they would have everyone moving on one plane, preferably on wheels.

"Buildings are masculine and aggressive. You have to take the long view and assume they will last; therefore, they cannot be pretty—the adjective I least like applied to architecture. I am embarrassed when architects talk about beauty; like happiness it is only a by-product. A building should be handsome, elegant, strong, lean—beauty is too vague an attribute. A building comes from the inside out and has to be gutty, though if it becomes too gutty it becomes forced. To turn a building inside out to show its entrails is a short-lived fashion. Mechanical systems aren't that basic. Structure is the thing."

Weese is a firm believer in the values of urban living, particularly as a background for architects. "Architects should grow up in and study the city; architectural schools in towns of under a million people should be abolished," he says. "The only way you learn about form is to look around you." He does not believe in a white palette for buildings in the northern climate because this is to pretend that we have white cities or that buildings do not get dirty. He believes that new urban housing for family living is the city's only answer to suburban sprawl.

The Eugenie Lane apartments designed for Chicago's Old Town, completed in 1962, have an attractiveness and character that respect the residential scale of the building's four-story neighbors. They are free of the ephemeral, and far from the antiseptic living environment often associated with a more industrially-oriented approach to architecture.

Two recent projects in Chicago further show his imaginative approach to the urban housing problem: a proposed redevelopment for a slum area in Chicago's Loop, and the Scott Street apartment tower.

The La Salle redevelopment has a mixture of high- and low-rise dwellings. Before tackling the project he said, "Private developers aren't much interested in houses in the city; overly-generous zoning laws lure them into the air. But they are interested in infiltrating their slabs into vintage town streets—which, of course, destroys the very environment they seek." His aim was to replace blight and stratification with units offering a wide range of rentals, while at the same time stabilizing the best values in the existing community.

The Scott Street apartment tower, with four apartments per floor, provides luxury in-town urban living "for one hundred families who want fireplaces, high ceilings, panoramic views (even from kitchens), unlimited storage, and floor-to-ceiling windows. It is for those who seek interesting street scenes, the dog-walking, people-watching vitality and interest of a diverse neighborhood . . . appropriate, too, for the contemplative life above the city. This tall house is a home and the character of Chicago shows in its ribs."

Weese currently is working on several projects across the country and finds distance a negligible handicap in the performance of his contracts. His office of about forty people is large enough, with careful scheduling, to accomplish all his purposes. He uses outside consultants as much as possible, but believes in setting the comfort standards for a building himself — otherwise, "they take refuge in the most conservative and often most expensive standard."

The handsome Arena Stage Theater for Washington, D.C., in 1962, is, for Weese, a direct expression of function; the octagonal volume, enclosing a rectangular stage surrounded by four tiers of seats, is clearly separated from a rectangular structure that contains the foyer, lounge, offices, dressing rooms and workshops. The theater form was the product of Weese's listening to hours of tape on how a theater works. This project has led to the commission for a concert hall to seat twenty-two hundred in its main auditorium, as part of the Milwaukee Center for the performing arts. Other facilities will include a great hall overlooking the river for the audience at intermissions and for banquets; an atrium garden; a four-hundred-seat recital and symphony rehearsal hall; and a two-hundred-and-fifty-seat theater-in-the-round and opera rehearsal hall.

"I believe in working on a problem within a narrow context rather than approaching it from all directions, but a context that is wide enough to ensure that we don't omit any really valid possibilities," says Weese. "For example, if we have a junior college to build on an urban site, it requires a tremendous movement of people—yet rather than buy all kinds of mechanical devices, like escalators, we want to take advantage of human foot power. So we start out with a six-story ceiling, and put the laboratories that are used for long periods of time at the top."

The Elvehjem Art Center, in Madison, is a nine-million-dollar complex for the University of Wisconsin. Designed around a large formal space, considered the center of the University, it contrasts to the more open nineteenth century campus of free-standing buildings on the adjoining hill. Weese, trying to create a simple urban core, said: "This is a city, that's a park, and like all urban patterns the only ones you appreciate are the strong ones. The design is shaped by building 'lines' formed by the grid-iron street pattern; 'lines' not only on the ground but also in the air— we maintain the existing cornice line." The six-story complex will be a concrete structure with local limestone infill panels, strongly expressed as three functional divisions.

Art education occupies the two top levels. The roof has many skylights over the art studios and, since it will be seen from the hill-

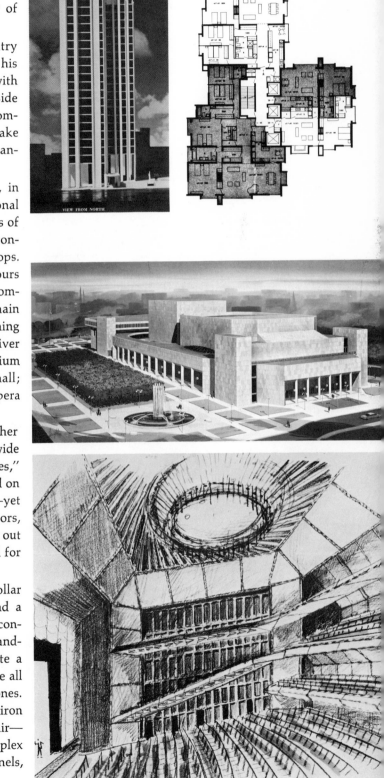

Scott Street Apartments, Chicago, Illinois.

Center for the Performing Arts, Milwaukee, Wisconsin.

side, it is thought of as another facade. This two-story layer establishes a continuous cornice around the whole site. Slung between it, free of the terrace below, is a two-story element that contains the offices, lecture hall, concert hall and art gallery; considered as wall-bearing structures, they are independent of the columns supporting the art studios above. The terrace level provides easy access to this middle layer by connecting with bridges across the adjoining community streets, carrying pedestrians right through the entire complex. In addition, it separates dissimilar functions and provides the acoustic isolation necessary for the assembly, exhibition and auditorium elements at its level. The bottom layer consists of two classroom levels, with skylights set in a sloping wall, merging this layer into the surrounding landscape while providing a gentle transition to the vertical columned structure above.

Weese believes that we have moved away from the Depression psychology where every square inch had to count, away from the psychology that modern architecture is the architecture of revolution, and are starting to concentrate our attention on the best way of doing things. Looking from his office window at busy Michigan Avenue and the backdrop of Chicago, he said: "Human nature is the constant; doctrinate rationality is one thing, and human logic another."

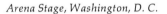

Arena Stage, Washington, D. C.

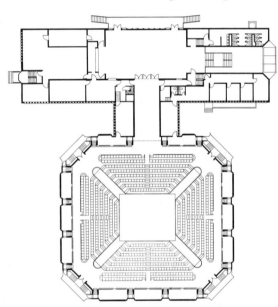

Elvehjem Art Center, Madison, Wisconsin.

BERTRAND GOLDBERG

The relatively simple procedure of placing elements one upon another is one of our earliest building principles. Refined, it becomes the post-and-beam structural system based essentially on the logic of right-angled geometry. It has been employed for centuries, with relation to prevailing structural techniques and materials, and remains the most universal method of building. Steel added a new dimension to this established vocabulary, by virtue of the possibilities inherent in stronger and lighter framed structures, as demonstrated by the early Chicago skyscrapers and Mies's later refined expression.

With the development of reinforced concrete came the possibility of molding or pouring structures whose strength and rigidity derived from shape—continuous warped or folded membranes, gaining their strength from continuity. The engineers Nervi, Torroja and Candela have all employed this method in sophisticated, statistically indeterminate, shell structures, as has Soleri, in a more craft-oriented manner, in his "earth houses." Wright used to demonstrate the character of post-and-beam structures by placing his index fingers in the form of a "T," then moving them slightly to show the instability of the connection. Conversely, he would show that strength can be derived from form in a continuous structure, by interlocking his fingers and trying to pull them apart. The architectural implications of the two structural approaches are vastly different.

Bertrand Goldberg is a native Chicagoan whose work is particularly interesting because he has been experimenting with the potential of continuous structures in central, urban locations. He believes that Gropius, Le Corbusier (until 1950), and Mies are architectural romanticists who have made the right angle a cult and refined its expression into a creed. "Our time," he says, "has made us aware that forces and strains flow in patterns which have little relationship to the rectilinear concepts of the Victorian engineers. We have become aware of the almost alive quality which our structures achieve, and we seek the forms which give the most life to our structures."

Goldberg's present direction goes beyond the realm of preoccupation with shape and structure per se, to derive from such other factors as, for example, his interpretation of the spiritual significance of our role in urban society. He believes that our epoch is experiencing a rebirth of faith not unlike that of the fourteenth

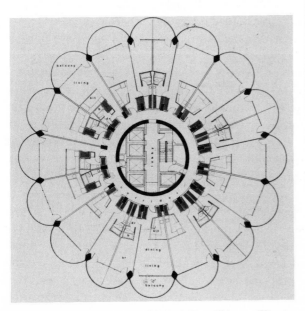

Marina City, Chicago, Illinois.

century whose social patterns we can increasingly identify with our own: "a creative drive toward urban life, a renaissance of faith against the previous system of rigid and formal doctrine, the growth of the city-state with its power to tax and its need to provide, and the growing value of intuitive forces in our life." Our ideas today are a projection of those postulated over a century ago, when "Darwin took the history of mankind away from the Bible, Freud took the soul of man away from religion and Marx took the government of man away from the individual." Goldberg contends that from the nineteenth century we have inherited neither the inner order nor the integrity that leads to unity.

Born in 1913, Bertrand Goldberg studied at Harvard University in its Beaux Arts days prior to Gropius. He proceeded to the Bauhaus where he was exposed to a totally different set of social, economic and aesthetic values—and to the German mind at work, which "was quite spectacular, particularly as developed as it was at the Bauhaus." He came under the influence of Mies to the extent that he believed that all architecture should be Miesian. "We used to say casually that Le Corbusier was an artist and Mies an architect; this marked the German distinction between the two." He returned to the United States and pursued the study of structure at Chicago's Armour Institute of Technology. For a decade he tried to solve spatial and structural problems as he thought Mies might have, aware yet unconcerned that this approach was not a personal expression. In design he continued the German tradition in which the architect also functions as an industrial designer.

In the 1940's Goldberg became absorbed with the industrial process and its application to architecture. He designed prototypes for prefabricated houses where the stressed skin became part of the structure, a relatively new idea developed primarily for the aircraft industry. His involvement had come through his development of gun crates of stressed skin that could be converted into houses. These subsequently led to his design for plastic freight cars where structural strength could be derived from form, with a freedom that architecture does not often offer. The dynamics of movement and kinetic energy, "the fact that a force of only millisecond duration is not a force that we analyze and handle in quite the same way as the dead load forces in architecture," became the focus of Goldberg's attention.

Then studying mechanical equipment in light of the industrial equation, Goldberg designed a prototype for that great symbol of American materialism, the bathroom, as a unit house appliance in molded steel. From the lesson of making steel flow under heat, pressure and impact into a new form he "became aware, at a sensitive level, of the fact that strength can come from shape rather than weight. If you deform a piece of sheet steel you have a sculptural form with a new moment of inertia, where shape can give strength. In the automobile, designers have been decreasing weights of steel while producing increasingly stronger forms. Produced automatically and endlessly, but in straight lines, the rolled steel forms we were working with from my Miesian background became a very clumsy tool. Whereas we had been talking for years about the machine in architecture, as part of the old Bauhaus tradition, it had more potential than anything we had given it credit for. We could virtually build anything we could imagine. The post-and-beam suddenly became a hangover from the Victorian tradition where the machine had been an expression of the human arm at work, from left to right and up and down. I

Project for Kansas City Apartments.

felt almost like a primitive looking at the machine that could create a material by a process that did not exist before—produce a magic that was not there before."

Involvement with the industrial process made Goldberg acutely aware of the influence that mechanical systems can have on a building, "either at a subconscious level, or quite directly. Kahn, in the Richards Medical Towers, designs around a mechanical system. The great extent to which electricity freed my design at Marina City is without question."

In the 1950's Goldberg began to apply the lessons of his industrial explorations to high-rise housing. A project for Kansas City, in bearing masonry, was never built because the sponsor ran out of funds, but it did win the 1954 *Progressive Architecture* prize for the best apartment building. Rectilinear in form, it was "like a Henry Moore sculpture" where the outer space penetrated the entire structure to the core. Goldberg concluded that post-and-beam structures were all indeterminate forms, cellular in development, nature and expression; size resulting from the multiplication of bays, their number determined by the final aesthetic proportion one desired. So began his interest in geocentric form "where utilities are centered and varying functions are spread out equidistant from the center."

The next significant development, the Astor Tower Hotel in Chicago in 1958, had a central core with the exterior still expressed as a conventional rectilinear form. Goldberg tried to overcome some of the problems inherent in curtain wall facades by using outside louvers, which, when cranked, presented an accidental and changing quality to the building facade. "I tried to develop a building that would go back to the classical light and shade concept on the exterior." Goldberg adds: "It always bothered us to try to express the structure along with the requirements of the curtain wall which, by reason of codes, had to be non-structural and therefore of glass. The glass creates a certain aesthetic expression that is undaring, limited, even boring, and in many ways a denial of those things that have some kind of human significance: light, shade and texture. Although the glass wall has a texture of its own, it is not one that readily communicates with the world around it."

Marina City, in 1959, is a thirty-six-million-dollar project built on only three acres of land in the heart of Chicago's Loop. A dramatic landmark in the Chicago skyline, it culminated thirty years of thought and development for Goldberg. Each of the twin, sixty-story towers has four hundred and fifty apartments in its upper two-thirds, with the lower third a continuous parking ramp that spirals upwards, accommodating four hundred and fifty automobiles. Since the residential level starts at the twenty-first story, magnificent views of the city are enjoyed from every apartment. The towers are as popular with Chicagoans as the "corn on the cob" they are caricatured as in Goldberg's office.

For many years Goldberg had felt there were advantages in the use of circular forms: the aerodynamic properties in a cylindrical high-rise structure; the structural equidistance from the center, and therefore uniform function of all parts; the absence of special corner conditions; and the creation of centrifugal or "kinetic" spaces resulting from non-parallel walls. The towers derive much of their rigidity from the 35-foot-diameter cylindrical core that houses each building's services and utilities like a vertical street. Service spaces in apartments were grouped toward this core, giv-

Astor Tower, Chicago, Illinois.

ing living areas the light and view. The construction of the core preceded that of the floors, providing a rising foundation for the erection crane, thereby saving many working days. The project is all-electric, with heat and hot water individually produced in each apartment.

The other elements of the "city within a city" are a sixteen-story office building; a one-thousand-seven-hundred-and-fifty-seat theater and a seven-hundred-seat auditorium; stores, restaurants, bowling alleys; a gymnasium, swimming pool and skating rink; a marina for seven hundred small craft; and a sculpture garden at the base of the towers—all overlooking the Chicago River. Built for an economical ten to twelve dollars a square foot, Marina City is Goldberg's response to the urgencies of urban redevelopment. It reflects his interest in the use of "geometry to create a new aesthetic experience," and his prediction that "it contains many of the design concepts which will continue to predominate in building construction for the next forty years."

"Many nineteenth century value judgments in art contained words like functionalism, practicality, utility, mass production. These terms originated in the science by which that century knew the world. In contrast, one of the first of the new words used in modern art appraisals is dada; others are surrealism, abstract, infinite and indeterminate. The change is here. The words materialism, pragmatism, planned society, regimentation, begin to carry an apology; while spirit, soul, beauty, God, humanity are very ' in' words. When William McFetridge, President of the Janitors' Union (the sponsor of Marina City), said before his bankers, 'We want to pay to make it beautiful,' we are suddenly through the sound barrier of Victorian commercialism and rationalism. We dare to say to each other that we are people with dark and sometimes questionable values, with dreams and needs for aesthetic response that we cannot analyze scientifically.

"Into the earlier forced clarity of the twentieth century architecture, into this perversion of the meaning of order, comes the creeping mystery of indeterminism. A TWA terminal by Saarinen, or a Ronchamp chapel of deep, mysterious forms by that former champion of right angles, Le Corbusier—we are no longer able to know what these buildings look like by inspecting their floor plans. The three-dimensional mystery of spatial architecture is with us once again, and it has brought with it the exploration of method. Never in the past five hundred years has there been so much invention in art and architecture. Never in the last three thousand years has the post-and-beam been so limited in its ability to construct the spatial dreams of our architects. Our new architectural forms abandon the concept of system for system's sake and produce totality of building; a monolithic quality, a statement of design with a beginning and an end, which finds kinship with the fourteenth century High Gothic Summa aiming at the totality of one perfect and final solution.

"Our pace of revolution is unprecedented in history. A single lifetime today brings more radical change than centuries created in Egypt, Greece or Rome. The physical proof of our regenerating urban society is that in the United States today there are more than 600 urban renewal projects for our 'dead' cities. The City, the Victorian enemy of the people—facing Wright's prophecy, in 1930, of extinction through decentralization of industry and overcrowding—now becomes synonymous with civilization. Suddenly the city becomes the place where Aristotle said 'one could lead the good life,' where specialization of labor provides the leisure which men may use to their benefit.

"Central city populations remain fixed while our suburbs have grown. Yet the city provides increasingly more of the services which the small suburban community cannot afford: generation and control of utilities, law and government, higher and specialized education, social welfare, recreation, and cultural development. These services now provided for the many suburban areas require the cities to increase their taxes, and consequently their power. Many cities have annual budgets which today exceed our former national budgets. Our cities have become city-states.

"City planning, along with architecture, reached a peak of development in the fourteenth century. The planners broke many fences, in spirit and in mind, and in the administration of affairs. It was possible for men to develop according to their abilities. This was a time for the specialist and his special city. Mumford describes the medieval city as the congeries of little cities, each formed so naturally out of common needs and purposes that it served to enrich and supplement the whole.

"The fourteenth century urban specialist is being redeveloped today. As the university gave an education to the bourgeoisie in the fourteenth century, and developed lawyers, doctors and philosophers, so our universities are educating artists, bankers and operators of the machines that replace the common laborer.

"The increase of taxation will force new solutions to our planning problems. We cannot burden either business with buildings used only thirty-five hours a week, or apartment buildings used only at night and on weekends, with our total tax loads. We can no longer subsidize the kind of planning that enjoys only the single use of our expensive city utilities. In our 'cities within cities' we shall turn our streets up into the air, and stack the daytime and the nighttime use of our land. We shall plan for double-shift cities within cities, where the fixed costs of operat-

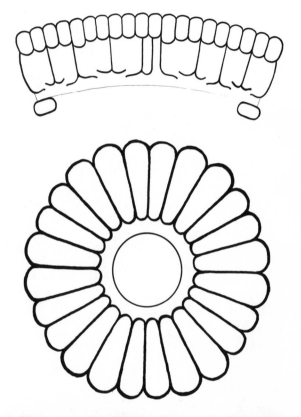

Public Housing for the Elderly and Family Housing, Chicago, Illinois.

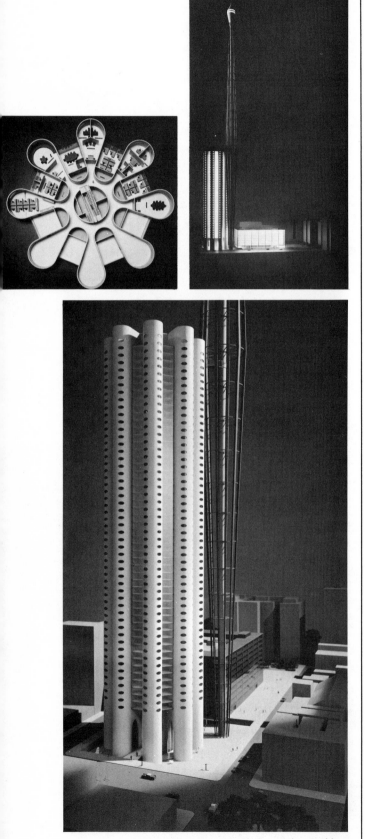

ing a city can be shared by commerce, recreation and education at the lower levels, and housing above. As we spread taxes and other fixed expenses over a wide use, we shall diminish the traffic problems that are caused by the journey to work. Our specialists living and working in the same building complex will need only vertical transportation.

"For our future we should no longer build separate buildings in our center city. We should think rather of building environment, total environment for the total men our modern faith has just reclaimed. Our future environment could repeat for us a great humanistic renaissance and should give us the building of cities within cities for these men of faith."

Within Goldberg's office staff of fifty, the architects work directly with structural and mechanical engineers. There is a particular effort to try to inject construction experience in the field into future designs, so that there is an empirical accumulation of knowledge.

The geocentric form has been used by Goldberg again, in part, in his recent proposal for the Chicago Housing Authority. Housing for the Elderly is in cylindrical towers where the form is conceived as "biological." In the Family Housing he uses "indeterminate" curved slabs, a combination of irregular shell forms.

Marina City is a centripetal, geocentric form where the core is a shell, and extending from it is a radical system of columns and beams. In a proposed office building for New York in the design stage, this separation does not occur. Here the loops never meet, and the building is a single vertical shell, "a beautiful and economical shape developed from structural need." After analyzing the function and design of New York office buildings, Goldberg concluded that most were built along a nineteenth century loft space concept, where today's tenant subdivides the interior into the smaller spaces of contemporary office arrangement. Goldberg saw his office building proposal as mainly a policy-making or programming center for highly-trained specialists, served by diminishing numbers of office workers. Improved methods of communication would permit the storage of information and bookkeeping machinery on less expensive land miles away from the office center.

Goldberg's solution was to design a series of defined spaces tailored to the needs of the policy-maker and his attendant office personnel; an efficient sequence in which policy, production and conference spaces could be directly related. A counterpoint in spaces is created where those of policy-making are more enclosed, oriented towards the introspective, highly-trained individual; with production workers, needing as much daylight as possible, occupying the open glazed areas.

After analysis by an independent concern, Goldberg's design was shown to be highly feasible from an economic standpoint, having a more efficient floor area in relation to usage than the more typical, modular office building.

Looking at the model of the New York office tower, Goldberg said: "We feed things into our architecture and in turn it feeds things back into us." And reflecting on his concern to develop further an approach derived from the idea of the geocentric structure, he continued, "I have moved beyond or out of the Miesian post-and-beam expression without being at all aware of such a move; so this was not self-conscious, but inevitable."

Project for a New York City Office Building.

Ralph Rapson

RALPH RAPSON

"The total environmental space created is the essential thing to me; this was always so." Primarily a product of the Midwest, Ralph Rapson was born in Michigan in 1914 and received his architectural training at the university there; understandably his early source of inspiration was the Chicago School of Sullivan and Wright. Rapson considered studying with Wright at Taliesin, but was discouraged by "the somewhat feudal nature of the setup." He received a scholarship to Cranbrook Academy of Art to study Urban and Regional Planning under Eliel Saarinen, but, he says, "we were much more influenced by Le Corbusier's planning principles than the 'satellite' planning ideas of Eliel." There he joined Saarinen's son Eero and Harry Weese. During his two years at Cranbrook, Rapson worked on several competitions with Eero, to continue their association when he later returned to the Saarinen office for some two years.

The influence of Mies was very strong. "I admired his precise, beautiful, structural expression," says Rapson. He agreed with Le Corbusier's thesis that from answering the functional requirements and social problems, and understanding the honest use of structure and materials, distinguished architecture would evolve. "I was leaving out the highly personal quality. I thought the art of architecture was more of a by-product; later on it became obvious to me that this was the important thing and was supplied by the individual and the personal magic that he could bring to a job."

In 1942 Rapson was appointed head of the architectural workshop at the Chicago Institute of Design. At the time Laszlo Moholy-Nagy was director of the Institute and his dedication to Bauhaus ideas had a considerable influence on Rapson. In 1946 he went on to teach at the Massachusetts Institute of Technology where he met Alvar Aalto. Aalto's belief that "probably architecture can do more to humanize life than any other art," struck a response in Rapson equalled only by his admiration for the Finnish architect's brilliant use of form to create and organize dynamic spaces.

In 1951 Rapson himself moved northwards when, at the State Department's request, he designed the American Embassies at Stockholm, Sweden, and Copenhagen, Denmark. Both had limited budgets and came at a stage in the United States' program for embassy construction when "it was a tough job to convince our government to do a contemporary structure." The expression of a straightforward office building, "essentially what an embassy is, was stronger than a more personal, sculptural and plastic approach." Rapson's apartments in 1954 for embassy staff in Boulogne, France, done with less interference and restraint from Washington, remain more to his satisfaction.

That same year he returned to the United States to become head of the School of Architecture at the University of Minnesota, where he has led the school to a highly respected position. Rapson says: "We believe, somewhat like Wurster, in a school policy of

Tyrone Guthrie Theater, Minneapolis, Minnesota.

U.S. Embassy,
Copenhagen, Denmark.

U.S. Embassy Staff Apartments, Boulogne, France.

Tyrone Guthrie Theater, Minneapolis, Minnesota.

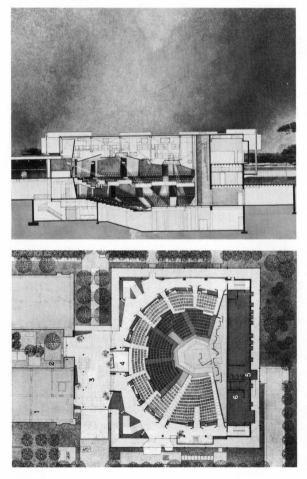

ordered conflict within a fairly rigid overall framework which allows for individual growth and personal expression." His own great drawing ability has inspired many of the students to such a degree that Rapson said, "in some cases they draw almost too brilliantly and sometimes delude themselves." Since he believes it impossible to teach architecture without practicing it, Rapson maintains a small office of eight, accepting work when he feels it can lead to architecture of value.

One lively result of experimental theater's move away from what has been described as the incurable invalid of Broadway is Rapson's new home for professional repertory, the Tyrone Guthrie Theater in Minneapolis—a place for the "delight, anticipation, gaiety and the mystery and drama of theater." With Sir Tyrone Guthrie, the former director of London's Old Vic, as its figurehead, it exemplifies the fruitful confrontation of two strong minds, each dedicated to his role in the project—neither willing to compromise where theater ends and architecture begins. There was a conflict all the way through between "function and abstract architecture," says Rapson, and "the final shape grew out of the function more than any other building I have worked on."

Guthrie's unconventional approach to theater suggested to Rapson that the building should "prepare the participants and put them in the frame of mind for unconventional theater. I tried to understand the client's interests, needs and aspirations, but it is finally the architect's obligation and prerogative to interpret these into appropriate forms; it is his responsibility to produce a building, or a piece of art, that goes beyond functional mandatory requirements. I would almost be arrogant on this point."

Two disciplines were the prime determinants of the new structure. First, the external form had to attach to the existing, rather overbearing, rectangular, three-story brick Walker Arts Center, and the desire to be a "good neighbor" suggested a strong, rectilinear discipline. Second, the internal theater form resulted from Guthrie's preference for the open stage, around which can be grouped a larger audience with a better view. Guthrie's program was to be classical, and he believed that an open stage rather than the more conventional proscenium stage was better suited to this. His aim was not to create an illusion, but to present a ritual of sufficient interest to stimulate the audience's attention. In an age when movies and television offer dramatic entertainment it seems important to stress the difference between such media and the stage.

The interior is an open stage within a 200-degree seating arc— an amalgam of the Elizabethan stage and the Greek seating plan. One of its striking achievements is the great degree of intimacy and proximity between actor and audience in a space that seats over fourteen hundred people. This is particularly important since the stage arrangement often presents an actor's back to a segment of the audience. An asymmetrical and exciting interior space evolved from Guthrie's comment that the gallery viewer was often a second-class citizen. Rapson integrated the balcony and orchestra levels by the ingenious method of having the seats on one side of the stage rise steeply and continuously to wrap around as a balcony. In some of the earlier studies seats fused from either side of the stage into the balcony. The more dynamic final solution, where the view and impression from seats on a changing floor level are always different, places certain limitations on the production, but Rapson prefers to think of these as a challenging opportunity for the director.

While realizing that the interior should not detract from the play itself, Rapson was determined that it have sufficient strength and architectural quality in its own right. When an interior is dark in color, as this one is, so as not to reflect light and distract from the stage, much of the form and quality of the space is lost; he counteracted this by a highly-animated treatment of walls and ceiling planes—the variety of angular relationships developing from acoustic considerations. Similarly, banks of seats, grouped around the irregular-shaped stage at the orchestra and multifaceted balcony levels, are covered in fabric of ten different colors creating a confetti-like pattern.

Rapson carried the drama and spirit of the predominately gray interior to the highly animated gray-white exterior, with white lobbies, having bright red and orange doors and charcoal carpeting, designed as transitional spaces. From outside, the form of the auditorium is seen through a glass facade, in front of which is an abstractly-shaped screen. Conversely, coming from the asymmetrical interior, one sees the undulating wall of the theater, or the "big toad" as Guthrie calls it, and across to the glass and screen wall with a garden space beyond. The lobby promenade at the balcony level was "floated" free of the walls and glass on either side, permitting an interpenetration of the two levels of foyer space, continuing the sense of integration between balcony and orchestra levels inside the theater. The screen has been the most criticized aspect of the building. To Rapson the effect of transparency was important: he wanted varying framed views of people promenading in the spaces. "We hoped," he says, "to provide an exciting and provocative overall character that anticipates the fantasy and stimulation of the theater itself."

"Architecture is both a fine art and highly precise social and physical science. It is the creative process of organizing and ordering total environment and relating it to man for his physical and spiritual use, comfort, and pleasure. The elements of the urban landscape—streets, neighborhoods, commercial and industrial areas, street furniture and billboards—all must be shaped, controlled and given order. This order is far more important than the individual architectural piece.

"The architect is faced with a great dilemma: on the one hand he must solve the intellectual problems of program, use, structure, and technical, social and economic aspects; on the other he must work as an artist. Without the art of architecture there is only building. Le Corbusier has written that 'architecture stands beyond the realm of utilitarian things,' and Wright said that 'architecture which denies aesthetics is like food in capsule form.' It is relatively easy to satisfy the function and stability, the commodity and firmness of a building, but it is rare that we find high aesthetic satisfaction—particularly in our times—in our environment.

"Art has been defined as the conscious, creative and imaginative act whereby man expresses his emotions. If architecture is an art, then it is an emotional expression; it then becomes my concern with the shape and form of our environment and expresses my deepest feelings about the way men live, work and play. The intellectually-oriented planning and structural factors are inseparable from the emotional content whose responses are stimulated by the intellectual processes: it is a constant interaction. We know that art is not necessarily beauty, and that the architect should not try to make his work superficially beautiful. But beauty as a

Chateau Coop Dining Club, Minneapolis, Minnesota.

Pillsbury House, Wayzata, Minnesota.

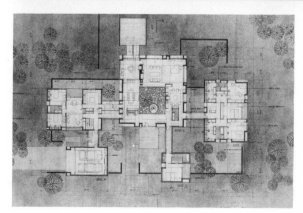

result of the essential nature of the problem—of logic and order—cannot be denied. Leon Battista Alberti said, 'I shall define Beauty to be a harmony of all the parts in whatsoever subject it appears, fitted together with such proportion and connection that nothing could be added, diminished or altered, but for the worse.' Aristotle, in his writings, held that beauty is the chief duty of free men. Whether we accept Aristotle's premise that beauty is the basis of all morality or not, it is true that the striving towards perfection in one's relation to the world is characteristic of both morality and art. If beauty is defined as that which approaches the ultimate satisfaction of human ideals, then beauty is necessary to human existence.

"Scientific and technical progress has placed in our hands the means of creating a truly superior environment. We have the ability to control architectural form at will, and limitations to the interpenetration and continuity of space are all but dissolved. We have many buildings that compare with the best in history, that are lost in some of the meanest and most shapeless cities known. If architecture is the true gauge of a culture, then this purposeless denial of human dignity is a devastating commentary on our world today. Invariably culture lags behind technological advance. While we cannot today derive much consolation in the fact, this lag is true of most periods. We are just not able to absorb the ever-expanding and ever-increasing scientific and technological innovations. As we add more and more gadgets to our way of life, we do so under the delusion that this is culture. We flatter ourselves that this is real progress, when so often it is only escape. Rather it is, as Wright says, 'a cheap substitute for culture, hired and paid for by the hour. Accumulation, not realization. Purchase, not production. A despair.' Our nerves are literally rubbed raw by this harsh indulgence of a way of life that worships the concept of 'built-in' obsolescence, this year's model, and the mediocrity of the paper cup, throw-away attitude.

"This is not to banish all lights, signs, noise, odors and dirt: the gaiety, the bizarre, the honky-tonk that we experience in our 'Times Squares.' The problem is to control and contain these elements. The sanitary, sterile and puritan characteristics that so many of our modern architectonic projects propose so morally have little real understanding of the intricacies of human life. There is a need for contrast; our environment cannot be played in a single key—richness, variety and complexity should be woven into an orderly composition. We should recall Wright's statement that 'the architect should help people to feel that [great] architecture is a destroyer of vulgarity, sham and pretense, a benefactor of tired nerves and jaded souls, an educator in the high ideals and better purposes of yesterday, today, and tomorrow.' Much is being done through the many urban renewal programs, but not much of real quality related to human aspirations.

"The creative act must always govern. Wright has given the process: 'In the arts, every problem carries within itself its own solution, and the only way yet discovered to reach it is a very painstaking way: to look sympathetically within the thing itself, to proceed to analyze and sift it, to extract its own consistent and essential beauty, which means its common sense truthfully idealized. There lies the heart of the poetry that lives in architecture.' However, the physical synthesis is quite another thing. Creativity is neither consistent nor predictable. The magic which the individual architect brings to architecture will vary, but is nonetheless his grave responsibility to society."

State Capitol Credit Union, Minneapolis, Minnesota.

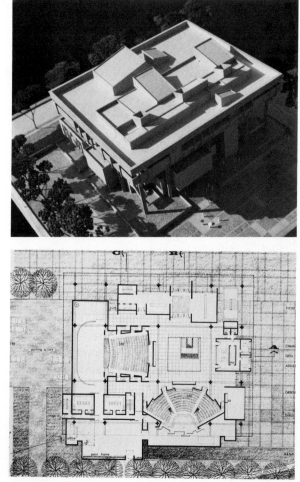

Performing Arts Center, Minneapolis, Minnesota.

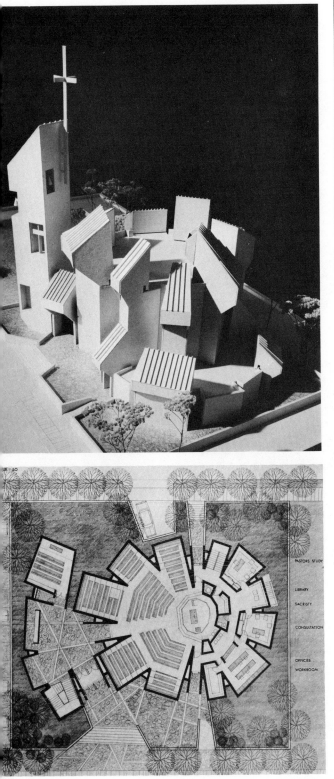

Hope Lutheran Church, Minneapolis, Minnesota.

Rapson has always considered the de Stijl spatial concepts of Van Doesburg and Rietvelt significant. At the Chicago Institute of Design he worked in collaboration with sculptors, painters and photographers on the problems of articulating and creating space. It reasonably follows that he should be primarily concerned with the shaping of space, its external and internal relationships rather than the enclosure of space. The de Stijl principles of design are particularly evident in two of his most recent projects: the Pillsbury House and the Chateau Cooperative Dining Club. Both are interesting in that they attempt to create exciting spaces in quite different surroundings—the house on a magnificent lakefront enjoying beautiful views, and the Chateau in a rather nondescript residential area adjacent to the University of Minnesota.

The Pillsbury House in Wayzata, Minnesota, is composed of five separate linked pavilions, with courts between, taking full advantage of the views. The arrangement was suggested by a "logical breakdown of functional requirements" into living area, private quarters, guest room and kitchen, family bedrooms, and garage. The Chateau is a simple cube in overall form, with its interior an intricate series of levels—interrelating varied spaces with changing views. In both projects the walls and ceiling undulate, as Rapson says, "almost nervously, almost cubistically."

Rapson believes the State Capitol Credit Union Bank and Office building in Minneapolis to be most typical of his approach. Here, in a more relaxed building, the nervousness of the two prior projects is under tighter reins, while the richness and variation of spaces and surfaces remain. A disciplined square plan, delineated by a concrete roof that is supported on sixteen cross-shaped columns, is set on a raised concrete podium. This provides the overall framework within which brick and glass screen walls richly modulate as they articulate and define spaces. In all three buildings various skylights, integral with and related to the ceiling pattern, introduce natural light to certain localized areas.

Rapson's most recent projects represent a strong continuity of these ideas, as can be seen by his Performing Arts Center and Radio-Television Facility, and the Hope Lutheran Church, both for Minneapolis. In the Performing Arts building, similar to the State Capitol Credit Union Bank, Rapson has employed a structural grid to support a fairly regular "cornice" element, both establishing a larger framework within which the lower theater elements are independent, and space is freely articulated. The church, since it is located near the airport and in a direct line with jet take-offs, is a solution to a difficult acoustical problem. Here, the heavy masonry structure is modulated for acoustical and aesthetic reasons, with great absorptive hoods also functioning as light sources. Many principles of light, acoustics and sight lines learned from the Tyrone Guthrie Theater were directly applicable, says Rapson.

Although Rapson respects the need for structural integrity and tries never to allow his work to deviate far from its ordering influence, a strong structural expression clearly is not central to his buildings. He does not consider himself a structural innovator. While he believes in good functional planning neither is he a "narrow functionalist; you cannot consider function without producing a good plan, and I put a great emphasis on abstract beauty in a plan."

For Rapson, individual creativity can be summed up in a prescription found in Buddhism: "Develop an infallible technique and then place yourself at the mercy of inspiration."

Kaufmann House, "Fallingwater," Connellsville, Pennsylvania.

FRANK LLOYD WRIGHT

During the ninety years of his life Frank Lloyd Wright saw the population of the United States expand from thirty-eight million persons to nearly five times as many, with seventy-five percent of these people living in urban centers. It was an urban expansion that coexisted with central deterioration; a need to escape from the automobile rather than with it; a lack of privacy, of community, and perhaps worst of all, a lack of dignity in the individual; an atmosphere of collective foreboding and individual helplessness stemming from the threat of total destruction.

Wright remained essentially a nineteenth century, anti-urban romantic. As Walt Whitman wrote in "Song of the Open Road": "Now I see the secret of the making of the best persons. It is to grow in the open and to eat and to sleep with the earth." This, too, was Wright's world. To him, not even democratic institutions could liberate men who were not free in their own spirit. He saw the rule of the mass, a democracy he would later refer to as "Mobocracy," curtailing the liberty of the individual to live freely and act creatively. The threat to individualism that Kierkegaard called the "tyranny of the multitude," was to Wright a reality. His ideal was "unity through individual creativeness," where "a new ideal of civilization arises based upon the freedom of man's mind guided by his conscience." Architecture he loved "as romantic and prophetic of a true way of life. . . . Architecture is that great living creative spirit, which from generation to generation, from age to age, proceeds, persists, creates according to the nature of man, and his circumstances as they change."

Wright was quite definitive about the role of the machine in civilization: "We must not dramatize the machine but dramatize the man. . . . Science is inventive but creative never." He saw the machine as a way of rendering traditional forms extinct, and a means of realizing new opportunities, methods and forms.

If Wright did not like the bureaucratic power of the modern state that came with the Industrial Revolution, he liked the detachment from nature even less. His liking for oriental and primitive cultures is easily explained by their unity with nature, where man could feel his life an organic whole. In the machine Wright saw the potential to transform the environment in harmony with nature: around him he saw it separating man from, and destroying nature. "We may deduce laws of procedure inherent in all natural growths to use as basic principles for good building," wrote Wright; "we are ourselves a product of such natural law." Emerson left the Unitarian church and found God again in nature: Wright also sought his principles in nature, for, to him, they were not only organic, but eternal.

Wright's disapproval of the whole system of architectural education led him in 1932 to found the Taliesin Fellowship, establishing a formal arrangement for the acceptance of resident apprentices. From the initial group of some twenty students, some one thousand students have benefitted to date from the educational environment he created. As a result, the sounds of construction at Taliesin East (Spring Green, Wisconsin) and Taliesin West (Scottsdale, Arizona) have never ceased. Because Wright was such a tremendous creative force, the Fellowship has often been criticized for producing only Wright disciples—architects who paradoxically did not assert themselves as individuals.

On three occasions, when he was starting the Fellowship, Wright invited Bruce Goff to become his chief assistant. Says Goff: "The

Taliesin West, Phoenix, Arizona.

first two times I begged off with excuses, but the third time I said: 'Mr. Wright, you honor me . . . therefore I feel I should tell you the real reason why I believe I should not accept your offer.' 'Yes . . . do,' he said. Then I told him: 'I have known people who have worked with you in the Oak Park days and since, and they all seem to fall into two categories; one group thinks you have ruined their lives . . . that you have stolen their ideas and that you are a devil. The other believes that you are a God who can do no wrong and that their lives are useless unless sacrificed for you. I don't want to think of you in either of these ways . . . nor can I ever be a 'disciple.' I need to be away from you far enough so that I can get the proper perspective.' He did not answer for an interminable time . . . then finally he put his arm around me and said 'Bruce, I wish others understood me the way you do.' Thus we remained friends. Later when people asked him if I had studied with him he would say, 'Bruce Goff has studied with me always.' "

Work at Taliesin East and Taliesin West is conducted today by two separate but parallel organizations. The Frank Lloyd Wright Foundation, headed by Mrs. Wright, directs the educational program. The architectural practice is conducted by Taliesin Associated Architects, of which William Wesley Peters, as President and Chief Architect, is the directing force.

Taliesin at present finds itself in the position of being almost flooded with commissions; twenty-six buildings are currently under construction. The total amount of work is much greater than ever before in the history of their endeavor—a success they attribute to their high dedication to Wright's principles which they are resolved will not be compromised in the work of the future.

Frank Lloyd Wright was born in Richland Center, Wisconsin, in 1869. He died in Phoenix, Arizona, in 1959. He cut short his professional training, restricted to engineering since no school of architecture was nearby, when he left home for Chicago at the age of nineteen. He was soon working in the office of Adler and Sullivan where he became Louis Sullivan's chief assistant. There, Wright explained, they worked with the imagination of true artists toward what no other architect at that time dared to even preach: buildings that owed their "style" to the integrity with which they were individually fashioned to serve their particular purpose. Sullivan's ideas, expressed with such eloquence, became integral to Wright's thinking, to the extent that Sullivan remained the only architect Wright ever acknowledged as an influence.

Wright was entrusted with the office's domestic architecture. One of the best of his early houses was the precise and very urban Charnley House, in Chicago, in 1891. Its compact powerful massing was reminiscent of the feeling of permanence and solidity of Richardson's architecture, while its very restrained, delicate embellishment reflected Sullivan's influence. Wright never quite forsook his liking for ornament. In employing it to accentuate surface continuity, he sought in turn to heighten the continuity of space. Ornament, for whatever reason, became increasingly criticized by European architects. Later, when the purist discipline of machine art swept architecture clean, the exuberant texture and detail in Wright's architecture seemed to belong more to the nineteenth century Art Nouveau. For Wright, like Sullivan, ornament was a part of architecture. Although, he wrote, "I cannot believe in adding enrichment merely for its own sake. Unless 'enrichment' by detail adds clearness to the enunciation of the architectural theme, it is always undesirable."

Larkin Building, Buffalo, New York.

The Beaux Arts architects in Chicago found geometric order in classical precedent, producing an architecture of effect with formal detachment. They pursued form as an end in itself. Wright's approach was more viable in that his geometry came increasingly from a response to purpose, structure, material and site.

In 1893, the year of Chicago's World Fair, Wright opened his own practice. During the first decade of this century, in the eclectic wake of the Fair, Wright designed three extraordinarily fine buildings: the Larkin Building, Buffalo, New York, in 1904 (demolished in 1950); the Unity Church, Oak Park, Illinois, in 1906; and the Robie House, Chicago, in 1909. Wright describes the Larkin Building as the first in which he "consciously" tried to beat the box. He found this liberation by pushing the staircase towers out from the corners of the principal mass, making them into freestanding elements. "I had 'felt' this need for features quite early in my architectural life," he wrote. A central, skylighted, four-story well was a narrow, "soaring" focal space, encircled by office galleries. Structure and the horizontal brick planes of the office galleries all "worked" as one to define the internal space, which was also expressed, with the staircase towers, in the exterior form.

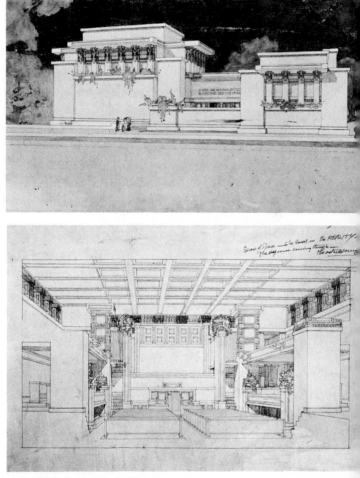

These ideas were more powerfully realized in the poured-concrete Unity Church. The diverse functions of assembly space and parish house were articulated as distinct masses, a square and a rectangle, respectively, without losing the "harmony of the whole." The independent yet related volumes were linked by an entrance loggia that allowed people entering the building to approach either space. This direct organization, clear separation and distinct expression of functions were to become one of the preoccupations of the functionalists in Europe.

Wright cites this church as his first real expression of the idea that the space within creates the reality of the building. There is a sense of the assembly space, or great room, coming through: "Space not walled in now, but more or less free to appear," said Wright. The interior treatment of the great room had the feeling of subsequent developments in Europe. It is indicative of Wright's philosophy, and indeed his powers of persuasion, that the liberal pastor gave up the symbol of the little white church with its steeple pointing on high, for Wright's conviction to build a great room. "A *natural* building for natural Man." The strong articulation, functional division and richness of geometric modulation that this building showed has, a half a century later, been given a new pertinence and vitality through the work of Louis Kahn.

Unity Church, Oak Park, Illinois.

By the time Wright designed the Robie House he had departed radically from his tight and formal early houses into an expression that was referred to as Prairie architecture. Here, extended horizontal lines, hugging the ground, related building and site. Interlocking and seemingly moving brick planes combined with broad overhanging and sheltering roofs to create compositions of rich surface and spatial variation. Cantilevers heightened the dramatic impact. These houses were almost private introspective worlds; although space "moved" continually outward, "leaking" to the exterior, it was essentially on its own secure terms. Horizontal strip windows, directly beneath eaves, and glazed interior angles that prevented horizontal walls from touching, allowed glimpses of the exterior, ensuring that interior space was never quite contained. Yet there was not the openness, lightness and transparency that European architects were later to achieve through the use of large glass areas; the almost dematerialization that can be seen,

Robie House, Chicago, Illinois.

for example, in some of Neutra's houses. Broad terraces and low garden walls followed the long horizontal brick planes of the houses, and in conjunction with integral planters, made a gentler transition from architecture to landscape.

The cruciform plan with wings radiating from a central space, bringing house and landscape into a more intimate relationship, was a favorite device of Wright's in these houses, and one that Neutra was later to employ with considerable success. The heavy masonry mass of a central fireplace, with its psychological overtones of security, provided a visual pivot. The strongest impression of these houses is one that almost compels movement in an ingeniously interwoven, horizontal sequence of spaces.

The Robie House culminated Wright's early experience in Chicago. He left for Europe to supervise two publications of his work, in 1910 and 1911. As Giedion wrote, "Wright had already achieved a body of work great enough and influential enough to assure him his place in history." Mies and Le Corbusier were only beginning their careers, working in Behrens's office. In such examples as his Robie house, Wright's freely related interlocking rectangular masses and interpenetration of space must have seemed powerful practical achievements to the Cubists who were then exploring a similar direction, one that the de Stijl movement was later to refine.

Parallel with Wright's concern for the relationship of spaces was his interest in materials. "In architecture, expressive changes of surface, emphasis of line and especially textures of material, may go to make facts eloquent, forms more significant," he wrote. His love of nature inclined him toward natural materials, which he used for the beauty of their natural pattern and texture. He relied generally on pre-industrial, non-synthetic materials, and in this sense his buildings came closest to developing a sense of tradition. This eventually led some European architects, coupled with their rejection of embellishment, to criticize him for not adopting a new attitude in response to the potential of the machine. This difference in attitude toward materials became clear in Wright's furniture designs: his rather complicated, very "constructed," wood furniture is in contrast to the slender elegance and greater comfort of Mies's and Le Corbusier's steel furniture. Designing a building as an organic entity, it was necessary for building and furniture to be in harmony.

Upon his return from Europe in 1911, Wright started to build his own home in Spring Green, Wisconsin; a complex of local, rough-textured stone and low-pitched roofs with broad overhanging eaves, grouped to create a series of interrelated courts. Wright added to this house all his life, twice having to rebuild almost completely after fires. "No house should ever be 'on' any hill or 'on' anything. It should be 'of' the hill, belonging to it, so hill and house could live together each the happier for the other." This was Taliesin East, a rural retreat "of" the brow of a gentle hill, with views outward, far over the landscape. Wright referred to his approach as a search for "Organic Architecture"—indigenous, of the soil, the time, the place and of Man.

The Midway Gardens in Chicago, in 1914, a restaurant and outdoor concert hall, was a large urban complex (demolished in the unprofitable prohibition years) that Wright designed even to the furnishings. A central, open space was surrounded by various terrace levels and buildings of highly animated, ornamented planes. The interplay of horizontals and vertical planes had become more abstract in Wright's work since his visit to Europe.

Taliesin East, Spring Green, Wisconsin.

Midway Gardens, Chicago, Illinois.

Imperial Hotel, Tokyo, Japan.

Millard House, Pasadena, California.

St. Marks Tower,
project for New York City.

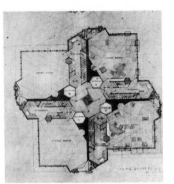

Taliesin West, Phoenix, Arizona.

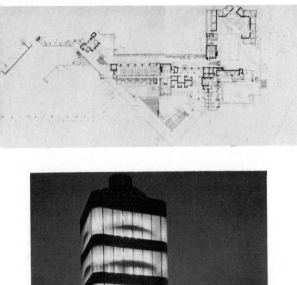

Johnson Wax Building, Racine, Wisconsin.

Receiving the commission to design the Imperial Hotel in Tokyo, Wright spent most of his time from 1916 to 1922 in Japan. The hotel was a very romantic and heavily ornamented series of interlocking horizontals, often in broad cantilevers, with vertical masonry planes producing a rich variation of building masses and spaces. The structures survived the earthquake that destroyed much of Tokyo in 1923, principally because of the structurally independent foundations that Wright had devised.

"Design is abstraction of nature—elements in purely geometric terms," said Wright. It naturally followed that the "box," being unlike an organism in nature, was becoming too rigid a limitation on both man and space. Wright thought of structure as an organic response to creating space and was highly critical of the emerging European rectilinear architecture.

The Millard House, Pasadena, California, in 1923, was his first project to be constructed of hollow, patterned precast concrete blocks, reinforced with steel and filled with poured concrete. Although it produced a homogeneous, continuous skin it was still fundamentally a built-up, rectilinear construction and not the plastic expression he was seeking.

His idea of organic structure is well illustrated by the proposed St. Mark's Tower for New York, in 1929. From a central structural core, rooted deeply in the earth, radiated four bearing walls, with floors cantilevered out from these to a non-structural, external glass skin. Wright had reverted to nature for his vertical structure, employing its principle of the tree. Although never built, it was a prototype for the Price Tower in Bartlesville, Oklahoma, in 1953. Curiously, Sullivan's "abstract" structural skeleton for a high-rise structure was an approach that Mies would carry to a new level of excellence: Wright had delved deeper into nature for what he thought was a more integral, more organic expression.

In 1931 Wright amplified his idea of "organic" in an essay directed "To the Young Man in Architecture." "Beauty remains the essential characteristic of architecture itself. But today because of scientific attainment the modern more clearly preceives beauty as an integral order; order divined as an image by human sensibility; order apprehended by reason, executed by science . . . it is in architecture in this sense that 'God meets with nature in the sphere of the relative.' Therefore the first great necessity of a modern architecture is this keen sense of order as integral. That is to say the form itself in orderly relationship with purpose or function: the parts themselves in order with the form: the materials and methods of work in order with both; a kind of natural integrity—the integrity of each in all and of all in each."

Wright's idea of "organic" naturally led to his dislike of an urbanity that for him resulted in the severance of man and nature, of man from his rightful heritage, the land. In his 1935 project for "Broadacre City," he proposed an agrarian society of an acre per family that was something of a self-delusion, a rationalized suburban sprawl. Over a decade earlier, Le Corbusier—always more aware of the problems of urban life—had designed a proposed city for three million inhabitants; a vertical concentration at a very high density, that also respected the importance of contact with nature. When Wright did tackle the problem of density in his 1956 project for a "mile-high" Chicago skyscraper, his romantic tapering tower, five hundred twenty-eight floors high with a daytime population of 130,000 inhabitants, although structurally possible, was unrelated to any comprehensive and realistic consideration of urban problems.

The 1936 Kaufmann House, known as "Fallingwater," in Connells-ville, Pennsylvania, is acclaimed as one of the great houses of any architectural period; a sheer poetry of structure and space, and one of the most compelling examples of a man-made episode united with the landscape. It is a structure of cantilevered concrete balconies and vertical stone walls. The interior spaces open through large glass areas to balconies that project dramatically as simple horizontals from the rock base above the water.

In 1938, in a quite different landscape, Wright again showed the full maturity of his genius. "The desert is where God is and Man is not," said Wright, quoting Victor Hugo. And in the desert near Phoenix, Arizona, where there is a splendor and excitement in the landscape that seems larger than life, Wright started to build a winter home, school and office in one—Taliesin West. On the edge of a plain and at the foot of a mountain, it was a place in the sun, a place where the "sovereignty of the individual" was secure. Battered walls of poured concrete, with large desert boulders as aggregate, formed a base for the redwood trusses and canvas screen structures placed upon them. Terrace gardens and shimmering pools complete a powerful, constructed drama in a most beautiful setting. Here Wright developed a wonderful, progressive spatial experience: a sequence of events in approaching and moving through a building—landscape, terraces, the tight space as a prelude to the high, expansive one, the dark space as an overture to the bright, illuminated one. "Space," he wrote, "the continual becoming: invisible fountain from which all rhythms flow and through which they must pass. Beyond time or infinity."

Having explored the use of triangular and hexagonal modules in his domestic architecture, in 1936 Wright designed the Johnson Wax Building in Racine, Wisconsin, on a circular module. Here he achieved the liberation of space he had been searching for, in a hall of slender, mushroom-shaped columns that were surrounded by a shell of alternating bands of brick and glass tubing. There was "no sense of enclosure whatever at any angle, top or sides. You are looking at the sky and feel the freedom of space. The columns are designed to stand up and take over the ceiling, the column is made a part of the ceiling: continuity." In 1950 he added the laboratory tower, again designed on a circular module, a beautifully clarified, forthright statement of the earlier St. Mark's principle in which he abandoned much of the richness of surface and detail that had characterized his work.

The circular theme continued to preoccupy Wright, and in the Guggenheim Museum in New York, which he had started designing in 1946, he created a continuous spiral ramp as both gallery exhibition space and the means of circulation through the building. It is a building at odds with its environment, and its purpose—a place to view art. It is almost a tribute to Wright's sense of humor that many critics interpret the building as indicative of his respect for both. But he was too proud an artist for such a purposeless gesture. Wright never lived to see the Museum quite completed, but at last concrete technology had enabled him to realize his search for continuity in structure and space. A search that had begun with the early static surfaces of the Oak Park Houses ended with the dynamic spiral on Fifth Avenue.

In the twilight of a truly magnificent career that had produced nearly five hundred structures (and projects for as many more), a dozen significant books, and established an educational foundation, Wright was able symbolically to root space deep into the earth, spiralling outwards from it, to infinity.

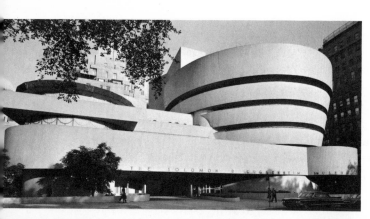

*Solomon R. Guggenheim Museum,
New York, N.Y.*

Triaero House, Louisville, Kentucky.

Crystal Chapel, project for the University of Oklahoma, Norman, Oklahoma.

BRUCE GOFF

Bruce Goff's architecture cannot be categorized with any of the mainstream approaches to design. Much of his work has been called strange and freakish, and has gone unappreciated. "Some people like the differences in it; some can't stand it," says Goff. "This feeling comes not so much from the public as from other architects and critics." Goff is criticized primarily because he practices with a flexible romantic freedom that he unashamedly refers to as having sentiment without sentimentality, and a catholic license that he considers necessary if an architect is to establish the essential character of each project. He is accustomed to this criticism and is unconcerned by it, having built up an immunity necessary for his own survival. Influenced by Wright, whom he was close to and greatly respected by, he has not aspired to emulate Wright nor, of greater significance, has he misinterpreted the spirit of Wright's work. It is the feeling that architecture should be organic that they share. "If I have any influence at all," says Goff, "I hope it will encourage people to realize that they have the right and freedom to do creative things; that they need to explore more fully man's potential; and that they must understand the nature of materials, structures and design."

Goff is a warm, rather retiring Midwesterner with a respectful appreciation and wider knowledge of architecture than is often assumed. He is deeply interested in oriental cultures and has an insatiable appetite for music. He likes to quote Debussy, whom he admires: "Music is not, in its essence, something which can be forced into strict traditional forms. It consists of tone colors and time values—of elements which the sensitive artist has only to pluck out of the air, from the great treasure store of nature."

Bruce Goff was born in Alton, Kansas, in 1904, and was an architectural prodigy. He was apprenticed to the firm of Rush Endacott & Rush in Tulsa, Oklahoma, at the age of eleven and had designed several houses "in the manner of Wright" before he even knew who Wright was. His first house was built when he was fourteen. One day, a passing car stopped before it, and its occupants started to laugh, saying, "Look at the crazy house!" Goff ignored them, when reassured by the words of a colleague: "When you are in the trenches doing what everyone else is, no one will pay any attention to you, but the moment you get into no-man's-land they are going to start shooting at you from all sides." Goff was soon aware that his buildings sometimes shocked people, but he maintains he has never designed one for this purpose.

Goff had the opportunity to pursue a formal academic training, but was skeptical of the eclecticism being taught at the time. He wrote to both Sullivan and Wright to ask their advice. Sullivan

Ford House, Aurora, Illinois.

replied that he had had precisely that same education and had spent his life trying to live it down. Wright sent a terse note: "If you want to lose Bruce Goff go to school." Not surprisingly, Goff stayed put, later to become a partner in the firm, which had to be dissolved during the Depression. He then went to teach at the Chicago Academy of Fine Art, and also had a small practice mainly engaged in residential architecture. The war terminated this, and in 1941 Goff enlisted in the United States Navy. He spent eighteen months in the Aleutian Islands, exposed to an environment "that wasn't spoiled by civilization," where he could contemplate "what was basic to design in any time, place, or person's work," and build with indigenous and "found" materials: "It made me respect all materials. There's not any one material that is *the* material."

After the war Goff went to California, where there were opportunities but building materials were scarce. He was glad to accept a teaching position at the University of Oklahoma in 1947. A year later he became chairman of its School of Architecture, resigning in 1956 to concentrate on his practice. Wright visited the school many times, and though he did not like any school, "he liked ours better than most," says Goff. Eric Mendelsohn too was impressed by the school and Goff's work. "I tried to teach the students to learn from what had been done, but more important, to think their *own* way as much as possible," said Goff. It is hard for students to distinguish between inspiration, influence and imitation; Goff's buildings were to inspire, influence and be imitated. There was no design formula in the school, in fact work was jokingly referred to as "the same old unusual stuff." The unusual became the usual, and "if a student's work was unusual, he earned the reputation of being a follower of mine," said Goff. "Students are generally considered as receptacles in which to pour prefabricated education rather than persons to bring something out of. This kind of education seems totally inorganic to me. We tried to relate our work to potentials rather than accomplishments."

The Triaero House, near Louisville, Kentucky, in 1941, and the proposed Crystal Chapel for the University of Oklahoma in 1950, show Goff's design licence, and why his work is hard to categorize. The Triaero House is triangular in plan, with the roof cantilevering from a central core that contains utilities. Walls and ceilings are redwood strips and copper, with black, venetian metal blinds shielding windows. The Crystal Chapel was to have been a stainless steel structure, with glass insulated by a pink, glass-fibre blanket. Structural piers and the chapel spire were to have been of Oklahoma pink granite.

"The design problem always differs from one building to another. If you work freely with a broad vocabulary of design elements and materials, all disciplined towards the order and character of each problem without a preconceived formula, you will arrive at a solution that will fit that particular problem. Saarinen said the solution lies within the problem. I am sure that he knew there was more than one solution; any good architect can design many solutions to any one problem.

"Mies says that he has no use for an architect who thinks he has to invent a new style of architecture every Monday morning; I think you have to invent one for each building, whether it is Monday morning or not. The differences in my work worried me at first because they did not seem to add up to a personal style— as did the works of Sullivan, Wright, Gaudi, Mendelsohn and Le

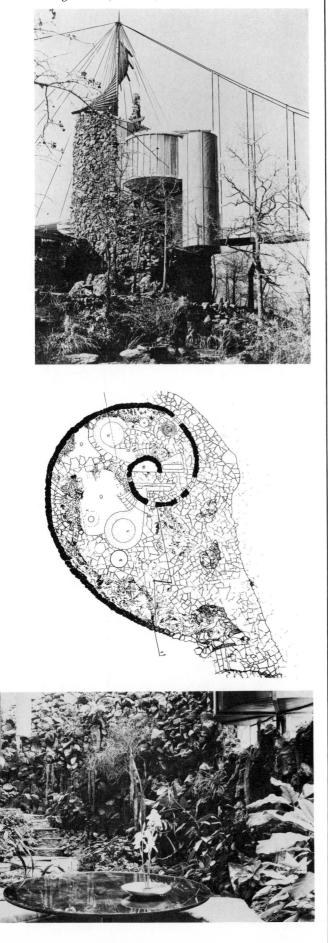

Bavinger House, Norman, Oklahoma.

Corbusier, no matter how different the individual styles of their buildings looked. Now, I realize that if each work of an artist has its own style, they collectively represent him. Music helped me to understand this. Stravinsky has a style. You can total his many very different works and say this is his style; that is more the result than the cause. As each thing is done the cause too has its own style; each piece has its own spirit, life and form. I began to realize that the objective is important; that the handwriting is not enough. Le Corbusier was able to rethink each problem as he did it. To me that is more vital, alive and important than to say 'I will never do this or that'—like some painters who will never use viridian in their palette, and feel very self-righteous about it, when sometimes it is the very thing they need.

"The particular expression of my buildings usually derives from working with individual clients and using their character as part of a starting point, with the functional requirements, site, budget and climate—always different in each project. I try to work out each for its own sake, while recognizing that there have to be certain abstract values that go beyond these to create architecture. When we look at Egyptian architecture we cannot begin to see it as they did. We see the residue of its more abstract quality, rather than its functional quality. I am interested in trying to extend this approach, without giving up the personal one derived from each client, while using technology to solve the problems that the personal approach cannot. I am not consciously motivated by a need for self-expression, it results from the natural way one works.

"Wright felt that he was architecture and architecture was him—that it was all within himself. Sullivan felt that architecture was something to strive for beyond himself; I admire this more. Wright believed that architecture was on the brink, and science was ruining it as it had ruined religion. I see no more reason why science should ruin us than the machine providing we can master the machine and think of science as an inspiration.

"This is an opportune but difficult time for architects. There is an emphasis on materialism, and the belief that only through conformity can you have harmony. The result is 'commonism.' Our sense of rhythm is sterile too; we feel that it is not rhythm unless it is monotonously regular. This applies in particular to architecture and popular music. Our time is more complex rhythmically than architects seem aware. We should not restrict buildings in height, material or color. If a building is truly a work of architecture, then it will be harmonious; works of architecture can co-exist as do works of nature. There should be no 'background' buildings. However, I am interested in the problem of overcoming obsolescence in commercial buildings. The centers of cities are dying, and the commercial buildings that once served their purpose are now obsolete. I am trying to use new techniques, technology and materials to develop commercial buildings that can be easily converted for a new purpose, thus flexible in their space concept.

"Buildings should not be 'dolled up,' but they should reward you like a person. Some people make a fine initial impression, but often the more you know them the less rewarding they become. The most interesting people are those one knows less while wanting to know them more—you never solve the mystery. Many buildings stop too soon, they are not carried through but remain a kind of outline where something should happen but usually does not. In Wright's greatest work, however, you can see where he has carried through into the finer details, so that one is rewarded close up as well as at a distance. A building should never really stop, a whole building can be an ornament or have ornamental aspects. Color is also important. You cannot design a building without being aware of this, and an architect cannot afford to have prejudices about it. Similarly, if he limits himself to certain theories, he ties his own hands behind his back."

Goff's 1949 Ford House in Aurora, Illinois, was designed for an artist and her husband. Mrs. Ford is "a very dynamic woman," says Goff. "She wanted guests to be able to gather in groups, and liked the idea of having the kitchen and her studio centered so she could work and talk at the same time." The need to centralize many elements suggested a circular scheme: "I tried to get the same order in section and plan, so I used domes." The kitchen, dining and outdoor barbecue space are in a sunken portion in the center of the house. Above this is the studio on a cantilevered balcony with a direct skylight. Two bedrooms are in domed units adjoining the principal space. The domes are standard Quonset ribs, lined on the inside with cypress boarding. Outside they are covered with copper, green-black stained shingles, and red-painted steelwork. Solid walls are of coal: "I don't consider it unusual to use hard coal and glass cullets in a wall, but since it is uncommon some people do."

The following year Goff built a house near Norman, Oklahoma, for Gene Bavinger, an artist teaching at the University of Oklahoma. The Bavingers' unusual requirements were both challenging and inspiring for the house they wanted to build themselves with the help of student labor. They had been living in the "usual conglomeration of little boxes with holes cut in for doors and windows" and found it restricting. "They wanted a large open space, and liked the idea of living on different levels; they wanted many interior plants, and preferred natural rather than synthetic materials. Gene was a hard-working, strong painter, as against the weak, delicate type, so I knew he needed a rugged kind of house," says Goff.

The site was beautiful. It was a ravine at the edge of a stream with crystal, sandstone and red clay strata, where the many trees were "busily textured and looked rather hectic." The rock shelf had a natural curved space, "like part of a helix," that became the first level of the house, with the native rock exposed in places in the interior. Since the clearing was small, and the Bavingers wanted different levels anyway, Goff thought it would be interesting to design the space growing upward, out of the rock, and winding around to echo the helix effect. The result was a 96-foot continuous wall in the form of a logarithmic spiral, which coils around a steel pole from which the entire roof, interior stairway, living areas and bridge are suspended. "I never design a house starting with a form idea," says Goff "but rather arrive at it, as I did here."

The interior space, which cannot be seen in totality from any one vantage point, is thought of as a conservatory for plants, within which the five principal areas are suspended in an upward progression: the living space; the parents' sleeping area; the dining area with a stairway leading up to a child's play space off which a suspension bridge crosses the stream to a flower garden opposite; the child's sleeping area; and at the top, the painting studio with a large west-facing window, from which the distant town and the magnificent sunsets of this part of the country can be

Bachelor's House, Bartlesville, Oklahoma.

viewed. The areas are shaped like carpeted bowls, stepped up at 3-foot intervals, each area with its own "satellite circular revolving closet of copper."

The planting areas, around the perimeter of the stone wall, are illuminated by a continuous glass skylight above them. Another skylight follows the stairway, upwards around the inner coil wall. The space within the house is dynamic and everchanging as the walls, ceiling and floors are never parallel. "Here, more completely than in any other house of this time," says Goff, "is an architectural expression of the way of life of the client; a sense of three-dimensional living space, the furniture integral with the house, and harmony with nature, indoors and out—a do-it-yourself architecture using available materials and a limited budget."

Wright sought spatial continuity in his houses, but often only in the more open public spaces, whereas private sleeping areas were usually in an adjoining wing. In the Bavinger house, Goff's client did not require any strong separation, which allowed Goff to design a continuous, flowing space. "I wanted to do something that had no beginning and no ending," says Goff. "Gertrude Stein says we begin again and again; this house begins again and again. She talks about the sense of not being in the past, present or future tense, but in the 'continuous present.' I was thinking in those terms."

Like many of Goff's buildings, photographs of this house suffer from the limitations of the camera, which can only record a limited view. Here, the space and interest is panoramic. The rich color palette that is central to his architecture is also lost in a black and white media.

In his Bachelor's House near Bartlesville, Oklahoma, in 1957, Goff returns to a triangular geometry in a design whose colorful exterior comprises gold anodized aluminum roof and sloping walls, and coal and glass-cullet masonry walls. The sumptuous living space is "somewhat representative" of his predilections for the treatment of interiors.

Goff's most recent design proposal is for the Phi Kappa Tau fraternity house at the University of Kansas, at Lawrence, where buildings, grouped around a central circular pool, are also laid out on a triangular base plan. The main building has dining and lounge areas on a lower level with a chapter meeting room above, and is flanked by a separate building for the housemother and an attached service building housing the kitchen. Connected by enclosed passageways that provide access up half a flight of stairs to the study areas, and down to the bedroom areas, are ten separate buildings, each accommodating eight students. Intended only for sleeping and quiet study, spaces are purposely small to encourage social contact in the central fraternal building. Sleeping areas are planned in two groups of four residents, separated by the stairway and bathroom. The concept of separate, linked smaller units has the advantage that the complex can easily be expanded by the addition of more units, and unoccupied units need not be mechanically serviced.

Goff's work is highly personal, though he will add that "the perfection of a piece of art is its most impersonal quality." He quotes Debussy: "The struggle to surpass others is never really great if disassociated from the noble ideal of surpassing oneself, though this involves the sacrifice of one's cherished personality."

"Music alone is able to make the improbable visible and alive," Debussy said. Goff, in his architecture, has extended that.

Phi Kappa Tau Fraternity House,
University of Kansas, Lawrence, Kansas.

Greene House, Norman, Oklahoma.

HERBERT GREENE

Herbert Greene was born in Oneonta, New York, in 1929. He started his architectural studies at Syracuse University, but left at the end of his first year when he found little emphasis there on Wright's approach to architecture—a characteristic common in architectural schools both then and now. On learning that Bruce Goff had just taken over at the University of Oklahoma, Greene transferred there. He was immediately exposed, through Goff, to the ideas of Wright. However, the work of architects like Sullivan, Le Corbusier and Mies was not neglected, as Goff always emphasized the need for a broad background.

The realization of space in Wright's building was of prime interest to the students, and their projects took on a complex spatial organization. Certain functions of a building were handled as complete enclosures within the larger framework of the whole. The aim was to express vividly the different functional requirements and aesthetic purposes of a building; Goff's own work at that time was just such an orchestration of individualized parts that respected the fact that they were "parts of one organism, like that of the human body." This might be construed as copying nature, and indeed nature was endlessly interesting for its sense of organization. However, most of the students understood their work as attempts to abstract from nature in an effort to understand it. To copy nature, Greene notes, "was as undesirable as it was impossible." He was particularly intrigued by the way in which Wright's plans seemed to have an almost symbolic pattern: "You could hang up the floor plan of a Wright building and enjoy its organization as a pattern. In those days his plans seemed to me to be expressive of some ultimate abstraction of nature."

Greene's appreciation of Goff's own work increased markedly after he realized that Goff's buildings were totally conceived in the mind and that his drawings were just diagrams of the idea. "I did not appreciate the Ford House on paper, but when I saw the actual building, I was very impressed."

At first, Greene was wary of being too influenced by Goff's work but then he "relaxed and tried to do what came naturally." After graduating from the University of Oklahoma in 1952, Greene worked in California and then in Texas before returning to Oklahoma to teach at the university. He has worked intermittently for

Goff; now he both practices on his own and teaches at the University of Kentucky.

"I am often baffled by the lack of attention that local color has received, both in school and in practice. Many architects put forth an ubiquitous technology which, like taxes, is only a man-made structure, as a defense against regionalism. Despite its present mass and momentum, it should not be regarded with the finality of an ice age. In the future, one task for technology will be to elicit individuality from local environments and thereby increase the possibilities of subtlety and choice. Freedom of choice is a necessary condition for any advance of life among the higher organisms. One of the problems we face today is to discover how architectural form can be made receptive to and evocative of happenings, architectural or otherwise, that have had their histories on or near the site of the building. To deny the importance of this consideration is to place limits on creative memory.

"Technology is essentially neutral. It is impossible to explain the differences in Roman, Romanesque, and Gothic architecture by their masonry technology alone. The state of mind exerts an organizing influence on the deployment of materials and technology. We may utilize forms 'as found,' or we may employ technology to produce new forms to solve new or even old problems. In architecture, our problem is to use technology for human purposes. One such purpose is the preservation of certain conditions of former space and time in the texture of our newly-created conditions or happenings in our immediate space and time. Let us call this a historic reference principle, one which is analogous to the transference of identity within organisms undergoing evolution. However, I am not advocating that the functional attainment and ethics of materials and structure be violated in the interests of this preservation.

"It is in the proper incorporation of local detail, along with the broad demands of more general principles, that modern architecture is weakest. And I suppose it will remain weak until we correct an oversimplified conception of the status of general or universal principles. This concept stems from the belief that the value or enjoyment of a form or idea is undying and absolute, even when divorced from the actual environment of human activity that created it. This classical concept is gradually giving way to the organic concept, which lays stress on a particular environment in a state of change or evolution. Since the actual environment intimately influences the content of human thought, general principles must always be renewed or restated for the immediate present.

"Modern methodology available for the analysis of an architectural problem presents us with enlarged means for understanding and realizing regional values. We are now able to deal with structure, to think about materials, about color, form, plan and purpose, either as separate elements or in related wholes. We should theoretically be able to attain a synthesis never imagined by older civilizations. Such is the power associated with the rise of abstract analysis; yet most of us would admit to a general lack of architectural quality on a par with that of older civilizations. Somehow we have to discover how to put our abstractions together to produce architecture.

"Architecture should attempt to get closer to the world of substance, the concrete world of natural phenomena. The best way would be to use intuition, screened by reason, to appropriate ab-

Greene House, Norman, Oklahoma.

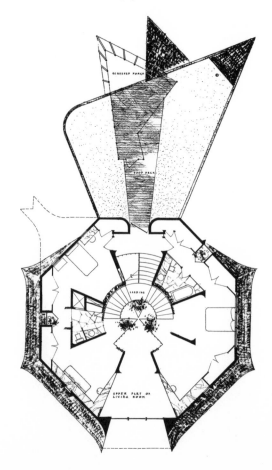

Joyce House, Snyder, Oklahoma.

Joyce House, Snyder, Oklahoma.

stractions that seem architecturally best suited to solve a particular problem. Traditional topics of architecture have been accounted for. Structure, the nature of materials and the relationship between building and site are major topics, as is the client's state of mind. Geometry is important because of the relatively new fact that more than one geometric description of the physical world is now possible. In mathematics, geometry has expanded to include the cross-classification of relations (for instance, color and shape) common to diverse circumstances. This fact has meaning for architecture as well as mathematics. A technique is now available for at least a partial analysis of our feeling for the relativity in the world. The new geometric understanding should warn us that in determining form we have neglected important aspects of human understanding. Our habit has been to let limited sets of geometric conditions, sanctified by time and usefulness, superimpose themselves upon our concepts of form and perhaps prematurely limit them.

"We need the creation of character in architectural form. How can we give a courthouse a judicial character, or a dress shop femininity? This can be achieved in some powerful way analogous to the contrasts we feel in nature, regarding the qualities and characters of different things. Modern architecture has discovered the power of abstract design. Now we must be careful to draw our abstractions from significant experience. Currently there is wide concern as to what constitutes meaningful experience. The 'duration' or 'instant' of a basic unit of experience within a concept of cognition has increasingly excited artists, scientists and philosophers as a part of nature requiring expression. The recent expansion of geometric understanding should encourage us in the attempt to give form to our concepts of relations and processes that make the character of experience vivid.

"There are levels of interpretation, private and public, that are coordinate to an act of experience. No two people experience the same thing in exactly the same way. In the last analysis we must respond privately to the public world of form and tradition. Since everyone's past experience is different, one person will see something another will not. Architecture needs to enliven these various responses as a function of an aesthetic aim."

Like many other architects, Greene is still concerned with expressing the elements of a building, but without superimposing an organizing geometry too quickly. His approach in establishing a

Anne Frank montage.

Cunningham House.

structural system and in organizing the relationships of a family of forms is similar to Wright's and Goff's. Greene says, "You try to arrive at your choice of geometry through characteristics of the problem, shape and character of the site, and even the nature of clients." Greene shares with Wright and Goff an interest in nature, the study of organisms and natural patterns. It is important to him to see analogies among patterns of organization in science as well as art—to try to see how one organizes, consciously or otherwise, diverse experiences in relation to these patterns.

In order to explore ideas, Greene spends much of his time painting. His recent paintings are photomontages associating fragments from different times, assembled for symbolic meaning. Robert Rauschenberg has placed, in his recent screen collages, contentious symbols in ambiguous relationships, mirroring the incongruous and irrational in everyday life. However, Greene's is a more surrealistic preoccupation in which visual pattern and cross-reference of images stimulate us to think about what we see. Familiar things are seen in new ways—relating subjects or objects often unrelated in everyday thought. Greene says, "The finished work is in the realm of art, yet the subject matter, in attempting to show relations in diverse spheres, is of philosophic outlook, and concepts of space, time, mind, matter and form appear as topics for contemplation."

This has, in turn, heightened Greene's desire to relate this experience to architecture. In the Joyce House, at Snyder, Oklahoma, in 1960, Greene tried to account architecturally for the continuity of thought and experience. He designed a "composite" that would "by a disposition of parts seem old, yet not be old." In the same way that his photomontages meaningfully associate different times and happenings, the Joyce House creates a similar reference by using the client's collection of Swedish objects and Victorian furniture, even to the inclusion of fifteen stained glass windows. Greene believes that his solution is reminiscent of the low eaved roofs of Scandinavia, the shingled extravaganzas of Victorian times, and in the screened porch, the design forms of native Indians. "The client enjoyed the objects, kept them with loving care, so they really became things to try and account for in the design." Greene did resort to a "standard"—the unifying background of white plaster. But objects were not placed in sanctified, museum-like repose. Their shape, size and characteristics were directly accommodated in the total design that is a response to them. Bruce Goff says that Greene incorporated the objects so skillfully that in the end people thought he had had them specially made because he wanted them that way. And Greene says, "This accommodates the past more creatively than anything else I have done."

For many architects the client becomes a convenient scapegoat for lack of accomplishment in a project. To become one's own client, as Greene did in designing his own house at Norman, in 1960, is to lay one's own predilections unavoidably bare. This is particularly so in an exercise as unrestrained as an isolated house in which a do-it-yourself approach supplements funds. The house is an all-out attempt to appropriate and evoke the character and texture of the Oklahoma region. "From prairies to barns, from birds to buffaloes and from wagons to planes—the poise and soft texture of birds are as valuable as the silhouette and woodiness of wagons—all this shows and is embodied in the design by its very geometry, texture and color," said Greene. "It is the conventionalization of natural phenomena, much in the tradition of Wright's conventionalization of nature." Greene tried to express these symbolic projections in the construction, aware that he was "not imitating nature but trying not to be so far removed in the abstraction that you cannot see it coming from nature." Greene says that this house "strives to promote thought about the content of what we might call composite or extensive characters, involving thoughts about regional things spread through time." Again his main theme is the notion of character as inseparable from time. He points out that the theme is expressed in A. N. Whitehead's comment: "As the past perishes, so the future becomes."

In contrast to the rough-finished natural quality of his own house, is the more polished and formalized Cunningham house recently completed by Greene in Oklahoma City. The dramatic curving roof, sweeping down into vertical wall planes, dominates the design. The curved forms have acoustic advantages, explains Greene, and create warm, indirect light sources. He attempted to "evoke a certain kind of aspiration. Materials and function must not be sacrificed in this process but there are, after all, in addition to elegance or strength, other qualities which may need expression." The house is set into the sloping site to create a feeling of privacy. Living, dining and kitchen areas are at the ground level on the garden side, with bedrooms above on the street entrance level. The living space, two floors high, has clear views of the landscape between brick piers and steel trellises which will eventually be covered by vines to protect the interior from the afternoon sun. The red-brick escarpment, similar to the brick used to build the house, is a strong visual "anchor" to the landscape.

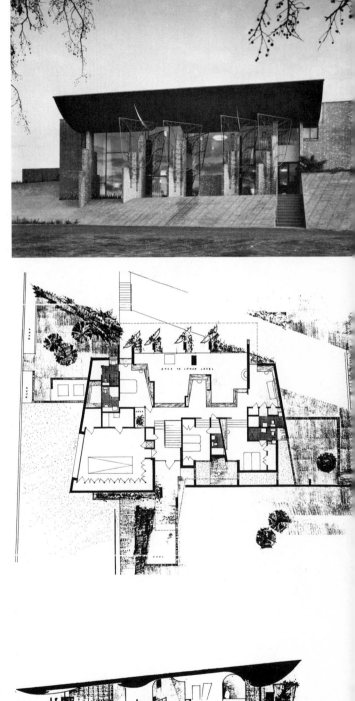

Greene thinks that the idea of getting deeply involved with the present and existing situation is in the tradition of William James, and very much an American concern. He certainly found it one of the most important characteristics of education at the University of Oklahoma in the Goff era. While certain predispositions from background and experience are inevitable, these are to be held without imposing them on the problem—a noble ambition, but possibly one demanding too great a degree of detachment. "This is very important in the American conception and differs somewhat from the European conception in which certain structural relations or formulations of space are thought of as being the mold in which architecture is cast," says Greene.

Both the Joyce and Greene houses have their general contours shaped to respect the 80-mile-per-hour "northerners" of the wind-swept prairies; they are elevated slightly, and through generous window openings they enjoy endless views that become an occupation and provide a sense of joy. There are also snug retreats from the almost overwhelming panorama of space. The warm, rich hues of these houses merge into the burnt-gold, gently undulating Oklahoma landscape; their vivid architectural silhouettes are accentuated and dramatized in intoxicating, orange sunsets.

Both Goff and Greene are concerned with the simple elements of life, often working with very limited budgets in rather sparsely populated areas. When thinking of their work it is appropriate to remember the words of Sullivan: "The greatest poet will be he who shall grasp and deify the commonplaces of our life . . . those simple normal feelings which the people of his day will be helpless otherwise to express."

Cunningham House, Oklahoma City, Oklahoma.

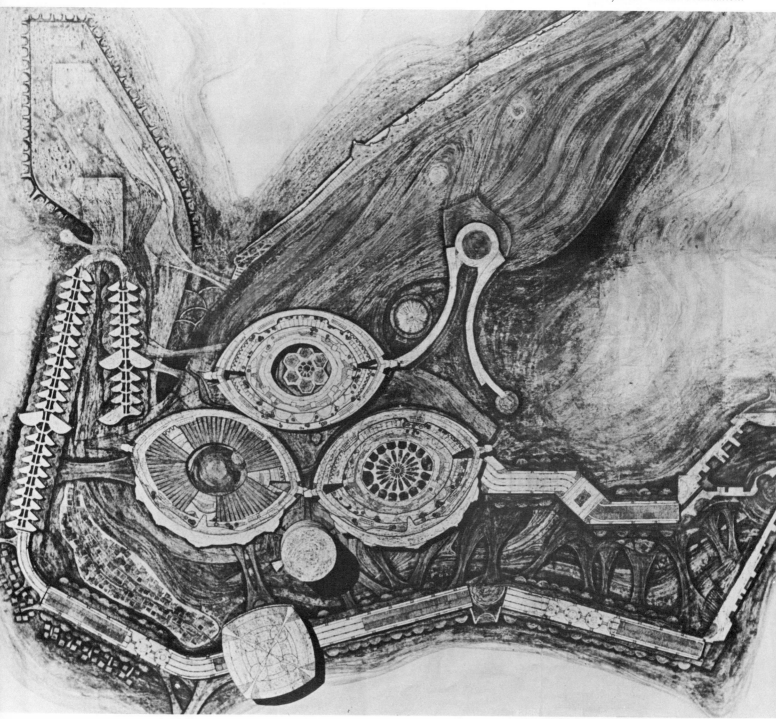

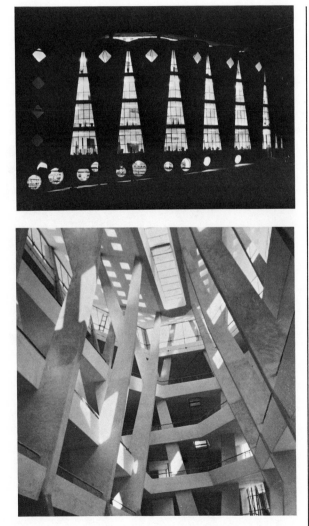

Ceramics factory, Vietri-sul-Mare, Italy.

PAOLO SOLERI

"Environment—the meeting ground for dispassionate nature and compassionate man." Dispassionate nature, in this instance, is the hot, arid Arizona desert; the compassionate man, Paolo Soleri. Born in Torino, Italy, in 1919, Soleri received a Doctor of Architecture degree (with highest honors) from the Polytechnic Institute of Torino. He came to the United States in 1947 to study for a year-and-a-half under Frank Lloyd Wright at Taliesin West— a short distance from where he now lives. "Mainly my activities were manual, because it is impossible for me to work on other people's designs," reflects Soleri.

Soleri is an artist and a visionary who has withdrawn to a world shaped by his own sure and fluent hand. His aptitude extends from the translation of his ideas into beautiful drawings, to the instinctive and rapid way he scribes clay molds for his bells— his principal source of income in recent years. How he seeks to transform a craft approach into an aesthetic approach can be seen in such diverse projects as his bells and earth houses, and in such exciting designs as the one for a tubular reinforced concrete bridge, and a Mesa City.

In 1951 Soleri and Mark Mills, another Taliesin member, built a striking, glass and aluminum domed house in Arizona. During a short stay in Italy in the early 1950's he designed a ceramics factory on the Amalfi coast. The sculptured exterior of tapered shells reflects conical shapes indigenous to the region. The interior is a simple five-story space, encircled by spiraling ramps, supported by a structure of reinforced concrete trees. This house and factory, plus his own desert structures, are the extent of Soleri's built architecture.

"The scientific revolution came upon man in all its force, and overwhelmed, he bowed to the new gods—Structuralism, Functionalism, and Rationalism. It is a mistake to deify scientific determinism unless one's ultimate goal is a statistically-determined future efficiently interpreted by man. I am concerned for our future in this time of technological change, political upheavals, and the last flaring-up of nationalism. Man is engaged in the transformation of the universe, which to him is statistical, mathematical and scientific, into a human environment. He seeks a post-rational or post-scientific position.

"This is directly connected with architecture in terms of structure. We had a period, which we may still be in, where we felt that if a structure was sound it must be beautiful. This is a fallacy. Structure is the nature of the universe, and as such lacks the human quality which we are trying to build into the universe. Architecture is not structure per se, but is based on structural elements, and goes beyond any structural achievements. A structural achievement is a poor reproduction or copy of more sophisticated structural systems which nature offers in the micro and macro cosmos.

"The making of a human universe is what we are unconsciously striving for, to achieve harmony out of disharmony or out of the statistical procedures that nature offers. In approaching this we should remind ourselves that there are *instrumentalities* and *finalities*. Technology is instrumentality; science, in its purest form, may have some kind of finality. The tools we are producing are instrumental—shown by the way in which they become obsolete. Aesthetic expression does not become obsolete because it has a finality in itself—which we tend to ignore or forget in our attempts to define the true nature of things.

"We must distinguish between the system we are employing and our reason for its use, or we will muddle instrumentality with finality. This is why we feel a car can be a work of art. Perhaps it can in a few instances, but generally a car has to be considered an instrument or a very simple tool—today a very obsolete tool. As such it should be planned in a scientific and technological way, instead of in an aesthetic way. Cities should become finalities because they are the basic elements of our civilized life. Also I do not think that the finalities of man need to be agreeable or happy by today's definition of these terms. Subconsciously we are looking for something much more complex, and possibly much more painful to realise because of our constantly confusing the system we use with our reason for choosing it. It leads us to mistaking an instrumentality for a finality.

"If we want to move really ahead we will have to change our approach to scale. We cannot keep thinking in atomized terms. The individual is very important because he is fitting into an increasingly complex society. It is basic, therefore, for the architect to think in terms of environment rather than single buildings.

"I approach environmental considerations in two ways: the pure, aesthetic approach, which is only theoretical, and the traditional craft approach. By craft, I mean making small objects to the largest structure that I can afford. The craftsman's way is the most secure, and closest to nature but it is not the fundamental way. The aesthetic way is the fundamental approach for mankind. To approach environmental problems in the broad and fundamental way would require organization, total involvement, and clarity—the very skills, for example, of the computer. Statistical research and data could be analyzed by mechanical systems thus providing the answers we need. Then the human touch would transfer them from a statistical structural position to a human position.

"Frank Lloyd Wright meant the craft approach when he spoke about 'in the nature of materials.' One works in the nature of materials when working as a craftsman, but not necessarily as an artist. The aesthetic world lies beyond the nature-of-materials world. Mies is regarded as having best expressed a sense of ra-

Earth House, Scottsdale, Arizona.

View from studio into ceramics workshop, Scottsdale, Arizona.

tionality and application of technical means, yet he colors those very rational systems with very aesthetic ones, somehow negating the original thought.

"Science, and possibly religion, may be objective, but the aesthetic world is subjective. It becomes objective only when a subjective sense is sufficiently strong and pure to extend it to the universal. One might write a precise history of science with such detail that it is science. One cannot write a history of art, one can only make descriptions. The only way to describe a piece of music is by playing it; similarly, each piece of art is an aesthetic element that is so involved with the artist that the only way one can talk about it is by doing it.

"In the arts self-expression generally comes first. There may be a few holy spirits for whom this is not true, but if so, their position is almost self-contradictory. I cannot imagine a detached or altruistic person achieving very much. If an architect's ego is very small, he is done for; if it is vast then he might make some very important contributions."

Soleri's earth houses are craft constructions, probably the closest expression of "in the nature of materials" possible, where the principle and system of construction itself is developed directly from the natural environment. In the first structure live his four apprentices; the second is his drafting room, which he believes to be his best structure to date; the third is a model-making and general working space.

The method Soleri uses in casting his ceramics and bells is, in principle, the same simple construction procedure for his earth houses. The firm desert sand is mounded to make the formwork for the shell, then steel reinforcing is laid in position and the concrete poured. After the shell has set, a small bulldozer is used to remove the sand from under the shell. Excavated sand is then placed over the shell, and planted, gently merging it with the landscape and providing insulation against the extremes of desert temperature. The structures, cool during the day and warm in the cold desert night, open onto landscaped working spaces, defined by embankments of compressed, watered sand that form a sequence of sculptured spaces, while also ensuring privacy. Elementary in procedure, these structures are born of the desert and suggest the age-old search for shelter. "Crafted construction is the open, at times over-emotional, acceptance of environment, out of which and within which, the building is born. Reflecting a love for the

Double cantilever bridge with dwelling facilities.

Tubular bridge with tourist facilities.

Dam model with botanical research laboratories and greenhouses

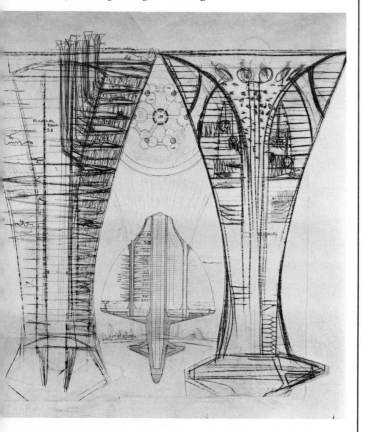

Project for a Mesa City.

material used locally, and a sensitivity towards the surrounding conditions, the building could not have been conceived for any other place. It is in the nature of materials, the totality of materials being the environment itself."

In 1958 Soleri began work on his concept for a Mesa City that would house some two million people on about 55,000 acres, a nucleus 13½ miles long by 6 miles wide. There is good historic precedent for such a venture. The creation of an ideal environment for man has challenged the imagination of many highly creative individuals, and although few of these visions have ever been realized, this in no degree minimizes their validity, for through their medium has come an abundance of ideas that have been inspiration for others. Soleri has filled many large sketchbooks and has hundreds of feet of drawings on rolls of butcher paper that explain his ideas and show his stunning draftsmanship.

Soleri chose a mesa for his site because large elevated plateaus are typical of the desert landscape to which he is so attuned. Soleri's use of water, essential to such a site, is self-suggested as a basic, unifying theme. Since a mesa is usually an isolated plateau, it allows the development of a homogeneous, self-sufficient community that might answer Soleri's search "within the awesome setting of nature, for a manly setting within which we can sense the grace of being and becoming."

The concept is one of megastructure groupings: a theological and philosophical center, an administrative and business center, and a center of higher learning, all ringed by residential groupings that will house up to four thousand persons in a single structure. The idea is basically constant in each center: Within very large structural systems, each having its own spatial impact and appropriate image, the intent is to produce a micro climate in which activities can then be developed. "Each organism is something that is between nature and man. The megastructures are the construction of a second nature on a very large scale, within which man as a family unit intervenes individually and sets up his own life. This will avoid the air-conditioned approach which tends to isolate man from nature biologically and spiritually, in a drastic and possibly unhealthy way." The theoretical suggestion of a different approach to scale and functional groupings will suggest new

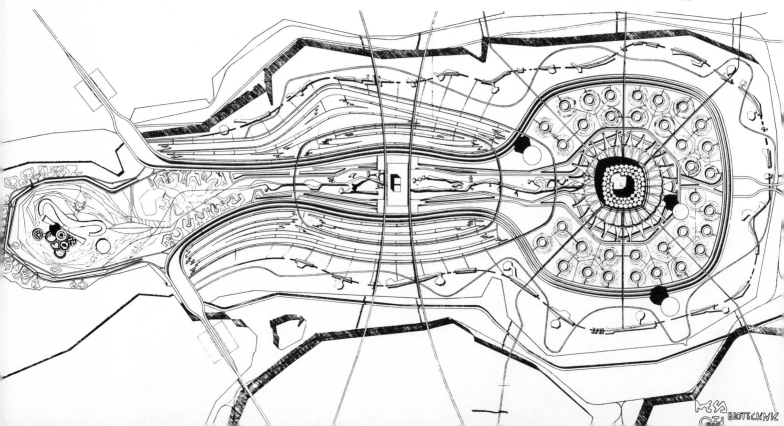

activities, thus evoking the aesthetic quality of the city, explains Soleri.

Architects and planners are divided over the merits of concentrating like elements, as against fragmenting them through the fabric of the city. Soleri, as his concept for Mesa City shows, prefers to group them. "With the complexity of the city you have to work as if you were trying to produce a higher organism, rather than a lower society of cells. In nature we see many examples of society—functionally just about perfect—but static. Probably the very perfection of their organization prohibits further evolution. Coral, for instance, has no significant organization, as its cells, with only a structural connection, are very independent and self-defined. In higher organisms, however, like the mammal, a very complex organization of interdependent organs is necessarily integrated. Society is organized in the same way, and cannot be spread thin any more than the organs of man can. Wright—who reflected the optimism of man at the beginning of the technological explosion—made this mistake in his Broadacre City concept. To achieve the more rewarding and complex quality we are seeking, we have to develop and build our culture, physically three-dimensionally."

Closer to realization is Soleri's Cosanti Foundation in Arizona, intended as an enclave where man can develop the finer aspects of his existence, a place for the study of the visual and fine arts in association with other cultural endeavors. Its raison d'être is the development of architecture as environment, in harmony with man. The Foundation will be organized on the atelier system, with groups of student apprentices working with an architect, sculptor, painter, etc. It would provide a place, explains Soleri, where youth could experiment with a minimum of compromise and a maximum of learning, and where more mature artists could live and work in an atmosphere free of academic formalism. "The discovery of self comes slowly and painfully, but the willingness and ability to project beyond it is the concern of youth. To be open, passively, is to be not open at all. You must inquire, act your part as intensely as you can."

Soleri is aware of the problems of leadership for such a foundation: "There exists the danger that Taliesin fell prey to. When there is one person guiding, it is a theocracy. Two things might happen: he surrounds himself with mediocrity where his authority is never questioned, but where the end results are questionable; or he gets really valuable people, possibly generating so much strife that things break down through inner conflict. I do not know what the answer is, yet."

The challenges and frustrations of the artist in society are well-expressed by Soleri. "One is, and also contemplates. One is joyful, and also desperate. One gazes upon one's labor from both the tremor of the inner longing and the indifference of the whole universe."

In our hasty age there is a place for the vision and values of Soleri, and his like, who, when he talks of environment, infers a creative symbol of man's cultural achievement. "Whether we set ourselves and our cities organically within nature, or whether we conceive a man-made second nature, boldly confronting nature itself with a perhaps too premature wish of a humanized universe, we must do so as metaphysical beings and not as cunning humans divided between the pursuit of comfort and the smugness of the 'foolproof.' We must exist and grow as finalities, not as instruments. Not even as the instruments of highly-improbable gods."

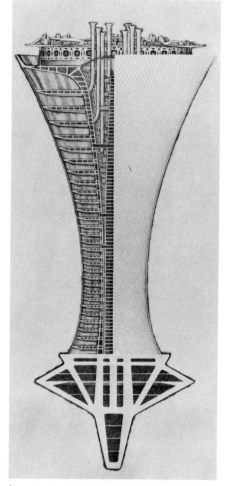

Mesa City: higher learning center, mega structure.

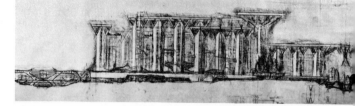

Mesa City: business center.
Mesa City: theological complex.

Mesa City: grounds village.

THE GROWTH OF MODERN ARCHITECTURE IN CALIFORNIA

"Like all Nordic barbarians we want to go to sunny Hellas, or to the land where the lemon blooms and no icy storms trouble us." So wrote Richard Neutra in his unpublished autobiography. The informal relationship between man and nature that California architects have pursued with such zest has proved an increasingly contagious idea to architects generally. It has developed from taking advantage of the most fortunate climate of large areas of California, and has resulted in an architecture that is casual in character. The climate, the fertility, the vastness and changing character of the mountains, forests and desert are all elements of a spectacular panoramic landscape that has attracted the largest and fastest-growing population in the Union. Its distance from the European-oriented East Coast has allowed it a certain degree of insularity, attracting a people more receptive to the idea of leaving behind them some of the traditions of their ancestry.

At the turn of the century, when the creative vitality of Chicago's architecture was in decline, California architecture was taking a distinctive direction. In the San Francisco Bay Region, Maybeck and the Greene brothers were developing a vital expression in a regional idiom that was to have extensive influence. In Southern California, Gill and later Schindler were developing an architecture with a strong affinity to the buildings of the early modern movement in Europe, although Gill's inspiration was said to derive from California's Spanish missions. The early example of these men, who struggled to make modern architecture acceptable, gave impetus to the work of the succeeding generation.

Our more liberal outlook today is evident in the way we are prepared to recognize the achievements of Maybeck for example; and, although on a different continent and in a different art, the strikingly parallel career of the German composer, Richard Strauss. A brave new world, after the Second World War, dealt harshly with their luxuriant brand of romanticism and somewhat nostalgic inclinations toward the spirit of a vanished age. Both enjoyed longevity to survive the era of their interest and close the curtain imaginatively and triumphantly upon it—which is what we find fascinating today. To the lyricism of Berlioz and Brahms, Strauss added a realism which drew its strength from modern ideologies and the naturalism of modern art which he used to enlarge the symphonic form. Similarly, Maybeck's work had an inventiveness and naturalness in the grand manner but without a stifling academic formality. He fell almost cruelly between the judgment of both the classical and the modern: the fact that he was not a strict interpreter of Classical architecture separated him from the former, and being an eclectic who looked for beauty in traditional architecture ostracized him from the few moderns of the time.

The Chicago Exposition of 1893 held for Bernard Maybeck (1862-1957) "the deep idea of beauty." He was apparently unaware of the architectural revolution, or at least was unconcerned by it. Having studied in Paris, he was enamored of the Greek and Romanesque monuments and the Gothic churches of Europe. Maybeck's idea about the relationship between architecture and science was that "architecture consists in doing things right. Science consists in inquiring how to do things right." His liking for Gothic churches led him to use pitch roofs in many of his houses, creating spacious and somewhat mysterious interiors. "There was an honesty in his approach to structure," Esther McCoy has written, "that was little understood because of his apparently conflicting interest in decoration." He used timber extensively, often in conjunction with concrete and synthetic materials. His Christian Science Church in Berkeley in 1910, recognized today as a very significant work in the development of the "Bay Region Style," had factory sash windows and asbestos panels in combination with concrete and local redwood.

Maybeck's sense of the grand manner was fully expressed in 1915, when he designed the Palace of Fine Arts for the Panama Pacific International Exposition. The commission was secured for him by Willis Polk, one of Maybeck's former students and the head of the Exposition's architectural committee. Polk was to design in San Francisco in 1918, the Hallidie Building with an all-glass facade, a structure without parallel in California during the first half of this century. Maybeck's idyllic Palace of Fine Arts, constructed of chicken-wire netting tacked to a board structure and plastered over, was romantic in silhouette, and also as a mirrored reflection in its foreground lake. Today it is a crumbling ruin—soon to be rebuilt in enduring materials despite Maybeck's comment, "Let the thing fall down in peace."

Schooled in the classical tradition at the Massachusetts Institute of Technology, the Greene brothers—Charles (1868-1957) and Henry (1870-1954)—came to California in 1893 and began their practice in Pasadena. Their work soon developed an indigenous and individual character that reflected their love of nature and its materials, particularly timber, and their appreciation of the simple wood buildings of Japan and Scandinavia. They boldly expressed their timber structures, whose structural members were of a generous proportion, with roofs and walls clad in shingles. Broad overhanging eaves, an extension of the roof structure, created sheltered terraces and sleeping porches, unifying their buildings and giving them a horizontal emphasis. The Greene brothers thought of their timber structures as an assemblage of many elements to be individually expressed and strongly articulated as a design motif, meticulously refined in collaboration with craftsmen. The garden became a dominant design element; outdoor spaces or patios were defined by indoor spaces, each related and complementing the other. However, the cool sheltered interior spaces were considered as separate entities, related through similar door and window openings to the exterior—space did not interpenetrate. Theirs was a relaxed but sensitive architecture, as inviting to the touch as to the eye.

Irving Gill (1870-1936), originally from the East Coast, arrived in San Diego in 1893, having worked for two years in Chicago for Adler and Sullivan. He captured the spirit of the rapidly-growing West when he wrote: "In California we have the great wide plains, arched blue skies that are fresh chapters yet unwritten. We have noble mountains, lovely little hills and canyons

Christian Science Church, Berkeley, California.

Gamble House (Greene brothers), Pasadena, California.

waiting to hold the record of this generation's history, ideals, imagination, sense of romance and honesty." Gill's houses had a close relationship to their gardens, usually developed through transitional outdoor spaces defined by pergolas, arched porches and patios.

In the first decade of this century he explored the possibilities of concrete construction in monolithic structures, and did much to advance its technology. His was a spirit remarkably parallel with that of his contemporary Adolf Loos, in Vienna. In 1916 Gill wrote: "There is something very restful and satisfying to my mind in the simple cube house with creamy walls, sheer and plain, rising boldly into the sky, unrelieved by cornices or overhang of roof. . . . I like the bare honesty of these houses, the childlike frankness and chaste simplicity of them." The San Diego part of the Panama Pacific Exposition of 1915, in the Spanish Colonial style, created great public interest in buildings with rich ornamentation; it turned the tide, much after Sullivan's experience with the Chicago Exposition, against Gill's simpler, more modest, rational architecture.

By 1920, with the Greene brothers and Gill doing very little work, R. M. Schindler (1887-1953) was sent from Wright's Chicago office to supervise the construction of the Holyhock House in Los Angeles. Schindler had studied both engineering and painting in Vienna and was interested in the work of Cubist painters; in 1912 he wrote, "The old problems have been solved and the styles are dead . . . the architect has finally discovered the medium of his art: space. A new architectural problem has been born." An admiration for Wright's work and an excitement for the opportunity in America drew Schindler to Chicago in 1914. Three years later he joined Wright's office. The work of the de Stijl and Bauhaus groups was after Schindler had left Europe, and he later wrote of it that it was "an expression of the minds of a people who had lived through the First World War, clad in uniforms, housed in dugouts, forced into utmost efficiency and meager sustenance, with no thought for joy, charm, warmth."

The Holyhock House completed, Schindler remained in Los Angeles to start his own practice. His interest was in the movement, penetration, depth and flow of space. This is well illustrated by his reference to the Pointillist painters' sense of color plasticity: "What the poster color squares of the patchwork-quilt school fail to do the Pointillists achieve by joining dots of receding and advancing colors, which 'leave' the surface of the canvas and create a color world in depth. The use of a similar technique allows the architect to dramatize his space forms, change their apparent proportions, heighten their three-dimensional qualities, soften their outline, and give color to the void." Schindler was pragmatic rather than academic. He wrote that "the sense for the perception of architecture is not the eyes—but living. Our life is its image."

With Schindler the relationship of interior rooms to exterior garden changed from defined space, as in Gill's work, to interpenetrating flowing space. In 1922 he built, with a friend who acted as contractor, a house for their respective families in Los Angeles. He described it as "a simple weave of a few structural materials which retain their natural color and texture throughout." The interior, on the same level as the garden, opened directly to it through canvas sliding doors (since replaced by glass doors). Interior partitions, free of the structure, were movable. Clerestory windows were used to frame high views, to ventilate and to admit light

Scripps House (Irving Gill), La Jolla, California.

deep into the interior. The construction was of 4-foot tapered slabs, poured in a horizontal position and lifted into place. Between the wall panels were 3-inch spaces, filled either with concrete or left open and glazed to allow light to penetrate to the interior. Schindler's interest in relating the interior and exterior spaces is a clear factor in the design. He wrote that "joining the outdoors with the indoors spatially to satisfy a new attitude toward nature and movement cannot be achieved by merely increasing the size of the conventional wall openings."

Where houses had a limited budget Schindler sought economy in structure, so that he could provide what he considered the vital luxury of three types of living areas: indoors, enclosed court or patio, and roof terraces—each relating directly to the other. In his design for the Lovell House in 1926 he used structure as a visible organizer within which solids were placed and space penetrated. The living space, above a beach, was contained within five, freestanding reinforced concrete skeletal frames. In the design of the Wolfe House on a steep hillside in 1929, Schindler abandoned "the conventional conception of a house as a carved mass of honeycomb material protruding from the hillside, and created a composition of space units to float above the hill." With the "Health" House designed in the same year, Neutra showed a similar concern.

In the 1930's Schindler developed a preference for using skin construction as opposed to a structural skeleton, because of the flexibility by which forms might be organized without having to respect a structural grid. Through this freedom, he felt, modern architecture might achieve what the past had referred to as "style." "Once an architect begins to worry about tying things down and about correct spacings, he arrives only at formal harmonies, and these have little to do with living." The Rodakiewicz House in Los Angeles, in 1937, was a fine example of Schindler's spatial ideas of form and movement. In his later projects, largely houses that merged with their hillside sites, some of the crispness of his earlier work was lost as the overall forms became more fragmented and nervous. At his memorial exhibition the written tribute referred to him as "the least understood and the least appreciated of the American pioneers of modern architecture."

THE BAY REGION

San Francisco is both the end of the trek westward and the gateway from the Orient. At a time when industrialization and communication have tended to erase local architectural differences, the Bay Area is one of the few examples of regionalism in America. It has produced an architecture neither quaint nor sentimental, but one which draws its vitality from the natural landscape and a stable climate. Gentle evolution rather than abrupt revolution, a pertinent progression from within, not arbitrary change, has been the characteristic way of advance. Here, having the good sense to work with the natural pattern enables much anonymous and even mediocre architecture to make a positive contribution. Further, it demonstrates that too often modern architecture has been alien to its immediate context and has overlooked the necessity to respect both appropriateness and continuity in the man-made environment.

San Francisco, located on a peninsula surrounded by its Bay and the Pacific Ocean, is itself very compact. Physical insularity has developed an urban cohesiveness of great character. Streets, laid out in a grid, run up and over a rolling terrain that is hugged by low buildings, few of them over four stories. If planned today, these streets would be likely to follow the natural contours rather than cut across them geometrically; yet a great visual drama comes from this abstract "strip-skeleton" that lays the steep slopes bare. "San Francisco, to me, is a city that has vertical chaos and horizontal order," said Wurster. It is a "uniquely comprehensible city." From one of the many hills a visitor can "know exactly what the city is. He can look down a street and see water. The architecture is the same way: it is what you look at and not what you live in that is important. This puts the kitchen to the street and the living room to the view, often making things backwards." From one of its many hills or from across the Bay, San Francisco tends to compose into an abstract montage: overlapping white rectangles emphasize the verticality of its hills, often crowned by tall structures, and are woven together by a web of shadow, punctuated, confetti-like, by spots of color. It is an animated panorama of light, undulating in sweeping curves with the sculptural topography, all registering against water, mountains and sky.

The only water-level entrance to the enormous, hot central valley behind the city is through the Golden Gate. Cool winds and fog are drawn inland from the ocean, in effect making San Francisco a giant air-conditioning duct. As well as ever-changing views, San Francisco has an astonishing variety of microclimates, each reflected in its architecture.

Across the Golden Gate to the north, hugging a beautiful coastline and backed by the magnificent redwood forests of Marin County, are the communities of Sausalito, Belvedere and Tiburon; and east, across the Bay, lie the hill towns of Oakland, Piedmont, and Berkeley, where the University of California has its main campus. Here, weathered timber houses perch precariously on steep slopes or bask half-hidden among trees. The enjoyment of nature and open-air living has fused garden and architecture. The direct use of natural materials reflects the informal life in an unpretentious domestic architecture. "We don't have the problems of cold that the East has," says Wurster. "You come against different conditions and you have to meet them differently. We have patios here; this is partly due to climate and partly due to the fact that houses are small and we can borrow from the outside space for the inside." Wurster believes that the so-called oriental influence in houses that suit the customs and climate "rather than a formula may not be oriental at all—but it is the same slant. The Japanese house doesn't fit Japan very well climatically, fits Honolulu better, California even better."

Bernardi House, Marin County, California.

WILLIAM WILSON WURSTER

When Lewis Mumford attacked what he called the "sterility" of the International Style, he pointed to the virtues of the "Bay Region Style" of architecture, referring to Wurster as its greatest exponent. "I don't think it is so much a style," said Wurster, "but merely a growth—certain things have evolved in their independent way." The Italian magazine *L'Architettura* wrote that Wurster ". . . is an exceptional artist for the degree in which he seems 'natural'; he is truly modern exactly because his buildings have the flavor and detachment of the works of the old masters."

William Wilson Wurster was born in Stockton, California, in 1895. After graduating from the University of California in 1919, he worked in San Francisco and New York and spent a year traveling in Europe before opening his own office in San Francisco in 1929. One of his first commissions, the Warren Gregory Farm at Santa Cruz, California, was a simple, carpenter architecture—a far cry from the classic-romantic vein then so much in vogue.

Theodore Bernardi became his partner in 1945, and Donn Emmons, a year later. Since then their firm has expanded to a present staff of ninety. Their office is an old warehouse near the San Francisco waterfront, which, says Wurster, "is a wonderful space for architects. There are no smooth spaces, nothing too polished or crystallized in political space. It is easier to make evaluations in rough space."

The Bernardi House in Marin County, California, in 1951, is an excellent example of a post and beam skeletal construction. It has exposed framing members, overhanging eaves, broad terrace decks, and vertical cedar board walls both inside and out. Located on a small lot on a steep, secluded wooded hillside, its informal ruggedness seems very appropriate.

A more precise yet equally persuasive example of the virtues of the Bay Region vernacular is the Center for Advanced Studies in the Behavioral Sciences at Stanford University, built in 1954. Simply-detailed, redwood-framed buildings with broad overhanging eaves were grouped informally to create a series of quiet courts.

The Pope ranch house in 1958, in California's hot central valley, has an effortless feeling that demonstrates the skill of an experienced designer. While apparently corresponding to the traditional image of the landowner's home, it does so with an unpretentious directness. Its 2-foot-thick adobe walls, with a few, small openings, and the encircling wide porch, protect against the intense heat. All the principal rooms are at the upper level, where the view extends across the plain to the horizon. The main staircase, rising from a landscaped mound, relates these rooms readily and pleasantly to the ground.

Of a similar scale, the all-white Coleman House in San Francisco, in 1962, is a steel frame structure with cement plaster exterior walls. Its two-story facade to the street becomes four stories at the back as it accommodates the slope at the site. The design focus is an interior garden court at street level, around which the house is wrapped. A circular stairway, encased in a curved wall of glass, connects the three main floors, providing additional views on the court. Across the entire back of the house, the main rooms are open on all four floors to magnificent views of the Bay and the Marin County hills beyond.

The same directness, lack of pretense, and skillful use of familiar forms that characterize the firm's work are evident in the concrete and redwood structure for the First Unitarian Church at Berkeley, in 1962.

Like Maybeck, whose work they especially admire, the partners believe that it is possible to learn from the past and use it, while being free of it and appropriate to our time. "The position of architecture is getting stronger now," says Wurster, "as the disciplines come together more to consider the problem of environ-

Center for Advanced Studies in the Behavioral Sciences, Stanford University, Palo Alto, California.

Gregory Farmhouse, Santa Cruz, California.

Yerba Buena Club, 1938 San Francisco Fair.

ment." It is of interest to see how these architects, accustomed to designing primarily on a domestic scale and in the timber vernacular, are tackling the new challenge of large urban commissions. This is the real test of the pertinence of a regional vernacular. The firm is presently engaged in two such undertakings for Monterey, California, and San Francisco.

The Custom House Project is an urban renewal proposal for 17 acres of Monterey. The site is bordered by the Bay, picturesque Fisherman's Wharf and the "Cannery Row" area of John Steinbeck's novel—now a tourist attraction. The new buildings are designed to harmonize with the historic adobes within the area, in both materials and scale. The complex will include a major department store, motels, restaurants, offices, apartments, convention facilities, theaters and parking garages. Old buildings will be preserved and their gardens improved. Outdoor cafés, fountains, intimate courtyards, and major parks and plazas will add interest and variety. The core of the project will be kept free of automobiles, and a "minibus" service will take visitors to all points within the development.

The San Francisco Redevelopment Agency, realizing the tremendous opportunity presented to the city in the Golden Gateway project on the city's waterfront, appointed an Architectural Advisory Panel to appraise the schemes of eight developer-architect teams. The panel (which included Kahn and Yamasaki) was concerned primarily with concepts which made the most significant physical and cultural contributions to the area. They suggested that the environment should be intimate in scale, with buildings and space varied to avoid repetition, and that a number of talented architects could be assigned various parts of the overall project to help achieve diversification. They advised that the project be made an integral part of the city, recognizing its grid plan. The creation of urban plazas and park areas had been ignored in the growth of the adjacent business district, dictating a need for these amenities for citizens working in this highly-congested area. The panel considered the separation of pedestrian and vehicular traffic mandatory, and the existing elevated freeway unsightly and environmentally detrimental.

They agreed unanimously that the proposal by developers Perini-San Francisco Associates, and architects Wurster, Bernardi and Emmons, and DeMars and Reay, was "exceptionally successful." The scheme has five tower, and three slab apartment buildings, and town houses. The buildings are located above parking structures that cover an entire city block, whose roofs are formally landscaped with planting in tubs and boxes, and interconnected by bridges, forming a continuous upper circulation level for pedestrians, 20 feet above the vehicular streets. A central city block is left open as a park at street level, connected by bridges to the upper level. Apartments and shops can be approached from the upper circulation level and from street level. The walls of the three-level parking garages have "interesting variations of grille treatment and serve as a unifying element at understandable human scale along the street," said DeMars, speaking for the group. "These walls, topped by the gardens of the town houses and visually like the retaining walls that line the roads of an Italian or Mexican hilltown, are never over a block in length; are interrupted by the entrances to apartments or shops; and always lead, beyond the next corner, to the greenery of a park or open space, much as do the side streets that lead to the squares of Bloomsbury."

Pope House, Madera, California.

Coleman House, San Francisco, California.

First Unitarian Church, Berkeley, California.

Custom House Project, Monterey, California.

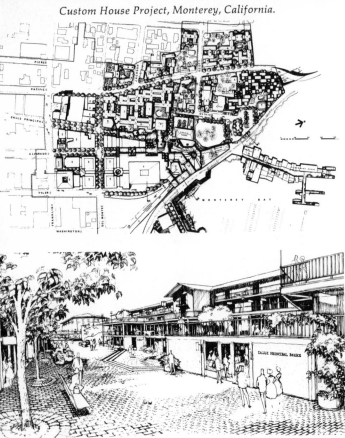

The town houses are thought of as not merely a token of urban tradition but an essential design element. DeMars explained that "the garage rooftops were a possible liability—bleak if untreated, expensive if maintained as decorative landscape." The use of these areas as gardens for the townhouses and ground floor apartments reduces the areas requiring maintenance as well as heightening the visual interest from above. The town houses have been criticized for encroaching upon the space necessary to provide the towers with a proper setting; that their gardens do not have privacy from the apartments above; and for the picturesque variations and lack of unity between the town houses that the two principal firms, and Anshen and Allen, have designed. As such, the town houses might appear more of a romantic gesture than an integral element of the total development.

In addition to the two principal firms, and Anshen and Allen, Skidmore, Owings and Merrill have designed an office tower for Alcoa. This twenty-five-story building, which will dramatically terminate the long vista down San Francisco's Front Street, is sited on the roof of a three-level parking garage, flanked by plazas. Although Wurster, Bernardi and Emmons are the architects for the garage structure, Wurster says that "S.O.M. presented such a beautiful scheme for the plazas that we have followed it, particularly since the whole plaza area relates so closely to their building."

The fact that several groups of architects have collaborated to work within an overall concept on the design development of various buildings might, "to a well-ordered mind, mean chaos," said Wurster. "It doesn't to me, because I think the beauty of the city is in variety. It is better that the Alcoa Building be differentiated and stand out as a powerful enterprise, by the episode of braces on the outside, against the residential buildings." Added DeMars, "We think it is entirely possible that a valid and non-synthetic variety may be achieved within the control of our associated firms. Principles and considerations effecting economy can be respected; at the same time, interesting digressions in detailed design solutions might be exploited, rather than be compromised out of existence for the sake of uniformity and a unified design solution."

Concurrent with his busy architectural practice, Wurster has been deeply involved in education. He was Dean of the School of Architecture and Planning at the Massachusetts Institute of Technology from 1944 to 1950; and Dean of the College of Architecture at the University of California in Berkeley, continuing as Dean when it was renamed the College of Environmental Design (combining the Architecture, Landscape Architecture and City Planning Departments), from 1950 to 1963. The problem of education is in trying to equate the narrow and deep as against the broad and superficial, thinks Wurster, while "opening some of the doors and making it possible for things to happen." He achieved this by a policy of "controlled chaos," where the student was exposed to diverse and often opposed ideas of architectural professors. "A DeMars, an Esherick, a Callister or a Soriano— you must have this diversity or results will be to too directed an end. If you have this variety something will happen."

Wurster's firm recently completed the San Mateo, California, branch of the Bank of America. As a tribute to its late founder, A. P. Giannini, the center mural bears the inscription: "His achievements were the result of his understanding of the needs of his fellow man." This, too, has always been the first concern of Wurster's firm.

Golden Gateway, San Francisco, California.

DeMars House, Berkeley, California.

VERNON DeMARS

An issue often inflated to the magnitude of a dilemma is that of the house versus the apartment. To the bleak anonymity of a minimal apartment, facing across an asphalt parking lot into the vapid face of another such lump, any sensible person would obviously prefer a house with a garden, sun, fresh air, quiet and privacy. The price paid, however, has been high: sprawling cities that use land uneconomically, extended services, and unreasonable commuting for the individual. To satisfy the psychological and material housing needs of the individual places both a direct and indirect burden on the nation's resources. Housing is the principal urban land user, and approximately one quarter of the nation's wealth is invested in it.

The real issue is good living conditions versus bad living conditions; the way people would and could live if we made it possible, and the way they are in fact forced to adapt to available housing as best as they can. Beyond the domestic needs of the individual, there exists a need to participate in certain collective activities on which material and spiritual livelihood depend. These needs are integral and inseparable. Invariably the speculative builder, whose tract houses are often mass-produced with little imagination and the expedient single-mindedness of the sorcerer's apprentice, has concentrated on the house as an object of sale, trying to fulfill practical or imagined wants. Public housing authorities have often developed community facilities, presuming to give the public what they deem is good for it. Both have largely ignored the more complex urban relationship, total living patterns, and any really rewarding quality.

Sadly, complacency reigns; not only in the long-outmoded patterns that seem self-perpetuating, but even in some of the more venturesome solutions of recent years. Despite the wealth of information available on housing, there are "few, if any, developments in the speculative field which carry conviction to the observer—that here at last is twentieth-century living within the economic reach of most of the people." So says Vernon DeMars.

DeMars was born in San Francisco in 1908, and since graduating from the University of California he has been earnestly involved with many aspects of the housing problem in a responsible and imaginative manner. As District Architect in the Western States for the Farm Security Administration program, between 1937 and 1943, he was responsible for the design of over forty farmworking communities, including transient and permanent housing, schools, clinics, and farm buildings with all their utilities. They had to be acutely realistic, quick, and cheap answers to the desperate needs of the migratory farmworkers. Many were emergency solutions, supplying the barest kind of shelter. The pathos and fortitude of these displaced citizens, subject to such desperate stress, were conveyed with great compassion in John Steinbeck's novel *The Grapes of Wrath*. "This is when I became interested in doing little pieces of environment in which there was a hierarchy of needs and uses," said DeMars. Looking back on the simple, modest timber buildings that comprised most of these communities, he reflected, "We could have been generous enough to give them something that would have recalled their own homes, but we were puritanical; we weren't going to provide any of the picture-book inheritance which would have made things familiar to them. Where we went wrong was in applying *avant garde* solutions to the most disadvantaged economic and social class." Referring to the 1930's and its moralistic attitude towards design, he continued, "At the start of a revolution when you know you are going in the right direction it is easier to be crystal clear in your solutions. Many people think I am muddled currently because in our buildings we have tried to recapture and provide for some of the things that ordinary people put values on."

Farm Workers' Housing, Farm Securities Administration, Yuba City, California.

While visiting professor at the Massachusetts Institute of Technology in 1947 to 1949, DeMars collaborated with Koch, Kennedy, Rapson and Brown on designing the Eastgate Apartments (now called 100 Memorial Drive) in Boston. At M.I.T. he met Alvar Aalto and found much to admire in his approach. "He basically has a functionalist approach, but allows his emotional, intuitive nature, which is grounded in functionalism, to suggest things. His work never has shallow whimsicalities or irresponsible arrogance even when he is at his most arbitrary. His materials are traditional ones that have a tactile quality, which he manipulates with a subtle switch from the way it might have been done traditionally."

DeMars's Easter Hill Village for Richmond, California, in 1954, in association with Donald Hardison, is a move away from the regular "architectural diagrams" of his earlier communities toward evoking some of the more kaleidoscopic quality of the laissez-faire cityscape, while "combatting the family's lack of identification with where they live." In this public housing community of three hundred row houses there are changes in color, materials and fenestration. Details that are "familiar and part of people's experience" are consciously injected. This approach has many tenuous threads with other arts of the time, thinks DeMars, such as action painting and some music, where the element of accident has taken place within certain rules.

"The architecture of the 1930's, based on the belief that utility is beauty, form follows function, and less is more, seems to be lacking something today. I am grateful that at present some of our colleagues are exploring the very frontiers of aesthetic expression in the new architecture, with a heavy emphasis on architecture as

Eastgate Apartments, Cambridge, Massachusetts.

Easter Hill Village, Richmond, California.

sculpture. But most architecture must be much more than sculpture. In a problem well solved, since the aesthetics are by definition built in, there is ultimately a pleasure that is part sensual and part intellectual which comes from experiencing the rightness or appropriateness of a solution, rather than concise formal relationships. If this is true in single works of architecture, it is even more so in the collective architecture of the townscape.

"Jane Jacobs, in her book *The Death and Life of Great American Cities*, says, 'When we deal with cities we are dealing with life at its most complex and intense. Because this is so, there is a basic aesthetic limitation on what can be done with cities: *A city cannot be a work of art.*' Although she concedes that art is needed in the arrangement of cities and in a host of other things that illumine life, she continues: 'To approach a city, or even a city neighborhood, as if it were a larger architectural problem, capable of being given order by converting it into a disciplined work of art is to make the mistake of attempting to substitute art for life.'

"There are some deep and disturbing ideas here. We have all had the experience of disappointment, emptiness, and boredom in great designed pieces of environment. But what are the urban environments that do delight us? Why, usually the seemingly *unplanned* situations: the free-for-all of San Francisco's North Beach or New York's Greenwich Village. Yet, is 'unplanned' the word? Few human activities take place without planning, and the planning of these areas must have been good—that is, right for the situation. Yet, most likely, the planning was actually a collection of little plans, each sensitively solving the little problems and coming up with a collective solution for the whole area. It is true that when you experience these solutions they form an entirely different kind of visual composition from the 'big design' of the Architect and Planner; the result is much closer to the way our sister arts, painting, music and literature, put things together today. Are there no lessons for us here?

"If an architect is doing a new development—and I agree with Jane Jacobs on this—it must have diversity: diversity in everything possible, from a variety of dwelling types to a mixture of so-called non-conforming uses that people need in everyday life, within a wide range of income levels, interest and orientation. This means different types of buildings in close proximity, almost as in real life. It poses more interesting opportunities for compositions of visual interest. Still, to the architect, 'diversity' is only the framework that presents him with design problems. How to deal with diverse uses and the inevitable and necessary repetition of uses? What price variety?

"A special problem today is the questionable aesthetic of repetition under mass production. It has always been a temptation to plead for industrialized housing by comparing houses with automobiles, overlooking the fact that the products of many companies are scrambled together in the natural environment of the auto, whether parked or in motion. The tract house has been left on the assembly line right where it was built.

"There is, however, a special phenomenon in architecture through which repetition develops added aesthetic impact up to a point. Repeated elements—arches, columns, windows—are the basic materials of design. Repeated entities, whole buildings such as the twin churches on the Piazza del Popolo in Rome, are heady stuff and were used with caution by the ancients.

"Other than in housing, the doubled or tripled building is a rarity.

Marin City Redevelopment, Marin City, California.

From earliest times, however, dwelling units have been repeated, but with two quite different approaches. One is to use repetition to form larger compositions, as in the facades of the Palais Royale in Paris or in the crescents and circuses at Bath, England. In the other, dwellings are repeated without any expectation of forming a composition, though they often do, as in the town houses of London's Bloomsbury or Washington's Georgetown. There was probably little conscious effort in either of these approaches to achieve variety. In the first case, builders were trying to construct bigger and more impressive unities to set apart the aristocracy from the hoi polloi whose dwellings then had all the variety; in the second, speculators were seldom able to get more than a half-dozen houses built in a row at one time anyway. The resulting subtle changes of minor detail from one group to the next is one of the delights of this housing type. Repetition, then, is not the automatic way to successful urban composition; on the other hand, its merits should not be overlooked by the designer who is overzealous for variety.

"What architectural character should the rest of the facilities have that make up a city? The same question of variety and interest prevails, but in a different framework. Can there be an aesthetic equivalent of time in urban compositions? This is not a question of synthetic aging, but of a purposeful attempt to design compositions with the scale and change of pace found naturally in old streets that have witnessed changes in use for generations. Nor is it a matter of some new eclecticism or other artificial approach, but rather a matter of scale and design invention—variations on a theme, all done with strength and conviction. In a new development, for instance a university, regional shopping center or urban renewal project, how can we put the breath of life into something we might describe as 'instant city'? My answer is still diversity, but certain problems arise as we get into architecture with a capital 'A.' Housing, or the residential texture of the city, should be just that—a texture, interesting enough but still principally a background for other things of shared community interest, focal points such as churches, schools, civic halls, cultural and even commercial institutions.

"If we have a complex, for example, a civic center or a cultural center, is unity desirable in such a case and if so, how can we achieve it? One solution is to have only one architect, which politics may not allow. If we have several architects, will they agree to play the same tune? There are several ways to play it.

"Architecture has been called frozen music. The single building, modest in scope and scale, is the solo performance, unaccompanied. The more ambitious single building, where one can still perceive and appreciate all its parts, is the string quartet. The highly-unified complex of buildings by one architect is like plainsong where a group sings the same melody in unison. Such a building complex is Saarinen's General Motors Research Center, Mies's Illinois Institute of Technology or Kump's Foothill College. The unison approach has tremendous initial impact. It is immediately understandable, inherently non-confusing and therefore offers serenity. Its one lack is perhaps its inability to sustain interest beyond a certain size. There is also the question of how many of man's varied needs and activities can be made to fit into nearly identical shells. Or conversely, whether this oversimplification does in fact express the reality of man's complex activities, or even respect his ability to understand and enjoy complexity within order.

"With the concept of harmony, different instruments or voices, while making their own sound, combine to make a greater and unified totality, a blending in which the whole is definitely greater than the parts. Earlier periods of architecture have seemed more capable of achieving harmony than our own; in architecture as well as in music true harmony is only achieved by agreeing on some rules. Beyond a certain scale, the work in music or architecture cannot be comprehended at the first hearing, or viewing, but must be experienced serially and then repeated for fullest appreciation.

"Another analogy is counterpoint, where a work can be composed in two ways: by unifying the component parts, or by contrasting them; the same artist may use either approach depending on the occasion or his purpose. Counterpoint involves one complete melody or theme played against another. To achieve harmony there must be an internal structure or order that acts as common denominator to allow the themes to live together. In both architecture and music dissonance can add to the palette by serving to heighten contrast. In jazz, accident or the mood of the moment calls for improvisation within a predesignated framework. Music depends on remembering what has gone before. Architectural compositions must be experienced by passing through them and around them long enough for them to be absorbed and registered. Can we say that such widely-accepted concepts in one art form have no counterpart in another—one that is closely allied and similarly structured?

"The concept of accident so pervades contemporary artistic expression that we must assess its role in architecture and the environment; it is the strongest force determining the appearance of our cityscape, and sometimes, the most creative and visually interesting force. Chance often determines the final use of a property in the city—which client buys it, what he decides to build, which architect he chooses—and a change in any one of these factors means a change in the end result. One may well ask if there is any predictability at all in the look of a city. I think there is. One can try to effect certain desirable things, and try to control those that are not desirable. But a planner's expectations must allow for a wide range of acceptable alternatives within the established framework. The architect should not try to impose preconceived ideas of order, but should give to real situations the forms they desire and need and even suggest."

Since 1951, DeMars has been teaching at the University of California. He believes, like Wurster, that the widest experience is necessary for the student to develop both an intellectual and intuitive design sense to be equipped to discount wrong approaches and invalid criteria, on his own initiative. He believes the student should be exposed to both architectural convictions and confusions: "We shouldn't pre-digest, or shield the student from the traumatic experience of making wrong decisions." In 1955 DeMars went into partnership with the English architect Donald Reay, then visiting critic at the University. Their office has grown to a staff of eighteen, their busy practice covering a wide range of building types and planning problems.

The concept for the Marin City redevelopment project, in 1958, was derived from DeMars's proposal for the Fort Drive Gardens neighborhood development for Washington, D.C., fifteen years earlier. The layout takes full advantage of an attractive site sloping to the Bay. The combination of various types of residential

Santa Monica Redevelopment, Santa Monica, California.

units—garden apartments, private homes and small rental units—provides for a wide range of incomes and an environment of variety and interest. Carefully landscaped walkways relate residential buildings to recreation and rest areas and community amenities, with a minimum of roads to cross.

The high-rise apartment building per se, so popular in the 1930's, achieved high densities. But, at best among parklands, it had a disturbing monotony when repeated; at worst, in the all-too-gruesome, concrete city "parks," it was, and remains, absolutely without soul. An urban flavor does not come from a building alone but its relation to attractive and stimulating urban spaces where activity and variety are, and make, city life.

The Golden Gateway project, designed by Wurster, Bernardi and Emmons, and DeMars and Reay, recognizes this realistically and responds architecturally. The proposal (again in association with Perini Developers) for Santa Monica's Ocean Park is an even more significant advance in the search for a healthy environment that respects community and privacy, individuality and choice, with a hierarchy of urban scale, neither sacrificing urbanity nor excluding the automobile. The proposal for this 19-acre site, which leaves sixty percent free of buildings, has terrace apartments built around "man-made hills" that contain five levels of parking, with slender apartment towers rising from the apex. Nearly half of the dwellings are terraced apartments, each having parking space for two cars at its entrance, a convenience equalled only in the private home. Spacious private patios, skillfully planned so that decks cannot be seen either from above or below, have planting in boxes and tubs to increase privacy while adding interest to the "hill." The basic element is a one-bedroom house to which "smaller pieces are plugged in to add extra bedrooms. You are free to plug them in anywhere. This is a valid way to make a composition—in the context of what I call 'action architecture.' " Parking for the apartment towers is within the "hills" directly accessible by elevators which connect to spacious entrance lobbies at ground level. Open-air terraces and steps around the "hill" provide varied circulation paths for pedestrians that give access to all terrace apartments, quiet rest spaces, and many of the recreational facilities and public amenities.

DeMars actively seeks what he refers to as the quality of the "accident" or "action architecture." He tries to allow the "accident" to occur within a framework that makes the mosaic coherent in its organization. This approach is clearly seen in the University of California's new Student Center at Berkeley, a commission won in a limited architectural competition, in collaboration with Hardison and his partner Reay. The Center is a complex of four buildings: with a Student Union, a Dining Commons and a Student Office Building completed, and an auditorium-theater under construction. These are grouped around a large paved plaza, always active because of the good all-year-round climate, which in turn relates to a series of other outdoor spaces. A pedestrian precinct at the natural heart of circulation, the Student Center will be the meeting place and heart of the twenty-seven-thousand student community and, when including local residents, may have significance for an even larger number of people. The amenities available, from barber shop to book shop, and ballroom to bowling alley, all combine to express DeMars's idea of a "small piece of deliberate city-like environment."

Wurster referred to the Center as "absolutely charming and particularly successful in its human quality." The critic Allan Temko, a firm advocate of Mies, has called it "a schizoid creation, torn between rational planning premises and their irrational architectural expression." While acknowledging the excellent general site arrangement and organization, Temko considered the Student Union and Dining Commons as "fatally at odds," making DeMars's doctrine of "Planned Chaos" painfully clear. DeMars, however, believes that "if the vitality of an accidental or semi-planned urban situation pleases us, may we not analyze its special qualities and relationships and perhaps evoke similar experiences in a fragment of cityscape under single design control?" He hastens to add that he is not trying to create the usual urban chaos of incompatible buildings, but rather the spirit of "the random buildings which stand compatibly side by side in such a place as the Piazza San Marco . . . We find more delight in this atomized accretion than we do in the self-conscious great unities that result from another design approach." A Piazza San Marco occurs from the natural process of historical accumulation; the Student Center, however, was executed by one architect at one time—to which DeMars replies, "if one end result is more desirable then the architect must build in these changes of pace."

Since the Student Center buildings accommodate quite different functions, this change of pace has naturally evolved from choosing to express this architecturally, through changes of material and form. Just as there are positive and negative elements in the urban landscape, DeMars's buildings are a "positive and a negative": for example, the Student Union is a formal, centralized structure intended to dominate the square, complemented by the Dining Commons, a visually-active and loosely-defined, glass-enclosed space beneath a sequence of hyperbolic paraboloids, relating to outdoor dining terraces.

The philosophy behind the Student Center is the antithesis of Mies's. DeMars says: "It is all a fragment of an urban situation with purposeful changes of pace, vista and materials at the scale and tempo necessary to evoke the experience of an urban situation; a synthesis of streetscape and plazascape, great building and small, shop and pub, terrace and mall. This implies complexity, and cannot be achieved with the doctrine of 'less is more.'"

Student Center, University of California, Berkeley, California.

Duncan House, San Francisco, California.

CHARLES WARREN CALLISTER

Tradition is not a museum, a reiteration of the past. To retain its pertinence and potency, each generation has to remake, so to speak, its own image of the past in the perspective of its own problems. Tradition, then, is a convenient if vague term for the process whereby a generation uses valid elements of its inheritance to be interpreted for its own purpose. The problem is to strike a balance, without compromising either, between relevant tradition and essential innovation.

A regional vernacular develops from the appropriate continuation of local traditions and sensitivity toward local conditions. Finland's Alvar Aalto has been an inspiration to other architects who see in him a brilliant innovator singularly conscious of his origins. The Bay Region tradition became an architectural force through the collective endeavors of serious architects who consolidated an authentic regional vernacular, mainly in handsome, naturally-weathered redwood structures. In the face of the International Style, the Bay Region's tradition has remained an important development in modern architecture. Its unpretentious informality has a certain romance and responsiveness that many cannot see in a more impersonal, "universal" approach to architecture.

It represents an indigenous school of thought. An architect does not adopt a style, but matures through his experience to certain architectural convictions; this is where the Bay Region itself is so persuasive. In thinly-populated areas, looking from wooded hillsides across the Bay to metropolitan San Francisco, architects had small practices and did not engage in the design of large constructions. Until the 1930's major commissions went to the large Beaux-Arts firms. When modern architecture won through, these architects suddenly found themselves with the challenge of building in urban situations. In what is a rapidly expanding region (it is predicted that the Bay Region will increase from four to ten million persons by the year 2000), what is basically a pre-industrial vernacular is of necessity being replaced, or at least modified, by an industrially motivated one. Regionalists cannot afford to be completely bound by their tradition. It is not so much what they must reject, however, but what they can legitimately retain from their heritage that will show to what extent regionalism can remain a vital force in modern architecture.

An important factor in the region's architectural expression is the way in which its architects have been able to employ certain elements of another area's vernacular and recast them in its own image. The somewhat eccentric eclecticism of Maybeck's Christian Science Church, probably the Bay Region School's tour de force, is a fine example. It is with this spirit, using today's "methods and materials," that Warren Callister carries forward the vigorous tradition that Maybeck himself in part appropriated from the Bay's timber structures. "I use new techniques within the traditional sense, but my concern is not with recreating the old," he says. "Rather, I seek to create our own unique eclecticism."

Charles Warren Callister was born in Rochester, New York, in 1917. After graduating from the University of Texas in architecture and fine arts, he spent four years in the Army, opening his own office in San Francisco in 1946. In 1956 he moved his office across the Golden Gate to a beautiful secluded wooded hillside, overlooking the small cluster that is Tiburon. From here, where time seems suspended, Callister and Associates have designed more than a hundred residences, principally in the Bay Area and Northern California. The office is a stone's throw from Raphael Soriano's waterfront location. The stones however—intellectually— have an upward trajectory, for to architects like Soriano, regionalists like Callister have never recognized the infinite potential of a scientific and technological discipline. Callister believes that a reliance on technique has led to an impasse: "There just isn't time today to become familiar with all the techniques available; the architect should involve himself more with the sphere of meaning." To many, and his contented clients are many, who are finding a brave new world impersonal, Callister's talent offers an immediate discernible warmth and romance, a refuge.

"As soon as I could I studied painting and sculpture at the university, and have approached architecture from the point of view. There also has been a strong religious influence on my way of viewing things, stemming from a religion whose evolution had a history very similar to that of American architecture of the late 1800's. Mary Baker Eddy advocated a Christianity that, like Sullivan's approach to architecture, was quite revolutionary at the time. The similarity of their terminology is phenomenal. The ideal of the prevalence of good, and the superiority of principle over any limitation, has given me an attitude; the true examination of conditions will find the true revelation of the spirit of religion or the art of architecture.

"Architecture is a very impermanent art. Today, even a decade is a long time for a building to survive. So the statement is not in the building but in concepts and these are more permanent than materials, techniques or devices. Content, the comment a person makes, is the important thing. The concept is the thing you understand in Japan; every decision was a process of great joy, and when you see this the architecture is immaterial. A great piece of architecture, through which a man vitally communicates with you, is far more important than the purpose it might serve. We have come to the point where we have tried the spectacular structures and rare materials, and they are not satisfying unless they really make some comment. Maybeck's Palace of Fine Arts is a tremen-

Onslow-Ford House, Inverness, California.

dous example—it is a completely fake plaster building that has no purpose now. The only value in this building is a spirit of communication with Maybeck. This communication with the author, coming from his inspiration, is the validity of architecture. We vitally need this. We need to feel that buildings express our views and have evolved from this intention of communication.

"There is a greater attitude and logic to architecture that is above all techniques. It is absurd to say that you plan, and then engineer, and then have architecture. You start with architecture. It is not building a shelter, but a mood, a feeling, a sense—these are the basic, vital things. There is no such thing as modern or traditional architecture, or style—there is only Architecture. There are techniques, but the architect only uses these to achieve the reality, validity and truthfulness of his architecture.

"Architecture can be likened to the cinema. The architect is like the director, absolutely dependent on everybody who contributes. He tries to instill a direction in them, the vitality all coming together to produce a result which he then edits. The great directors are those who have the insight, sense and feeling that can persuade and move your attitude—make you weep, make you laugh. These are the things that architecture can do, but it is almost forgotten today. This is where education is failing. It teaches a process divorced of feeling, and the feeling is more important than the knowledge.

"Architecture is a social art, and self-expression is dependent upon communication with our fellowman. If I have a client with a particular attitude or manner, I say 'this is the project that so and so could work with very well. . . .' That is architecture. Choosing people who might work well together will heighten the architecture better than any detail. For this a client must be willing to divulge his attitudes and feelings. I do not rely on interpreting the site or the program, but the people associated with me—the client, contractor, and so on. If there is an excitement here it is expressed in the building.

"It is not necessary to concern ourselves with originality. This is absurd. We are going to see the development of teams of people who are working together to reveal some circumstance, the greatest essence that they can possibly establish. This is all they have to worry about; architecture, form and means will follow. All we have to have is the intention.

"It is necessary that we have such a thing as regional approach. Materials, textures, forms and colors have social and historical connotations that should not be overlooked. We are going to have to search our beginnings and allow these things to grow stronger and be more expressed; not necessarily in terms of the climate, site or materials, but in terms of cultural differences that are important to maintain and enlarge. Architects come to the Bay Region with the idea of doing 'missionary work' and are overwhelmed by the region. It is the most organic architecture I can think of. I do not mean the locale, but the attitude and manner of the region, and the repose you may feel—this is far greater than architectural relationships. As communication and mobility increase we need small areas of participation where we can make contact and feel response.

"Changes are coming in everything as a result of the expanding population. I am anxious to start the consideration of these things in the higher echelons of evaluation. Working on a proposal for a community of two hundred and fifty thousand people, I am aware

Neidig-Prendergast House, San Francisco, California.

of how ill-prepared we are as architects to know the real activity that should determine this design. It is not the buildings, or their shapes—these are superficial to the vitality and meaning of life. The environment will be created by creating these new activities.

"Suburban areas are boring because they do not stimulate a situation of human contact and activity. The problem today is not privacy but too much privacy. We have never examined how we might be together profitably. The cable car in San Francisco is an example: it is crowded and inconvenient, yet exciting; people are full of life just because they are on it.

"Architects have to change the criteria by which they are practicing. They have to move architecture from a profession to an art. We must teach not techniques but evaluation, and a basis of evaluation commensurate to the scale of whole cities. This is going to change the architect, or he is going to be lost. The rush is on."

Within his rapidly expanding office, at present forty-five people, Callister has absolute faith that interaction rather than the imposition of dogmatic ideas will reveal the essentials to advocate in a project. An oriental influence in Callister's work is often noted, though people are quick to ascribe this to any timber structure, particularly if its roof has some distinctive shape. The influence of the Orient and Pacific, which Callister recognizes in his work, is a cultural one that he believes will heighten and increasingly influence the whole country. His relaxed interpretation of the region's tradition, his belief that human culture has roots deep in tradition, and his desire to provide a significant character and splendid setting for our activities, all motivate his work.

The Duncan House, built in 1961, is located on a narrow sloping site on top of one of San Francisco's hills. Movement through the house focuses attention on a magnificent view of the city, while excluding views of the houses on either side. Where glass is usually a transparent protection against the elements in most of the Bay's modern houses, Callister deliberately frames views with mullions that are often more than a foot in depth. The shape of Callister's roofs is invariably a direct reflection of his interior spaces. Here the built-up beams support a curving, laminated wood roof, with the overlapping edges of each layer visible.

In the 1962 Onslow-Ford House, in Inverness, California, the roof again is shaped, even in such a small building. The concrete columns that support the laminated wood roof beams retain the spiral curves left by the paper forms in which the concrete was poured. Callister's timber structures are designed with the idea that time and sun will enhance and mellow the wood. Members are deliberately bold and coarsely-textured to counter the unevenness of weathering—similar to the work of the Greene brothers.

In the small Neidig-Prendergast House in San Francisco in 1964, the unfinished, rough-sawn redwood siding has already weathered to a dark patina. This house presents an almost closed appearance to the street because its small site suggested the house be oriented inward. But the interior does open to a view of the Bay through large glass areas that flank the fireplace. A central clerestory bathes the interior in light.

The Cove Apartments in Belvedere have views across the Bay to San Francisco, from living areas and contiguous wide decks, and from hooded dormer windows to second-floor bedrooms. There are seven residential units in two buildings that are supported above the water on piles. They are designed, says Callister, with

Rossmoor Leisure World, Walnut Creek, California.

Cove Apartments, Belvedere, California.

a strong bold form and reflect the regional tradition and character of wharves and barns. The rather angular, almost carved look of the buildings has a simplicity that is emphasized by the restraint of using only one exterior material.

One of Callister's largest completed projects to date is a retirement community at Walnut Creek in Northern California. Ultimately ten thousand housing units, intimately grouped around small courtyards, will create individual neighborhoods surrounding an eighteen-hole golf course. Community facilities, connected by covered walkways, are grouped around a central plaza.

Callister is presently working on his most challenging project to date, a proposal for a community for two hundred and fifty thousand inhabitants, to be possibly located between San Francisco and Los Angeles. He is using it as a practical vehicle to explore new ways of living and the values we want to propagate in our society. The preliminary design studies for buildings show his intention of relying upon the Bay Region vernacular on a grand scale.

To preserve our rapidly disappearing natural landscape, communities must be concentrated: "We cannot let our confusion absolutely surround us, we have to have areas of relief," says Callister. "We can build next to these areas and they will provide the open spaces that are truly great in scale." This is precisely his approach —he is trying to preserve the agricultural plain and build islands of great concentration in it and around it on the hillsides, with the mountains and the plain thus retained as a backdrop and an open green-belt. It is a most healthy and enlightened reversal from the usual approach where housing covers the entire plain and luxury homes encroach on the hills.

A look at the relief, orientation and strong scale that the Bay itself gives to the whole San Francisco area is an obvious comparison. It is an instance of taking a cue from nature and establishing a man-made restraint. Moreover, man relates naturally to an intimate sense of scale and needs, too, the contrast that a panorama of open space can provide. Creating a total environment, as a single operation, is becoming a not uncommon challenge to California architects. Callister is trying to approach the problem, finding his inspiration in the rugged and beautiful landscape, the "tradition and pride we have grown from."

Proposal for a community for two hundred and fifty thousand inhabitants.

JOSEPH ESHERICK

James Joyce recognized that there are many ordinary phenomena that are just as important as those we have always alleged to be tremendously important. He does not establish great analogies of good or evil; his families are fuzzy and blurred in their structuring; he does not diagram things in an oversimplified way. Joseph Esherick, who greatly admires the works of Joyce, thinks this is the proper approach to designing—that architecture should be composed of common objects, consciously preserving conflicts and ambiguous qualities. It is Esherick's contention that most design theories of the nineteenth and twentieth centuries have directed their energies essentially toward a certain appearance of the end product; that such energy and focus are external to man, not sensitive to his needs, purposes and will. He advocates a scientific and systematic approach to the resolution of architectural problems. He seeks a solution that starts from the general, but is based on the particular nature of the individual problem—contrary to the classical system that depends on a universal law.

Joseph Esherick was born in Philadelphia in 1914. He graduated in architecture from the University of Pennsylvania in 1937; his was a Beaux-Arts background with the teaching of Paul Cret as the main influence—although that of George Howe was starting to be felt. Esherick discovered early that it was not just how a building looked that was important, but how people utilized and reacted toward it. While studying architecture, he spent much of his time sculpting and making anatomical drawings for the medical school. This was a first and vital insight into a tremendously sensitive functional structure; it led him to discover that the human body was neither the ideal structure nor the general case that was naively illustrated in anatomy books, but one that developed in an individual, particular and highly-specialized way.

In 1938, after working briefly for Howe, Esherick came to California. After four years in the Navy he opened his own office in 1946. Because of the limitations of specialization Esherick believes that an era is beginning where the physical and social sciences are uniting in the search for common methods. At the University of California in Berkeley, where he has taught since 1952, Esherick has studied mathematics, scientific method (within the philosophy department), operations research, systems theory and, to pursue the application of these to architecture, computer programming. In 1960 he studied sculpture and painting at the San Francisco Art Institute.

Impressed by the clarity of the structure of mathematics, Esherick tended to despair when he found no real structure to architecture. "It is one of the major tasks of architecture to study what this structure might be," a task at which he is presently at work, while also exploring methods of teaching such a system. He believes that the architect must develop a sensitivity to life around him. For Esherick this is "Main Street" rather than "Mykonos." In teaching he thinks one needs to be very precise and give the student enough to worry about for ten years, after which time he can

Bermak House, Oakland, California.

111

Larsen House, San Francisco, California.

generate new worries for himself. Esherick sees the architect's mentality as analogous to that of the junk sculptor, whose techniques he can use in a more purposeful way. Instead of wandering the streets for objects, the architect can choose directly from a catalogue. To Esherick, there are more important challenges than to fuss with small things and try to change them.

"Form is what it wants to be; what things are and what they do. We need to discover realities and meanings. I do not want to be mystical about this—while I find Kahn's ideas stimulating and respect them, I think the mystical part is something that will be transformed or disappear. Things have purposes, and this is why you make them. What they want to be, in a way, is as efficient and effective as possible. You can measure the success of a design in terms of its responsiveness and effectiveness. Effectiveness means the degree to which an object satisfies each one of the inputs, however small, to which it responds. Form, then, is a composition of satisfying structure, with the "wants-to-be-ideas" suggestive of some kind of purpose; what you have to do is find it out and then design very specifically for it. Form should not be judged by some arbitrary standard, but only as good or bad in relation to a specific purpose. If you think otherwise you so limit your interpretation of the past, present and future that it ceases to be as complex, and as interesting, as you ought to be able to think it is.

"One of the great problems with modern painting is to know when a painting is finished, and with architecture, to know when a problem is solved—often an architect does not know that because he does not know what the problem is. Aware that a problem exists, yet not knowing what it really is nor having any real method to approach it, architects are inclined to invent one. The Beaux Arts education invented problems, mostly aesthetic ones, and also the rules for solving them. Aesthetics is a man-made problem, whereby you can define rules just as in chess.

"We have tended to look at the end products (buildings), or one might even say the by-products, of architecture, when the way to look at architecture is as a complete process. We have been concerning ourselves with expressions instead of realities. It is much more important to find out what a designer thought he was doing and relate this to the outcome of the building as a phenomenon being used by various people. If you eliminate the process of design and look at only the building, you idealize it into something that it is not. A building is really little more than a background, a set of diagrammatic ideas; how well these ideas are communicated is what makes a building interesting.

"One of the difficulties of the design process is that many of us have been trained primarily in convergent processes. The Beaux Arts system, with the idea of the *esquisse* that you generate in a short period of time and subsequently refine, produced an essentially focal architecture. For example, Callister focuses on his buildings so specifically that the rest of the situation disappears. If the design process is a formative or modifying one, it always begins with fairly specific ideas about fairly specific objects; these objects then are used to describe existing situations as representing either a satisfactory state or a state in need of development or modification. Thus one deals exclusively with known images, using them to develop a design solution that consequently is limited to a modification of past solutions. Our immediate design heritage, and the Bauhaus exemplifies this, is from a group who began by seeing the need to destroy the past and its formalism, but who managed, in so doing, to substitute a new formalism. It does not matter that it is not the fault of the Bauhaus; but it is sufficient warning to us that it has happened, and that a new and rigid academy of form has appeared. It is the old problem of being unable to understand meanings, to grasp at forms. I would describe this as convergent thinking, when what we need to do at the outset of any idea is to think divergently. This is the only way that innovation is possible.

Mc Intyre House, Hillsborough, California.

"We need to establish a system having two characteristics: that the system itself does not structure our view either of the environment, formulation or solution of the problem; and that the design and decision processes are embedded in the problem itself, and man-oriented. We ought to generate many divergent thoughts and a number of different alternatives, and then develop some method of selection that is not arbitrary but has a definite criterion. You have to prove that A is better than B under some quite particular terms. To do this by the usual architectural system of drawing is too hard and time-consuming. We should be able to produce a general or abstract case in some way and then manipulate it. When you look at a formula in mathematics you can see the limitations of how a change of any one symbol alters a particular phenomenon. By specifying what the design problem is in a loose, general sense, you quickly define the domain and the limits without specifying the solution. The result is the opportunity to predict outcomes and work on a variety of alternatives, and on refinements that you do not normally have time to consider.

"We tend to limit the industrial process, a functional element of architecture today, again with preconceptions. One of the great things about the industrial process is that there is a higher degree of individualism possible than with the hand-made process—not individualism in the sense of personal expression, but rather in the satisfaction of individual and particular needs. Consider the frequently stated relationship between functionalism and the industrial process. The prewar buildings of the Bauhaus group, and the postwar functionalist buildings in this country—the Seagram Building, Lever House, Crown Zellerbach—are claimed to be expressions of the industrial approach; in fact they represent merely a handcraft approach, the only change being that machines are used to do what otherwise would have been done by hand. A machine aesthetic has been constructed, and while this has transient importance in indicating future possibilities, it is still an aesthetic system and therefore a limiting thing. The industrial process has nothing built into it that suggests a modular system. There are modular systems in certain related activities, such as cataloging, distribution, shipping, and warehousing, but the industrial process can be as fluid as we want it to be.

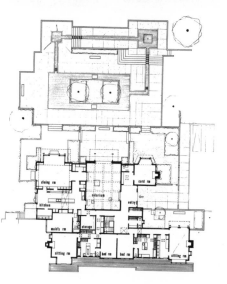

"There is a new cult in architecture, for the most part subjective and trivial, that concerns itself only with aesthetics: beauty for beauty's sake, at all costs and no matter how arrived at. [In this category Esherick referred to an approach like Stone's or Yamasaki's, who he feels are moving absolutely in the wrong direction.] Beauty is a consequential thing, a product of solving problems correctly. It is unreal as the goal. Preoccupation with aesthetics leads to arbitrary design, to buildings which take a certain form because the designer 'likes the way it looks.' No successful architecture can be formulated on a generalized system of aesthetics; it must be based on a way of life. Nothing irritates me more than to hear people talk about noble materials—any material can

Cary House, Mill Valley, California.

be noble. Why anyone should think that marble is one bit better than concrete, or that red brick is more human, is something I have never been able to understand—although there probably is a point where you can say that people respond to red brick in a different manner than they respond to concrete. I am more interested in getting people to respond to the beauty of a sidewalk, or an asphalt street, than I am in getting them to understand the beauty of bricks or plants— I am notoriously unsuccessful in this respect.

"What is most useful for our particular time is to produce things that are subject to a kind of ambiguity that can be interpreted in several ways. Then people are not forced to participate in a rigid, preordained way. Any environment you produce should not become dominant; people are far more important. The very ambiguity of the social science problem, and I take design to be a social science problem, its wooliness, its vagueness, all of these elements of the problem are in fact elements of life itself. Our designs must preserve this capacity for ambiguity.

"A building itself should change. For example, Kahn has argued against too much color because you cannot see the subtle and marvellous changes of light and shadow that take place throughout a day. All these things change over a long period of time; it is important to allow this to take place and to allow people to see it. All aspects of a building should be considered for what they are; nothing need be relegated to arbitrary categories. Architecture could then move on to a plastic, free approach where the building itself disappears and we sense only our primary media of space, light, and time."

Esherick, seeking the fastest way to generate a wide variety of alternative solutions to a problem, tends to design while drawing. A fairly traditional relationship is for the architect, having discussed a problem with his client and arrived at some preliminary ideas, to present him with the refinement and development of these in the form of presentation drawings. In explaining and interpreting the drawings, the architect is often placed in a defensive position; whereas the client, in questioning them, is often actually in an attacking position. In many instances, the more attractive presentation drawings are, the more they are liable to act as a barrier, because they have developed a significance of their own. It focuses a client's attention on the drawing, where ideas, purposes and materials intended to be realized volumetrically are not easily communicable, rather than on the building.

Esherick tries to obviate these problems by an individual and somewhat circuitous design process: he starts with a series of conversations seeking to establish in general terms the client's motivation to build; after broad objectives are clarified Esherick draws, during client discussions, what are basically diagrams of the building—"thinking always in terms of space." No drawings are prepared between meetings, and only blank sheets of paper are brought to them. Gradually, he says, "the ideas pile up and the form emerges. I found you could do this quickly and arrive at a level of communication not possible otherwise." It is only after the main problems are resolved that drawings are prepared in the office for client reviews. There are difficulties in this means of approach: the effort and participation required of the client—and apart from residences, clients are often anonymous; moreover, it is possible to secure a client's reaction to immediate needs, but very difficult to get a prediction of future ones; many architects

Bermak House, Oakland, California.

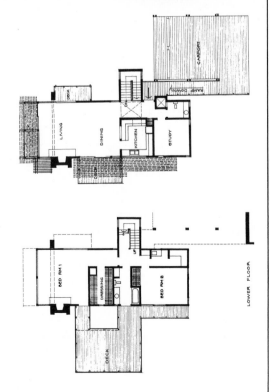

find such an intense personal involvement with their clients restricting; then, too, the creative process being directly before the client, can itself be so intriguing as to be distracting.

Esherick's recent projects show a probing approach to the "eventuality" of architectural form. Respecting San Francisco's white rectangular urbanity, Esherick designed the surprisingly spacious Larsen House in 1960 for a small site. The main living spaces, in the rear of the house, are open through glass walls to panoramic views over the Bay. The house—materially black and white—is a good character.

Esherick also sought a simple form for the 1962 McIntyre House, in Hillsborough, California. However, the parents required three independent suites, for themselves, their two sons, and two daughters, necessitating a separateness that to Esherick "was the quintessence of complication; if anything were to be expressed it would be complication. Every part is dealt with as a particular unit. The rooms are almost separate pavilions, the roofs change, and each door and window is related to the particular conditions around it. It is a clearly changing house; things are happening constantly. Our intention was that your eye should not light on any one thing at any special time."

In contrast to the intimacy and privacy of the compartmented suites, the main social space is an almost formal solarium, sheltered by twenty, domed, transparent skylights. Opening onto a terrace, garden courts, and a water garden, it is a very distinguished space that can be used all year round. In hot weather the entire room functions as a giant ventilating duct, with air entering through vents just above floor level and emptying through the roof space. "There was a great little lesson in this solarium," says Esherick. "With pre-cast concrete you can say, 'The beam is the gutter, and the gutter is the beam.' You can't do this with any other material. But it has to be used in the most complete way, not just to express the structure. There is no reason why the structure should be made into a thing apart. It actually doesn't need expression—it has nothing to do with the people living in the house. Here, in pre-cast concrete the wall is the beam, then the overhang, and eventually becomes the roof. Form can be absolutely everything."

The houses at Mill Valley, for Dr. and Mrs. W. Cary, and at Oakland, for Dr. and Mrs. G. E. Bermak in 1963, are somewhat in the vernacular and spirit of the skeletal, redwood-shingled tradition of the Bay Region. Both hardly disturb the hillside sites on which they are almost delicately placed. The houses have spectacular views, from windows that tend to isolate and focus attention on them. Sun-shading devices, particularly against the brightness and heat of the late afternoon sun, are designed as a functional element of each window. Esherick considers this more "vital" than the extension of the roof as an overhang, which he thinks of as arbitrary and aesthetic in derivation. In both houses, within a rectangular envelope, he sought an ambiguous quality; a literal attempt to destroy or fragment the form in order to achieve varying interpretations. "You can look from different points," says Esherick, "and rearrange the structure in a dozen ways. We tried to make it hard to tell what is wall and what are merely links between openings." Coupled with Esherick's almost passionate desire to have his buildings continuously reflect the changing qualities of nature, this inevitably leads to many changes within the building itself. "I am against the jewelry school where you try to produce one gem that is constant under all conditions."

With larger projects Esherick tries to develop an intellectual framework within which "meaning, purpose and objectives" can be stated. In the case of Wurster Hall to house the College of Environmental Design—principally the departments of City and Regional Planning, Landscape Architecture, Architecture, and Design—at the University of California in Berkeley, this took two years for its architects, DeMars, Esherick and Don Olsen, to develop. Completed in 1965, it is a relatively inexpensive building. The exterior is pre-cast concrete, using a basic standard form which is modified to accommodate the variety of functional conditions within the building. All projections are on the exterior to preserve maximum flexibility within the building. The interior is rough and intentionally changeable. All ductwork, piping and mechanisms are exposed — without constraining or modifying their "insistence will." Where interior walls are not exposed concrete they are covered with rough plywood to which drawings can be tacked. To many it is a brutal building; to Esherick it is frank.

The architects agreed that the building itself should not be an influence, and should be almost impossible for the students to copy. This is in contrast to Rudolph's Art and Architecture Building at Yale, says Esherick, where seemingly "the building is intended explicitly as an example. One of the great values of the Yale building will be the antagonism set up, but the difficulty is that since the building is so narrowly explicit, the reaction is likely to be equally narrowly explicit." Wurster Hall summarizes Esherick's approach; it endeavors to be factual and functional, but at the same time very ambiguous with a seeming consistent irresolution. "It attempts to be the most precise and best thing we could possibly do, and, although very precise, I thought you should never be sure where the building is exactly. I am interested in seeing where things are more or less independent—conflict should be preserved and not resolved—and I try to point out the individual differences and individual likenesses; this is what I mean about the fuzziness of boundaries." To Esherick, a building should be like a forest where you can stand outside and sense the nature of the spaces inside without really seeing them.

Esherick vividly recalls a lecture series some years ago at Berkeley entitled "The Struggle of the Modern," by Stephen Spender, who said that it is possible to define something with absolute clarity by saying what it is not. This theory appears in mathematics, and Clifford Still, a West Coast painter, explored this approach too. It is possible to interpret Esherick's buildings as combinations of what they are and what they are not, a vibration of positives and negatives. Esherick's is an unsentimental view that accepts realities rather than dwells on idyllic visions, and embodies the idea of beauty as incidental, or *as will*. It should be noted that some architects would contend that Esherick's position is rationalized irrationality, one which might fearfully duplicate the picturesqueness of late nineteenth century Victorian extravaganzas. The crucial question is to what extent should a strong central discipline at least control, if not resolve, conflict?

Esherick's buildings develop an intense aesthetic, an almost sculptural impact, and display a liberalism and soul-searching that hold a certain fascination for our generation. Whether it is enduring is another question. But the theme itself spans the centuries: Only what is true can be beautiful. He is probing, searching, with great integrity.

Environmental Design Building, University of California, Berkeley, California.

ERNEST J. KUMP

While "house" implies certain utilitarian functions, "home" goes beyond this to encompass intellectual, emotional and spiritual considerations, and broader environmental relationships. "Home" expresses a total condition—this is architecture. "Science and technology are the means that have made possible solutions that can be rationalized and intellectualized," says Ernest J. Kump; and to achieve a total condition we must not ignore that "architecture expresses aspirations and emotions, is subjective, and is the goal." Because function has both utilitarian and emotional aspects, Kump believes that, to Louis Sullivan's edict "form follows function," we must add "as fitness and feeling." Architecture goes beyond science to become art, he thinks, and the rational solution will never automatically create art, because art requires choice, which is intuitive. Kump is an avowed regionalist, attacking impersonal architecture because it is devoid of "individuality of expression with respect to the roots and traditions or the nature of its surrounding environment, and is creating an architectural desert."

Ernest J. Kump was born in Bakersfield, California, in 1911. He graduated from the University of California at Berkeley, in 1932, and studied for a year at Harvard University before returning to Fresno to join his father's office. The firm, which now numbers about thirty, is in Palo Alto, with a branch in New York City. Kump's approach to architecture derives from a philosophy that seeks the "truths and principles" underlying architecture—what he refers to as "a new architecture for man."

"To understand, teach, and do good architecture, I have sought: to understand the true nature of man, of architecture and their relationship to each other; a clear definition of architecture, and the universal principles underlying its expression. Man, by nature, is an indivisible physical and spiritual entity endowed with the powers to feel, think, and act. By his nature he is a creature of space—in which he lives, moves, and has his being. I understood that architecture evolved from man's concern with the natural spaces in which he found himself, and from his desire to order these spaces better to suit his physical wants and spiritual needs.

"The fact that man can feel what he desires, coupled with his ability to think and act to attain the object of his feelings (in this case his concern with the spaces surrounding him), led me to what I believe is the true definition of architecture; 'the expression of feeling through ordered space environment.'

"Certain principles govern all of the activities of man and the universe, and three of them are the generative elements of all cre-

erbert Hoover Junior High School, San Francisco, California, 1955.

Carmel Junior High School, Carmel Valley, California, 1962.

117

ative activity: center of consciousness, or a judgment sense; organic unity, or an object in view; and vocabulary, or the parts between. They are manifest in music by the key tone, tonality, and scale degrees—in literature by the subject, object, and a vocabulary of words, and without them, neither music nor literature could be. In architecture, they are manifest in function, form and a vocabulary of building parts; and in the architect as the judgment sense, his objective as form, and a vocabulary of emotive parts.

"From these come four additional elements, or principles, that are inherent and manifest a quality: order, from the discipline and the right relationship of the parts; design, as the expression of the ordered arrangement of the parts; harmony, from balance and quiet; and form, as the expression of the objective materialized, implicit in the idea of organic unity.

"Everything in nature is endowed with dual physical-spiritual properties, exactly the same as those inherent in the nature of man, to which we are all sensitive. Since it is generally understood today that all of the universe was created from a simple microcosmic unit of energy, the same indivisible duality of physical and spiritual (or emotional) properties must be inherent in it also.

"In my first attempts to apply these principles I lacked a clear understanding of 'vocabulary' and 'order.' I decided to divide and conquer. I had always felt the importance of order and I chose to work on this principle first—mindful of Pope's great admonition: 'Order is Heaven's first law.' My first attempts to apply it were in the physical or dimensional order of the structure and parts of my buildings. I experimented with various dimensions of modules and used modular design in all my work; this gave direction and discipline, and resulted in efficiency and economy in the use of structural parts for building, and in a quality of work that could not be captured in any other way. It was, in itself, an expression of good design and achieved an organic integration of all the physical elements that went into a structure. It also provided better organization of working drawings and office procedure.

"Nature contains an infinite variety of matter and form, and underlying it all are laws of natural organization and growth. All nature is built of repetitive units—and the nature of each thing depends on the nature of the units composing it. What is the true nature of the unit or part that makes up the vocabulary of architecture? I realized that whatever this unit or cell was, it had to have characteristics parallel to those cells which nature has created, complete entities in themselves, capable of self-reproduction, self-energizing, and being put together into larger unities. If architecture, then, concerns itself with the spaces of man, the natural unit or cell of architecture is a unit of space. So the basic unit of architectural vocabulary could not be a material unit but must be an ordered unit of space environment. Thus architecture is 'a cellular organization of organic units of space environment.'

"Here was the basis of a true vocabulary for architecture. But if it was to be sound in design, it must allow infinite variety and freedom within unity and have both physical and emotional properties. The physical properties would include the three-dimensional size of the space unit, the physical environment (visual, climatic, etc.), while also having the quality of organic flexibility for the organization of subspaces within it. The emotional quality would be achieved through the proportion, profile, scale, color, texture, pattern, and finish of the space-defining materials. Each space unit must also be self-energizing, containing its own inte-

Basic Space Module School.

Miramonte High School, Orinda, California.

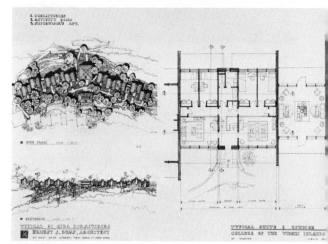

College of the Virgin Islands, St. Thomas, Virgin Islands.

grated mechanical and electrical system for heating, lighting, acoustical control, etc. Finally it must be possible to join these space units in multilateral combinations to allow three-dimensional freedom in space organization. This is the basis of cellular construction in nature, and therefore must apply to cellular space units as a vocabulary of architecture. Within this concept there are limitless mathematical possibilities in organization and form in architecture, for true, organic, three-dimensional planning, with simplicity, economy and a better and higher quality of space environment for all of man's activities."

The projects of Ernest J. Kump Associates cover a broad architectural spectrum, but it is in answering the nation's urgent need for educational facilities that the firm has gained most recognition. While schools need to be functionally efficient, technologically modern, and structurally flexible and adaptable, they do not necessarily have to look like "an antiseptic clinic or a light industrial plant," says Kump. By employing the "space module" concept he has found that construction and operating costs are lower; additions can be more easily and harmoniously planned; space is more flexible, which is most important in view of the largely unpredictable and changing teaching space requirements; and, the schools have aesthetic variety—he is proud of the firm's unique solutions to the complex problems of many school districts.

Kump's space module concept is basically a simple principle: a common denominator of space, size and shape is established that will accommodate combinations of the functional spaces required (with a smaller, regular module for subdivision); complete flexibility is preserved within this by designing it as a column-free, unobstructed space that can be divided to meet specific needs or be rearranged as purposes change with time; this space unit is then repeated throughout, each one incorporating all mechanical utilities in its structural envelope. Flexibility extends also to site planning, where the basic space modules can be grouped to form rows, clusters, or courts depending on topography and planning requirements.

The Miramonte High School in Orinda, California, completed in 1957, was one of Kump's first structures based on his space module (a 56-foot square, 9 to 12 feet high, due to the sloping roof, using a 4-foot component module). Corridors between the basic space modules are flat-roofed to emphasize the individual units—although in subsequent schools Kump has more frequently employed a continuous, low-pitched roof line for greater simplicity. The large, defined basic space modules are framed in wood, with columns on the external wall plane; this provides a greater visual unity and clearer statement than the more common, small repetitive module of many modern buildings. Kump's Carmel Valley Junior High School and his renowned Foothill College, both in California, are recent examples of this principle.

More than a high school but less than a university, and needing its own identity as such, the junior college has become a solution for those adults who seek to pursue their education inexpensively and close to home. Whereas the traditional university campus has tended to seek isolation and a certain detachment as an atmosphere conducive to scholarship, the junior college is, of necessity, an integral part of the community. As such it is potentially a considerable, formative local cultural force. Foothill Junior College in Los Altos, an excellent example, was completed in 1961 by Kump Associates in association with Masten and Hurd, with site and landscape planning by Sasaki, Walker, Associates. Here,

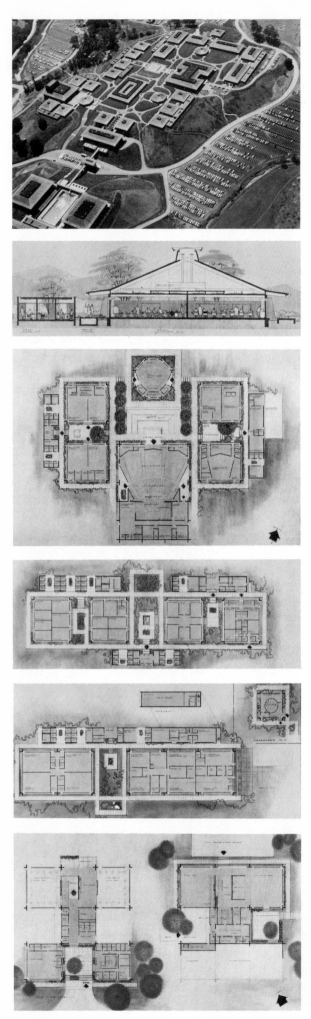

Foothill Junior College, Los Altos, California.

Kump created an environment on a grand scale with great unity, dignity and respect for the individual, that accommodates an enrollment of thirty-five hundred young students (eventually six thousand), on a 122-acre site.

The importance of Foothill College is not the individual buildings, although there are many useful lessons to be learned from these, but the total environment, which is an excellent example of its type and character. The whole campus is planned on a very subtle radius, with some forty buildings grouped around a similar number of outdoor spaces. A formal court in front of the library is used for outdoor assemblies, and is the focal space for other large, informally-landscaped outdoor spaces around which buildings are grouped. The broad, overhanging eaves of the buildings shelter outdoor corridors that lead to smaller, intimate patios scaled in size to the classrooms and offices that open out to them. This relationship of internal to external space, and the variety and sequential movement through spaces as one experiences them, are masterfully handled.

Since the college buildings are on a gently rolling hilltop, there is vertical as well as horizontal variety in the transition of space. The natural terrain has been sculptured to form earth mounds which enhance the variations and echo, at a more intimate scale, the larger forms found throughout the surrounding valley. The nature of the site has been advantageously exploited to create a quiet world for the pedestrian: automobiles must be parked in one of the several landscaped parking areas at the foot of the slope. Walking up the gentle incline there are dramatic, changing views of the buildings. Then, entering the campus beneath the sheltering eaves, one discovers a natural world of warm informality—monumental, yet without academic solemnity. Brick buildings, which house services, administration and offices, have been located around the perimeter of the complex to form what is almost a compound.

The individual structures have a harmony and discipline that comes from the consistent handling of space, both around and within them, and the restrained vocabulary of materials. The basic space module is 60 feet by 68 feet by 10 feet, defined in the buildings by V-shaped, exposed aggregate concrete piers, with a 4-foot component module. The structural piers support redwood-shingled, hipped roofs that are visually dominant and neatly contain all mechanical equipment. The academic buildings have rough-sawn walls of redwood. Three octagonal lecture halls, whose proportions also derive from the basic space module, provide focal points of interest for the major spaces, and visual foils to the rectangular buildings grouped around them. The physical education complex, with an Olympic-size swimming pool as its focus, is well-placed; slightly apart from the main campus on an adjoining knoll, it is dramatically approached by a pedestrian bridge above the main automobile approach road. A pavilion midway across the bridge is a pleasant shelter where students who have automobile pools may wait for transportation.

For this number of buildings the architecture may appear too "woodsy" for some tastes, and certainly it would be inappropriate in most urban situations. Yet the rapport between location, site planning and the individual buildings, the result of order, unity, strength and coherence, make this scheme a worthy crusader in our present search for a better and more humane environment for our activities.

Foothill Junior College.

Mira Vista Elementary School, Richmond, California.

Mabel McDowell Elementary School, Columbus, Indiana.

JOHN CARL WARNECKE

The central role that legislation can and should play in the shaping of our urban scene is of acute interest to John Carl Warnecke. He has responded to the need for radical changes in the practice of architecture, implied by the enormity of our present problems and opportunities, by developing an organization of professionals with diverse backgrounds and abilities. Their work, he explains, is guided by his conviction that every effort must be directed towards improving the quality of life in our society. The scope and prodigious output of Warnecke's comparatively youthful, ambitious office, reflect a personal astuteness and pragmatism that have resulted in one of the largest and most successful practices in California.

John Carl Warnecke was born in San Francisco in 1919. Before completing a liberal arts degree at Stanford University and continuing his architectural studies at Harvard University, he had worked in his father's office—this practice, in the Beaux Arts tradition, undoubtedly did much to create a good foundation for his own firm which he started in 1946. Warnecke was not really aware of the significance of the Bay Region's indigenous architecture until the Harvard exposure to the International Style had broadened his architectural background. These various influences are reflected in the diversity of his architecture, in an approach that stems essentially from a carefully-studied awareness of "local truth and continuity."

The Mira Vista School in Richmond, California, built in 1957, showed Warnecke as a skillful exponent of the Bay Region vernacular. Classrooms, enclosed by broad sloping roofs punctuated by large skylights, stepped up the hillside to merge gently with the terrain. The large hovering roofs, airy interior spaces, open galleries and terraces—with an intimate sense of scale—all were to become recurrent themes in many subsequent projects.

The McDowell Elementary School in Columbus, Indiana, in 1960, was deliberately built in a drab neighborhood. It has apparently done much to create a new sense of pride, in addition to providing a pleasant gathering place for local residents. The school is arranged in four clusters of three classrooms that are axially placed around a more dominant group of common-use rooms. The steel frame buildings, faced with brick and glass, are all defined by peaked roofs cloaked in shingles. Covered walkways, connecting the elements, tend to orient the school group into its own enclave of four play yards; but, beyond these, the spaces extend visually outwards to the community.

McDowell is the fourth school in Columbus designed by outstanding firms across the nation. In 1956 J. Irwin Miller, head of the Irwin Bank, and Cummins Diesel Engine Co.—Columbus' largest industry—established a foundation that offered to pay the architectural fees for any new local school whose designer was selected from a list of firms independently nominated by Belluschi and Saarinen. From Miller's influence this small town of twenty-five thousand is a showcase of modern structures, with buildings by Eliel and Eero Saarinen, Weese, T.A.C., Barnes, Pei, S.O.M. and Warnecke.

The Del Monte regional shopping center for Monterey, California, completed in 1952, is probably his most compelling group of buildings based on the clustered-square theme. Warnecke, as usual, reduced site-grading to a minimum by having his carefully-related "squares" follow the terrain of the hillside. The structures form intimately-landscaped malls, with terrace levels linked by short flights of steps, softened by planting and enlivened by fountains. One of the most pleasant and lively shopping environments in the country, it represents an achievement all the more significant since this commercial building type is often a brash intrusion on the landscape. The great hipped roofs are sheathed in large buff-colored concrete panels that look most gracious seen against the sunny wooded slopes. The roof trusses, spanning the large interior volumes, rest on precast concrete beams and columns, sandblasted to expose the natural texture and color of their aggregate. Similar to Foothill College, to which it has a close affinity although without quite the same structural directness, it demonstrates how the Bay Region's vernacular can still be meaningful.

Warnecke relies on his "local truth and continuity" theme whenever he works in environments of special quality and character. An excellent example is his United States Embassy designed in 1957 for the hot, humid setting of Bangkok, Thailand. Warnecke found his point of departure in an old hospital there that had been successfully adapted to the climate. "I noticed the large roof overhangs, the floating balconies and the details of beautiful, precast concrete railings of modular design. The overhangs kept sun and rain off the flat wall surface. The whole building had an attractive, lacy feeling. Here I saw the possibility of creating the main elements of design with the technique of modern, flat slab concrete construction which could give an even lighter feeling to this concept of design."

Warnecke's white, airy pavilion, in a space screened by rich, green rain trees, is raised above a small man-made lake, with the excavated earth used as fill for a future annex and parking lots. The open ground floor, approached by vehicular causeways from the side and a covered walkway from the rear, is a large sheltered entrance area. Above this, protected from the sun and rain by balconies, rise three levels of glazed-wall offices, open to views of the rain forest over precast balcony rails. A central well, letting natural breezes circulate through the open ground level, helps to cool the building, and reduces appreciably the air-conditioning load for offices.

This particular idea was carried to a more mature expression in 1961, when Warnecke designed the Capitol for Hawaii. A considerably more complex functional problem, serving both legislative and executive functions, it required the creation of a symbol

Del Monte Shopping Center, Monterey, California.

U.S. Embassy, Bangkok, Thailand.

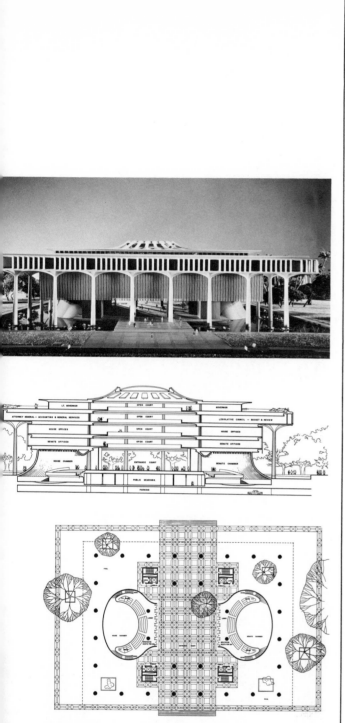

Hawaii State Capitol, Honolulu, Hawaii.

of government in an historic setting of tropical splendor. The center of the building is again a hollow entrance well, rising through the four levels of executive offices to a domed skylight. Visitors have direct access from the entrance level to spectator galleries that overlook the House and Senate Chambers, and from four formally-placed elevator cores to the balcony floors that surround the central well. The enclosing arcade of concrete columns that stand in the reflecting pool gives a loftiness to the structure, but somewhat at the expense of a clear structural system. This is the first major governmental building in the United States that has been entrusted to a modern architect, an acknowledgement long overdue. Seen in contrast to the recently completed and patently ludicrous Rayburn office building in Washington, Warnecke's Capitol should give officials some food for thought.

His simple and sensitive solution to the challenge of designing the Kennedy grave in Arlington Cemetery reflects Warnecke's meticulous care and thought. It was a task where any preconception would have been an easy but dangerous companion. Speaking of his approach to the problem Warnecke said: "The first thing we did was to record first quick and intuitive impressions, which I value, of any and all possible solutions. We made an exhaustive research of the history of graves in the Christian tradition for more than three months, in order to gain insight and direction for the development of a design concept. The grave had to be unobtrusive, with a timeless quality, a sense of repose, dignity and nobility, and yet be a grave, a symbol of death. As we developed the design we separated the emotional, religious and symbolic elements of the grave, eventually eliminating things that were inappropriate either to the traditions of Arlington, to the site itself, or were symbols with meaning for only a small section of society. We wanted to present something that the majority of people could come to, could understand and identify with. The eternal flame was the central and given design element. From all the possibilities we tried to find the most appropriate for this particular President, in this particular place, representing what he represented. But this was extremely difficult to try and capture in a symbol of his death. When you work with the symbolism of death, another dimension is lost because there is no function, architecturally, of death. It is very presumptuous to say, 'this is death,' or 'I understand what death is and it should be symbolised this way.' By separating all the problems over a period they began to resolve themselves."

In essence the solution is a sculptural landscape, looking across, symbolically, to the Lincoln Memorial. Visitors are led through a gentle sequence of varying emotional and visual experiences, all carefully created so as barely to disturb the natural scene. A circular grass forespace bounded by an ascending path is the approach; a curved bench directs visitors to the right, with the path to the left retained for ceremonial visits. An elliptical space becomes a prelude to the grave site. There, a slightly elevated marble platform contains simple slate markers for the President and his two deceased children, and the bronze font with the eternal flame; behind this is a terminal wall bearing the Seal of the President of the United States. After leaving the sanctuary and passing down the steps into the elliptical area again, visitors will stand before a great overlook, the floor of which is slightly inclined and terminates in a ledge engraved with words spoken by the President.

The color and texture of granite paths progress from dark gray on the approaches, medium gray on the overlook, to the white marble of the grave platform itself. Walking back down the curving path the visitor will have remembered and, as all would wish, taken something with him.

"The liberty for personal expression can almost destroy a total environment: the Yale campus is a good example. Washington is an environment that has been cared for by many people in which there is an inherent overall continuity and form. There must be a sensitivity to such an environment; an architect should not do just whatever he wants. Yet he can still display great diversity and creativity in his work while respecting the environment in which he builds.

"By search, research and studying each client's needs, from which we expect to draw inspiration, we eventually form with the client the unity of a team that is unique for that moment. We have faith that out of this approach will come an expression of the client's requirements. We have made demi-gods of some of the architects just preceding us—Wright, Le Corbusier and so on. Their very personal, individual expressions pointed to different directions in architecture. This has been helpful because it has shown the great freedom which is possible. But there is a point-of-no-return here beyond which real chaos lies. It is time to begin establishing a series of directions, where we might cooperate and find a common unity, and begin working toward these.

"Each generation of architects is presented with a different set of circumstances that are not particularly evident, but are always there. The problem a generation ago was the great change of techniques that came from a new technical, industrial society. Mies and Le Corbusier had a great opportunity that grew out of the changes in the physical world and our perception of it. It was easy for a 'new world' of mass media to understand and visualize their singular buildings—thus their impact was revolutionary. Our generation accepts the fact that technical changes will probably go on for ever. And although there will always be a need for singular buildings constantly exploring new forms, structure and materials, we have been confronted with a whole new set of problems: The pressures of time; of practicing in different areas of the country; of projects such as universities, and urban centers, that once were developed over decades. Ours is not a problem of an avant-garde solution for every commission. We have to recognize where we should preserve the architecture of the past and build modern structures in direct, harmonious relationship with it—such as Lafayette Square in Washington. [Warnecke has designed new buildings around Lafayette Square, an area that contains many buildings of historic and architectural interest, and is a setting for the White House itself.]

"The architect of a decade ago could take a single idea or expression, study and simplify it, and then apply it to types of buildings. An architect today, who understands the rich diversity of America, is bound to be interested in all of man's institutions and their individual, unique expressions. He inevitably becomes interested in architecture as a social science relating to all men. Had I not come to Washington and had the opportunity to work with politicians—at the level of social-political scientists—I might not have realized the direct relationship between our efforts in architecture and those of the politician. We are both basically involved in creating a better way of life for man on earth. There is a direct parallel in purpose. President Kennedy had a tremendous ability to understand his role as a leader in every aspect of American

John F. Kennedy Grave, Arlington, Virginia.

life, and the role of a patron of the arts. In all great periods there has been an artist-patron relationship. He stepped into a vacuum that had existed for decades, and gave impetus and direction to all the design professions through public policy statements. Just as important, he understood the continuity of the past, present and future.

"As an architect recognizes the scale of problems today he is drawn to the conclusion that the individual building is of little consequence. Yet, actually, the reason he is trying to solve these larger complex problems is to create an environment that will encourage and enhance outstanding individual buildings. It is the quality of the specific thing, the number of them he does or that all architects do together, that really counts. It is the small individual building of excellence that is the true test of whether the larger problems have been solved. The architect today lives in a paradox of having to solve gigantic problems while at the same time coming to a peaceful coexistence with himself so that he can, at the same time, solve the small individual problems. The architect must not lose sight of the total picture for which architecture has always existed and within which it will always be evaluated.

"The type and size of one's practice is a major problem facing the architect today. If we are to solve the problems of our time we must have an office that is equipped to do so. This is quite different from the architect a decade ago, who could have a small office. Trying to solve our problems effectively and efficiently while still producing buildings of merit has completely revolutionized the practice of architecture. Today we must have an office large enough to handle the largest problems because generally these are the most important and critical. The diversity of problems necessitates an office of highly-specialized people having equal respect for each other's discipline—recognizing that there is basically one design profession rising above the separate design disciplines. Another factor of our time is the ease with which we can move about. It may be better to work across the country with a client who will understand you than work in your own area with one who is not sympathetic."

As Warnecke gains larger commissions, particularly in the comparatively new area of master-planning for large tracts of urban environment, his office continues to expand. His San Francisco office has grown to eighty-five people. Partially due to his friendship with President Kennedy, he opened a branch in Washington, with a staff of forty-five. In Honolulu his office numbers eighteen. Within this office structure Warnecke accords his design staff great latitude, not because of lack of personal involvement, but rather because of a desire for initial responses to the solving of problems. If the office has any set principle, it is the freedom it allows in a building's expression, dictated by its prospective environment. Where the environment is unique and has great natural beauty, the Warnecke group try as much as possible to retain it. Where it has been created over the centuries, they try to have their work become part of a chain of events. In the general environment of cities, where there are no distinguishing qualities, they try to express the unique requirements of the particular client.

In creating a new academic empire, California anticipates by 1975 the expenditure of a billion dollars that will turn barren land into bustling college and university campuses.

Warnecke's College of San Mateo, fifteen miles south of San Francisco, is a new junior college designed as a single planning

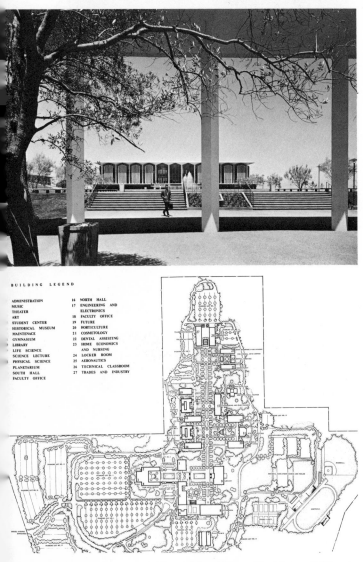

College of San Mateo, San Mateo, California.

operation. The one hundred and fifty-three acre site is on the crest of a hill, commanding superb views in all directions. For its first stage of development the college was designed for four thousand students; ultimately it will expand to eight thousand full-time students in liberal arts and vocational training programs. The campus is laid out on two main axes: one, along the spine of the hill affording some protection against the chilling winds from the Pacific Ocean, is a tree-lined mall along which academic buildings are related around colonnaded courts; it is crossed at the point of greatest student concentration by the other axis which is terminated by the library and fine arts center, and is flanked by the student center, administration and athletic buildings. The peripheral road for automobiles does not cross pedestrian routes to the buildings. All parking areas and sports fields away from the academic enclave are directly below the crest of the hill. The buildings are all of reinforced concrete, based on a 16-foot module that is repeated in the linked, colonnaded courts. Although this is a strong unifying theme and brought economies to the construction, it has not produced a flexibility of space division and expression comparable to that of Foothill College.

The proposed University of California at Santa Cruz, on a beautiful wooded, sloping two thousand acre plateau with magnificent views out to the Pacific, makes even the San Mateo college seem a somewhat diminutive challenge. The project is planned to create a series of residential colleges of two hundred and fifty to two thousand five hundred students, related to a university center. The natural, open parkland areas of the campus will insulate the colleges without isolating them, allowing informally-grouped academic clusters to develop individually within a unifying landscape.

Probably because San Francisco is the center of one of the fastest expanding regions in the United States, with so much of its natural beauty disappearing rapidly, our urban challenge seems dramatized there. It emphasizes that the real architectural problems today lie in creating whole new tracts of urban environment—such as college campuses. These are the forerunners—contemporary symbols of our potential to shape our environment at a new and expansive scale; even a glimmer of hope that we might find some convincing answers. Warnecke has wisely sought to establish an organization that is large enough and diverse enough in its skills to work on this scale.

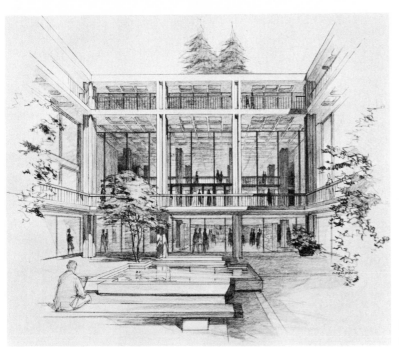

University of California, Library and Master Plan,
Santa Cruz, California.

RAPHAEL SORIANO

Raphael Soriano is a man of insistent beliefs with the enviable achievement of their consistent demonstration. Born on the Greek island of Rhodes in 1907, Soriano came to the United States at the age of seventeen, bringing with him a passion for music which he has never lost. He continually finds inspiration in the structural organization and simple variations on a central theme present in the music of Bach and the Spanish flamenco. Graduating from the University of Southern California in 1934 and working in Richard Neutra's office for a few months, Soriano built the Gato house, his first steel house, in 1936. Against the current tide of taste and prejudice toward a material with "cold" and industrial connotations, his house had an appropriate lightness and strength. Soriano has unswervingly pursued the articulate use of steel in residential structures, with elegance and restraint. He has consistently exploited technological means and industrially-produced component parts with striking virtuosity.

In 1952 Soriano left Los Angeles for a waterfront location in Tiburon, from where he enjoys a splendid view across the Bay of San Francisco and the Golden Gate Bridge. His romantic surroundings, like his appearance, seem to belie the sophistication of his architecture. A lone figure, gazing out over the Bay, simply clad in sweater and beret, he appears more like a fisherman patiently awaiting a bite than an industrious architect. To the few who know him and have been exposed to the vigor of his ideas and his characteristic outspokenness, he is something of a legendary figure. Unlike many who indulge in caustic criticism, Soriano is ready and equipped to advocate alternatives: "Technical innovation and the ensuing high mortality of obsolete materials and techniques require methodical investigation, greater precision and accumulation of meaningful findings to provide the impetus for further progress. Only through scientific thought liberation comes." These ideals he has admirably advanced in his work.

"The architect cannot possibly perform and serve society unless he understands his own society and his relationship to it. History and the richness of centuries must be understood in relation to their societies. Many of our colleagues are still lost in the Renaissance, involved with the Middle Ages, or even the cave period. This is a serious and important problem. Very few architects have thought about it, and if they understand the implications of history they do not show it.

"If a person designs a building and puts a mural on it today, how, why, and what is this mural doing? He has to answer the questions he himself puts, and if you search deeply you will find there are no answers. What we call 'art' today was not called 'art' in the past; it was simply a magical or ritualistic statement of the society. Development depends upon liberation from symbolism; therefore, 'art' does not enlighten but creates confusion and enslavement.

Leaver House, Mill Valley, California.

Today we have tremendous means of communication and propagandizing—newspapers, radio, television, even satellites. It seems incomprehensible to use a mural to record or communicate our accomplishments. If you carve or paint anything on your buildings, then you have to say what you are doing with these non-architectural things. At best they become a decorative aspect or an appliqué. Alain, the French thinker, said that women will usually put trinkets on, especially the older they get, to detract from their creases—that is exactly what we are doing in architecture.

"As civilized people we organize in order to make a statement. The totality must be well organized in order to make sense—and this has nothing to do with 'art'—otherwise there is chaos. For instance, Japanese gardens are superb because they are extremely simple; they do not give you too much and are always well related. If you analyze the houses, they are structurally designed and have marvellous spaces, but there are areas, too, of complete mysticism. I cannot admire the Japanese house as a total accomplishment; there are areas where it fails because of that mysticism. Shrines and decorative motifs having symbolic implications of the past are retained, and neither bear any relationship to structural integrity, or present-day architecture. Many sophisticated Japanese architects follow this procedure blindly, accepting it as part of an 'everlasting' architecture. We cannot make sense of past rituals today any more than an Inca boy can make sense of the ruins of his ancestors. They are completely removed from the reality of this civilization.

"Many people accept Plato's statements as truths needing no verification, yet we have enough knowledge of the world today to know that many of his ideas are untenable. For this reason I will not indulge myself with philosophies, novels, and poetry; they are principally personalized interpretations—misinterpretations of what we already know. When you think, you negate a lot. A Frenchman once said: 'To think is to say "no".' The artist is not making a statement about the world, but a personal statement, and I take it as such. The tragedy is that people take it seriously and think the artist has to be involved with society, that he has the answers and provides another dimension of understanding. Many scientists fall into the trap of thinking that 'art' brings another dimension, without analyzing the implication of art—what it was for originally, and what it means today. They take it as part of our heritage, something we cannot question, like religion.

"In architecture there are requirements of our society that must be solved, and we must tap the knowledge of our society to do this. We are not doing this as architects; we still think we are painters or sculptors, and we indulge our whims. The physicist does not solve problems through whim. Ours is an objective dissertation of structural integrity that has nothing to do with whim or self-expression; all we do is apply our collective, tenable knowledge to the solution of a problem. The sensitivities of a person are obscure and misunderstood. But because we do not understand the phenomena of the world does not mean that we have to project mystical interpretations about them. We cannot indulge the 'I' attitude because the subjective mode tends to be inaccurate; everything we use or select has been given to us by another person, another intelligence.

"When I put two things together I see relations, and I try to discover how well these relations work, not only here, but with other, broader ones that have to be discovered; this sets the

Gato House, California.

Hallawell Seed Building, San Francisco, California.

tempo, and it is an architectural decision. That is the way serious composers work. In the case of Bach, two or three notes probably started all kinds of reactions and relations that, in turn, demanded still others. This is how architecture should be approached. The totality of the instruments work together in concert, so that you are not conscious of the instruments, but their workings. Alain said that in the music of Bach you find the drama of sound, but in other music that is not serious music really you find the drama of man; meaning that one is the structural thing and the other is purely descriptive self-expression. Debussy tried to describe the waters; it is impossible. You lull yourself into thinking you are creating the impression of waters. This is precisely the attitude architects practice today when they involve themselves with the 'art' or self-expression in forms devoid of structural basis.

"Many architects are working hard making fantastic curvatures and shells that do not work. You have to ask: Why are you making this type of curve—self-expression? Social need? Or structural statement? If it is self-expression or a whim you are on dangerous ground. The sculptural approach is death to architecture. Saarinen's TWA Terminal is a good example of what not to do. It is an untenable concept structurally—nothing but a sculptural whim. You cannot learn from whims—in fact it is a regression—after that all you do is adopt more sculptural attitudes.

"An interesting example of aping comes to mind. Nearly every architect loves the Ronchamp Chapel. Here is something that is completely disastrous; the great Le Corbusier, and look at his misconception. 'Phenomenon of visual acoustics . . . The shell of the crab . . . In the brain the idea is born, indefinite it wanders and develops. On the hill I had meticulously drawn the four horizons. . . . It is they which unlocked, architecturally, the echo, the visual echo in the realm of shape.' [Soriano was quoting from Le Corbusier's book on his chapel at Ronchamp.] These are all marvellous-sounding words—but just find the content. If this is not voodoo I would like to know what is. What you learn from Le Corbusier's appliqué of the shell of the crab, with respect to architecture, is nothing. The tragedy is the blind imitation of the young and old disciples all over the world—making Ronchamps of all sorts of buildings. To imitate just does not make sense. People start out on the wrong track if they express themselves by abstract feelings, and the triviality and involvement of impressions that they do not understand. Corbusier's study of the shell is completely unscientific. It is a good thing our scientists, physicists and mathematicians do not follow these methods. Frank Lloyd Wright was one of the worst offenders, by creating arbitrary geometric patterns. This is completely contrary to our civilization, and to architecture.

"Only scientific learning will bring us intelligence and prevent our preoccupation with trivialities. We do not understand the sun, but then, in a sense we do. We are human beings and our bodies make use of its energies. If we want to study parts of it, as scientific men, we can know a lot about it with accuracy and precision; this should be the attitude of the architect. You cannot study abstractly the economy of integration and the devising of a particular relationship of elements without scientific help to see if your decision is working. An abstract thought must be immediately put to the test of whether it is tenable. As a personal concept alone it is not sufficient; if the concept is tenable as a universal concept then we have something. Saarinen's TWA Terminal is a good example: it was tenable as his concept only, there-

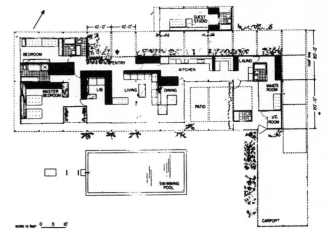

Curtis House, Bel-Air, California.

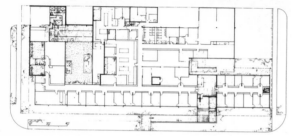

Adolph's Office Building, Burbank, California.

fore it was a failure as an architectural accomplishment. Frank Lloyd Wright's Guggenheim Museum is another such example.

"The mathematician and scientist have a large common ground, although they disagree in small areas. With the architect it is just the opposite: it is in the big areas that there is disagreement. We have never established an accumulative source of knowledge enabling us to go into higher realms of investigation. Anything we do must be a working condition, and in order to be this, it must be a structural condition; if you divorce the two you have death— a pile of materials but not a structure. The more I observe life and nature the more I find this to be true.

"Our society is large and complex today, and the type of cities we have to plan is not something you can arrive at with beautiful pictures that have nothing to do with the ultimate functions of the city. Pisa was a marvellously designed geometric fortress, but the society was small. An urban system now can be approached only by the most accurate analysis of tremendous amounts of information by precise instruments.

"I do not think that there is any hope for architecture as practiced in the large offices. There is too little control of anything.

"We are making a mess of an exciting and beautifully rich future by being schizophrenic."

Soriano has a small practice that involves him personally in every decision. His first influence was Neutra. It is often said that Soriano's work has been influenced by Mies but, although he

Shulman House, Los Angeles, California.

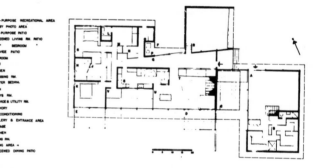

admires Mies's work very much, he did not become aware of it until after he had designed his first steel houses. His similarity to Mies is in his striving to clarify and simplify details. Actually, the direction of his slender, prefabricated industrial components is quite unlike and independent of Mies's more visually durable, monumental architecture. In turn, Soriano's "clean" steel houses have themselves been a source of influence.

One of the first obstacles Soriano had to overcome was the usual prejudice toward unfamiliar building techniques. In his steel structures, bids were so high that he was forced to seek bids from subcontractors and undertake the construction himself; however, this enabled him to maintain the complete control over workmanship which he considers essential. For the Hallawell Seed Building, built in San Francisco in 1939, he was able to undercut the lowest bid by a third. He prefabricated the building in Pasadena and shipped it to San Francisco in large sections of 12-foot by 12-foot modules of steel members. "It was an illuminating and enriching experience to learn the problems of prefabrication and the problems that exist in every trade. I constantly think of progress in the use of materials and try to avoid the wastage that exists in conservative ways of building."

Soriano tries always to simplify his structures, and to develop simple, flush details: "After I have found the best solution for a detail I don't vary it. I always thought things should be mass-produced and I have been constantly gearing myself to industrialization. That means you must have a methodology in structure, simplification, and the fewest parts possible." The Curtis House in Bel-Air, California, in 1949, rapidly assembled from prefabricated industrial components, and based on a 10-foot by 20-foot bay module, demonstrates this. Internal divisions are created by storage walls that were rolled into the house on dollies after the floor and ceiling had been finished. When these cabinets are in place the rooms are delineated, thereby using the wall functionally, rather than parasitically: "It is a logic which can integrate the whole body of the house." The speed of erection and close tolerances could hardly have been achieved with anything but steel. It demonstrated that two factors, once considered incompatible, were not: standardization and flexibility. Soriano believes that future houses will have modular frames with standard parts and walls that can be rearranged as simply as furniture. "If you are looking for a solution to twentieth-century housing, the general and individual must be identical."

Soriano has designed many houses deriving essentially from these ideas, notably the Shulman House, Los Angeles, in 1950, and the Leaver House at Mill Valley, California, in 1958. His is the continuing emphasis on a *reasonable* discipline, houses rapidly assembled for an economical price, houses devoid of whims. An objective approach; performing houses, says Soriano, where natural human requirements can best flourish unencumbered by the acquired nostalgic misconception of living.

The same modular plan and prefabrication method have been employed in the Adolph's Office Building in Burbank, California, in 1958. Occupying one city block, the steel and aluminum structure is made of 20-foot by 40-foot modules, all assembled with prefabricated elements to precise specifications, and shipped from different parts of the country.

The use of aluminum was an easy transition for Soriano after his experience with steel structures. "It is a simple material where

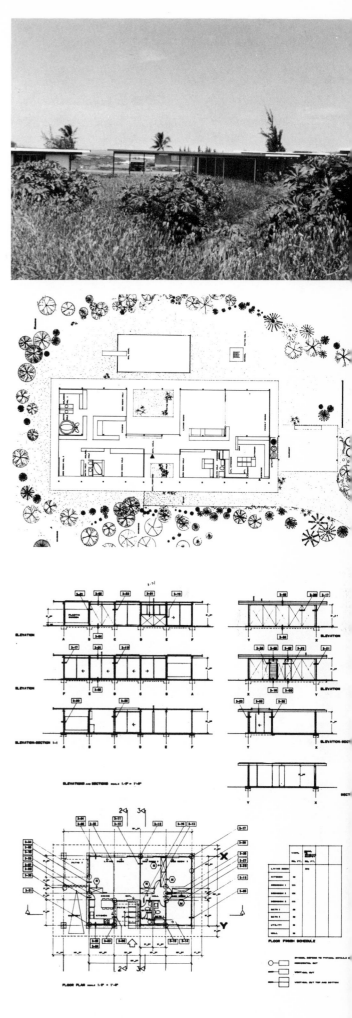

Low-cost housing for Hawaii.

you can do lots with a very little. You can have finished colors without painting, it is easy to manufacture, and you can drill it more easily than steel; at the same time it is easier to ship because it is lighter in weight—and I am interested in a world market." This interest was given impetus by Soriano's commission to build low-cost housing in Hawaii, with a pilot project of twenty-one houses. "The houses are prefabricated and finished here, and then shipped to Hawaii. This will be an interesting advancement; not only can you do the houses locally, but you can also have them shipped elsewhere to be assembled with unskilled labor. All they have to do is bolt them together. The details are so meticulously done that nothing is left to the whims of craftsmen to fill the gaps or make corrections with a molding. Everything is on an assembly line. I find no necessity for tolerances; if it does not fit properly there is something wrong and you notice it immediately."

Soriano has thoroughly analyzed the component parts to ensure the greatest possible economy. Using identical elements and modules, he has achieved a striking number of variations—from a two-bedroom house of 550 square feet to a six-bedroom house of 1,300 square feet. Few architects can afford to engage in the extensive study and analysis of small houses to the degree that Soriano has. With high quality, and a low cost of ten dollars per square foot, he is making a valuable contribution to low-cost housing.

Soriano has recently organized Soria Structures, Incorporated, a corporation for a world market that will produce aluminum (and other) structures for houses and even larger buildings, such as hospitals—all designed for a prefabricated assembly method. He has also just started design studies for an all aluminum structure, 1,000 feet high, for San Francisco. "I think it will be the first all aluminum structure of this height in the world," he says. He has used computors before to program construction and analyze structure. Now he is using one in the actual design of this structure.

Although Soriano will dismiss art unequivocally, he proceeds to demonstrate a quality in his architecture that comes close to being art itself—an analogy he would accept only if "art" were defined as a decision resulting from scientific investigation. Of his own investigations he modestly adds: "What I am doing now I still consider a horse-and-buggy type of exploration belonging to another century. Unfortunately we have to make small inroads to break the awful things happening today that are centuries behind our time. This may be a step toward the real thing which will only come through studies with computors, new technology, methods, and materials. We have to start with this to pursue the other—which is still unobtainable commercially."

Sanders House, Palo Alto, California, 1955.

THE LOS ANGELES REGION

San Francisco is a mature city, its basic configurations propitiously established long before the complex forces of our time could radically affect its form. Los Angeles, however, is a burgeoning infant by comparison, clearly reflecting the extensive ramifications these forces can produce, where allowed fairly free rein. A city mirrors the generating forces that continually affect its structure and mold its imagery. To compare Los Angeles with San Francisco, or certain European cities, in terms of environmental aesthetics, is a purely academic exercise—about as meaningful as comparing the horse and buggy to the automobile.

Los Angeles is fascinating because it demonstrates that only by understanding and anticipating the forces that shape the city can they be controlled and purposefully directed. Its new scale is dramatic, while also catastrophic. The comparative ease and speed of circulation by automobile, and relaxed living in close contact with nature, are good. They have been achieved however at the expense of a land-consuming, two-dimensional sprawl that makes its downtown center anachronistic—a fact clearly seen in its present state of despair—and any chance of initiating an efficient public transportation system unrealistic. So, the sprawl widens. With little apparent logic in centripetal forces, or at least the ability to generate any, the city is continually pressured outwards by centrifugal forces. One force dominates, that of rapid vehicular movement, and has created such an imbalance and lack of unity that Los Angeles is fighting both for and against itself.

It is hardly surprising that the best architecture in Los Angeles should be the individual residence—whose manageable scale and design detail make it an excellent vehicle in which to mature architectural skills. In the Los Angeles region Gill and Schindler have been followed by Neutra, and a younger generation that has benefited from the patronage of the Case Study Houses program.

In the 1940's, the experience gained from using new materials and techniques in the war effort was ready for creative application to the realization of a contemporary living environment. John Entenza, then the editor of *Arts and Architecture,* used the magazine as a sponsoring agent for a series of Case Study Houses, encouraging the propagation of good design and, by example, the education of public taste.

The program helped pioneer the steel frame house where dignified living conditions derived from architectural simplicity—simplicity implying a recognition of essentials, and a chaste, candid directness of statement. Since the houses are generally built-up from the simple, attentive joining of steel elements, with glass or solid infilling panels, they inevitably are classified as being in the Miesian manner. But Mies very precisely and authoritatively achieves a formal, highly-disciplined balance in plan organization and fenestration, whereas the Case Study Houses tend toward a more informal concept and slender, skeletal appearance, more intimately related to the landscape of adjacent living areas. Soriano's buildings are an excellent example.

One of the earliest, most publicized houses of the program is Charles Eames's own house. Although it was a unique solution, not intended as a prototype, it was in the spirit of the program since it was assembled from standard, factory-produced elements. The house showed that generally available, prefabricated component parts need not result in a stultifying monotony if they are imaginatively employed.

Eames House, Los Angeles, California.

RICHARD J. NEUTRA

Consistency, or an architectural discipline, will come from knowing man as a biological individual and concentrating on his basic physiology and organic responses, believes Richard Neutra. Not wishing to indulge in mechanistic metaphors, and thus oversimplify the issues of life, he believes that if one could design something based essentially on a response to human considerations, it would be almost timeless. "While unconscious of any artistic rules or following any abstract principles, I very early enjoyed falling thoroughly in love with the few prospective clients who showed faint signs of trusting me. My attention became so fixed on human relationship to surrounding circumstance and a physiological penetration of the client, that I began to perform, quite unconsciously perhaps, with an emphasis not on the fashionable, well-advertised installations, less on conspicuous shapes and materials, but rather on much more minutely sensitive values and responses which in subtle combination might go on and last over the amortization period or even a lifetime."

Born in Vienna, in 1892, "R. J. Neutra has preserved in practice the artistic integrity which emanated from the schemes of the early twenties," Sigfried Giedion has written. "The power to leave nature undisturbed and simultaneously to draw her into a specific emotional situation reveals the artist, no less than the power to transfuse a ferro-concrete skeleton with psychic value. In this transcendence from architectonic vision to a natural form of life R. J. Neutra's high rank can never be denied . . ."

Richard Neutra was in close contact with many of the leading figures in modern architecture. He admired Otto Wagner, and wrote a preface to a biography of him. Adolf Loos was a friend of his youth, and as a student Neutra worked for him. A mutual admiration for Wright's work drew Schindler and Neutra together at the Technische Hochschule in Vienna. In 1921 he met Eric Mendelsohn and, through one of their collaborations, they won first prize in the competition to design the business center for Haifa. This was not built, but Neutra used the award to come to America in the same year.

From New York he went to Chicago where he befriended Sullivan. At the latter's funeral, in 1924, Neutra met Wright, who invited him to Taliesin for several months. He went to Los Angeles in 1925, where he suggested to Schindler that they practice together. They collaborated on a competition design for the Palace of the League of Nations overlooking Lake Geneva, which was one of three entries selected for a travelling exhibition.

Kaufmann House, "Desert House," near Palm Springs, California.

While there is an obvious affinity in his and Schindler's work, one-and-a-half years working with Mendelsohn had little apparent influence on Neutra. Mendelsohn was moving from plastic flowing shapes into even more expressionistic curved forms, and Neutra clearly preferred Wright's open planning, spatial interpenetration, and more subtle manner of uniting building and site. But, although these concepts are basic to his work, Neutra's buildings are lighter and airier, employing in many cases a slender post and beam system of construction. The sensitivity and skill with which he has reconciled his architecture with the immediate site and the surrounding landscape approach those of Wright himself.

Lovell House, "Health House," Los Angeles, California.

"In former periods—let us say in the Middle Ages or in antiquity —there were few or no surprising moves in design. People went on with a well-established tradition and subtly improved on it piecemeal, intensifying what the consumer already knew and had responded to. Design in former ages was not a challenge, it seemed extremely natural; it has become a challenge for our time. Why is new design necessary for us? Well, the whole concept of 'new' is controversial. In a man, what is venerable or revered, is age. In an object, it is the contrary. The revered now, at least to many of us, seems mostly the new. This is characteristic of our time and its quick-turnover merchandising attitude.

"If I ask the question, 'Why do we have to have a new design?' there is a general ready-made answer today. 'Don't you know that there has been terrific technological progress?' We have so many new materials surrounding us, and having all these materials on hand is a very precarious situation, to say the least. It is even more precarious to have your thinking filled with these new materials, to the exclusion of everything else. I was once told that to have a girl in mind is more dangerous to man than having a girl on one's lap. This may be our situation in general.

"Newness in the sense of the practical man, of the engineer, of the man who is designing freeways and automobiles, has of course nothing to do with eternity; it has to do with amortization periods, with operational periods where the maintenance bills are not getting too high. Yet, the Egyptians, and even Plato himself, who thought of eternal ideas, were not wrong. It is not *all* that is corroding on the rubbish heap. We know better. It isn't really quite so futile, what man brings forth. Yet this contempt for eternity-aspirations is one of our great troubles in design. The great oversight is not to recognize the human being and other enduring organic fundamentals.

Project for "Rush City Reformed."

"Where we have employed our technological progress, it has usually been steered towards a techno-economically motivated standardization, and a frustrating monotony. Architects must have a heart for individuality. If they produce an unidentifiable sameness, they smother the individual and his creativity in a cage of monotony. As well as within chaos, the individual can become amnesic within endless 'order' and unmitigated standardized geometry up to the horizon. The architect preserves or even instills into the landscape, environmental characteristics; he furnishes self-identity by mnemonic means to his client, and makes his life within his own potential creative. When creative, an individual well-housed in all his activities becomes a blessing to mankind. His life's a curse when withered in amnesic sameness.

"Anti-individual sameness comes at a time when biological in-

Von Sternberg House, Northridge, California.

Amity Village project, Compton, California.

dividuality is more researched than ever before. In the last decade, thousands of papers in physiological and biological journals have been published all around the globe, with very pertinent observations. Today we have such an abundance of information on man that even the title of a book, *Man the Unknown*, is exaggerated.

"There is another factor facing the architect today. It is a philosophy born in our country, very much revered, and very expressive of our everyday thinking: pragmatism. Don't believe that I want to smear James or the Instrumentalists, or Dewey. But the fact is that many centuries of philosophical thinking have passed by without any such idea ever quite coming up. That a thing is true because it works, because it operates, and that a thing is beautiful because it functions, is a new thought. This may have been, until recently, one of the principles of our American thinking and of our design.

"Sullivan, who was really something of an idol to me, and still is, said that 'Form follows function,' and pronounced this the new principle of design. The expression that form follows function explains good form, but is a very unreliable guide. If form and function are related in this way, it puts them into two categories: Form being static and function being operational. And the shape is the consequence of the operation. Well, this division is one of the dualisms under which we are suffering. A bird's mating colors and dance do not follow but precede function! Form is not static at all, but instrumental, something which makes us function, makes us work. It has impact on all the sensorial equipment that we have. We are either activated by it or we are not; and this is what a designer has to know. That a function is mechanical is an idea of the nineteenth century. The truth is that the most interesting part of all functioning and operations is like 'our own human functioning and operation' and *form is markedly eliciting this*. The worship of new materials, of extraneous materials, contempt for eternity-aspirations, technological monotony, and this whole pragmatism of facts and 'money talks,' indicate a mid-nineteenth-century type of materialism that the twentieth century is, philosophically speaking, somewhat tired of.

"While I have experimented more than many architects with all kinds of material, I feel increasingly that human material is the most interesting of all. Take, for instance, the sensorial equipment of man. Man once was a creature of five senses; today we know he has a multitude of sense receptors of many modalities. And every year new sense receptors and new senses are being discovered. Well, as a designer, you are continuously tickling all these senses. People, too, have their inborn biological individuality comprising thousands of known parameters. There is a certain range of 'normalcy' but it is a tremendous range. I discuss and try to explore clinically just exactly these things, and they are the basis of my diagnosis and design.

"Among all these senses, which have been and are being discovered, not one is 'the sense of beauty.' 'Sense of beauty' is a figure of speech, which comes perhaps from the eighteenth century. It does not mean anything in our current terminology. On the other hand, there is no separation of utility and beauty. You cannot determine where a tree stops being beautiful and starts becoming utilitarian. To get over this dualism would be a great step for the designer pleading for the acceptance of design and shape as a prominent good for 'soul-body' per se. As long as it is an accepted axiom that there is utility on one side and beauty on the other, of course

Nesbitt House, Los Angeles, California.

Tremaine House, Montecito, California.

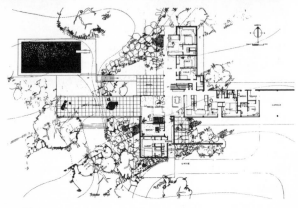

'utility will be first'—and if there is some consideration left, it may be beauty next. The designer has a very tiny chance, as if he were an impractical longhaired beautician.

"We are so full of adoration for our wonderful progress, which is really not progress but a huge, multiple cluster of piecemeal progressions, all in collision with each other. Under these circumstances there is one chance for us to get by; we must awaken the designing profession, the foundations and the universities, the government agencies and legislators, the political party leaders and the entire votership-consumership, to the thought that we shall survive only by a wholesome comprehensive harmonization of design of our rampant setting, so that it is, above all, humanly tolerable."

Neutra's house for Dr. P. M. Lovell, built in 1928, brought him international recognition. He called it the "Health House" because, beyond having differentiated outdoor play and recreation areas—a swimming and a wading pool, a tennis court, a gymnasium area and an outdoor stage for amateur theatricals—the structure is brought into a close relationship with the health factors of nature. Located on a landscaped, steeply-terraced hill, it has views of the Pacific Ocean, the mountains of Santa Monica, and at night the city of Los Angeles illuminated in the foreground.

The construction of the house itself, unfamiliar to contractors, had to be personally organized and supervised by Neutra. It began with a prefabricated light steel frame that was erected in forty hours. The "floating" floor planes, constructed of expanded metal reinforced and covered by concrete applied from a compressed air gun, were suspended by slender steel cables from the roof frame; they express the changes of floor level strongly, following the contours of the site. The swimming pool, at the lowest level, was also suspended within the steel frame, from U-shaped reinforced concrete cradles. The Health House was a landmark in modern architecture in that it showed the potential of industry to go way beyond mere utilitarian considerations.

During the 1920's Neutra explored the possibilities of a planned metropolis for a population of one million, which he called "Rush City Reformed." The linear layout was conceived so that each method of transport would be stratified and segregated: the ground level was devoted totally to vehicles; pedestrian areas, relating to shops and other facilities, were above and reached by elevators at street intersections. The plan incorporated a variety of housing from eleven-story apartment buildings to single-story houses. If it seems rather rigid in its separations and idealistic in concept today, it did explore a system within which urban problems could be resolved—a concern, fortunately, that is again being generally considered.

It employed several principles that were to reappear in Neutra's work. For example, the 1939 Amity Village project for Compton had its houses with front lawns landscaped as common space, facing onto a green parkway that was separated from automobiles. The outdoor area surrounding each house was broken down more intimately into a play and social court, separated by the bedroom wing yet linked beneath a pergola, and a service and entry court, defined by the landscaping in the parkway. Even at this modest scale we find the seeds of the four garden spaces later to be beautifully realized in the grander Kaufmann and

Tremaine houses.

In two other houses, the Von Sternberg in 1936 and the Nesbitt in 1942, Neutra employed a different palette of materials: the first house had a skin of aluminum-coated steel; the second, built during the war years when material was very restricted for private buildings, was of local redwood and brick. The entrance hall in the Nesbitt house has a pond and planting, interpenetrating the front garden and hall, all visually uninterrupted by a plane of glass. This eliminates an "entrance door" as such, while privacy within the house is maintained by the plan arrangement itself. A floor-to-ceiling flush mirror increases and emphasizes the illusion of space—a favorite device of Neutra's, which he employs with the greatest skill.

From Neutra's many outstanding residences, two, in his adopted California, select themselves for discussion: the Desert House designed in 1946 for Edgar Kaufmann (Wright had shortly before designed the "Fallingwater" residence for him), set in the hot arid desert surrounding Palm Springs; and two years later, the Tremaine House in the sweeping, tree-shaded, rock-strewn meadowland of Montecito. Both have pinwheel plans with the living-dining area at the hub; wings of one-room depth, designed to obtain natural light with views on at least two exposures, extend outwards and open to terraces and patios that in turn merge into the rich garden landscape. They respond quite lyrically to their natural surroundings, without ever compromising their architectonic integrity. The natural scene is so married to the interior space that the barrier between occupant and landscape is illusory. The roof "hovers" above a polished terrazzo plateau, and interior space is barely defined and never contained by the glass screens that slide open at the touch of a button. The large areas of fixed glass, mitred unobtrusively at the right-angled junction, give the occupant a great sense of intimacy with the landscape. This effect is further emphasized by the juxtaposition of glass areas to solid, yet almost ephemeral planes that are attentively detailed and, at night, skillfully illuminated. Relationships, while environmentally casual are architecturally intentional; privacy is never sacrificed, but inherent.

Neutra believes that the architect should strive for a response to space and time that may be only fleeting, yet in its intensity becomes truly memorable. Both houses have such: a chance reflection in the pool, or glass in shadow; the roof "hovering" above the sunset, or a rock silhouetted in the sunrise; the stillness of the desert, the rustle of leaves; the first breath of morning air as glass walls slide apart. Some buildings can capture this poetry in nature and make it part of themselves, they endure in our memory. Executed with restrained taste and casual elegance Neutra's houses respond to what contemporary living patterns could be but so seldom are.

Although Neutra's name is primarily associated with fine residences—certainly he seems to be at his very best here—he is not simply a designer of beautiful Californian houses for wealthy clients. To all his work he brings the same concern for human response, climate and site. This can be seen in his recently completed Mariner's Medical Arts Building, where it is hard to imagine a more agreeable place to endure the rigors of losing a tooth.

From 1949 to 1962, completing a wide range of projects, Neutra was in partnership with Robert Alexander. The "Ring Plan

Mariner's Medical Arts Building, Newport Beach, California.

Ring Plan School, Lemore, California.

School" built finally in 1962 for Lemore, California, aptly named the Richard J. Neutra School, was originally designed in 1925, with a model of it exhibited at the Museum of Modern Art's exhibition of modern architecture in 1932. Neutra has always been cognizant of, and sensitive to, the stresses in modern life; in *Survival Through Design* he wrote, "The man-made setting reacts through an infinite number of stimuli upon the nervous system of every member of the community." In the Ring Plan School an elliptical center court is an oasis of retreat; each individual classroom has its own library, teaching materials and washroom, creating a small community feeling for the young, insecure child. Flexible seating, even use of the floor, also helps to eliminate the tensions between teacher and pupil that can come from a more formal arrangement. Around the perimeter, the classrooms open to patios, separated by planting, thus allowing the educational activity to extend into the outdoors.

In the Los Angeles County Hall of Records building, a system of louvers—each 125 feet high, 56 inches wide and weighing 3,000 pounds—adjusts automatically, opening and closing like the petals of a flower as it responds to the "signals" from the light-sensitive cells on the roof that follow the sun's rotation. When clouds obscure the sun the louvers open fully so that all available light can reach the offices. An instrument records wind velocities and automatically closes the louvers when high winds threaten damage.

In larger projects Neutra tries to apply ideas that he has first explored and developed in his residential architecture. He seems to be searching for an intimate scale consonant with his approach, which he calls "biological-realism," which is not always easy to reconcile with the demands of larger spaces and a more involved structural system.

His ideas have spread, as witness the world-wide Richard J. Neutra Institutes, which were "founded by friends and patrons of endeavors of half a century." And in California his own concern for the universal design determinants of man and environment, and the zest with which he has employed new techniques and procedures, have had a tremendous influence on the younger generation of architects.

With a flowing shock of white hair Neutra resembles a younger Albert Einstein. Both came to the "New World," found fellowship, and responded by enriching the American scene.

Corona Avenue School, Bell, California.

Los Angeles County Hall of Records, Los Angeles, California.

Goodman House, San Bernardino, California, 1952.

Rosen House, Los Angeles, California.

CRAIG ELLWOOD

When James Stirling, a most talented English architect, and Craig Ellwood were Visiting Critics at Yale in 1959, their approach to architecture soon identified them to the students as the "thick man" and the "thin man," respectively. Stirling's buildings, with their robust visual strength, and use of materials "as found," convey the urgency and full significance of their concept, with a minimum of interference; in sharp contrast are Ellwood's slender, almost frail structures that are cleverly detailed and beautifully executed and finished. Ellwood, at least, can smile when accusations of monumentality are aired. If some of his structures seem vulnerable to anything stronger than a gentle breeze, it is because we are still unaccustomed to seeing the great strength and economic expression of steel. At a time when many architects would wish to see regional traditions exercise greater influence on modern architecture, Ellwood envisions developing the means of our highly-industrialized country into a truly "industrial, American vernacular"; modular, prefabricated elements derived from new building techniques and materials, refined and unified to develop the discipline of a new, *real* machine aesthetic. This was the direction that Neutra and Soriano were pursuing locally, and it is natural that Ellwood should have been influenced by their logic.

Craig Ellwood was born in 1922, in Clarendon, Texas. In 1946, after four years in the United States Air Force, he went to work for a construction firm, one which contracted the best jobs in the Los Angeles area. This introduced him to the work of Saarinen, Eames, Wurster, Harris and particularly that of Neutra and Soriano. In three instances clients approached the builder directly for a house, and Ellwood was asked to design it. As a result, in 1948 he started his own design practice, and the following year he began night classes in structural engineering at the University of California in Los Angeles. A clearly expressed structure, which he has continually refined towards an increasing standard of excellence, has remained the discipline of Ellwood's architecture.

In 1949, the Hale House in Beverly Hills, California, immediately showed Ellwood's approach to architecture. Slender 4-inch "H" columns were rigidly connected to 4- by 10-inch wood beams (although a complete steel frame was considered, economy necessitated the partial use of wood). Non-structural, infilling panels of glass, and stud walls that stopped clear of the roof deck at the under side of ceiling beams, created a feeling of lightness and openness in a relatively small volume. The structure was exposed throughout the house, and like the steel entry-stair, was painted rust-primer red.

Ellwood's Courtyard Apartments, Hollywood, California, designed in 1952, were awarded first prize in the Collective Dwelling Category in the 1953-1954 International Exhibition of Architecture, at São Paulo, Brazil, by a jury that included Le Corbusier, Gropius, Aalto, and Sert. Four identical dwelling-units, opening to small entrance garden courts, are constructed of three parallel masonry walls, and rigid steel frames with exposed trusses at the open ends.

In 1955 Ellwood designed his third Case Study House (No. 18) for *Arts and Architecture* magazine. The house is basically a 32 foot by 72 foot rectangle with a prefabricated steel structural system. The 16-foot units were placed on 8-foot centers, and erected in 32 man-hours. The columns are 2-inch-square tubes, and the beams, 2-inch by $5^1/_2$-inch tubes. The same connection detail serves all exterior wall junctions—glass, panels, sash and sliding door units—with the columns. Blue, heat-absorbing wireglass is used to filter the sun over the glazed walls, and at night these glazed canopies are floodlit directly from above, giving a soft blue illumination.

Hale House, Beverly Hills, California.

The Smith House in West Los Angeles and the Hunt House in Malibu, California, both designed in 1955, are each approached from the street by an entrance ramp that is formally flanked by garages. In the Smith House, by designing living areas to be at street level, Ellwood was able to create a most dramatic vantage point for viewing the coastal city lights and ocean to the south. The house is a "T", whose horizontal faces the street, screening the vertical which contains the living and dining areas. Beneath this, within the space frame, will be added a master bedroom suite in the future. The summer house for Elizabeth A. and Victor M. Hunt is an "H"-shaped plan: the living, dining and kitchen areas, opening to an ocean deck facing the Pacific, are in one leg, and two bedrooms, separated by the entrance lobby, are in the other. The legs are linked by the extension of the entry lobby, providing access to the two bathrooms, with the fireplace as a terminal feature. Private decks on either side of this link provide sheltered outdoor spaces when onshore winds make use of the ocean deck impractical.

Courtyard Apartments, Hollywood, California.

The designs for the South Bay Bank, Manhattan Beach, California, in 1958, and the Carson/Roberts office building, Los Angeles, a year later, again show Ellwood's attention to details, quality of materials, and sun control for glass areas. In the office building the steel had to be encased in concrete for fireproofing; the clear articulation and direct expression of structure however still dominate the design.

Ellwood's largest project to date, an eleven-story office building for Beverly Hills, California, was designed in 1962, but never constructed because of complications in acquiring the site. To

Case Study House Number 18, Beverly Hills, California.

Smith House, Los Angeles, California.

comply with the building code, Ellwood had to provide parking space for three hundred and seven automobiles. He did this on the second, third and fourth levels, with a metal screen shielding automobiles from view while it also allowed required ventilation. Parking was also accommodated on half of the grade level, the other half being retained for commercial rental area and one basement level. Ellwood articulated the separation between office and parking areas by recessing the glass wall at the fifth level, where there is a roof garden, and at the ground level where glass is recessed behind the line of structure.

"The chapel at Ronchamp is a profound statement of rebellion against machine building. I do not believe that Le Corbusier necessarily meant this to be a prototype for a new architecture. I do believe, however, that the effect may have been well calculated. Ronchamp was Le Corbusier's reaffirmation of talent and genius —his testimony for creative architecture, beauty, romanticism and humanism. It was his reaction to the manufacturer-designed, look-alike, anonymous architecture of 'curtainwallism.' The building is sculpture—and as such it possibly succeeds. But it does not truly succeed as architecture. When Kahn said that while a painter can paint square wheels on a cannon to express the futility of war, and a sculptor can carve the same square wheels, but an architect must use round wheels, he was emphasizing the limits of architecture. True, great architecture is art, and the art in architecture is an immeasurable quality. But great architecture is primarily technique, and therefore a building must clearly reflect the order, the discipline, the measurable aspects of its being. Architecture must certainly be more than an expression of an idea. And the real art in architecture is not arbitrary style or ethereal symbolism, but the extent to which a building can transcend the measurable to the immeasurable; the extent to which a building can evoke pleasure and profound emotion; the extent to which a building can spiritually uplift and inspire man while simultaneously reflecting the logic of the technique which alone can convey

Hunt House, Malibu, California.

its validity to exist.

"The curtain wall became a crutch for the lazy architect. With this concept, however, we experienced the genesis of a true American expression: this was machined architecture; this was twentieth century American architecture. Mies's Seagram Building, for example, and a number of other excellent curtain-wall structures designed by Saarinen, Yamasaki, S.O.M., and Pei. We also have Kahn's powerful medical research building at the University of Pennsylvania which, excluding its masonry towers, is another kind of curtainwallism, another kind of creative, machined architecture.

"Structure is the only clear principle. Form is valid only when it is shaped by structure and possibly characterized by function, region, culture and climate. Structure does not necessarily mean the steel or concrete cage. The three basic elements of construction are solid bodies, slender members and stressed surfaces. The architect has a choice which can lead to vastly different forms, each with structural integrity and clarity. But today we see skeleton and stressed surface construction that appear to be solid construction. We see hyberbolic paraboloid umbrellas enclosed at outer edges with what could be bearing walls. We see fake vaults and phony, folded plates. We see decorative columns and simulated structure that carry no loads. An obsession for curvilinear form has led to impure structure, forced to withstand stresses in the least direct way—structure forced to fit any arbitrary form the architect can dream up. I greatly admire the poetic structuralism of Nervi, Torroja and Candela, but these men have worked within mathematical and geometrical disciplines, within the structural order of continuity and plasticity. And each has worked within a culture and economy compatible with his plastic concepts.

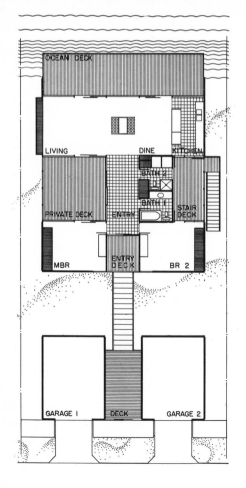

"*Discipline* is the key word. There must be something beyond arbitrary decision, some underlying force that motivates the forms of architecture. The moment that form becomes arbitrary, novel or stylish, it becomes something other than true architecture. Form must express logic, meaning and rationality, yet it cannot exist by itself; structure through technology is the only means to valid form. Materials and methods will certainly change but the rules must be timeless. As architects, one of our tasks is to apply the new machine technologies with sensitivity. Only through structure can we create new architecture. In nature, form and structure are one, and this should also be true in architecture. Nature is simple, but unfortunately it does not simplify. It is up to us to search for this simplicity, to express logic and clarity, and to understand structure. Form is structure, no matter what other names are given to it, and therefore structure is architecture.

"In architecture there has always been a need for integrated decoration, I do not mean applied ornamentation. Structure itself is decoration—the rhythmic expression of frame, arch or shell. Form is decoration—the rhythmic interplay of mass, volume and line. Material is decoration—the rhythmic emphasis of texture and color. Depth is decoration—the rhythmic movement of light and shadow. I say rhythmic because *rhythm* is fundamental in all design, whether natural or man-made.

"Confusion would be an understatement for the current status of architecture. There exists chaotic and critical disorder, a jumbled, turbulent, irrational mess. Impatience is part of our problem, as too many of us are caught in the race to be first in creating a new architecture. There seems to exist among our leading architects a mass denial for continuity. Each new project is treated as a separate essay in abstract design, without any affiliation to what the past has taught us, without any real concern for the present, without any relationship to the work of other architects. Le Corbusier titled a recent book, *Creation Is a Patient Search*. He believed strongly that the past exists first and foremost to justify and illuminate the present, that there exists a duty to accept what has gone before. Franz Kafka wrote that 'all human error is impatience, a premature renunciation of method, a delusive pinning down of delusion.'

"Also at fault is our moral and cultural climate. This is the era of the doctrine that fosters mass acceptance as the criterion of our culture. We are constantly plagued by the stupefying forces of mediocrity which result from our society's system of salesmanship. Too many of us are concerned with the extrinsic effect rather than the intrinsic solution. The desperate search for individuality is so intense that exhibitionism through fakery of form has become the rule rather than the exception. Form must have logic and conviction. Boris Pasternak beautifully stated his own philosophy of the quest for new means of expression: The most striking discoveries are made when an artist is so full of his subject that it gives him no time to think about it . . . and in his haste he proclaims his new word in the old language, without bothering his head as to whether it is new or old.' Pasternak elaborated on this by stating that Chopin, in the old language of Mozart and Field, said so much that was new in music that it seemed to be its second beginning.

"What do we seek? What are our goals? If we are truthful about it, self-aggrandizement is too often the prime aim, and unfortunately, a natural ambition. Creativity cannot evolve without ego,

South Bay Bank, Manhattan Beach, California.

but also it cannot evolve without order. Order is basic, there can be no freedom without it. Whether we like it or not, in our economy this order is bound to the machine and governed by it. Mechanization is here and we have helped to promulgate it. The craftsman is disappearing and we have helped to stifle him. Our economy dictates that machine products and machine techniques be the essence of our buildings. We cannot retrogress to handicraft methods or to forms that repudiate, or are incompatible with, methods of machine building. In another time we were moved by the Barcelona Pavilion, the early houses on the Mid-Western prairie and the villa at Poissy. Each was intrinsic crystal clarity, and expressed precisely and poetically a qualification of space, form and structure in direct relation to time and purpose. "Mies said: 'We cannot invent a new architecture every Monday morning,' and he is right. The development of great architecture is a carefully measured process, the slow and deliberate maturing and refinement of an order, the patient and unending search for moral beauty. Architecture is not a game of arbitrary novelty. Our prime objective then should be beauty through order. If we can create spaces and an environment which will help to inspire the passions of man and uplift his emotions; if we base our architecture upon an order that gives it the validity to exist in our time; if we search hard for truth and clarity; then the recognition, the reason to exist that we all seek, will follow soon enough. With these considerations it seems possible for us to produce an architecture that needs no rationalization: an architecture that applies the machine and its techniques with sensitivity, transcending the prosaic limitations the machine has seemingly begun to impose, expressing both beauty and logic. This will not come about through esoteric applications of the Indian mud pueblo nor white walls of hand-tooled, simulated arabesque stone tracery, nor in hand-formed concrete and hand-carved granite columns. It is time we stopped to reexamine our recent motivations, and evaluate the potential of the machine. In this we may find the way to valid new forms and to a properly qualified, truly meaningful architecture."

In his houses of the 1960's, Ellwood has shown an increasing concern for rhythm and symmetry—rigid aesthetic principles in the organization of space. This movement toward a vernacular much more classic and homogeneous in feeling, much closer to Mies, has naturally eliminated some of the "assembled" or "constructivist" feeling of his earlier work.

The Daphne House, Hillsborough, California, in 1961, is a symmetrical arrangement of a sleeping wing and a general living wing that are related by an entrance space behind which is a screened kitchen area. The wings flank a large swimming pool which is the major feature in the design. White steel columns, to which roof and floor fascia channels are welded, support the house, creating a pleasant rhythm; and by having the white marble walls and gray tinted glass recessed 7 inches behind them, the columns avoid awkward detailing problems while adding emphasis to the structural frame. The illusion of a pavilion hovering above the ground is created by recessing the foundation wall of the floor slab 3 feet to allow the sill fascia to be clear of the ground. The hovering effect is increased by encircling the house with black Mexican pebbles to contrast with the precision of the white sill, and other devices such as raising the entrance platform above a reflecting pool. The elevation of living areas also had the practical advantage of raising the house above the pool deck, keep-

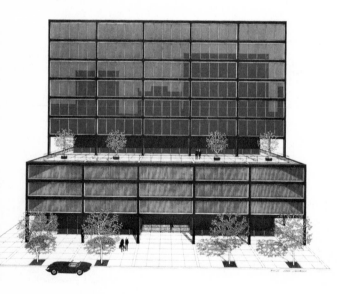

Project for an Office Building, Beverly Hills, California.

ing poolside furniture unobtrusively below the line of vision. The Rosen House, completed in 1963, is on a small plateau on the southern slope of the shrub-covered Mandeville Gorge in Los Angeles. Approaching the house up a curving road, one glimpses white lines and gray planes of brickwork turning against this tangled background, eventually revealed as a beautifully precise box "hovering" above an immaculately cultivated plateau. This is probably Ellwood's most complete statement of a steel house to date. The precision and attention to every detail—if God is in the details, as Mies says—is evidence of Ellwood's great discipline and mastery of the problems of this building type, in this vernacular. Whereas Mies's Farnsworth House and Johnson's own "glass house" were essentially for one person, Ellwood has attained clarity in the Rosen House while resolving the greater complexities of a family unit.

The symmetrical plan is a study in formal geometry: nine squares, each comprising eight 3-foot 4-inch modules, with the center square left open as an atrium. Yet, within the house, this rigid arrangement seems to be neither autocratic nor to compromise utilitarian needs. Not surprisingly, this machined object has an aged olive tree as the focus of the central void. The ambiguous (to a purist) structural condition of the floor slab in the Daphne House was to have been avoided here, by elevating the building 3 feet and carrying the water-worn black pebble "podium," which surrounds the structure, beneath it and right through into the atrium. The local building code required a firewall, which is recessed similar to that of the Daphne House, that interrupts this. The garage and swimming pool are on a paved "island", related to the house by steps but subordinate to its mass at the lower level.

Daphne House, Hillsborough, California.

The Chamorro House in the San Fernando Valley north of Los Angeles, designed while the Rosen House was under construction, is an even more dramatic statement of structure as architecture. Two retaining walls define a paved terrace, bridged by two steel trusses where the sleeping areas are contained. The living areas are underneath, opening to the terrace and a swimming pool.

Ellwood has carried this idea even further in his design for a weekend house near Los Angeles. Here the two trusses will span a gorge in what must be the ultimate dramatization of living within a steel structure.

The coherence and unity of a building depend on its detail and the extent to which it is integrated with and expressive of the basic architectural intent. Ellwood, a perfectionist like Mies, has tried to design his buildings as entities with the details inseparable from their motivating concept. References to his obsession for articulating elements and his fastidious attention to detail are obviously intended as criticism by those who see a preoccupation with such refinements as a devitalizing factor to architecture. But Ellwood's architecture is based on this paring down to essentials; the process of elimination and subtraction where structural and functional elements are so visible that they become the very essence and totality of his architecture. The roots of such criticism penetrate deeper, possibly stemming from a new emphasis on considerations that have been somewhat neglected in the struggle to employ the machine wisely. And, in moving closer to the Miesian idiom, Ellwood exposes himself to the criticisms of a section of the profession who feel that the master has taken this expression about as far as it will go. "Mies will not admit this—neither will I," says Ellwood.

The architect does live in a technological age that has produced a variety of new ideas and technical images, which the architect obviously cannot ignore if his architecture is to be valid in the twentieth century. *Economy of means*, or the elimination of the superfluous is an idea that has a very definite appeal. To a large degree it has become a canon of modern society. If production methods in the building industries have not yet adapted to this idea, making it rather expensive, this does not invalidate the approach itself. The expression of structure and methods of construction derive directly from the economy of means idea, and though architects may not finally desire a clear expression of this, it remains one of the principal approaches in design today.

The idea in America that the architect has a moral obligation to show a clear structural system and method of construction in a building may well have its origins in the Chicago period, when the concern, both aesthetic and emotional, was for simple, honest, form and expression. It is natural for the architect to want to express a well-proportioned and handsome structural system, but there is certainly no reason to believe that this will automatically result in good architecture. Yet a clear, true structure has been emphasized, by some, as almost sacred to modern architecture. In this light Ronchamp may well have appeared as a betrayal, almost an immoral act. Obviously an exposed structure can also be a severe limitation to an architect's creative intent; integrity can lie within, as well as exist on the surface. An architect in any event would be naive to believe a building could be built without certain compromises in its structure—this does not mean falsification—just as the layman would be naive to believe that an architect's

Rosen House, Los Angeles, California.

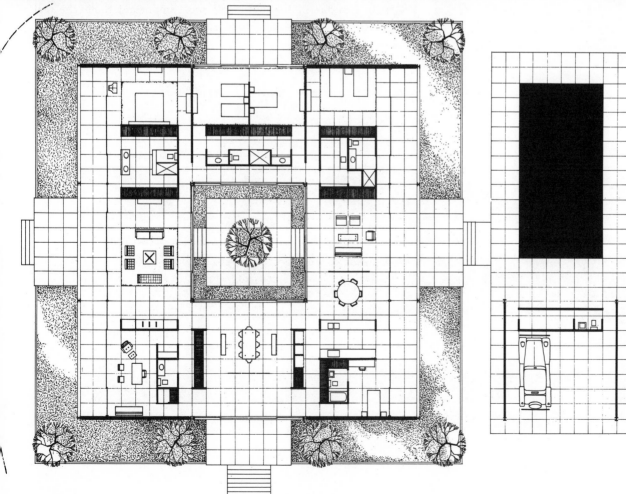

155

structure is not motivated by certain aesthetic ends. Mies's Berlin Gallery and Ellwood's house that spans a gorge may be absolutely moral expressions of structural concepts, but they are as much intellectually and aesthetically derived as they are structurally.

The idea that there is some virtue in exposing structure is comparatively recent. Historical periods were quite equivocal about it. The Greeks were so concerned with the refinement of proportion, details and optical corrections that it is often difficult to distinguish which of their expressed elements were structural. Although the Gothic period developed from a new principle of construction, many of the supposedly structural features were actually non-functional—merely decorative, to dramatize the mass. Renaissance architects concentrated their energies on architectural features—pilasters and the like—that may have emphasized structural forces, but were in themselves non-structural. Baroque architects freely employed or concealed structure, at will, purely for architectural effect.

Structure *is* a major discipline. It is also a means of approach for the average architect today. As a discipline it is one of the few really valid ones. The historical references are not meant to denigrate the validity of such an approach, but to point out that architecture and structure are inseparable considerations. As Le Corbusier wrote: "Architecture is a thing of Art, a phenomenon of the emotions, lying outside questions of construction and beyond them. The purpose of construction is to make things hold together, and of architecture, to move us." When an architect criticizes a building, invariably his criticism is based on how he would have approached the problem. This is meant neither to justify Ronchamp nor to criticize Ellwood, but to stress that while structure is one of the architect's most important tools, the real concern is to what architectural ends, encompassing human purposes, he uses it.

Project for a House spanning a gorge near Los Angeles, California.

Chamorro House, near Los Angeles, California.

Opdahl House, Long Beach, California.

EDWARD A. KILLINGSWORTH

"The present search for change in architecture is of great concern to me," said Edward Killingsworth. "Good buildings can result when using dynamic forms if they are handled by masters [we had been talking of Ronchamp], but generally only the clean, simple forms produce good buildings when handled by lesser architects. The Boston City Hall is a rather frightening direction. Apparently the thinking of our leaders is toward what is new in architecture rather than what is good. There is a search for strange forms which may be closely identified with a particular architect as his contribution or his 'style' of architecture."

Edward Killingsworth was born in Taft, California, in 1917. After graduating in 1940 from the University of Southern California, where he is now a critic in fifth year design, Killingsworth had five years of Army service before he started to practice architecture. In 1953 he formed a partnership with Jules Brady and Waugh Smith, also California-born and trained. The present firm of Killingsworth-Brady and Associate (Smith has recently retired) numbers about twenty, and its work ranges from single family residences to master planning.

Case Study House Number 25, Long Beach, California.

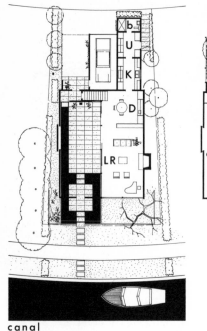

canal

FIRST FLOOR   **SECOND FLOOR**

The Killingsworth-Brady approach to architecture is quite consistent and unself-conscious. Simple post and beam construction, usually in wood, carefully detailed to overcome the problem of shrinkage and twisting, produces a simple exterior form and pleasant interior spaces that have a quiet, yet rich variety. Although Ellwood's present architecture reflects it more, like Ellwood they have discovered that the strongest influence on their work is Mies's architecture. Their buildings, however, in a manner that is reminiscent of Neutra's, reflect much more of the warmth and casualness of Southern California. Entrances are frequently through a pleasant outdoor garden overlooked from the interior spaces surrounding it. Reflecting pools and fountains are often used in these gardens to increase the spatial feeling of intimately-scaled and carefully-detailed spaces. Planting, in the best California tradition, is employed as a soft texture and irregular outline in contrast with the refined regularity of precise structures.

Killingsworth says, "The most flattering thing an owner can say about one of our buildings is, 'It's my building, I did all this myself, the architects only translated my thoughts.' There can be no greater tribute to an architect than this. It means the owner has completely identified himself with the building, and it is *his* building, not an architect's monument to himself. This means that we have been able to translate the owner's thoughts, desires, and needs successfully."

The 1958 Opdahl House, at Long Beach, California, is on a small 30 by 80 foot site. The house rises between solid, two-story flanking walls, set back 3 feet on each side to afford privacy from neighboring buildings. It is approached through a court space that also contains a carport. This leads to another garden area with a terrace and reflecting pool across which stepping stones lead directly to the two-story living room. The house also opens at the rear through a glass wall to another intimate garden area.

Case Study House Number 25 in 1962, at Long Beach, California, is also on a narrow, small lot. The principal entry to the house is by boat from a canal. A secondary means of access from a street at the rear leads to the house across stepping stones, over a shallow reflecting pool. Beyond, through a 17-foot-high entrance door, is an inner landscaped courtyard that is sheltered by an open sun screen comprised of 3-inch by 2-inch timber members. The living space and the master bedroom above it have a view of the canal through the branches of an old olive tree. These rooms

Case Study Triad, House "B," La Jolla, California.

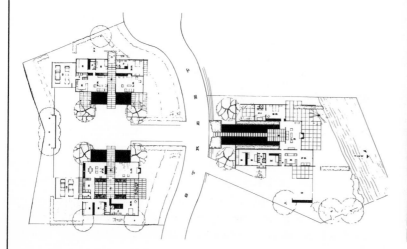

Cambridge Office Building, Long Beach, California.

Atlantic Research Plant, Costa Mesa, California.

in turn are oriented to the courtyard, giving this small house, similar to the Opdahl house, a great sense of spaciousness.

In the early 1960's, when the Case Study House program directed its attention towards the broader implications of quality in real estate tract developments, Killingsworth, Brady and Smith were commissioned to design three houses in close relationship at La Jolla, California. Each house has individual character and is distinct from the others; the siting, continuity of materials, form and landscaping establishing a sense of unity. An axial development has led to a balanced composition with the approach to the more delicate houses "B" and "C" centering upon the approach to the more elaborate of the group, house "A" at the lower level. All three houses have a sense of spaciousness, achieved by both distant views, and immediate ones into their landscaped courts. Generous ceiling heights of 10 feet, with the exception of certain intimate areas, augment this feeling.

Elements of their residential architecture reappear in such varied commercial structures as the firm's Cambridge Office Building and the Duffield Lincoln-Mercury Agency, both timber-framed structures in Long Beach, California; the Atlantic Research Plant, now under construction in Costa Mesa, California, and the recently-completed Kahala Hilton Hotel in Honolulu, a pre-stressed concrete structure, and the firm's most publicized design to date.

The Missile Systems Division of Atlantic Research is a 126,000-square-foot plant comprised of four buildings with seven hundred adjacent parking spaces, and facilities for engineering, manufacturing and testing, plus an administration building and cafeteria. The 15-acre site will ultimately be doubled to 30 acres, with 250,000 square feet of floor space. The buildings are being constructed on a 4-foot module for easy expansion. Specimen trees and plant groups will be used extensively and employees will have access to garden areas adjoining the cafeteria. A reflecting pool and fountains will set off the administration building which, with its delicate columns, lightly-scaled overhang, and narrow strip windows, contrasts to the other windowless buildings. The general effect of the entire complex "will approximate that of a university campus."

Hilton Hotels asked the architects to design a building which reflected the quiet and casual elegance of old Hawaii; a luxurious retreat in a most romantic setting. Although concrete is generally a heavy material in appearance, particularly in comparison to wood structures, the aim was to produce a delicate and graceful building. This was achieved by close attention to detail and by the avoidance of visually robust forms in preference to those that were long, straight and slender.

The main ten-story structure, in the shape of two offset rectangles raised above the ground, contains three hundred guest rooms and suites. This is approached through a grand, 30-foot-high lobby the principal feature of which is three, shallow elliptical domes, each establishing a parallel axis: on the first, is an elliptical pool; the second coincides with the main entrance and the double row of royal palms along the entrance driveway; on the third, there is a long view over a broad lagoon, stocked with tropical fish and fed by several decorative waterfalls that also serve to aerate the water. Throughout the design are framed views of the gardens "that have been laid out according to the traditional principles of the Italian Renaissance," says Killingsworth.

Duffield Lincoln-Mercury Agency, Long Beach, California.

Trellises of precast, pre-stressed structural concrete cover the roof and the sides of the guestroom wings. These trellises support the lanai balconies, but they were primarily designed to cover the entire building with flowering vines that will grow upwards from a big "flower box" on the lower level of the building, from pots on each balcony, and downwards from planters on the roof. Thus the structure itself will never dominate, blurred and softened as it is by trellises and vines. The architects feel that their aim of an unobtrusive environment will be attained if the guests remember only gracious rooms, lush gardens and elegant informality.

Killingsworth says that "architecture is space and delicacy." His work shows a meticulous, romantic concern for both, and, similar to Ellwood, with a consistency and refinement that comes from familiarity. And there is an avoidance of the "style for the job" notion that is so often sentimental rather than architectural. Again the Mies axiom comes to mind: "I would rather be good than original."

Kahala Hilton Hotel, Honolulu, Hawaii.

162

Jones House, Los Angeles, California, 1954 (destroyed by fire 1961).

A. QUINCY JONES

Today more than half of all American families own their own homes, the majority of which have been purchased from speculative builders. Proportionately, the number of individual architect-designed houses has declined in relation to builders' houses, where mass production allows fees and costs to be amortized over a number of houses, and the "package" consists of land, streets, utilities, landscaping, and a long-term mortgage loan. The speculative builder has answered a need, and despite the limitations of his specific product, the advantages of owning one's own home and being able to enjoy sun and fresh air are obvious. Unless the advantages can be retained while eliminating many of the disadvantages, the new systems of living that respect the needs of the individual with relation to those of the total community will not be created; we actually have the means to create these new systems—and our circumstance demands that we must.

The problems of our proliferating suburbs are well-known: they necessitate the costly spread of services such as roads and utilities; force such community facilities as there are to be meager and far-flung; and do not permit any economical, adequate transportation system, thereby obliging complete reliance on the automobile. As a result, the countryside is consumed with a monotony of similar houses and a web of streets supposedly laid out to secure the maximum number of lots per acre, and commuters are faced with inordinate hours of commuting (although it is well to remember that the onerous physical conditions under which one commutes are the real factor here).

Of course, the monotonous areas would be monotonous whether houses are similar or not; in fact houses can be quite similar but the overall neighborhood containing these houses may be anything but monotonous. And the web of streets, usually a grid pattern, is not necessarily the most economical in terms of getting

163

more lots. Planning a community on other than a conventional grid pattern can provide more lots, but such planning requires good rules to operate within, because possibly several lots or blocks may need to be considered as an entity rather than as separate units unrelated to each other.

These concerns are central to the work of A. Quincy Jones. A Los Angeles architect, Jones practices in a city that is only slightly over a hundred years old, one that has developed its own pattern and texture independent of historic prototypes, where the way of life is related particularly to the individual house and the automobile. Within its city limits, Los Angeles actually has over fifty percent of publicly-owned land devoted solely to the use and storage of the automobile. Los Angeles may also be the forerunner of a new type of city where people live in relatively self-contained communities and seldom need, or wish, to go to the city center.

A. Quincy Jones was born in Kansas City, Missouri, in 1913, and when he was six, his family moved to Los Angeles. He studied architecture at the University of Washington in Seattle, graduating in 1936 (two years after Yamasaki). After four years in the Navy, he opened his own office in 1945. Two years later came the opportunity that embarked him on a serious study of the development house—over 5000 of which have been built from the many prototypes designed in his office. The project was a shopping center related to seven hundred builder's houses on the fringe of Tucson, Arizona. He asked to be allowed to design the houses as well, but plans that fitted Federal Housing Authority requirements had already been acquired and construction was about to begin. Jones asked if he might consider the master plan overnight and make proposals, promising that enough design drawings of houses would be ready for construction to begin within one to two months. Streets were already under construction but Jones was able to rearrange the layout of houses to produce a better community, and to landscape the development. He designed the houses, but never did do the shopping center.

In 1950 Jones formed a partnership with Frederick E. Emmons, who was born in New York in 1907 and studied architecture at Cornell University. In the same year a house designed by Jones in San Diego won the First Honor award in the National Awards program of the American Institute of Architects. The house was 1000 square feet with all the rooms related to adjacent gardens. The idea had been to design an inexpensive house that individuals could build on their own lots. It was published in *Architectural Forum* as the Builder's House of the Year. The same issue contained a circular site plan by Anshen & Allen, designed for Joseph Eichler, one of America's most enlightened builder-developers, cited the Sub-Division of the Year. Eichler suggested to Jones that since they had respectively done the House and the Sub-Division of the Year they should work together—they continue to do so.

"We are living in a time when most knowledge is far beyond that which we are practicing within the profession of architecture. Part of this condition results from our attempt to operate under an out-dated set of rules. Building is the third largest industry in the country, yet our product is made the same way that it was three hundred years ago with the same prejudices involved. If we say that a house should be built of wood, brick, stone or shingle, we

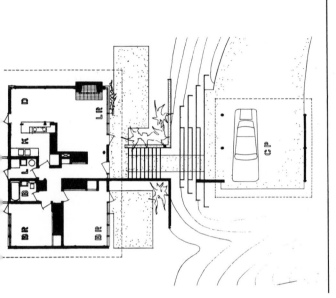

House of 1000 square feet, 1950.

never offend anybody, but most people have a negative reaction toward the synthetic materials such as plastics, steel and aluminum. We need to preserve the materials that enhance our environment in their natural form—trees, for instance—and work instead with the inert things that do not normally enhance the natural surroundings until they are utilized in a certain way. If we can follow this line of reasoning, we can add to the improvement of our environment, rather than subtract.

"Our inability to communicate the means available to us today of creating a delightful and livable environment has fostered a reticence and lack of understanding by people; so we have the schism between knowledge and potential, and the one does not capitalize on the other.

"Again, as with synthetic materials, we must break down the barriers of acceptance. An out-of-date organization, the almost anti-organization of our environment, has fragmented things. We seldom look at the broad picture, creating systems and hierarchies of order and relationships, then to beam in on smaller things. Although Jane Jacobs makes the 'accident' sound very romantic, it has a better chance of being a 'good' accident if it happens within an order and not chaos. For example, watercolor is a direct medium that has some order but certain of its qualities are dependent on the accident; this is so with action painting too. We have to start with an order and a plan. If we do, the accidental things that result may be 'great' and exciting. I think we are about twenty years away from the time when Los Angeles might be an interesting city. The automobile is the factor we talk about most, and it is going to force us into doing something more orderly than at present.

"Many people criticize Los Angeles without understanding that it has evolved as a reaction to a need and as a reflection of a potential. It is not ugly because it is an automobile city, as many critics say, but because people have not realized how to use the automobile. The freeway is not always a curse aesthetically and, in many instances, it is becoming an asset to the city. Some of the best open areas in our cities are where freeways have been built and trees planted. The problem is that the freeway should be designed more intelligently in relation to the total city. We have too many local planning commissions that do not coordinate their work. We need an overall planning body for the United States, not to execute work but to coordinate it.

"Usually, a commission is related to a particular lot. Even when working with one 'body' or client, such as a university, the architect-planner finds that land is often subdivided without recognition that it is vital to consider all buildings, all spaces, all circulation patterns, etc., as parts of a total entity. We are not too far away from the time when we can set up a different set of standards or ground rules for the architect. Today, we work with building codes and planning ordinances which accept property lines as the basis for regulations and restrictions.

"The first example of a recent breakthrough in this country from the strict adherence to present-day codes is the condominium apartment. Although the primary effort to gain acceptance for condominiums may have occurred partly for commercial reasons rather than for reasons of good design, the concept has a number of merits that can apply to urban development. With the condominium apartment, we are building within property lines but selling what I call 'buildable volume.' Somehow, we should be able to advance a step further and devise the legal means of saying to a land owner, 'You own a 100-foot by 200-foot lot, and you are permitted to build a six-story building which equals x-number of cubic feet of building.' If we can get to the point where ownership can be translated into terms of volume rather than area of land, and one is assured the right to sell or lease the buildable volume, but within a master plan, then we can develop our cities properly. With this kind of approach, we would make great advancements in our planning of urban areas. It has only to be administered intelligently.

Planned Community for Eichler Homes, Marin County, California.

Atrium House for Eichler Homes.

Greenmeadow Comunity Center, Palo Alto, California, 1955.

"Zoning regulations that arbitrarily establish front, side and rear yard setbacks, with no concern for the total community, are antiquated. They were established when densities were not a problem, when it was unusual to develop a single piece of property and sell lots without knowing who was going to build on the property or what they were going to build. These regulations are not compatible with today's process of building in large developments; they are detrimental to obtaining a better land use that becomes increasingly important with the higher densities that are now mandatory. Building codes that differ from one community to another are illogical, especially in these days of contiguous communities that comprise our cities.

"Here is an example of what is happening in many parts of the country. A developer owned a large area of land in the San Fernando Valley in Southern California. He took thirty acres, asked us to develop it and provide housing with at least the minimum equivalent of what could be bought in a tract house. We were to assume that we had a free hand, with no lot lines or street

U.S. Consulate General Office Building, Singapore, 1961.

St. Michael and All Angels Church,
Studio City, California, 1962.

patterns to worry about. We knew that one of the big cost factors here was the value of the land—about twice that of the utilities. The way to get the best cost factor was to get more houses per acre and, in turn, lower the cost of utilities by reducing roads, sewer lines, etc. Our scheme achieved a density of about twelve families to the acre, with a garden area equivalent to what they would have with an individual lot. We provided some community facilities, a pool and playgrounds. Ours was a logical scheme. We prepared our cost analysis based on the developer's land value of ten thousand dollars per acre and established that he could sell a three- or four-bedroom house for approximately twenty-five thousand or thirty thousand dollars. To build from our proposed scheme, the developer had to get the land rezoned from R-1 status to R-3 because some of the houses had party walls. After he obtained the rezoning, the developer came back to us and said that under the new set of circumstances, our cost analysis was all wrong. He explained that now, with R-3 zoning, the land was worth three times as much, or thirty thousand dollars an acre. He said he would have to add the proportionate amount of cost to each house. Here we were with the same piece of land, purchased for the same amount of money, but once the zoning had been changed, even before the houses were built, the developer could sell the land for three times its original value.

"Here is another example of regulations that affect building design. In an apartment building we designed for San Francisco each living room has a large balcony of about 120 square feet that can be used comfortably, in its exposed situation, only a few days each year. In the design stages, instead of balconies, which are not appropriate in every situation, we tried to enclose this same amount of space within the interior living area. Instead, the balconies were added because, as a Federal Housing Authority project, the owner gets a quarter-room count for a balcony; this amounted to about a one thousand two hundred fifty dollar allowance, although each balcony may cost only six hundred dollars to build. This gain was multiplied by approximately 150 apartments. The owner was unable to obtain an equal allowance with our initial design which eliminated the balconies and added to the interior living space.

"In this example the outdated rules worked against the architect and good design. By utilizing a sliding glass screen, we could have had the advantages of both inside and outside space at no extra cost. Of course, we should not use that as an excuse, no more than the automobile in planning, nor limitations of building codes, because as long as there are rules, we know that we can still design good things within them. But architects do not always do what they should in trying to get the rules changed. Too often we accept them without trying diligently enough to improve them.

"On the bright side, an example of how a variance from the restrictions produced a better community than the existing regulations permitted was in the Greenmeadow Community Center which Eichler Homes built in Palo Alto in 1955. The city had an arbitrary requirement of a minimum of 8,500 square feet per lot. The community originally was to have one hundred and eighty houses. We retained the city's density but, working with Eichler, we designed the community with approximately 8,000 square feet per lot. With the extra 500 square feet, saved from each lot size, we included a community center of approximately four acres.

Laguna Eichler Apartments, San Francisco, California.

169

Research Library, University of California, Los Angeles, California, 1964.

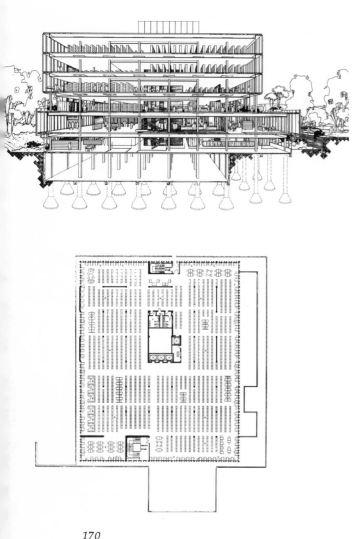

This community center provides a nursery school that also serves as a meeting place for adults, a swimming pool of Olympic size, park area with groves of trees and community pedestrian walks. Today, this community remains one of the best examples of what can be done with the proper cooperation of all persons concerned who make decisions that affect planning.

"My preference is for a 'performance' over a 'specification' type of code. Unfortunately, almost all of our present codes and regulations are based on a type of 'specification' code that defines requirements in measurable restrictions. The enforcement is made easier and the interpretation is less likely to be based on personal opinion, but such absolutes also limit the imagination and decrease the possibility of accomplishing the best and the highest use of the land in relation to the total community.

"Initially we should analyze a problem to establish what is possible within the rules as they exist. Then, we should analyze a problem and re-program it, based on the best use of the space and disregarding the rules. Next, we should spend time trying to get approved those particular design elements which are not within existing regulations. Whenever we can get one point across successfully, we have gained a little ground. These points eventually add up to major gains.

"Another important factor that the architect has to contend with today is that people still want architecture to be permanent. Certain buildings should be permanent, but there are also many buildings that should be temporary or designed in a manner that does not preclude another use. For example, in our library for the University of California at Los Angeles, we decided that the University should be able to use the building for some purpose other than a library. Maybe one day the books will be on microfilm, and everybody will have their little reading device; the number of books it takes to fill 250,000 square feet now, might well be stored in 1,000 square feet. This library building could make a fine science building ten years from now—there is nothing but space and columns—it is completely flexible. A building can be designed for permanence without being rigid on the interior. Things change so much that many buildings should not be static. It might even have been better to use a light steel frame for the library so that it could have been taken down.

"In some cases you almost penalize yourself financially by building because the increase in the value of the land does not correspond with the cost of the building you have erected on it. This is true of houses in particular. There are single family houses on 60-foot by 120-foot lots in Los Angeles where the land is worth more without the house than with it. As the density increases, the land that housing units sit on becomes too valuable to let it be used for low densities indefinitely.

"These are some of the things we should think about. The architect should be among the leaders and help improve the ground rules in order that we can build a better physical environment for the future generations than we enjoy at present."

Graduate Research Library, University of Hawaii, Honolulu, Hawaii, 1964.

State University of New York, Albany, New York.

EDWARD DURELL STONE

Edward Durell Stone was one of the first American architects to embrace the International Style and, as one of its talented exponents, soon emerged as a leading figure on the American architectural scene. Early accomplishment often corresponds with an early reassessment of a personal direction. Stone's reassessment led to a singular vision based on his idea and ideal of creating a more enduring, elegant and richer architecture. It resulted in a certain consistency in his buildings of the last decade. He is now considered a romanticist, which, "by definition, is one who reasserts imagination and sentiment and emphasizes individualism in thought and expression," he says. "This, at least, I have tried to accomplish, and I am willing to accept as part of my credo." But he prefers to be labelled, if he must be, a rational romantic. "I wouldn't propose to burden any client with whimsical things. It is my hope to provide him with a practical building, and, above all, a beautiful one that he will be proud to possess."

Edward Durell Stone was born in 1902 in Fayetteville, Arkansas. His was a leisurely affluent youth in the home of the State University, described by him as a "hotbed of tranquility." When eighteen, he visited his brother who was working for the firm that had been founded by H. H. Richardson in Boston. He was impressed by McKim, Mead & White's Public Library and H. H. Richardson's Trinity Church. On his way home via Washington, Stone was entranced by the lush tropical vegetation, the fountains, and brilliant colored tiles in the garden court of Paul Cret's Pan American Building. "This was the moment of truth for me," he says. "I decided if architecture could be like this then this is what I want to do." A year later Stone returned to Boston and studied architecture for successive years at Harvard University and the Massachusetts Institute of Technology. He never received a degree, a fact he often refers to with a smile. His ability, though, was such that in 1927 it earned him the coveted Rotch Traveling Scholarship, a competition for graduates of those two distinguished institutions.

In Europe Stone saw the "new architecture," and he returned to America in the inopportune year of 1929, with his imagination fired. He worked in New York on the Waldorf Astoria Hotel and then on the Radio City Music Hall. Stone's design for the Mandel House in Mount Kisco, New York, built in 1935, showed him confidently at terms with the spirit of the architectural revolution. The first modern house in the East, consonant with the restraint of the new idiom, it generated considerable excitement in architectural circles. The concrete and steel building had an open plan for the living area, strip windows that provided panoramic views of the countryside, and a semicircular-ended dining room, in which glass bricks were used, as the pivot of the composition. This, and several other noteworthy houses, brought to Stone and the late Philip Goodwin the opportunity to design America's first public building in the International Style: The Museum of Modern Art in New York in 1937. They placed the auditorium below ground level and the elevators and service spaces at one side of the building, so as to leave the galleries as a flexible, open sequence of exhibition spaces. The Members' rooms, opening through large glass areas to a roof terrace, became a design prototype for Manhattan rooftops.

In 1938, Stone designed a house for the then President of the Museum of Modern Art, A. Conger Goodyear. It showed signs of departure from the established norm of the International Style. Broad overhanging eaves sheltered floor-to-ceiling glazing from the summer sun—a practical necessity that Wright had recognized for over thirty years, Stone points out. The overhanging roof line, which he refers to as the "hat" or "lid," is now one of his aesthetic priorities. Today, Stone thinks of the International Style as essentially an impoverished approach to architecture, one of transitory appearance whose synthetic austerity was never really compatible with the American image of home. "It was too cold, arid and sparse" he says, "and amenities which might have grace and charm were forsworn."

Stone's architecture took a new course in 1940 when he visited Taliesin, Wright's Wisconsin home, en route to California. He was enamored with an architecture so attuned to the natural beauty of the landscape. This impression was reinforced by the Bay Region style in San Francisco, whose informal architecture used natural materials with ease and cultivation, romantically exploiting the casual relationship between interior spaces and beautifully-planted courtyards. However, the several timber houses that followed, with informal, picturesque results, were not fundamental to him. Although the concept of a more indigenous architecture was in his mind, so, too, was the memory of Europe's great historic buildings—his real enthusiasm. During the war Stone designed airports and companion military installations. If they did not afford much scope for design, they did familiarize him, he says, with some of the problems involved in large-scale housing and planning.

In 1946, Stone designed the El Panama Hotel in Panama City, a departure in hotel construction that created a precedent for the tropics. Only the central one-third portion of the slab, with rooms off its dividing corridor, is air-conditioned; the remainder has rooms on only one side of an open gallery. The hotel slab is oriented to catch the prevailing breezes and, with ventilating jalousies opposite each private open balcony, the rooms become

Mandel House, Mount Kisco, New York.

Goodyear House, Old Westbury, New York.

Museum of Modern Art, New York, N.Y.

breezeways. The rooms have studio beds and are converted to sitting rooms during the daytime, standard today in most hotels and motels. In this hotel, Stone attempted to minimize the space devoted to lobbies and corridors. He now tries to eliminate them altogether.

The Thurnauer House in 1949 substituted for the space-wasting hallway a spacious, top-lit playroom as an atrium providing direct access to all other rooms. The desire to eliminate corridors led to Stone's inclination to open rooms or smaller areas off a central focal space. He says, "In the basic conception of a building, I like to arrive in a very eventful space—an atrium, a garden, a great hall—to encounter immediate drama and the possibility to orient oneself. Corridors are the curse of the twentieth century and immediately establish an institutional dullness. You don't find them in classical architecture where one traversed a courtyard or, as in Versailles, moved from one salon to another."

In 1954 Stone designed the United States Embassy, in New Delhi, India. It was the first building to be guided by a new directive from Washington: "To the sensitive and imaginative designer it will be an invitation to give serious study to local conditions of climate and site, to understand and sympathize with local customs and people . . . yet he will not fear using new techniques or new materials should this constitute real advances in architectural thinking."

El Panama Hotel, Panama City, Canal Zone.

Stone took this edict very seriously, producing a building praised by no less than Wright, and considered widely as an elegant and dignified marriage of the tastes, techniques and cultures of East and West. For Stone it was a new design departure. He says, "Its formality, its simple repose, its richness, which was justifiable for practical reasons, embarked me on a new outlook. It was my own and it was unique, although, actually, it had its prototype in the classic temple."

The Embassy was on a raised platform, traditional in ancient temples, that accommodated services and provided a hidden area for parking automobiles sheltered from the intense rays of the sun. Stone's obsession with restraining the visual intrusion of the automobile is one most architects share. Embassy offices are on two floors around the rectangular periphery of a central courtyard which doubles as a water garden, reducing temperature both psychologically and practically. The courtyard is animated by a pattern of light and shadow produced by an open, overhead screen. An inexpensive screen of terrazzo blocks, cast and polished on the site, veils the glass areas from the sun, reducing the glare in the offices while maintaining the view outward. The entire building is shaded by an umbrella-like canopy that is separated from the second floor by a heat-dissipating breezeway several feet high, and supported on steel columns whose gold leaf finish "introduced a note of oriental opulence."

In the Embassy Stone introduced the grille into modern architecture, and although he has not used one for several years, it will always be thought of as his trademark. The practicalities and romantic appeal fascinated him, but he says, "perhaps subsequently I let this enthusiasm get out of hand. The fact that the grille has texture and pattern concerns some people because it was immediately called decorative, which is as vulgar as tattooing in some circles. Maybe if it had been all circles or all squares it wouldn't have been so disturbing to them." It was an inexpensive device that was widely used or—more exactly—widely misused. For Stone it is a closed chapter about which he will casually joke: recently, seeing a butchered version of the grille on a parking structure intended to mask architectural sins and give "zip" he quipped, "now there's a man with an idea."

In 1956 Stone completed the Stuart Company offices and factory in Pasadena, California, and the Graf House in Texas, continuing the richness of the Embassy into two other quite different building types. The former resulted from the client's desire to have a beautiful environment for his employees, apparently recognizing that good architecture is good business; the latter, enclosed by high walls with its rooms opening to courtyards, has its spiritual counterpart in the classical Pompeian house. The central space of the house is a living area between an elliptical swimming pool and a circular island for dining that is set within a rectangular lagoon. Stone has since designed several houses that are variations on this formal theme.

One of Stone's prime concerns is the organization and sequence of usually axially-arranged, formal spaces in his buildings. He seeks the beauty of eventful and exciting spaces by the simplest and most economical structural methods. "I haven't felt called upon to experiment too much with structure and it isn't my tendency," he says. "The elements of most buildings are small and the simplest way to accomplish the structure is by a flat slab, free of beams, with columns placed on practical centers. Structural tricks are expensive and do not prove too much." Stone views much of the current obsession with structure as mere mannerism.

A World's Fair almost obliged a display of structural dexterity. Stone's United States Pavilion at the Brussels World's Fair, in 1958, was no exception. To roof the 350-foot-diameter space Stone "adapted the principle of the bicycle wheel," connecting an outer steel ring to an inner one, 60 feet in diameter, by 2-inch steel cables, covered with translucent plastic panels. Until that time no circular buildings of this magnitude, free of columns, had been roofed over. The building was acclaimed as one of the most sophisticated at the exposition. "The exterior," said Stone, "had the feeling of gaiety befitting an exposition and a dignity appropriate to a government building." The structure was slender and translucent, almost discreetly fading back so as to concentrate attention on a display that was both tasteful and intelligent—a great contrast to its axial neighbor, the U.S.S.R. Pavilion, whose ponderous structure "packed in" an exhibition of astonishing naiveté.

The Huntington Hartford Gallery of Modern Art, in New York, opened in 1964, is one of Stone's most romantic, most embellished and—for these reasons—most criticized buildings. The building itself is "lost" in the visual chaos of Columbus Circle. Stone had proposed a circular plaza, to be lined peripherally with columns rescued from the late Pennsylvania Railroad Station (shades of the Roman Forum) to serve as a setting for the Museum as well as a distinguished approach to the Lincoln Center.

On its tiny, irregular island site "a miracle was needed to get an orderly, spacious gallery area," says Stone. His solution was a series of galleries, arranged as landings on a grand staircase. Speaking of the character and atmosphere of the gallery spaces Stone said: "The old monumental repository had long since gone,

Thurnauer House, Englewood, New Jersey.

replaced by the dramatic white, austere, brilliantly-illuminated areas, a tradition of the thirties. Yet I have long felt that one of the objectives of a museum should be to make the visitor aspire to have original works of art in his own home. With this in mind, the galleries were given warm, rich materials and comfortable furniture. In such surroundings it is not difficult to project works of art into your own environment." Referring to the treatment of the building's exterior, he says: "Compared with the current hygienic austerity of much of our architecture this building may be considered romantic—a radical departure, with its arches and use of rich materials. We live in an age of architectural transition and the more exuberant forms are finding favor in a new generation also enamored of the plastic possibilities of concrete. I believe too that people now yearn for fine materials and a quality of richness."

"There is too much conformity in contemporary architecture. I like to think of architecture as an individual creative expression; I get more pleasure out of my work if I carry through my own convictions rather than pursue a dogma outlined by some other architect. An architect should try to find his own expression. At one juncture the work of many people looks alike. The paintings of the Impressionist, for example, or of the Cubist, working in the

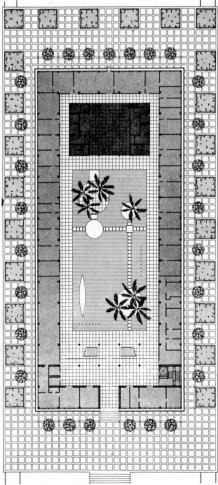

U.S. Embassy, New Delhi, India.

177

Gallery of Modern Art, New York, N.Y.

same movement at the same time, looked quite similar. As time passed, however, each worked into his own individual style. In this age of standardization, Americans need more than ever to cultivate the open mind. Those who assert their individuality should find greater tolerance from their fellow; if our flights of fancy found receptive audiences and each of us were encouraged to be an individual, our lives would be enriched.

"In the 1930's, figuratively speaking, a book-burning took place, and any thought, any reflection of what had happened in architecture through the ages was scorned. Unless one adhered rigidly to the then *au courant* functionalism, he was committing a sin. However, the purge appears to have run its course, and I may have been one of the first to repudiate it. I now find I have company among my greatest colleagues. Without shame, a laboratory building is inspired by the towers of San Gimignano (Kahn: Richards Medical Towers); a dormitory group, transparently motivated by the massing of Gothic structure, and an airline terminal inspired by Da Vinci's first efforts on a flying machine (Saarinen: Colleges at Yale and the TWA Terminal); a group of government buildings at a recent exposition was clearly detailed in the Gothic tradition (Yamasaki: Seattle 1962 World's Fair); the greatest of modern architects (Frank Lloyd Wright) was inspired in one period by the architecture of the Mayans; the greatest living painter (Picasso) went through a period when Negro art found expression in his painting.

"I am critical of the steel and glass monolithic structures, inspired by the work of Mies, particularly the type one finds along Park Avenue now, because I believe that architecture should be permanent in character. Looking at Chartres Cathedral or Bernini's colonnade in front of St. Peter's, or the Hagia Sophia, all these great monuments, which have naturally influenced me, have stood for many hundreds of years. Here in New York, Rockefeller Center has a feeling of permanence. Much of our modern architecture lacks this intangible quality of permanence, formality and dignity. It bears more resemblance to the latest model automobile, depending upon shining, metallic finish—doomed to early obsolescence.

"This obsession with monuments of the past may seem sentimental and pedantic, but I believe the inspiration for a building should be in the accumulation of history. Although none of my buildings copy classical examples, they have a formality and, I hope, a dignity that one associates with historic monuments. A knowledge of great historical buildings enables the architect to remain in the mainstream rather than be diverted by passing enthusiasms which can lead him to dead ends.

"When I came to New York in 1929, there were no examples of modern architecture. Obviously you cannot effect a whole conception or develop an architectural philosophy in the thirty-odd years since then. The perfection of the Parthenon, generally considered to be man's greatest symbol of architectural perfection, was achieved only after some five hundred years of work on the simple problem of a temple. It is ironic that we today are accused of a fixation if we work five years on the solution of a building type. This might also be cause for reflection for those who wish to place contemporary architecture in the straitjacket of a finally crystallized style. Modern architecture is still in its infancy. We have a right to be encouraged by what we have done, but not to accept it as the final architectural statement in the United States.

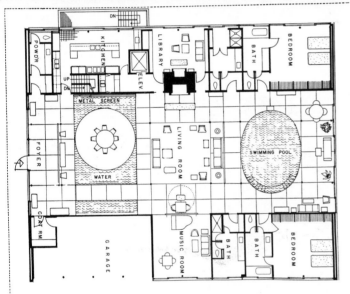

Graf House, Dallas, Texas.

U.S. Pavilion, Brussels, Belgium.

Stuart Company, Pasadena, California.

"It is my effort to seek what I call the inevitable, which I hope is distinct from the obvious. I believe, with some pride, that our buildings are well-planned and have an element of inevitability. I try to find an architecture that is hopefully timeless, free of the mannerisms of the moment. Architecture should follow a grander and more ageless pattern, and it can and should be approached simply. I try to search for the most direct, honest solution to a given problem. If an architect conscientiously takes into account the circumstances that are unique to each building, then careful analysis should result in an original architectural solution. I am afraid that we architects are too fond of saying that no two problems are the same, and yet we follow the same design pattern we have previously developed.

"Style has been overemphasized: there are books devoted to architecture that do not show plans explaining the basic conception. In the search for novelty, sensational effect and modish styling, the result seems contrived rather than a natural object of beauty. There is a temptation for architects to seize upon transitory styles and deny their own creative heritage. Architecture is not millinery. Fashions pass by, buildings remain to become grim reminders of transient enthusiasms.

"It is encouraging that so many of our significant thinkers have pointed out the unfortunate environment we have created for our people, and are proposing corrective programs. When such programs are inaugurated, architects can begin to fulfill their destiny. We will not be wasting our effort creating precious prototypes in the midst of chaos, but adding brilliant buildings in a well-ordered plan for the country as a whole."

The output of Stone's office is prolific for a group led by one man; his successful completion of a large number of projects is reassuring to the most nervous client. He also consistently meets rigid budgets: "We haven't failed in the last ten years," he says with pride, "and in most cases we have demonstrated that work of quality can be obtained within very limited means." His office is graced by an ever-changing procession of architectural models, photographs of completed buildings, and sketches of proposed ones. He employs about two hundred architects, the majority of whom work in two formidably-large drafting rooms on Park Avenue. Stone himself works with a small core of designers in an old brownstone just off Fifth Avenue. He likes to think of his relationship to his design staff as similar to the Renaissance relationship of a master to his school. "I wouldn't say that I have a genius for organization," he says, "but I have the fortunate faculty for providing leadership without generating resentment."

Currently Stone is deeply involved in two most significant commissions: The State University of New York at Albany, and the John Fitzgerald Kennedy Cultural Center in Washington.

The University campus, for ten thousand students, was an opportunity long sought by Stone—to plan a formal composition on the grand scale, in a pastoral setting. Here, free of all save economic limitations, he was able to group the academic buildings essentially under one continuous roof in a series of quadrangles, with colonnades providing covered passage from one building to another. As such he made one unified statement, avoiding the expression of isolated, individual structures. All vehicular traffic is routed around the periphery of the campus, and the entire academic complex is on a platform beneath which service deliveries are made, and utilities are compact and readily accessible. Dormi-

State University of New York, Albany, New York.

John F. Kennedy Center for the Performing Arts, Washington, D.C.

tories for six thousand students are arranged in four three-story quadrangles, each of which has a twenty-story dormitory tower overlooking the beautiful countryside.

Preliminary designs for the John F. Kennedy Cultural Center were started in 1958, when it was called the National Cultural Center. After the tragic event of November, 1963, it was fitting that the nation's cultural showplace, the center for the performing arts, should be renamed as a memorial to one who had been a great patron of the arts in his lifetime. "It really should represent twenty-five hundred years of Western culture," said Stone of the building, "rather than twenty-five years of modern architecture." As Washington is primarily a city of white buildings in a park-like setting it naturally follows that Stone's will be a white building (he seldom departs from the "classic purity" of the all-white building), set in an eleven-acre park on the banks of the Potomac.

Stone developed two schemes, each placing the opera, concert hall and theater under one roof. Since all three functions have highly specialized requirements and overlapping schedules, it was considered advisable to provide separate facilities for each—with direct access to parking facilities beneath the building for some fifteen hundred automobiles. The first scheme placed the auditoria around a grand salon, over two hundred feet across, which would itself be suitable for state balls and formal receptions, and would open to a banqueting space with broad terraces overlooking the river. Stone thought of the salon as an appropriate, formal setting, worthy of receiving foreign dignitaries who could be escorted by motor launch from the airport to the Center. Although admired, Stone's scheme at an estimated cost of seventy-five million dollars was considered "too grandiose."

In 1962 he was asked to prepare a new scheme nearer the region of thirty million dollars. He designed a rectangular building 650 feet long and 350 feet deep, with the three auditoria arranged in a row, separated by entrance lobbies. One grand entrance foyer runs the length of the building, overlooking the terrace to the river. The enormous area of the flat roof is devoted largely to two restaurants, one for formal dining and one for tourists. Between these is a flexible area with a sliding roof to be used for band concerts, balls, theater and exhibitions. Stone is dedicated to the idea that his design will symbolize the cultural maturity of a great country.

Stone believes that great architecture should lift the spirit, feed the soul and transport people out of themselves. It is this presence that he searches for in his own work, and he has virtually limitless opportunities to realize it. In an essentially materialistic age, he expresses some of the more romantic yearnings that an affluent society can indulge and, if his work in the poorer regions of the world is any indication, even the developing countries desire.

Jeddah International Airport, Saudi Arabia.

MINORU YAMASAKI

Yamasaki, searching for a quality of "humanism" in his buildings that stimulates a climate of rapport with man, voices strong discontent with forceful buildings that lack compassion towards man. He also deplores the meanly-contrived architecture of accommodation—the catalogue- and code- motivated architecture that regards its occupants as a statistic. Yamasaki's dislike of the "regimented patterns of glass and porcelain-enamel rectangles" is not an indictment of Mies but of those who take him as an easy, rubber-stamp remedy. He cites Mies's Seagram Building, with its dignity and majesty, as the one building in the United States he would most liked to have designed. Admiring the order and calm of Mies's architecture he says, "Mies showed us that machine-made buildings can be as beautiful as the hand-made buildings of the past."

Minoru Yamasaki was born in Seattle, Washington, in 1912. His was not the idyllic boyhood that his buildings might suggest. The son of a poor, immigrant family, he had to spend five gruelling summers in Alaskan fish canneries to pay for his architectural education. He graduated in 1934 from the University of Washington, where the excitement for architecture "was immature and introverted," says Yamasaki. "No one there, not even the teachers, knew what was going on in the architectural world. We didn't even know about Mies's Barcelona Pavilion." He came to study for a year at New York University at a time when the Depression left little scope for useful employment. Then, for nearly a decade, Yamasaki worked in the drafting rooms of large offices. Although it was boring to work on "designs of anonymous value," he gained considerable technical skill, to the point where he could produce work quickly and became chief draftsman of a hundred men. In 1945 Yamasaki became chief designer for Smith, Hinchman & Grylls, a Detroit office with a staff of six hundred draftsmen. At that time he became friendly with Eero Saarinen, and he remembers the intensity and energy with which Saarinen studied a project.

Architecturally, Yamasaki made his mark in 1951. He and two colleagues from the office of Smith, Hinchman & Grylls had formed a practice of their own, when they received the commis-

World Trade Center, New York, N. Y.

sion to design the Lambert-St. Louis Air Terminal. The building, endeavoring to create an entrance worthy of a city, set a new precedent for the design of airport terminals. Three lofty shell concrete vaults enclose the main space, with interspersed glazed areas through which daylight floods. At night the vaults, reflecting artificial light, stand shimmering white against the sky. The shell vault structure solved the two major problems of flexibility and expansion: there is no need for supports other than at the four extreme corners of the shell, and the terminal floor area can be doubled by the simple addition of three more shells.

In 1954, the assignment to design the United States Consulate in Kobe took Yamasaki first to Japan and subsequently around the world. His impressions on this first time out of America were to set his direction. He found that there was great emotional experience and involvement possible with buildings of the past; he felt this was achieved, not necessarily through form or ornamentation, but from a clear, cultural concept executed in the building technique and technology of the times.

The wonderful change of pace and the element of surprise in moving through spaces in the buildings of Japan impressed him as it had Wright. Then, too, there was the feeling of kinship and warmth for a building that "made you want to touch it," not only physically, but mentally. In a Japanese house "the materials are elegant—the *tatami* mat, the *shoji* screen with such slender mullions, the natural wood post so highly polished—everything has a marvellous touch." After this the use of concrete inside a building seemed very crude and unpleasant. "I don't mind an architect using rough materials outside," he said, "but inside—there, I think, you are violating a person's feelings." He was overwhelmed by the simple way nature had been enhanced in the Japanese gardens, and by the delightful serenity achieved. From the intensity of these kaleidoscopic impressions, and particularly the formative experience of comparing the Taj Mahal with Le Corbusier's Chandigarh, Yamasaki formulated a design philosophy which has remained essentially constant.

"There are a few very influential architects who sincerely believe that all buildings must be 'strong.' The word 'strong' in this context seems to connote 'powerful'—that is, each building should be a monument to the virility of our society. These architects look with derision upon attempts to build a friendly, more gentle kind of building. The basis for their belief is that our culture is derived primarily from Europe, and that most of the important traditional examples of European architecture are monumental, reflecting the need of the state, church, or the feudal families— the primary patrons of these buildings—to awe and impress the masses. This is incongruous today. Although it is inevitable for architects who admire these great monumental buildings of Europe to strive for the quality most evident in them—grandeur, the elements of mysticism and power, basic to cathedrals and palaces, are also incongruous today, because the buildings we build for our times are for a totally different purpose.

"There is another, much less desirable aspect of this effort toward monumentality. There are examples of architectural 'muscle-flexing' that evince a desire to be stronger, more powerful, more exciting than the buildings of competitors. The result of this thinking inevitably ends in crudity, to the point of brutality. When we have the machine that can make very precise parts, it

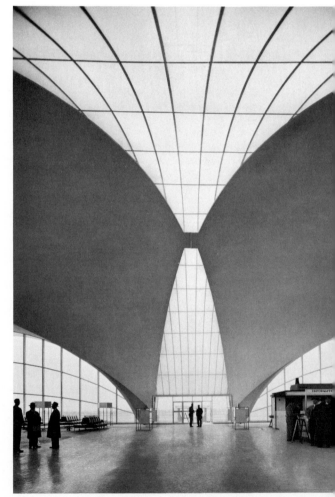

Lambert—St. Louis Terminal, St. Louis, Missouri.

does not make sense. Shockingly, in Japan, with its background of sensitive and intimate architecture, there are now many such buildings. These can never be appropriate to a democratic society; they are much more fitting as an image for the totalitarian principles which we abhor.

"For the same reason I question even as great an artistic example as Le Corbusier's High Court at Chandigarh. Though I admire its tremendous visual impact, its power and crudeness create the feeling of a great pagan temple where man must enter on his knees. This kind of egocentric reasoning is one of the major causes of the confusion in architectural thinking.

"Experimentation is vital and necessary to all our fields of endeavor, but experimentation which is not controlled by the cohesive force of an underlying philosophy—a purpose which goes beyond structure, stability, utility and economics—can only produce anarchy. In England the Renaissance expressed the beginnings of the dignity, pride, and humanity that is the great heritage of the English-speaking people today. So should an architecture for our society be totally consistent with our way of life and ideals—it should elevate the spirit of humanity and sympathetically express its ideals.

"An architecture to implement our way of life and reflect it must recognize those human characteristics we cherish most: love, gentility, joy, serenity, beauty and hope, and the dignity and individuality of man. This idea in its essence is the philosophy of humanism in architecture. We must strive to enhance life through beauty and delight, and reflect the nobility to which man aspires. We must provide—through order—a background of serenity for today's feverish activity, and scale architecture to frame man happily in his environment. Finally, we must be truthful in expression of structure and purpose, and advance today's industrialized technology for the benefit of society.

"Many of the qualities basic to older architectures—good proportion, elegance of detail and nobility—exist in distinguished, historic European buildings. These qualities must be translated into our idiom, and we can be inspired by and learn much from European examples. However, in the understanding of serenity and scale, I believe we must turn to Japanese architecture. I am aware of the impracticality of trying to house twentieth-century civilization within the framework of traditional Japanese architecture. Its materials, scale, and structure are inappropriate for the demands of our time, and the discipline of total simplicity would be impossible for us. Yet the complete emotional satisfaction of my many experiences in Japanese architecture convinces me that there is a great deal we can learn there.

"The chaos brought on by political turmoil, mobility, the population explosion, and by the tremendous impact of the machine, demands that man—if he is to retain his sanity—must have a serene environment. But with serenity we must have delight —the delight of the interesting silhouettes, of waterplay, of variety in outdoor and indoor spatial experience. But serenity, the physical manifestation of the belief that man can live in quiet dignity, must unify the whole.

"There are other qualities which we need, such as excitement— but excitement is fragmentary, and the basic qualities of architecture must be more encompassing and enduring. We may be enthralled by the excitement of Broadway or the Ginza at night, but we can hardly aspire to these as a permanent diet.

McGregor Memorial Conference Center (right)
College of Education Building (center),
Wayne State University, Detroit, Michigan.

Reynolds Metals Office Building, Detroit, Michigan.

"The understanding of scale in our buildings which will enable man to live proudly and make him feel that he is in touch with his surroundings—a kind of over-all security—is much more difficult to pinpoint. Yet the experience of buildings such as those in Japan where this is true should assure us that it is possible to translate this quality in our environment in our own terms."

Called a romantic, Yamasaki is frequently categorized with Stone for his supposed neoclassic predilections. Though their aims have a similarity, their architecture has distinct differences. Where Stone's buildings have a formal dignity and relaxed repose, Yamasaki's have a casual, almost nervous animation. Stone's architecture is more akin to the classic in spirit, with economy valued above profusion, restraint above license, and the system of construction and structural technique subordinate to formal perfection and an ideal of beauty. Yamasaki's architecture is closer in spirit to the Gothic for more fundamental reasons than just his liking for pointed arches. Structure particularly, and the emphasis on construction, are his most powerful design themes, and he uses them to dramatize and achieve certain aesthetic ends that at times are clearly more important than the nature of the structure itself. He usually emphasizes the slenderness of structural elements, making them stand alone by contrasting them to areas of glass. Spatial excitement derives from the contrast of small to large, enclosed to open, light to dark—a drama extending even to a lively silhouette.

The pleasure in architecture for Yamasaki is discovering a specific concept. This was Saarinen's concern too. "If you can find the concept which is appropriate to a particular problem, then you can devise an architecture appropriate for it," he says.

Yamasaki's concept for the McGregor Memorial Conference Center for the Detroit campus of Wayne State University, completed in 1958, was that the building should be a gateway and communication point between the city and the university. A two-story central gallery, glazed at the ends and with a skylight above, divides the building. From this conservatory-like lobby it is a short flight to the conference rooms lining either side. The folded concrete slab structure is expressed, tooth-like, both inside and and out, with its geometry echoed in the skylight. From the gallery is viewed a fine garden-pool, a welcome oasis on a drab campus. This was Yamasaki's first project after his trip around the world.

Yamasaki had seen Stone's United States Embassy in New Delhi and was very impressed. In Detroit in 1959, for the Reynolds Metal Company Building, he, too, used an exterior grille as a sunscreen, behind which were metal walkway, window-cleaning platforms; but here Yamasaki used gold-anodized aluminum. He was criticized for the screen's "costume jewelry" effect, but was justifiably applauded for the interior arrangement: two levels of office space wrapped around a skylighted, central well area. The lobby and display floor is a raised podium surrounded by a reflecting pool and approached across an entrance bridge. It is an island of retreat in a bleak, asphalt landscape.

Yamasaki's second building for Wayne, the College of Education Building in 1960, is across the street from the McGregor Center. Its exterior effect is derived from a precast concrete, non-structural facade of rows of pointed arches. He himself passed the harshest judgment on this building: on presenting the model to

Reynolds Metals Office Building.

the Wayne Board of Governors, he then produced a small, wedding-cake bride and groom which he placed on top.

The exploitation of structure for aesthetic effect, still using pointed arches, was explored by Yamasaki in a series of buildings in the 1960's. The United States Science Pavilion, for the Seattle World's Fair of 1962, had a fretwork of arches, described by its critics as mere artistic caprice—a mass-produced facade in the Gothic idiom, without the Gothic logic. Having a central courtyard with a pool and fountains, it was a pleasant place of refuge and rest for weary visitors, and the most popular building at the exposition. The soaring entrance court of Yamasaki's Pahlavi University, in Iran, has Gothic arches developed from the more gossamer-like ones of the Fair. Here, the proposed master plan shows his continued interest in using water to good effect, and creating pleasant places. The Civil Air Terminal, in Dhahran, Saudi Arabia, was constructed of precast columns that spread outwards to form the roof structure, shaped as segments of a Moorish arch. A narrow strip of glass separates precast infilling panels, with stiffening ribs reminiscent of traditional Arab forms, from the structure.

In the North Western National Life Insurance Company Building in Minneapolis, Yamasaki's columns form a monumental portico, eighty feet high, as a noble entrance to the building and as an approach to a park beyond. Here, a narrow band of gray glass, revealing the interior floor levels, separates the dark green, marble infilling panels from the structure of white columns. The sanctuary of the Synagogue at Glencoe, Illinois, is formed by sixteen fan vault shells that are expressed both inside and out—unlike a Gothic fan vault, which was covered externally by a pitch roof. The vaulted forms have a double glazing of translucent amber glass in their interstices that allows a rich muted light to enter the space.

Yamasaki notes that his is an old form used in a new way—a way that was not possible before—and insists that we should not be inhibited about learning from history. "I would argue against the frantic search for new forms, a search that avoids any form done in the past. If we avoid the use of Roman or Gothic arches, for instance, we are denying ourselves two of the most logical and beautiful means of construction available. Actually, these forms are better done in concrete than in stone. I hope of my buildings no one will say: 'It could have been done fifty years ago.' I think you can choose from the entire palette of forms as long as you have that rule."

The twenty-eight-story white tower for the Michigan Consolidated Gas Company, Yamasaki's first high-rise structure, is a building of distinction for a utility company that has injected much-needed inspiration into the rather drab skyline of Detroit's Civic Center. The facade is a series of precast concrete sections between columns. For Yamasaki, this represents a movement away from the machine monotony of the conventional curtain wall towards the more three-dimensional possibilities of richer shadow effects, and a functional yet "mechanically-produced ornament." The hexagonal windows are floor to ceiling—"in a high building it is terribly important to keep the sill as low as possible so that those at the farther end of a room can see what goes on." But while their narrow width of twenty inches prevents the feeling of acrophobia, it also tends to limit views outwards. Yamasaki has gone to great lengths to ensure that the noble

Federal Science Pavilion, Seattle, Washington.

Temple Building, North Shore Congregation Israel, Glencoe, Illinois.

Pahlavi University, Shiraz, Iran.

North Western National Life Insurance Company Building, Minneapolis, Minnesota.

Dhahran Air Terminal, Dhahran, Saudi Arabia.

Woodrow Wilson School, Princeton University, Princeton, New Jersey.

I.B.M. Office Building, Seattle, Washington.

twenty-five foot entrance lobby is elegant in material and detail. A clever arrangement of tiny suspended lights gives it a delicate, almost unreal, nighttime brilliance. Yamasaki's attention to detail is evident when close to or inside the building, but from a distance, as in the Reynolds Aluminum Building, the small detail of the facade is lost. Instead of the vertical mullions, the marble-clad columns and the horizontal spandrels become dominant.

Yamasaki's nineteen-story I.B.M. office building in Seattle is an extremely refined addition to a new trend in American skyscraper design—the external bearing wall. The "wall" is comprised of high-strength steel pipes, four-and-a-half inches in diameter, encased in precast concrete and spaced at twenty-eight inch centers. The floor slab spans clear from these to the central circulation and service core, providing open office floors, free of columns. By keeping the spandrels at the same plane as that of the gray-tinted glass, the vertical lines of the building are strongly expressed. Although slightly smaller, this building resolves many of the visual problems of the Michigan Tower. It is more direct in design concept, simpler in structure, construction and detail, and gains from a clear termination against the sky. The structure meets the plaza level via marble-clad steel arches in a way that, at the corners, almost dares you to breathe.

Faced with the predominantly Gothic flavor of the campus of Princeton University, Yamasaki designed a rather restrained, more classic structure—similar in spirit to the I.B.M. Building—for the new Woodrow Wilson School of Public and International Affairs. The faculty offices are in a sandwich-like structure, spanning the full ninety feet, which forms a strong cornice to the building. They are carried on sixty columns that form a twenty-eight-foot-high colonnade around the entire building. The lofty first floor is devoted to a library with a double mezzanine on one side of the skylighted entrance lounge, and an auditorium and dining room for two hundred on the other side. A below-grade floor accommodates the small conference and seminar rooms, and service areas. The structural scheme allows non-bearing walls for the ground floor, with the exception of those around stair and elevator cores which provide lateral stiffness. Yamasaki believes this to be the first time that such a structural scheme has been used.

A large proportion of Yamasaki's staff of seventy are designers who seem to be continuously making, dismantling and reassembling beautifully-executed study models. Yamasaki does not like to take on more than four or five commissions at once, so that he can devote his full attention to all aspects of each project. From his early office experience he is conscious of the need to carry a project through as a totally integrated product, considering all aspects from the outset. Yamasaki has his own mechanical and electrical engineers in the office, and constantly uses John Skilling, of Seattle, as his structural consultant, to whom he readily acknowledges a great debt.

"I like to make a column the exact size it needs to be and the correct structural form to perform its function." But Yamasaki's concern for richness in architecture has led him to take excessive liberties in exaggerating structure for pure effect. He has been called a "cosmetician" and "exterior decorator," and even he has said: "My colleagues and I have built some rather shallow things." Yamasaki continually criticizes his work, often rather disarmingly during his public lectures. In his recent designs he has been

Michigan Consolidated Gas Company, Detroit, Michigan.

more wary of "effect," and has placed greater emphasis on more disciplined design and an honest use of structure.

Yamasaki's commission to design the World Trade Center, with the New York firm of Emery Roth and Sons who are producing the working drawings, may prove as significant for him as it inevitably must for New York. To be located on Manhattan's Lower West Side, it will house anyone and anything connected with world trade. The program presented to Yamasaki, who was selected over a dozen other American architects, was quite explicit: twelve million square feet of floor area on a sixteen acre site, which also had to accommodate new facilities for the Hudson tubes and subway connections—all with a budget of under $500 million. The vast space needs and limited site immediately implied a high-rise development that will make the adjacent drama of Manhattan's business tip seem timid in comparison. It also raises all the old questions of concentration—is it just too big? Can the city cope with the ensuing congestion?

After studying more than one hundred schemes in model form, Yamasaki decided on a two-tower development to contain the nine million square feet of office space. One tower became unreasonable in size and unwieldy structurally, yet several towers became too approximate for their size and "looked too much like a housing project"; whereas two towers gave a reasonable office area on each floor, took advantage of the magnificent views, and allowed a manageable structural system. The twin towers, with 110 floors rising 1,353 feet, will be the tallest in the world. From observation decks at the top of the towers it will be possible to see for forty-five miles in every direction. Apart from sheer height, the visual impact on the skyline of twin towers, on what is essentially a one-towered island, will make them really count. One distinct advantage of the project's enormity is the architectural opportunity to advance the art of building. Yamasaki reexamined the skyscraper from first principles, considering no ground so hallowed that it could not be questioned, especially in view of the potential of modern technology. The usual economic prohibition on "custom-made" was out, as virtually anything made for the Center would automatically become a stock item. "Economy is not in the sparseness of materials that we use," said Yamasaki of his $350 million estimated cost, "but in the advancement of technology, which is the real challenge."

The structural system, deriving from the I.B.M. Building in Seattle, is impressively simple. The 208-foot wide facade is, in effect, a prefabricated steel lattice, with columns on 39-inch centers acting as wind bracing to resist all overturning forces; the central core takes only the gravity loads of the building. A very light, economical structure results by keeping the wind bracing in the most efficient place, the outside surface of the building, thus not transferring the forces through the floor membrane to the core, as in most curtain-wall structures. Office spaces will have no interior columns. In the upper floors there is as much as 40,000 square feet of office space per floor. The floor construction is of prefabricated trussed steel, only 33 inches in depth, that spans the full 60 feet to the core, and also acts as a diaphragm to stiffen the outside wall against lateral buckling forces from windload pressures.

The other primary obstacle to be overcome in the skyscraper is the elevator system, and Yamasaki has shown himself equally imaginative here. A combination of express and local elevator banks, called a skylobby system, it is particularly efficient because it requires fewer elevator shafts—thus freeing approximately 75 per cent of the total floor area for occupancy; had a conventional elevator arrangement been adopted, only approximately 50 per cent would have been available. The building has three vertical zones; express elevators serve skylobbies at the forty-first and seventy-fourth floors; from these, and from the plaza level, four banks of local elevators carry passengers to each of the three zones.

From the outset, Yamasaki believed that there should be an open plaza from which one could appreciate the scale of the towers upon approach. There is little or no sense of scale, for instance, standing at the base of the Empire State Building. Yamasaki's plaza will be sheltered from the river winds and contained by five-story buildings which will house shops, exhibition pavilions and a 250-room hotel. This lively area will wrap around the base of the towers, hopefully to be used for international festivals and a gathering place. Despite its huge size of 450 by 300 feet, it should have an active atmosphere, judging by the buildings' projected working population of 50,000 and the more than 100,000 persons who will pass through the space each day.

Yamasaki has responded to the initial design challenge with economy, quality, and a direct inventiveness. To maintain a design standard through the myriad of details will be formidable in the extreme. On Yamasaki's side is his single-minded optimism—the optimism of the Manhattan skyline. "The World Trade Center should," he said, "because of its importance, become a living representation of man's belief in humanity, his need for individual dignity, his belief in the co-operation of men, and through this co-operation his ability to find greatness."

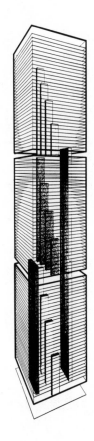

World Trade Center, New York, N. Y.

WALTER GROPIUS

Where artistic and architectural expression has attained a comparatively full revelation, there has usually been a consensus of opinion on certain principles, and a hierarchy of values which have had the patronage of leaders whose authority produced action. In Greece, Pericles summoned the resources of the Golden Age to erect the Parthenon. The mid-twentieth century artist and architect, however, does not have such a synthesis; in a constructive sense he is seeking a tradition, even a role in society, and presented with the average citizen of inconclusive opinions, the means of implementing his ideas.

What seemed a unified effort in the early heroic days of modern architecture has become apparent as a series of diverse interests. Originally it was a fight against outmoded ideas to establish a whole comprehensive body of relevant formal, technical and social ideas—but these ideas no longer *appear* to be at stake.

Wright, Mies and Le Corbusier have pursued personal visions that begin to show our possibilities and point towards the formulation of a meaningful vocabulary for our age. With them, Walter Gropius is recognized as one of the great pioneers of modern architecture, for his parallel roles of educator, critic and designer. Mies and Gropius have both tried to establish a common denominator of expression, appropriate to the spirit of a technical age. But where Mies has tried to show *a* way, Gropius has sought for a more flexible approach based on creative teamwork.

Central to his approach has been a search to appreciate, both as a human and industrial equation, the specific as it relates to the larger context: the individual as part of the collective, where the very complexities of our social circumstance imply collaboration and common method; the elements of industry, the products of the great power of mass production, assembled to form the machinery of our world. The circumstance where one individual creates one object is becoming rarer; in industry it almost never occurs. An individual, however, can still control the design of an object without designing all its individual parts, or being deeply involved in each of its design processes.

If some architects are not particularly enamored of Gropius's conclusions, they must credit him with trying to explore the truly important issues, and the methods to tackle them. The idea of uniting art and technology within the social context of our daily

"Werkbund" Exhibition, Cologne, Germany.

Fagus Works, Alfeld, Germany.

lives has remained his central theme. It is one that is fundamental to the ideals of the modern movement.

Gropius believes that group consciousness can be the means for developing the tradition and continuity that he considers the precondition for cultural growth. "It is true that the creative spark originates always with the individual, but by working in close collaboration with others toward a common aim, he will attain greater heights of achievement through the stimulation and challenging critique of his teammates, than by living in an ivory tower," says Gropius. "Synchronizing all individual efforts by a continual give and take of its members the team can raise its integrated work to higher potentials than is represented by the sum of the work of just so many individuals." For such teamwork to be effective Gropius believes that it requires: an unprejudiced state of mind; a belief that the team benefits from the different pursuits, interests and reactions of other members during group meetings; and, voluntary participation growing out of mutual respect and liking, with individual leadership and responsibility to maintain artistic integrity.

To safeguard design coherence Gropius says that final decisions, after support and criticism, must be left to the member in charge of a specific job. The idea of teamwork as a group of architects simultaneously trying feverishly to design a building is quite misconstrued. To be effective a design team must obviously have a framework of reference, certain common or related patterns of thought and action that are compatible, whereby diverse minds share a certain mutual understanding. Then, believes Gropius, the collective personality can, like that of the individual, be clearly sensed.

Where Mies has established a team in the sense that his office understands his method of problem resolution and objectives clearly, and reacts as a homogenous unit, Gropius has tried to establish a broader and more diverse basis for collaboration, not only between architects but also artists, technical experts and so on. With his advocation of teamwork Gropius has taken a stand on one of the greatest dilemmas facing the architectural profession today: how to relate the creative act, which almost of necessity remains, at least at the very initial and vital design stages, an individual and to a certain extent a private process, to the collective effort that seems implied if our real challenges are ever to be tackled realistically.

Gropius's emphasis on collaboration extends to building procedures and techniques. "Architects in the future will refuse to be restrained from a natural urge to take actual part in a team effort with the industry to produce buildings and their parts." He indicates that the twofold task for the younger-generation architect is: "To join the building industry and to take active part in developing and forming all those component parts for buildings; and to learn how to compose beautiful buildings from these industrialized parts."

Too often the emphasis on industrial standardization is presented as a fracture between those architects who are interested in the specific building, who are design rather than socially conscious, and those who are interested in system building, who are socially responsible but unconcerned with design. This is a distorted view. "Design," "system," "social responsiveness" and so on, can co-exist if we really want them to. Gropius's direction is more towards shop-production and site-assembly, recognizing that man will always rebel at an over-mechanization that is contrary to life. His ideas of prefabrication appropriately emphasize that total prefabrication, the monotonous mass production of whole house types that would inevitably result in exclusive systems of building, is to be avoided. Instead there should be a standardized mass production of component parts that can be assembled into units giving the architect the maximum functional and aesthetic flexibility in responding to the needs of a particular building. Technical ingenuity alone, or "instant houses," would produce rigid responses to particular problems.

The real dilemma here is that there must be a more directed industrial production initially, as Gropius has advocated, if industry is to produce the right type of simple components. Charles Eames's own house, constructed from component parts available in standard manufacturers' catalogs, shows the possibilities of the "assembled" approach. The Eames's house, however, had to be assembled in such particularly designed and modified ways—precisely because of the lack of collaboration between industry

Bauhaus Building, Dessau, Germany.

Gropius House, Bauhaus, Dessau, Germany.

China set, Bauhaus.

and architecture—that construction costs were inevitably greatly increased. It is well to remember that industry rarely distinguishes between what is simple and beautiful, and what is simple and ugly. It remains, still, for the architect to work closer with industry, without being subject to restrictive pressure. If industry is to offer products on a take-it-or-leave-it basis, the architect's flexibility will most certainly continue to be impaired.

Flexibility is probably the key. Because assuming components themselves are well-conceived, details and elements must always be an integral part of a complete, unified architectural statement. It is an extremely difficult problem because, as Gropius explained three decades ago, we must combine the greatest possible standardization with the greatest possible versatility.

The architect, as designer, has not only been separated from industrial methods and factory production, but also from contact with contractors and therefore the actual process of building. Gropius saw the need for closer ties, but they have not developed. The widening gap between architect, builder and manufacturer has resulted in high costs for unfamiliar methods of building, lack of communication and acquisition of new skills within each group, and lack of organization method to respond to the quickening rate of technical advance. Gropius sees the architect as the natural leader to coordinate the building process, but he would probably be the first to acknowledge that such leadership must be the reward for the greatest capability. To use technology more effectively implies a closer organization and relationship between architect, builder and industry, with method and technique implemented at a much greater scale than at present. Then, too, industrialized building methods and procedures cannot effectively be grafted onto a building industry that is structured to meet traditional tasks. The dilemma revolves around what is almost the cliché theme of our time: it is not science and the machine that are destroying the quality of our life, but our inability to direct their products. The collaboration that Gropius has long advocated seems ever necessary.

Walter Gropius was born in Berlin in 1883. After studying architecture in Berlin and Munich, and working as chief draftsman for Peter Behrens from 1908 to 1910, he opened his own office. His first large commission was the Fagus Works, a shoe-last factory near Alfeld, Germany, which he designed in collaboration with the architect Adolph Meyer in 1911. Brick columns and steel beams supported floors that were kept back from a "taut" glass facade. Instead of the traditional manner of meeting a solid column, the glass curtainwall turned the corner giving the building a great sense of transparency and lightness.

At the 1914 Cologne Exhibition, the Fabrik model factory and office building for the Deutscher Werkbund, a group interested in the design of machine-made products, was another tour de force for Gropius and Meyer. Spiral staircases were sheathed in a glass membrane that continued directly into the curtain-wall facade of the rectangular building. Emphasis on an analysis of function and the purifying role of rationalization motivated the approach in these designs. Although they established Gropius's reputation, they were still isolated and visionary achievements in German architecture.

Berlin-Siemensstadt, Berlin, Germany.

Project for a Total Theater.

However significant these buildings might have been in the evolution of modern architecture, their influence cannot compare with what history may well record as Gropius's greatest achievement —an educational center. In a Germany recently fled by its Kaiser, where the social, political and economic order had just collapsed, a country where art was preoccupied with the romantic, mystical overtones of Expressionism, Gropius sought a new way ahead. Possibly sensing a fresh stirring in cultural interests, in 1919 he united the schools of design and fine arts at Weimar, to form the Bauhaus. He directed the school's activities until 1928, assembling a faculty of outstanding talents that included Itten, Feininger, Klee, Schlemmer, Kandinsky, L. Moholy-Nagy, Albers, Bayer and Breuer. Gropius had the courage and vision to bring together, in a state institution, men who were then radicals, and who are now acknowledged as among the finest artists of their time.

The Bauhaus however was more than a roster of impressive talents. Gropius had recognized the student's need for contact with creative and enthusiastic minds, actively and passionately involved in their work, to help develop what is a basic requisite in a creative person—the capacity for growth through stimulation and curiosity. There is nothing so contagious in any time. Although architecture was never a full curriculum at the Bauhaus, Gropius emphasized that the building was the final objective of a universal design for action, rooted in sound principles and values. In trying to bring art and science together the Bauhaus developed what is probably the only comprehensive set of principles between the Beaux Arts and our own educational system today.

Gropius House, Lincoln, Massachusetts.

"The Bauhaus was not an institution with a clear program—it was an idea and Gropius formulated this idea with great precision. He said, 'Art and technology—the new unity.' He wanted to have painting, sculpture, theater and even ballet on the one hand, and on the other, weaving, photography, furniture—everything from the coffee cup to city planning," said Mies at Gropius's seventieth birthday luncheon in Chicago, in 1953. "The fact that it was an idea, I think, is the cause of this enormous influence the Bauhaus had on any progressive school around the globe. You cannot do that with organization, you cannot do that with propaganda. Only an idea spreads so far."

Gropius saw the schism between process and production, between the skilled designer and machine production that, although it was killing off the traditional individual craftsman, held the promise of a new way of life. Art and technology . . . the unity of art, machine and life . . . a synthesis of the mastery of form, space and skill of hand . . . a unity of discipline, a stimulating moral force towards a common goal. Principles, simultaneously aesthetic and moral in implication, that, from the coffee cup to the city plan, projected the image of a new way of living. The machine and industry implied that, through the medium of teamwork, there could be found new forms from new problems, techniques and materials, free of any preconceived ideas about form.

Gropius started workshops to ensure the understanding and development of practical skills in students, while freeing them from the isolation of paper design and giving them a direct feeling for form as it derives from material. Gropius also recognized that even if the aspects of art that are dependent upon the skill of the individual or the inspiration of the creative act could not be directly imparted to students, certain principles could; sound theoretical instruction in the laws of design of universal validity, since they derive from the laws of nature and the psychology of man. What the Bauhaus examined was not a romantic world of the machine—the illusionary world of Wright—rather, it attempted to face the realities of industrialization in terms of planning, architecture and design, and the psychological needs of people.

Gropius has designed most of his buildings as collaborative ventures. But in 1926, when faced with the antagonisms of reactionaries in Weimer he moved the Bauhaus to a new and intended permanent home in Dessau, he designed the complex alone. It is generally recognized as one of the most important buildings of the 1920's and a seminal building in the evolution of modern architecture. Giedion wrote that it "was the only large building of its date which was so complete a crystallization of the new space conception." The building's complex spaces were contained in three centrally-connected hooked arms, shaped like a pinwheel. Elements were grouped functionally and distinctly from each other, connected by overhead links. It was an asymmetrically balanced composition where interpenetrating volumes, to be appreciated from many vantage points, formed an architectural unit. The fragmented experience recorded by Cubist painters on their canvases, Gropius had achieved as a continuous, moving architectural experience. A reinforced concrete skeleton behind horizontal ribbons and planes of solid and glass—machined, transparent, hovering, a cool functionalism, it marked the emergence of what became labelled as the International Style.

The freshness of Gropius's vision was equally evident in the small faculty houses at Dessau. Their somewhat complex constructional image expressed a synthesis of function and space as much humanly as technically determined, where, for example, openings in the external wall were a direct expression of the functional dispositions and needs within.

What the Bauhaus looked for, said Gropius, "was a new approach, not a new style. A style is a successive repetition of an expression which has become settled already as a common denominator for a whole period. But the attempt to classify and thereby to freeze living art and architecture, while it is still in the formative stage, into a 'style' or 'ism' is more likely to stifle than to stimulate creative activity"—a point that many of art's "publicists" could well take today. Yet the creation of a style is precisely what the Bauhaus is presently accused of. "I realize that I am a figure covered with labels, maybe to the point of obscurity," said Gropius. "Names like Bauhaus Style, International Style, Functional Style have almost succeeded in hiding the human core behind it all." It is rather sad that Gropius feels the need to defend the Bauhaus today:—about as necessary as having to defend motherhood. Writing about Gropius, James Marston Fitch said: "Whenever any group of men agree upon a common method of accomplishing common tasks, a common system of expression (i.e., a style) will ultimately appear. Ours is the first period in history which this cultural certainty has embarrassed."

"You know that I, for my part, have always been identified since the early 1920's with the idea of 'functionalism' as the only straight and narrow line to take us into the future. But in the interpretation of those with only sectorially-developed minds, this line had become indeed so 'straight and narrow' that it led straight into a dead end. Its original complexity and psychological implications, as we developed them in the Bauhaus, were forgotten, and it was decried as a simple-minded, purely utilitarian approach

Harvard Graduate Center, Cambridge, Massachusetts.

U. S. Embassy, Athens, Greece.

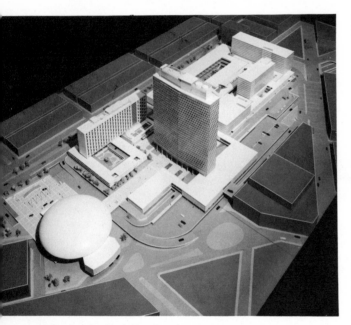

Project for Back Bay Development, Boston, Massachusetts.

to design, devoid of any imagination that would give grace and beauty to life. To this I can only say: The revolution of the 1920's was total and moral, and its creators looked at beauty not as something self-consciously 'added on,' but as something that was believed to be inherent in the vitality, appropriateness, and psychological significance of a designed object, whether it was a building, a piece of furniture or a stage design. We knew and taught that space relations, proportions and colors control psychological functions that are as vital and real as any performance data for structural and mechanical parts and for the use-value of a plan. If our early attempts looked somewhat stark and sparse, it is because we had just found a new vocabulary in which to speak out, and this we wanted to set in the greatest possible contrast to the overstuffed bombast that had gone before. Besides, we were often held down to a minimum of expenditure by a public which could be sold on modern architecture only when it promised to be cheaper, because it did not yet recognize its aesthetic qualities.

"As the evolution of form develops always in successive waves of reactions against preceding trends, it is only natural that these early testimonies to a newly-found freedom in architectural design have been followed by a wealth of new conceptions and refinements in the field of space relations and in the use of new techniques. If one compares the typical architecture of the 1920's with that of today, the most significant development lies in the increasing accentuation of three-dimensional plasticity. Structural boniness, curved shells, recessed and protruding building parts offer a rich play of light and shadow absent from the surfaces of the curtain wall, which for so long has become the one-sided trademark of modern architecture. Personal interpretations of these fresh experiences have enriched our vocabulary and pleased our audience, and the stage seems to be set for a major contribution to the evolving image of our time ... if we could only keep from straying into a new eclecticism or from adopting a sort of super-functionalism that borders on mysticism. Curiously, nothing seems harder to achieve right now than a sober, straightforward, balanced approach which would allow us to solve our design problems without bending over backwards too far in our desire to include all possible tricks of a scholarly or a technical nature which are at our disposal today."

Apart from Gropius's emphasis on teamwork and industrial production, four other general points emerged from the Bauhaus that seem particularly pertinent today.

First, visual education. It sought to put visual education on a broader and more contemporary basis and, through a more profound visual training, to heighten perception. Said Gropius: "A society such as ours, which has conferred equal privileges on everybody, will have to acknowledge its duty to activate the general responsiveness to spiritual and aesthetic values, to intensify the development of everybody's imaginative faculties. Only this can create the basis from which eventually the creative act of the artist can rise, not as an isolated phenomenon, ignored and rejected by the crowd, but firmly embedded in a network of public response and understanding." This is an initiation that Sir Herbert Read refers to as demanding vision—where vision means insight into the process of life. Said Gropius: "Considering the reservoir of rich talent and the wealth of technical and financial resources available today, it would seem that this generation holds all the aces in the age-old game of creating architectural form symbols for the ideas by which a society lives. Only a magic catalyst seems to be needed to combine these forces and free them from isolation. I personally see this catalyst in the power of education; education to raise the expectations and demands a people make on their own form of living, education to waken and sharpen their latent capacities for creation and for co-operation. Creativity of the makers needs the response of all the users."

Second, directness. Gropius called for directness in solving problems, which he described as "the attitude of a man who has been able to empty his mind of prejudice and all non-essential considerations and has thereby arrived at a state of new innocence which allows him to penetrate to the very core of his task." Complete detachment is obviously an impossibility. What Gropius referred to is the state of mind that great artists like Klee and Miro have achieved, allowing them a new, essential vision.

Third, method. "In architectural education the teaching of a method of approach is more important than the teaching of skills," Gropius says. "In an age of specialization, method is more important than information." In an automated age that is intriguing, and to many, foreboding, an age that to the political philosopher Raymond Aron calls for "the acceptance of instability," method seems more important than ever. Recently, A. C. Montieth of Westinghouse Electric stated that half of what an engineer now knows will be obsolete in ten years, and half of what he will need to know in ten years is not available today. A. N. Whitehead has written: "The fixed person for the fixed duties, who in older societies was such a godsend, in the future will be a public danger."

Lastly, the comprehensive vision. It was no accident that the Bauhaus integrated and coordinated the efforts of many disciplines. Gropius considered this interdependence of creative man, the con-

*Pan American World Airways Building,
New York, N. Y.*

centric rather than the sectional view, as the means to realizing an integrated society. He saw an increasing specialization impairing the ability to give direction to conflicting tendencies. People working in the artistic and scientific fields today realize that there is a crisis in communication, caused by the fragmentation of experience and dispersal of knowledge into self-contained—if not self-sufficient—disciplines, each developing increasingly private terms of reference. If our achievements are ever to match our opportunities we desperately need means of communication that offer us a sense of the essential structure between and within various disciplines. In the end most creative thought is dependent upon a general, clear and coherent vision. As Gropius said, it is not necessary to have the knowledge of a specialist in different fields, but it is necessary to reach a general level of competence in understanding them.

Gropius's ideal of the integrated society and the man who can visualize things as an entity may well be a mythical one. Like the unprejudiced mind, it is an elusive goal but an excellent aspiration, providing it does not impair the precise, pragmatic response essential to action in our fragmented society. The importance of the comprehensive vision is that it represents a very healthy catholic attitude of mind towards art in the broadest sense, and life. An attitude where the criterion is the achievement of something good, or the excellence of something supremely good. This remains the best extension of personality, and fulfillment, possible to man.

Gropius resigned as the director of the Bauhaus in 1928 to devote his time to practicing architecture; also, he felt that much of the enmity against the school was directed at him personally. Mies became the Principal in 1930, and remained to close the Bauhaus in 1933. Adding pitched roofs and other adornments, the Nazis sought, Canute-like, to "mask" the building. Their motivation was probably more to eradicate the implication of a way of life that the Bauhaus symbolized, rather than the stylistic tendencies themselves.

The penetration of Gropius's analytical approach to architecture combined with his perceptive vision are very evident in his thoughts for the Total Theater in 1926. There are three basic stage forms: the arena, encircled by spectators; the Greek theater with its stage projecting into the audience, with an arch of spectators; and the Renaissance open proscenium, where stage and spectators are apart. In the Total Theater Gropius tried to synthesize the advantages of each into one theater volume.

Gropius wrote: "The task of the theater architect today, as I see it, is to create a great and flexible instrument which can respond in terms of light and space to every requirement of the theater producer: an instrument so impersonal that it never restrains him from giving his vision and imagination full play, and a building whose spatial treatment lifts and refreshes the human spirit . . . I have tried to create an instrument so flexible that a director can employ any one of the three stage forms by the use of simple, ingenious mechanisms . . . the aim of this theater is not to assemble a number of ingenious devices. All of these are merely means to attain the supreme goal—to draw the spectator into the drama. . . . An audience will shake off its inertia when it experiences the surprise effect of space transformed. By shifting the scene of action during the performance from one stage position to another and by using a system of spotlights and film projectors, transforming walls and ceiling into moving picture scenes, the whole house would be animated by three-dimensional means instead of the 'flat' picture effect of the customary stage. This would also greatly reduce the cumbersome paraphernalia of properties and painted backdrops. Thus the playhouse itself, made to dissolve into the shifting, illusionary space of the imagination, would become the scene of action itself. Such a theater would stimulate the conception and fantasy of playwright and stage director alike; for if it is true that the mind can transform the body, it is equally true that structure can transform the mind."

Having left the Bauhaus, Gropius focused his attention on the problems of high-density housing in such projects as the Berlin-Siemensstadt in 1929. If his analysis and proposals based on the rationale of such calculations as sun and light angles seem rigid and inadequate today, it is well to recall the conditions to which they were a reaction.

In 1934, faced by the rapidly deteriorating situation that was soon to plunge Europe into its darkest hours, Gropius moved to England, where he formed a partnership with Maxwell Fry.

In 1937 a new chapter in Gropius's life began when he was invited to Harvard University. A year later he became Chairman of the Department of Architecture, a position he held for fifteen years. It would be impossible to assess the revitalizing influence on American architecture of those years; it is sufficient to remember the number of today's leading architects who were students there.

The educational structure of the Graduate School of Design was different from that of the Bauhaus, but this did not require any

University of Baghdad, Baghdad, Iraq.

change of emphasis in Gropius's basic approach—one of principles. He quickly clarified his position: "My intention is not to introduce, so to speak, a cut-and-dried 'Modern Style' from Europe, but rather to introduce a method of approach which allows one to tackle a problem according to its peculiar conditions." He also expressed his sentiments on the functionalism label: "Functionalism has to do not only with material things, there has always been a psychological side as well. Architecture starts beyond all practicalities. The prerequisites of the building have to be there. That is engineering. Architecture begins where engineering ends."

Gropius quickly added Breuer to his faculty, and in partnership they designed several fine country houses for the Boston area, including Gropius's own house in Lincoln, Massachusetts, in 1938. Here, the main volume remained an interpenetration of solids and voids similar to his European work, but was constructed of wood, although with vertical weatherboarding rather than the local tradition of horizontal clapboards. The screened porch, a traditional feature of the American house, became a dining extension of the living room. Built unobtrusively on a gentle slope, and looking out over the countryside from large openings and a roof terrace, it is easy to imagine the excitement that the first "modern house" in the vicinity of Boston must have caused. The Chamberlain cottage in nearby Wayland, in 1939, was one of the most modest and charming of the houses in collaboration with Breuer, whose design influence is very clear here.

In 1945 Gropius, with Norman and Jean Fletcher, John and Sarah Harkness, Robert McMillan, Louis McMillen, and Benjamin Thompson, formed The Architects Collaborative. The original association of eight architects, presiding over a staff of nearly a hundred, remained intact until the death of Jean Fletcher and the resignation of Benjamin Thompson in 1965. They were primarily a Harvard- and Yale-trained group, some Gropius's own students, who saw validity in a teamwork approach to architecture; they interested Gropius in establishing a group with a freer association, a few months after he had disbanded his office with Breuer. T.A.C. has not taken an esoteric approach to architecture; it has designed many buildings and tried to deal with very real problems. Since it is concerned with the social environment behind architecture, it has attracted clients for housing and educational buildings in particular.

Gropius has had to assume a major role in T.A.C.'s most important and challenging projects: the Harvard Graduate Center in 1949, where a series of individual brick dormitories, linked by covered walks, formed quadrangles that sought to conform to the spatial sequence and scale of Harvard Yard; a proposal for a new Civic Center for Boston designed in 1953, with Belluschi, Bogner, Koch and Stubbins; the United States Embassy, in Athens, 1961; the Pan American office building, in New York, in 1963, where Belluschi was also a design consultant to the architects, Emery Roth and Sons. And, on the banks of the Tigris, designed in 1959 and under construction for two years, the University of Baghdad —where the basic concept, explains Gropius, "has been the balance of unity and diversity, of integration and differentiation." Several rows of irregularly zigzagging dikes, about 10 feet high, are a distinctive feature of an otherwise level site. These dikes create a series of terraces to a main plaza, around which teaching and administrative facilities will be grouped, with various views of buildings and landscape. Buildings will be air-conditioned to counteract the excessive heat and tightly grouped to provide shade and to facilitate travel between each, creating various sheltered patios landscaped with plants and fountains.

We build on the legacy of a preceding generation, cognizant of the significance and essence of our own—only then can our contribution be valid. Wright died in 1959, Le Corbusier in 1965, and Gropius and Mies were both born in the 1880's. They not only did much to create our legacy, they also had the difficult and historically novel circumstance of living to build on it. To combine the difficult roles of pioneers and contemporaries they defined their themes in their early years and carried them forward with conviction.

If many lessons of the Bauhaus still seem valid, in retrospect we can see that action must be of a different magnitude and emphasis if it is to be effectual today. Our extraordinary advances in science, technology and industrialization could not have been anticipated then; nor could our rate of urbanization, consumption of the natural landscape, population mobility and expansion have been fully grasped. The Futurists bestowed a certain mythos on the machine which they regarded as a poetic life-force. The Bauhaus saw it as a challenge, a stimulating one of moral implication requiring a social awareness and direction of its energies. Our machine age of automation, electronics, new system and communication controls, and nuclear energy, awaits such direction. We have become emotionally adjusted to the machine age that the Bauhaus and the pioneers sought to come to terms with, but it is already obsolete. The great lesson of the Bauhaus today is that technology must not be the motivating force alone; there are other factors—not least, the human one. It was with purpose, principle and understanding that Gropius strove to effect a synthesis between art, technology and man.

University of Baghdad, Baghdad, Iraq.

Chase Manhattan Bank, Great Neck, Long Island, New York.

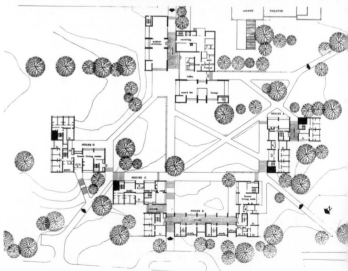

Buildings at Williams College, Williamstown, Massachusetts.

Buildings at Brandeis University, Waltham, Massachusetts.

BENJAMIN THOMPSON

Benjamin Thompson was born in St. Paul, Minnesota, in 1918. He studied architecture at Yale and was one of the founding members of The Architects Collaborative. In 1963, when he was appointed Chairman of the Department of Architecture at Harvard University, he found himself having to consider very objectively, as had Gropius at two vital and responsible moments in his own career, the basic concepts of architectural education. He is well aware of the shortcomings in the educational system today, which he refers to as being almost back in the fifteenth century.

In 1966 Thompson formed an independent architectural practice. He relinquished his major responsibilities as a partner at T.A.C. because of the teaching demands on his time. The Department of Architecture is undergoing organizational changes based on his plan for closing the gap between the architectural profession and the schools. "Office practice and school practice must work together. The plan is to use my own office as a special center for experimentation—a laboratory where both professional architects and students tackle problems together and, in the process, come up with new concepts that will hopefully advance educational and professional methods *in tandem.*"

"When T.A.C. was first formed in 1946, many people had suddenly become aware of the 'new architecture'—it caught the mood, particularly of young people. The implication was more than architecture for architecture's sake; it hinted at a reality to which one could relate. Yet looking back at the period, there was oversimplification of this architecture's derivations. We now know a great deal more about society and social problems; we realize architecture is the manifestation of its particular era and that the path of form following function is sometimes a six-lane highway.

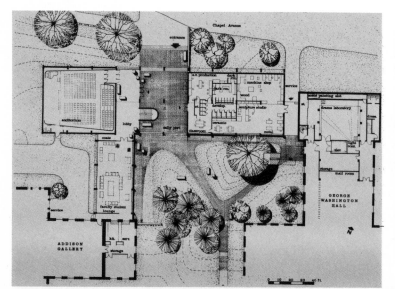

Arts and Communication Center, Phillips Academy,
Andover, Massachusetts.

"We need today a more careful structuring of the architectural planning problem and a deeper concern with the human aspects. We have the possibility of this now because research can uncover more information, and analysis may come, through the sophisticated use of computers. But there is an inclination to discount the analytical stage—partly a reaction against the 1920's and 1930's. This becomes a license for self-expression, a kind of anti-intellectualism. I am moving in just the other way—trying to find a method at Harvard where we can research, analyze, and synthesize. I feel that synthesis, so important to approach in architecture, may best be taught by both showing a certain structure of how to approach a problem, and then giving the student specific problems to apply this to. It is also necessary to get a cross-fertilization of different disciplines working together for generalized solutions. When presented with a too-hypothetical design problem, students do not relate to their world today; then they go to the magazines for research. We need to create a realistic approach that requires serious research at an advanced level. Then we must stimulate other disciplines to collaborate. I am also looking for a better approach to problem-solving. I believe that if we take urgent problems connected with, say, poverty or urban renewal, we will have motivated students. Architectural problems should grow out of the human needs of the time.

"The university can perform a role in society, which the great universities of the past have; then they will be reflecting and adding to the dimensions of the day. When we criticize the university as an ivory tower, this indicates it is not relating to its world. The swing of youth's interest towards the Peace Corps, towards racial problems, has been a remarkable evidence of the social orientation of youth.

"T.A.C. made a definite choice to select educational buildings as a particular interest. Recently we have become involved in the AID program and have been doing work in Africa and the Near East. Some of the problems an architect works on today are too frivolous, too unrelated. In an abundant society we must ask, 'Is this really worthwhile? Should I devote time to it?'

"Architecture is a slow process. You build with a certain method, you develop an attitude of how to put a building together. Slowly you refine. Things can be expressed in a quiet way, without effort to speak louder than the content indicates. Form is everything, but so is the unity of the work. The architect arrives at a certain level of performance in his work—not change for the sake of change; a painter does not suddenly decide to do the one great painting of his life. There should be continuity in a man's work, but we observe this to be unusual today—which is too bad."

Thompson's sincerity is to be seen in his work, and distinguishes his architecture. The Chase Manhattan Bank in Great Neck, Long Island, New York, and the buildings at Brandeis University, Waltham, and Williams College, Williamstown, both in Massachusetts, all completed in the 1960's, have a simple, direct vocabulary that reflects his relaxed yet firm approach to design.

At the recently completed project for Phillips Academy in Andover, Massachusetts, his task was to add to one of the oldest boys' schools in the United States an art center, a science center, a chapel and a library addition. He has maintained a sense of continuity with the existing campus, without being too strongly influenced to the degree of an arbitrary, romantic compromise.

Arts Center lobby, Phillips Academy.

The art center, linked to an existing museum, forms an intimate entry court, approached from the street by a pedestrian sally port beneath the art center. The new space forms a prelude to the larger-scaled courts of the old campus. An interior gallery opens out to this court through large glass openings, while the street facade is purposely "quiet" with predominantly brick walls along its length. The art center has studios above its workshops for wood, metal and photography, and divided levels create a stimulating working space. The science building has chemistry, physics and biology areas, grouped around a common service center; storage space is on a lower level, related to a lecture hall shared by all three departments. The nonsectarian chapel is in the remodeled basement of a neo-Georgian structure. The existing one-way slab system and the columns are left exposed, cleaned and painted white. Cavity walls are of dark red brick with a dark mortar. The outer face of the cavity wall is carried to the ceiling. The space between it and the lower wall is painted white and illuminated by recessed lights which gives the ceiling a floating effect.

The new buildings have a unified character. Concrete columns that are widely-spaced and strongly expressed support two-way concrete waffle slabs for floors and roofs, with coffers exposed on the underside. Column and parapet surfaces have a heavy texture from bushhammering that has exposed their natural aggregate. Slate floors and brick walls complete a basic vocabulary of materials. In modern architecture, employing synthetic materials often results in problems of aging. These new buildings, relying on traditional materials, are in harmony with the existing old buildings and will age well themselves. In the Andover buildings, Thompson has refined an expression that he is very much at ease with, with a degree of modesty that is unusual today. He explains, "I have worked very much in the 'less is more' theme, using fewer materials and ideas, trying to synthesize and simplify, so that what you see are fewer elements in a stronger way—it is an attempt for strength through calmness firmly stated through scale."

In addition to Thompson's involvement with T.A.C. and Harvard, he presides over Design Research, an enterprise that sells almost everything to furnish a modern home or office. To the Cambridge store, opened in 1953, he added branches in New York in 1963 and San Francisco in 1965. Furnishings can make or mar a building. Thompson has tried to create the means to a good environment with all its elements, furniture, fabrics and useful objects: in combination at D/R with flowers, music and people they create a lively and an unusual store. Thompson is sad that such unusualness is not more common.

It is in keeping with his attitude that art should be part of our lives; that its validity can be in everything that we do; that the architect needs the real world as much as the real world needs him. It is an attitude that he himself defined well in a recent lecture as "search and continuity." Concluding, he said, "Search implies a struggle with no absolute end and no fixed in-betweens. For those who search, the struggle is more important than the end, and once that end is reached, the search begins anew, somewhere else. And of continuity in design we can be sure, as long as we, as Sullivan proposed, are products of our civilization whose needs flow through our veins."

Chapel, Phillips Academy.

Science Center, Phillips Academy.

Senior Dormitory, Dana Hall, Wellesley, Massachusetts.

HUGH STUBBINS

In the medium-size design-conscious architectural office there are two practical approaches to the process of design which coexist or vary in their emphasis according to the office leadership. One method is to allow the designer working on a particular project enough freedom to feel that he is making a real contribution; the other is to impose a degree of design dictatorship to ensure that the projects of an office have general direction and consistency. Hugh Stubbins, who has a medium-size office of about forty employees, seems to very skillfully maintain a delicate balance between the two. He works with and encourages the best from his design group by giving them a sense of initiative and yet he himself is very involved with each project. In this way he effectively and cohesively directs the total work of his office.

Hugh Stubbins was born in Birmingham, Alabama, in 1912. After graduating in 1933 from the Georgia Institute of Technology, his natural ability was sufficient to win him a scholarship for graduate studies either at Harvard University or at M.I.T. He chose Harvard. Although they had never met, Gropius invited him back to Harvard as an instructor in 1939. In 1953 he became Chairman of the Department of Architecture for a year, before resigning to devote his whole attention to his expanding practice.

"I think of architecture not as individual buildings but as the whole fabric of our physical environment. Architecture is the man-made world in its totality. It is everything we have built around us—our cities, our suburbs, our sidewalks, highways, buildings, parks, signs, street-lighting, right down to the houses we live in, and the chairs we sit in—all of our physical aids to living. It is seldom, if ever, that one can design the whole fabric. Usually only a small part of it comes within the purview of the architect, and it follows that if order and all great attributes of the art of architecture are to be achieved then an important consideration is the relation of each individual effort to the whole.

"Alvar Aalto in Finland has consistently followed the approach of building within the whole fabric of his environment. He was strongly influenced by the background and geography of his country. I think that he is the greatest living architect. His always fresh, sincere and humble approach has influenced me greatly. Aalto never strives for 'newsworthy' architecture. He builds with a thorough familiarity with the problem and its situation, with a palette of homogeneous materials and logical structure. He draws on past experience with an eye on the future.

"In my work there are some guidelines or principles which I try to follow. I have a deep respect for function. The planning problem must be solved. The building must 'work' not only for the user but, if possible, be flexible for the future. Structure is of great importance. It should be forthright, logical, honest. A building should have structural integrity, which does not mean that structure must necessarily be expressed. A building should express in some way its purpose as well as have a unity in itself. It must be a whole thing, rather than a lot of pieces strung together. Integration within environment is of prime importance. I believe that to avoid the chaos we now have in our physical world, we must respect our surroundings—be they natural or man-made. We must be conscious of architecture as an expression of our time, built in our time for the use and enjoyment of our contemporaries, using our technology and experience.

"As a young architect, I used to look down my nose at the work of the practicing architects of the day. I felt they were selling our birthright as architects. I felt that architects who looked to only the future and never back were the best hope for our badly misunderstood profession. After living a while longer, gaining some experience and perspective, I began to realize that I did not know everything and that there might be room for more than one point of view. At any point in time, we are only a link between the past and the future, and must look in both directions to interpret the present. Today architecture is no longer an articulation of tradition or a search for a new style. One cannot design a building abstractly. Architecture is not pure sculpture. Fine architecture is not the fitting of things into a preconceived shell or favorite form. It is not a fashion, though many people look upon it in these terms. A complete solution involves many facets. In truth, architecture is an approach towards life. It is a social art.

"Responsibility to the community and client makes architecture completely different from other visual arts, such as painting or sculpture. This does not mean that it contains no possibility for self-expression. The first and most natural thing to do is to listen to one's own feelings, which are conditioned by one's approach to life. The architect is the only professional today trained to give some sense of order to our chaotic environment, by a continuous search for equilibrium and adaption. I am not so naive as to think that the architect can solve these immense problems by himself. Our rapid urbanization caused by an expanding population is such a complicated political, financial, social, and physical organism that architects often give in to the pseudo-idealistic approach to avoid the real problems.

"In bringing order and beauty out of this chaos, the coordination of many specialists is essential. The ability to see the woods as well as the trees is essential. There is a need for more people who are conscious of their surroundings and bent on improving them.

"This is, of course, inseparably tied to education. From the very beginning, each child should be taught to develop a perceptive awareness of the things around him. He should be taught to 'see' when he looks. Our high schools and colleges should have courses in architectural appreciation. We study the history of art, of music and of civilization, but never architecture, unless we are architects. In the final analysis, the environment of man is the consequence of what he believes to be important, the reflection of his own inner drive towards a greater awareness, and his concern for all human values.

Project for Brookline, Massachusetts.

Congress Hall, Berlin, Germany.

Undergraduate Dormitories, Princeton University, Princeton, New Jersey.

Senior Dormitory, Dana Hall, Wellesley, Massachusetts.

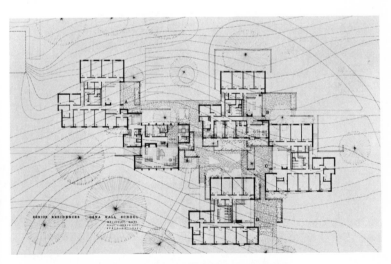

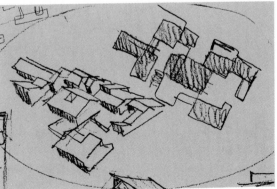

Loeb Drama Center, Cambridge, Massachusetts.

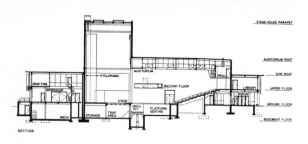

"To improve the training of architects, I believe students should specialize earlier in school. Only about two percent of architectural students are really designers, with that inborn natural ability that can be cultivated. Other students, having the desire to build, are talented in closely-related fields. Architectural schools should guide their talents into parallel channels of support, thereby filling out the 'design team' with architecturally-oriented and allied professionals.

"Hopefully, in the quest for beauty in our man-made world, architects will no longer stand alone with their demands for a better and more beautiful environment in which to live and work. We have managed to provide ourselves with large quantities of houses and offices and industrial buildings, but we have failed to provide ourselves with quality. We have failed to provide the kind of surroundings that create a feeling of delight, that banish drabness, light the voice of the spirit, and make the interplay of light and shadow a daily enjoyment.

"Who is to blame for this? It is not the fault of individuals. It is the lack of a clear and compelling goal that prevents us from moving toward a more comprehensive attempt at planning and rehabilitating our living sphere. Unfortunately a great many of our clients are not in the habit of extending their vision much beyond their own business concerns, principally because they have not been educated to do so.

"Architects today must also accept part of the blame, as some of them think that the client is a 'damned nuisance.' He has problems, however; he is concerned with the function of his plan, convenience, economy of operation, and cost of construction and maintenance. He wants a beautiful building, but this element is lower on his list than some other things. The client cannot be so neglected if we architects are to continue to be of service to our fellow men. The client is very important, and has a right to insist on certain things. Unlike former civilizations, the citizen in a collective sense is the client of the architect today. There is, in my opinion, nothing incompatible with good function, economics and beauty. In fact, all of these are ingredients essential to produce viable and beautiful architecture."

Stubbins's work is notable for his concentration on the sound design principles that have for so long distinguished the work of Alvar Aalto. His projects have been diverse, ranging from schools and other educational buildings to multiple housing, theaters, office buildings, and specialized projects such as the Congress Hall in Berlin.

Opened in 1957, the Kongresshalle was intended to express the ideal of "freedom in thought and expression." Stubbins's most publicized design, the building comprises essentially two elements; the architecturally-dominant main auditorium, seating one thousand two hundred, that rises to a height of 60 feet above a raised plaza beneath which are housed all the ancillary activities. The two huge concrete arches that support the hanging roof and shelter the auditorium walls rise dramatically upwards and outwards, visually continuing the gentle rise of the surrounding landscape. The raised plaza, overlooking the river and park, is a promenade and cafe terrace, sheltered by the overhanging roof.

Stubbins's work, however, has been principally in the New England area, using his favorite material—wood, in conjunction with brick and concrete. "Brick as a surface or skin material has never been bettered. I like to use concrete for structure, although I have been disappointed with a number of buildings where we have used poured-in-place concrete—I have had to rationalize that it looks good." Stubbins cites Pei's concrete work as being of extraordinary quality. Looking for a lasting quality, work that will age well and not be dated by fashion, he relies on and continues to explore the appropriate use of these preferred materials.

In a redevelopment project for Brookline, Massachusetts, in 1959, Stubbins proposed two curved buildings comprising six hundred and fifty-two apartment units that linked to form a crescent overlooking a landscaped park and lagoon. This attractive space, although privately owned and maintained, was to have been accessible to nearby housing, thereby helping to unify the neighborhood. Behind the crescent, built unobtrusively into the hillside, were to be two levels of parking, service areas, and a small shopping center. Stubbins limited the height of his building to preserve the consistent residential scale of Brookline. Economies were achieved by approaching apartments either directly, or up or down a level, from access corridors on the side of the slab away from the park view. This system of access also permitted apartments to extend through the full depth of the slab and enjoy two exposures.

In his recent dormitory complexes at Princeton University and at the Dana Hall School, Stubbins has been more concerned with a varied and intimate expression of space and individuality of grouped residential units. The undergraduate dormitories for Princeton form an intimate sequence of basically rectangular outdoor spaces, scaled to the present campus quadrangles. Changes in level, and the planes of the space-defining buildings, animate the surfaces of the interior court, which is central to the design. A changing silhouette is achieved by varying the number of floors in groups of units, staggering the wall planes, and particularly by projecting the edges of masonry bearing walls beyond the roof and wall planes. Stubbins has carefully designed his new buildings to be in sympathy with their neo-Gothic neighbors. Access is based on the traditional entry system where several suites of rooms open off individual staircases. Alternating between these stair towers and residential units are bathroom facilities that, like the stair towers, are recessed from the main facade plane of the residential units, further emphasizing a small scale.

The senior residences for the Dana Hall Schools in Wellesley, Massachusetts, appear to be a "tighter" cluster of buildings, related outward to the landscape rather than forming a dominant court space. The complex comprises four houses around a commons building with a central living room, recreation room and office space. Each house, accommodating thirty-two girls in single and double rooms, has a student living room, bathroom and laundry facilities, and a faculty suite. Each has its own small entry court, and is designed to step down a gentle slope, and group around a central common courtyard, connected by an intriguing pedestrian way. The houses are unified by walls, steps, courts and roof line. The variety of spaces and residential quality— brick walls, stone paving for paths and courts, copper roofs— give the new buildings a quiet unity and scale in harmony with the neighborhood.

Stubbins faced a similar challenge in the Loeb Drama Center, built close to the Harvard Yard, in 1960. A center for the production of plays and for student drama workshop activities, the

Bowdoin College Senior Center, Brunswick, Maine.

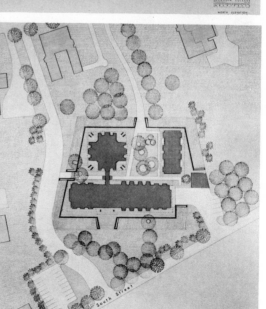

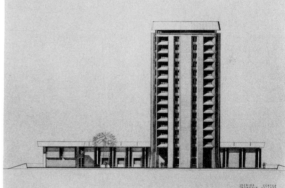

problem here was to fit the theater, seating six hundred, into a neighborhood which is predominantly colonial in character and residential in scale. Rehearsal offices and rooms encircle the auditorium at the second level, so that from the street the building appears as a two-story volume, where the projection of the auditorium and fly gallery over the stage is barely apparent. The red brick and bushhammered concrete structure, the low garden walls that enclose landscaped areas leading to lobbies flanking the auditorium, and a continuous grille on three sides of the building —a luminous, lacy thing that would attract attention, rather than using marquees or signs—are intended to harmonize the scale of the building with its environment.

The theater had to have a flexible stage and seating arrangement, to accommodate productions staged in a proscenium, Elizabethan or theater-in-the-round arrangement. This was achieved by having the seating in front of a cross aisle and closest to the stage, movable on motorized platforms at the right and left of the stage. The stage, also on lifts, can be converted into various shapes and levels. Although it is technically efficient, Stubbins has since found this mechanization a drawback for students, who have to be supervised to use it, and who prefer to improvise their own techniques for stage presentations.

Recent designs for the Bowdoin College Senior Center, and the Countway Library, show Stubbins achieving a more robust expression than in the earlier Loeb Center, and in a different vein from the Aalto-like design overtones of the Dana Hall residences.

For the small, classical quadrangle campus of Bowdoin College, in Brunswick, Maine, Stubbins has designed a tight group of three buildings, placed on a broad, defined podium. A symmetrical sixteen-story residential tower is combined with two, two-story high, separate structures, containing lounges and dining space, and a residential building for the director and visiting faculty members. The tower has four individual study rooms in four suites on each floor, related to the same number of common rooms, in each corner of the tower. The architecturally-dominant, projecting brick bays provide study alcoves in the towers. These are echoed in the lower buildings in the likes of the small dining alcoves. Also, the deep "cornices" of the three buildings help to unify them.

The Countway Library is one of Stubbins's most powerful designs to date. An even more compact and bold statement than the Bowdoin College complex, it continues the alcove theme. It is monumental in scale because of its importance in combining the Harvard Medical School Library and the Boston Medical Library (as the second largest such library in the United States, it will be a resource for the entire Boston medical community), and owing to its location, adjacent to the neoclassic buildings of Harvard's Medical School, where Stubbins thought it should be a forceful building if it was not to be visually overpowered. The small site almost dictated a square plan shape, and the symmetry and height of the surrounding buildings were an important design determinant. A warm-hued limestone, also the interior finish, is used to clad the reinforced concrete structure, relating the new building in material to the existing context.

The main entrance floor, reached by a bridge over a shallow court, contains the tools of the library; administrative offices, card catalogues, and reference sources. Two floors below this, the upper level lighted by the encircling court, is for journals, indices and abstracts; and the three floors above will house books and monographs. The two top floors will contain special facilities, such as office space for two medical journals, reading rooms, club rooms, a rare book room, and a multi-purpose auditorium. A skylit, interior focal court space gives the reader a sense of the library's total resources. Around this court, circulation areas are located that give access to book stacks; beyond these, on the outer periphery and acting as a sound buffer, are the quiet alcoves for reading. By projecting these alcoves between and beyond columns, glass areas are shaded in the deep recesses. The glazed walls of the floor beneath the cornice of offices are also recessed for sun protection. The strong shadows on recessed surfaces are intended to echo, in reverse, the shadow effects of the projecting cornice and columns of the surrounding neoclassic buildings.

Stubbins's respect for the character and scale of a context, his emphasis on the need to relate new structures—harmony without compromising contemporary architectural principles—makes good sense where the surroundings have a quality that is worthy of maintaining and continuing. Thoughtful architects are becoming increasingly aware of this need, and share Stubbins's concern. And so to a certain extent is the general public when it sees the destructiveness under the guise of so-called improvements, made without respect to existing quality in areas that are truly worth preserving and extending.

*Countway Library of Medicine, Harvard University,
Boston, Massachusetts.*

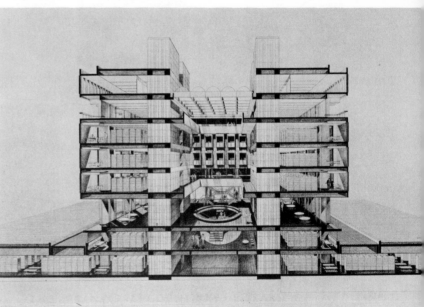

Central Lutheran Church, Portland, Oregon.

Equitable Savings and Loan Association Building, Portland, Oregon.

PIETRO BELLUSCHI

"My approach to architecture is based on the three great principles of clarity, proportion (not in the classical sense, but the proportion of things in relation to themselves) and integrity." Through these, explains Belluschi, he hopes to bring out the potential beauty in a building. The personal statement of the innovator, claiming that the human spirit must be given abstract expression beyond practical goals, is very important, but "knowing my limitations, my direction is not quite along those lines, it is my belief that there is a great deal of poetic potential in understatement, fully realizing that this can also be the road to dullness. But it is my road." In actuality it has proved a very rewarding and active road for Belluschi, who brings a highly professional touch to his varied roles as architectural consultant, advisor, and juror —indeed it scarcely seems a competition if Belluschi's name does not appear in some capacity.

He practices architecture in an unusual and flexible way. Before becoming Dean of the School of Architecture and Planning at the Massachusetts Institute of Technology in 1951, he had a practice of some forty people in Portland, Oregon. Since coming to Cambridge, he has operated a one-man practice, with varying personal involvement: from critical appraisals of other architect's work, to a completely free hand in establishing a *parti* for a project, dealing with the client, and having his solution carried through into working drawings and specifications by an associate architect. His collaboration with associates all over the country works well because rather than inject his personality in an abrasive fashion, he tries to create a homogeneous team. The disadvantage of this method is that while it allows Belluschi to engage in many activities, some details must escape his attention because of geographic diffusion and interrupted involvement.

Collaboration between the "designer architect" and the "production architect" is quite common today. In larger projects it is often necessary if an architect wishes to limit the size of his practice. Edward Stone, for example, had to open an entire office of some hundred architects to handle only the production drawings for the New York University at Albany. For the New York World Trade

Center, Yamasaki has avoided having to double his staff by associating with Emery Roth and Sons, while possibly benefitting practically from the firm's local experience in office buildings. But such firms, and the many others using associate architects, particularly in "out of town jobs", have an architect from their own office, familiar with their design methods, engage directly in the process of making production drawings. Belluschi obviously must rely to a much larger degree on the contribution of his associate architects.

Pietro Belluschi was born near Rome in 1899. After studying civil engineering in Rome and then at Cornell University, he worked as a mining engineer in the Rocky Mountains for "nine miserable months" before going to work in an architect's office in Portland, Oregon. There he remained for sixteen years as partner and chief designer, until the firm was dissolved in 1943, whereupon he opened his own office in Portland. Without a formal education in architecture, he searched for what might constitute the basic reality or integrity in a building. "I soon discovered, which is a clue to my development, that the backs of buildings were often more important than the fronts because there was less attempt to add externals."

An office building and a church in Portland, in 1948, were two projects in which Belluschi developed a clear expression of structure, in quite different yet distinctly modern vernaculars. The Equitable Savings and Loan Association was in many respects a pioneer building. The reinforced structural concrete frame, clad in light-colored sheet aluminum, had a maximum projection of only $7/8$-inch beyond the darker aluminum spandrels and tinted glass, creating a smooth exterior, machined and reflective in appearance. It was the first, sealed air-conditioned building in the United States. In sharp contrast to this, and the architecture of Rome, was the spirit of his redwood Central Lutheran Church. Belluschi was so enamored of the Northwest region's redwood barns that he became known as "the man who likes barns." They influenced the design of many of the houses and churches on which his early reputation was built.

"I am committed to a philosophy of simplicity, of understatement, but that of the saint, rather than that of the fool. It comes from deep understanding and purification, so that every time you omit saying something, or choose not to make a personal statement, you do it for good reason, for taste and restraint. I think in terms of what is appropriate—how to meet one's duty to a client's problem, and meet it with ingenuity so that the aesthetic of a particular project may emerge. The client, in turn, must be able to appreciate and accept the poetic values inherent, but not always obvious, in simple design.

"To search for the solution in an abstract way is very tempting but only a few extremely gifted, elected architects can do it. Even when they are gifted, they too fall on their face—as did Wright, in the later years, and Stone; Rudolph himself admits that he goes all the way to do what he thinks is an experiment, and then allows that he might fail. Architecture, as an art, must strive for roots and continuity but must not deny the man of genius his right to innovate if that is his moment, and his voice rings true.

"But we must also care for function, technology and social service. Architecture is more than sculpture or the means of giving pure expression to abstract human ideals. Our visual world is determined by 'forces' of a practical nature, not only by the

Library for Bennington College, Bennington, Vermont.

226

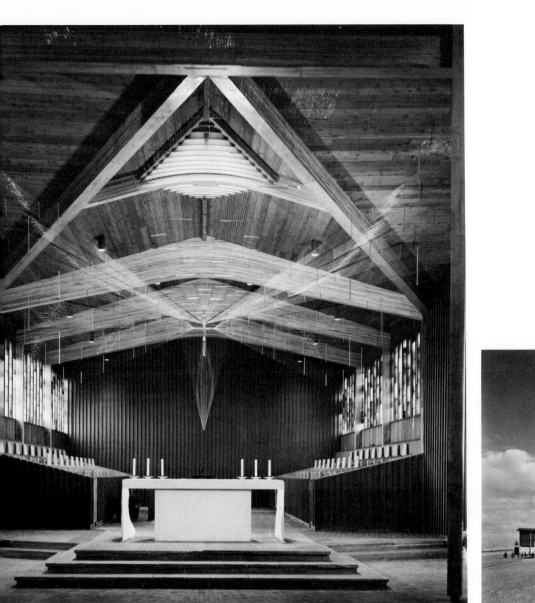

unique contribution of true artists. It has been said that the personal, sometimes arrogant acts of form-giving by our elite artist-architects, have damaged rather than helped our environment. It is easier to make a case for the need for wise technicians and honest craftsmen.

"It is part of man's nature for survival to wish to understand his condition, to find the means to adjust to it, to find and believe in some kind of order. It is in this context that we must view the artist-innovator. We need him as a spearhead in the search for formal order, even when his forms are tentative or abstract. He teaches us to see; he seeks new meanings, new songs to fit the words—and if the words are inadequate, he seeks to invent new ones. Through him, we gain that larger understanding needed to match the new dimensions of human knowledge. It can be argued that the form-giver, while sometimes pointing the way toward what we should do, at other times may reveal to us exactly what we should not do, saving us from bad ideas with which we may have been toying. Forms as well as ideas become crystallized through age or usage, thereby losing their strength and ability to move us. We rely on the artist to make them free and eloquent again. Admittedly, this is a most difficult task, particularly in a materialistic age when values continually shift and become confused. New, ephemeral philosophies arise, soon to become obsolete, and the taste-makers become bored and invent new fashions.

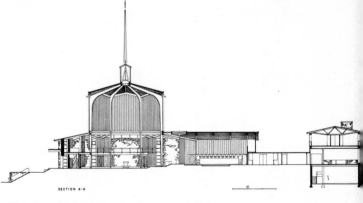

Church and Monastery for Portsmouth Priory,
Portsmouth, Rhode Island.

227

I have always felt that in the plethora of choices open to an architect, only self-discipline, the understanding of physical laws and sympathy for people's needs and desires would save him.

"I like to compare an architect's work with a writer's. In a novel there must be interest, readability, clarity, a body, a beginning and end, and the writer must have touched on deep things. In poetry, you have an entirely different problem. In architecture it is disturbing when someone tries to solve his problem in poetic terms when what is needed is the equivalent of a good report— well written, and to the point; it becomes even more painful when he has no poetic gifts and his ideas could have been conveyed in some clearer manner.

"Architecture, unlike other arts, is not an escape from, but an acceptance of, the human condition, including its many frailties as well as the technical advances of its scientists and engineers. It may rise to great art if it achieves unity, order, and form by appropriate technical means, and if it meets its purposes with conviction. I suppose only then will we have achieved the 'Great Society.' The great architect strives for comprehension, rather than originality for its own sake; a thorough study of a problem, made within the freedom that knowledge provides, is always the greatest source of originality.

Housing for the University of Rhode Island, Kingston, Rhode Island.

2ND FLOOR PLAN OF HOUSE

3RD & 3RD FLOOR PLANS OF HOUSE

4TH FLOOR PLAN OF HOUSE

TYPICAL FLOOR PLAN OF COTTAGE

"An architect should not be afraid to vary his philosophy to suit a particular project. We must accept the enormous variety of situations that our age has created, and try to find solace in the thought that nature has evolved the orchid and weed, the whale and the mouse, the eagle and the humming bird—all from a wonderfully complex yet orderly system. We should not attempt to formulate a rigid intellectual program for architecture. Anyway, it seems impossible for us to draw laws and conclusions that cannot be challenged.

"To have a certain consistency as a social art, architecture must have integrity and it must be based on what is possible, extracting whatever beauty may be hidden, while doing it in an understated way. Most important, probably, is structure. Not only the way in which a building is put together, or the simplicity of its structural idea, but how this is expressed without striving to make the bones be the whole answer. Structure that has been hidden, twisted or polluted as an idea, will seldom produce good architecture.

"Integrity is the kind of honesty to which some modern historians and critics attach very little importance. But honesty and integrity are great moral qualities in architecture, and necessary guiding beacons. At M.I.T., my colleague, John E. Burchard, thinks they are only the remnants of our puritan culture and mean nothing in our free-thinking age. I contend that only integrity will save us from chaos and that only the greatly gifted can defy it with some impunity, but not even they, for long.

"To give unity to our cities under today's circumstances is perhaps beyond our ability; the present variety of techniques, our complex problems, and above all the large dimensions of our activities do not allow for such unity. We have no alternative but to accept the fact that pluralistic society lives and grows on confusion and conflict. We are constantly reminded of the great symbols of past ages, and urged to create our own—but symbols cannot be contrived. They are born out of the deep passions of people who believe in their destiny, who have acquired the vision to find meaning in life, and the means to give it expression.

"Today's architects, for instance, find themselves in a schizophrenic state of mind when defending the old parts of Boston that are in danger of being destroyed by urban renewal. They do not like to admit that cities, like people, grow old and obsolete, must die and be reborn. The importance lies in the quality of what is rebuilt. The critic Allan Temko advocates that all new architecture should be anonymous, very rational and quite impersonal—all à la Mies; obviously this is not possible.

"However, it is clear that we cannot allow the disorder to get worse. Perhaps we can concentrate on creating humane oases in our bleak civic deserts. The shopping center is in this trend; when it is well designed and contains fountains, greenery and benches, it creates a gracious environment where one feels at ease. The Lincoln Center has been criticized, but despite its many limitations it creates an urban center of a scale that can be appreciated. Los Angeles is a typically modern city, but without form. It presents a frightening experience for the visitor—but there are auspicious countertrends, such as the proposed development of the Santa Monica Mountains to the southwest. So it is well for us to admit that while it is no longer easy to achieve beauty in the same way older societies did, we have a different and more dif-

New Equitable Center, Portland, Oregon.

ficult order to achieve. Our spirit will shine through only if we are true to ourselves and never forget that it is man that we must serve."

Belluschi firmly believes that architecture should respond to its setting. In 1959, with Carl Koch and Associates, he designed a library for Bennington College in Vermont. To fit the intimate white colonial clapboard theme of the campus, his was a wood structure, painted white, with horizontal, wood sun louvers. The lower floor was partially depressed to keep the scale of the new building in harmony with the existing two-story structures, and situated so as to continue the pattern of the rectangular spaces of the campus.

Belluschi has designed many churches—"but I have not done any two to which one can attach a particular principle, other than that of trying to create an atmosphere where the basic elements of light, materials and proportion may play their unifying roles." His 1961 church and monastery for the Benedictine Portsmouth Priory, Rhode Island, in association with Anderson, Beckwith and Haible, is built on a gentle slope overlooking a bay. The octagonal church is raised on a circular stone platform for visual authority, and is connected by a link containing the sacristy and retro-choir to the three-story monastery. The monastery has a concrete frame structure, and the church is constructed of laminated hardwood members; walls are made of redwood and Rhode Island fieldstone, with roofs of copper. The new buildings are grouped so as to dominate, yet harmonize with existing modest school and farm buildings, while merging into the landscape of small pastures and fields.

The new Equitable Center, recently completed in Portland, shows another aspect of Belluschi's versatility, and the breadth of his current practice. Much less austere than his earlier building for the same client, its recessed glass responds to the prevalent concern for glare and sun control in office buildings. It is interesting to see the similarity and also the subtle shift of emphasis in the two buildings, designed two decades apart.

Back in New England, Belluschi has collaborated with Sasaki, Dawson, DeMay Associates, and Kent, Cruise and Associates, on a design for the University of Rhode Island, for a ten million dollar housing complex to house sixteen hundred students.

The principal designer with Belluschi on this scheme, presently under construction, has been Hideo Sasaki, Chairman of the Department of Landscape Architecture at Harvard University, and a landscape designer who has collaborated with many of the leading architectural firms across the country. His emphasis on the need to design negative spaces as well as the containing buildings in a positive manner, to design in terms of total environment, met with sympathetic response from Belluschi.

In an effort to personalize the housing and create a meaningful climate for study and social contact, residential clusters have been created. The student rooms are designed so that each desk will have its own window, providing a study carrel; two double rooms share a bathroom; four double rooms share a living room with an outside balcony; each cottage houses forty-eight students with its own entrance and ground floor lounge and study areas; three to five of these cottages are connected, forming easily administrated groups of one hundred and fifty to two hundred and fifty students. The ground floors are expressed as concrete pedestals and support the brick-surfaced residential stories above. Both the concrete and brick are chosen to harmonize with the materials traditionally used on the campus.

Two of Belluschi's larger commissions have been in New York: the Pan American Airways Building which he designed with Walter Gropius, and Emery Roth and Sons, and the Juilliard School of Music at Lincoln Center which he designed with Catalano and Westermann. But in San Francisco are his most challenging commissions to date: the fifty-two-story Bank of America Building, at the foot of a hill, collaborating with Wurster, Bernardi and Emmons, and Emery Roth and Sons; and St. Mary's Cathedral, on top of a hill, in association with Pier Luigi Nervi, and McSweeney, Ryan and Lee. While trying to find an approach for the office building, the character of the skyline and the city's fairly consistent scale of whitish buildings stepping up the hills were foremost in Belluschi's mind. To treat a large skyscraper so that it will be well-scaled to its urban context is one of the easiest areas to fail in for an architect! The Pan American Building in New York has been greatly criticized, in addition to adding a quarter of a million daily visitors to an already densely-populated area, for its ponderous scale and for ruining one of the best vistas in New York, down Park Avenue. "I have no apologies for it," says Belluschi, "other than that the scale is too big and there are too many windows. Although they are a big statement of purpose, Yamasaki will find his twin towers (World Trade Center), when they are built, will be too large for the detail he has. You cannot relate them to any scale at all." Belluschi's concern in the Bank of America skyscraper was to retain the sense of the tower, provide the necessary square feet of office space per floor to accord with

Project for World Center of the Bank of America, San Francisco, California.

the high land value, and produce a building that would not appear "big and bulky." He also bore in mind the simple brownish palette that Mies had used, "the great simplicity which is the secret of Seagram, the most beautiful building of recent years," and the "light, crystal-like quality" of his own first Equitable building.

Belluschi's design is for linked twin towers, with a jagged, heavily-modelled reflective facade. He is very concerned with the sculptural appearance of the building. Architects are usually very wary of working with artists, but Belluschi says, "now that the design is established in principle I would like to have a sculptor work with me on it." The structural set-backs are a practical design choice and not the wedding-cake result of building-code light angles: "As you go up the elevators decrease in number, so there is some reason for the building also decreasing in size. I would like to have a symbolic value, but not purchased at too high a price. The important thing is to remember that the price is never too great in achieving good architecture."

"When I heard a new cathedral was to be built in San Francisco, I said, 'I pity the architect.' And then I was asked to take part in it," said Belluschi. "What we have now for the Cathedral is a concept. It is an idea and a strong idea, and we are all very much excited—but the fear of God hasn't left us!" As art and religion, each in its own way, seek to interpret the meaning or essence of our existence, so must religious architecture seek the essence of

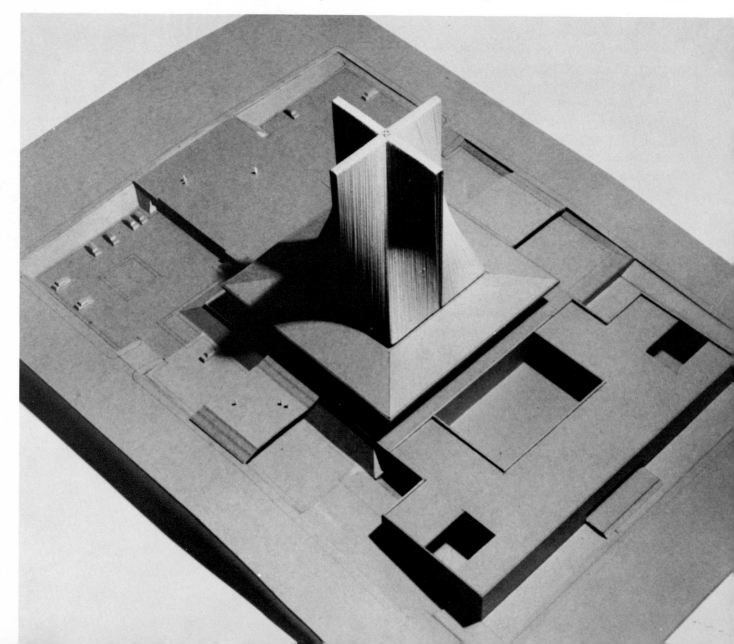

space, thinks Belluschi. "That is why space in a church acquires supreme importance," which Paul Tillich refers to as "Holy Emptiness." Belluschi regards England's rebuilt Coventry Cathedral as the most successful of recent years, with the reservation that it did not represent our current technical capabilities, which he particularly wanted to represent in St. Mary's Cathedral. He searched for a form that would be high enough in the interior to provide the quality of space necessary for a cathedral seating two thousand six hundred in its sanctuary; and on the exterior, to have the symbolic rising quality of the traditional combination of nave and spire, yet without overpowering the San Francisco skyline. He needed a form that would have height, dimension and drama, without bulk.

The solution for the Cathedral sanctuary came to Belluschi in Rome, where he had gone for discussions with the Archbishop who was attending the Ecumenical Council. Just prior to Belluschi's appointment, certain liturgical changes were introduced by the Council, prompting Belluschi to group the congregation around the main altar on a square plan, rather than in the more traditional rectangular nave plan. His solution is dramatic and simple. Four up-ended hyperbolic paraboloids rise from a square at the congregation level, creating the necessary large volume, to a slender cruciform apex. Light will bathe the interior space, through the immense overhead cross of colored glass which continues down the four sides of the structure, separating the hyperbolic paraboloids. The thin concrete shell may eventually be covered with white marble. The pedestal structure, containing several chapels, the sacristy and atrium, is still in the early design stages.

A church "should strive to express its purpose," says Belluschi; in a building type where practical considerations may be important but are certainly not paramount, this presumably implies being both simple and profound, at peace and yet moving. And while a church must be intimate, "it should be a segment of space which reminds the worshiper of the infinity from which it was wrested," said Belluschi. "Integrity, proportion and clarity—it is through them that Beauty will shine."

St. Mary's Cathedral, San Francisco, California.

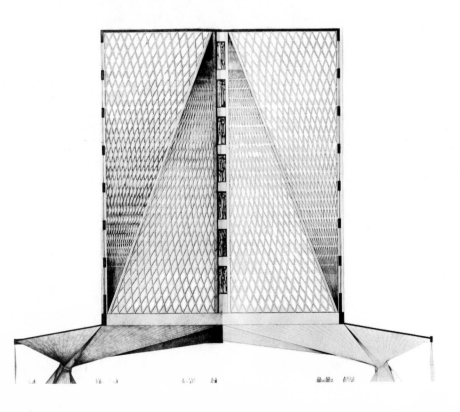

EDUARDO CATALANO

Le Corbusier wrote that "genius is personal, decided by fate, but it expresses itself by means of system. There is no work of art without system." He also wrote: "An attitude is not a system." Considering the evolution of modern architecture, from the Crystal Palace to the present, we have to conclude that while we have developed some good systems for small, individual problems, we still have only attitudes towards the important, universal ones.

Our inability—even our lack of seriousness—to devise appropriate systems that might enable us to confront comprehensively and responsibly some of our increasingly challenging problems is reflected in the absurdity of our "rhinoceros-like" attitude towards these problems; particularly towards technology and the resourceful accumulation of a pool of useful knowledge. Serious architects like Eduardo Catalano consider this a fundamental shortcoming of architecture today.

Eduardo Catalano was born in 1917 in Buenos Aires, Argentina, where he studied architecture. He came to the United States in 1944, where he received a Master of Architecture degree at the University of Pennsylvania, and another a year later at Harvard University. Returning to Buenos Aires he had his own practice, until 1950 when he went to London to teach for a year at the Architectural Association. Then, when invited to teach at the University of North Carolina at Raleigh, he returned to the United States. In 1956 he was appointed Professor of Architecture at the Massachusetts Institute of Technology, where he presently teaches the graduate class. He also has a small practice in Cambridge of about fifteen people, mostly former students.

To many of the students who have benefitted from contact with Catalano, he is an architect of great integrity and purpose: an advocate of order and system, who, like Berenger, resists turning into a "rhinoceros."

"I am trying to develop a direction for my work, searching for laws or norms of organization, performance and construction, consciously avoiding the anti-norms upon which architecture seems to be based at present. The architect today, isolated from society and at the service of individuals, confines his task to a reduced world which only allows him to express himself in a variety of moods within a very short period of time. The search for visual 'values' becomes the main objective of architecture to such an extreme that archeological resurrections are brought about for the sake of visual innovation. Thus, today, a new direction in architecture is to recapture any old direction.

"Architecture is still dominantly following the cyclic curve described by art, which Picasso explains as moving but not advancing. On the other hand, science and technology follow an upward curve of an ever-increasing verticality, parallel to the curve also described by the population explosion and the mounting social, political and economic problems we face all over the world.

"What is happening to architecture and art criticism is best exemplified in Ionesco's play *Rhinoceros*. The monstrous, aimless rhinoceros, through direct exposure or description through lectures, magazines, and art criticism, begins to be accepted and to replace man to such an extent that the few men who remain human beings, isolated in a minority, long to become rhinoceros to share the success of the new breed. The absurd of yesterday, through persistent exposure, becomes valid today.

"How do we architects respond to this? How responsible are the social and the art critics, especially the latter who are also making a living out of our failure? How responsible are the universities?

"We face a historic process that cannot be avoided. Cities are expanding beyond controllable sizes; government land control and financial assistance lead to the construction of large urban complexes, introducing new relationships that will, in a few decades, result in the vanishing of the isolated individual building, as it is conceived today, that satisfies individual needs and whims. Even in countries such as the United States, committed to individual freedom and private enterprise, government agencies are increasing day-by-day their participation in, and control of, urban development; thus we reach the status of genuine socialism.

"To cope with the vastness of the problem and simultaneously take advantage of it, architecture will have to move away from its cyclic curve and depend entirely on rationalized designs and systematized construction based on truly industrialized processes. For there will be no hope of solving our increasing social and economic problems if we do not put architecture along the curve followed by science, technology and industrialization.

"With the advent of new ideas, processes and materials, a new scale and visual values are born. The task we face is to discover, in scientific and technological forces, the inexhaustible resources that give architecture its lasting values. Assuming that there is a meeting of minds on the goals of architecture, which would be the forces at work that can make the strongest impact to reach that goal?

"In small private offices there is a misunderstanding of the role of architecture, and because of a limited amount of work and confined technical resources, the result is highly individualistic designs—cyclic work—a product of the master's mood. Large offices also fail to achieve such goals because they are no more than a juxtaposition of small offices, with all the handicaps and none of the advantages. There is no unity of purpose or continuity in either of their approaches that can lead to valid technological developments. Projects seldom reach the large scale that allows systematization in the design concept as well as in the construction methods. Every designer is acting like a small Picasso, 'moving' from period to period.

"The hope then lies in the universities and their coordinated work with industry. As everybody knows, but nobody really takes advantage of it, schools of architecture have at their disposal large human and physical resources: libraries, laboratories, workshops, teachers and students, and continuous work for experimentation, cross-fertilization and continuity in the development of ideas, and the accumulation of experience year by year. But in schools of architecture the potential resources are misused because, behind a screen of broadness and general education, the schools do not take a stand on the purposes of the studies. There is a tendency in academic life to believe that variety of purpose is the essence of a broad education. This belief exists because *purposes* are always confused with *approaches*. Thus, a school of architecture, instead of developing coordinated approaches to a common-purpose architecture, offers random approaches to a non-purpose architecture.

"An expectant generation, unfortunately not rebellious, is not interested in attending sophisticated trade schools—as *all* the schools of architecture are—but want instead to live in an atmosphere of experimental work, solidly supported by general, scientific and technological studies. They do not want to base their work on the temporary mannerisms that have dominated architecture and its teachers for a long period, but on permanent forces. They are also alarmed that architects today depend on an industrial production with which we do not collaborate. The largest industry in the nation produces building components that very seldom have been programmed, designed and engineered in a combined effort with architects and engineers.

"Schools of architecture can contribute nothing to industry because there is no tradition of research in architecture. Every problem, usually of an individualistic nature, starts from zero without a goal or the continuity and accumulation of ideas from year to year. Working with such an aimless attitude, teachers have sel-

House in Raleigh, North Carolina.

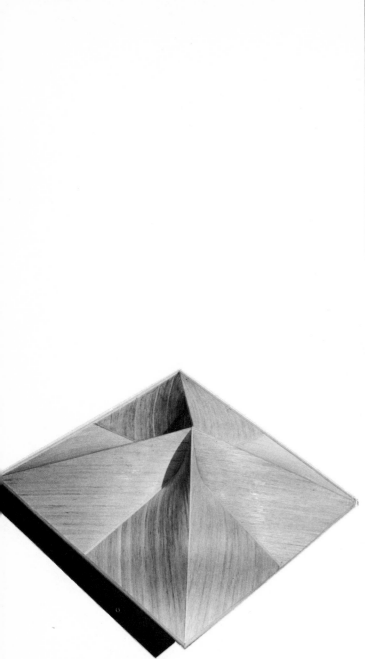

Hyperbolic Paraboloid. Fig. 1.

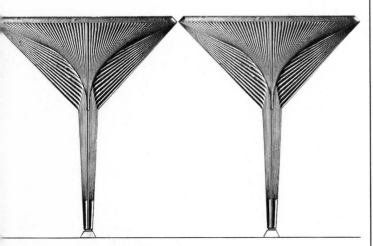

Hyperbolic Paraboloid. Fig. 2.

dom developed a method of research for consistent programming, analysis, evaluation and development of ideas; neither have they been able to establish a direct association with other branches of knowledge, especially industry, for the necessary cross-fertilization of ideas and methods. Schools today are only makers of day-by-day professional practitioners.

"The ever-increasing social pressures and the unavoidable command that science, technology and industrialization are taking in orientating and shaping our endeavors open new dimensions to architecture toward the solution of total systems of urban organization and construction. This has been my approach, as opposed to the usual one of designing isolated buildings, shaped by individual needs and the erratic mannerisms of the designers.

"I built a house in 1954, in Raleigh, North Carolina, as the result of some structural studies on warped surfaces made two years earlier while teaching at the University there. The house was an attempt to approach space and structure, both conceived simultaneously and with one as the expression of the other, as an indivisible event. A house is a small but rich architectural event, that more than any other type of building allows one to control the forces that shape it. In this design, as in most of my work, I wanted to emphasize the principal idea with a very strong and short sentence: the 'shelter' that dominates the landscape, provides order beneath it and allows the random needs of life to take their place without interfering with the main thought.

"Structures of readable and clear geometry, springing from the ground as if freeing themselves from the forces of gravity, are ever present in the buildings I design. The Raleigh house is the best example of it: a shell spanning 87 feet, supported on two points. The Student Center at M.I.T. is the latest example. Both buildings, each at its own scale, are generous in dimension and develop the idea of shelter as the main theme: both introduce the visitor gradually into the centers of life by putting emphasis on depth.

"I have always been very much attracted by the order, sense of continuity and structural qualities that pure geometry gives forms, especially those of the non-planar family. These four-sided forms have excellent structural properties, while their geometry allows great simplicity in construction—two paramount needs in architecture.

"The Raleigh house makes use of the basic surface unit called the hyperbolic paraboloid. After this experience I became interested in designing a variety of 'shelters' based upon the use of this four-sided unit, which I believe constitutes one of the simplest and richest geometrical-structural systems ever found by architects and engineers. This simple unit, by a change in its components—angles, lengths of sides, number of them, and their location in space—is capable of generating an unlimited number of spatial and structural solutions, thus becoming a true system.

"The architect is not a sculptor, but a designer and builder of systems. He has to find the freedom within the set of laws that regulate any system. In these examples of systems one combination of units generates others; each form is not a static form that ends with itself, but a live system that generates many other ideas. Figures 1 and 2 show two examples of the same combination of units with supports at opposite sides of the vertex. The simple inversion of the unit provides a different spatial solution to the problem of shelter. Figures 3 and 4 are based upon the same combination of units and same structural behavior, but the lowering of the vertex of Figure 3 to a plane that contains the edge of the structure provides a completely different spatial solution as shown in Figure 4. I have made many different 'shelters' that all originate from a single organization of units.

"I have enjoyed working on such side projects as the network of a city as a system. Here I was interested in developing a geometric system of circulation that would be able to grow, to change in shape and scale, while preserving its continuity and basic geometric properties. The system starts from a simple core not larger than one square mile: from a pattern of straight lines at this core, the system grows outwards in a curved pattern that preserves the continuity of circulation and the consistency of geometry. Here, as in all structures, the form changes as the scale changes. Within the large areas defined by the expanded network, a sub-system (neighborhood) can be developed. The peripheral roads for transportation, which also lead to industrial centers can be reached from any place in the city by turning a street only once; all the streets, roads and highways meet at right angles regardless of the topological transformation of the network. Continuity, growth, changes in scale and structure are combined into a single cohesive idea, free from construction inconsistencies, visual preconceptions or random moods.

"I have not seen yet an urban nucleus able to grow topologically, with consistency. The city of Washington represents the worst example of a preconceived geometric pattern, without the chance of expanding beyond a few terminal formal points.

"Architecture (the whole and the parts of an organized urban complex) constitutes a continuous three-dimensional event that

Hyperbolic Paraboloid. Fig. 3 and Fig. 4.

should originate, grow, change and be built according to a pattern of behavior and construction. That is architecture as system.

"In a very small degree, the transformation from custom-made design to systematized design and industrialized construction is happening in the most advanced technological nations. The transformation is part of the natural but slow interplay between the social, political and economic forces—forces that cannot be changed by theoretical architectural manifestos. The transformation needs to be accelerated and controlled to ensure that architecture is not a 'rhinoceros,' or a spectator, or at the mercy of a historic process, but that it is a responsible force that contributes to shape this process.

"There will alway be surgery to repair the sick organs of the city or to satisfy the very few specific needs that require specific solutions, but all of the creative and industrial resources upon which architecture depends so heavily cannot be oriented toward the few and ignore the many. This is where the schools of architecture are grossly failing.

"At the School of Architecture in M.I.T., I have been attempting to develop buildings as total construction systems, simplifying programs for generalized collective needs, searching for common denominators to set the genes of the systems, emphasizing industrialized building processes. When the scale permits, as in the New Campus for the University of Buenos Aires, done by Horacio Caminos and myself, we have systematized the use and construction of the buildings to such a degree that most of the activities of the campus will be developed within a single prototype design.

"The Student Center at M.I.T. is part of the general surgery that is transforming campuses today. With its simplicity, I have tried to achieve a more timeless architecture, rejecting the family of 'rhinoceros' that populate our campuses today. But it is a custom building for a specific program, following the individualistic approach that today dominates our designs. I wish it could have been approached with more vitality and flexibility in its function, and with more precision and purity in the interrelation between the structure and the mechanical services, to become a true system of life and construction.

"The main building at M.I.T., built in 1925, has a voice of seniority because of age, location and simplicity. Its dome, a symbol of compression, represents the elder brother, downward-looking, realistic, witness of the past and heavy-shouldered. The structure of the Student Center, with its large cantilevers—symbols of tension and defiance of gravity—represents the younger brother, looking upward, optimistic and a witness of the present. Two ages, two needs, two aims, separated by two generations of spatial and technological developments are sharing the same room; yet they are able to maintain a dialogue identified through their common height, generosity of dimensions, simplicity of form, visual strength and use of materials. Depth, sense of shelter, and an attempt to defy visually the forces of gravity are part of the new themes brought by the Student Center into the dialogue.

"Where do we go from here? By slowing the pace I am attempting to recapture the freshness that existed in my early work (if that is mentally and biologically possible), while working steadily in my office and in the University to help put architecture away from its cyclic curve."

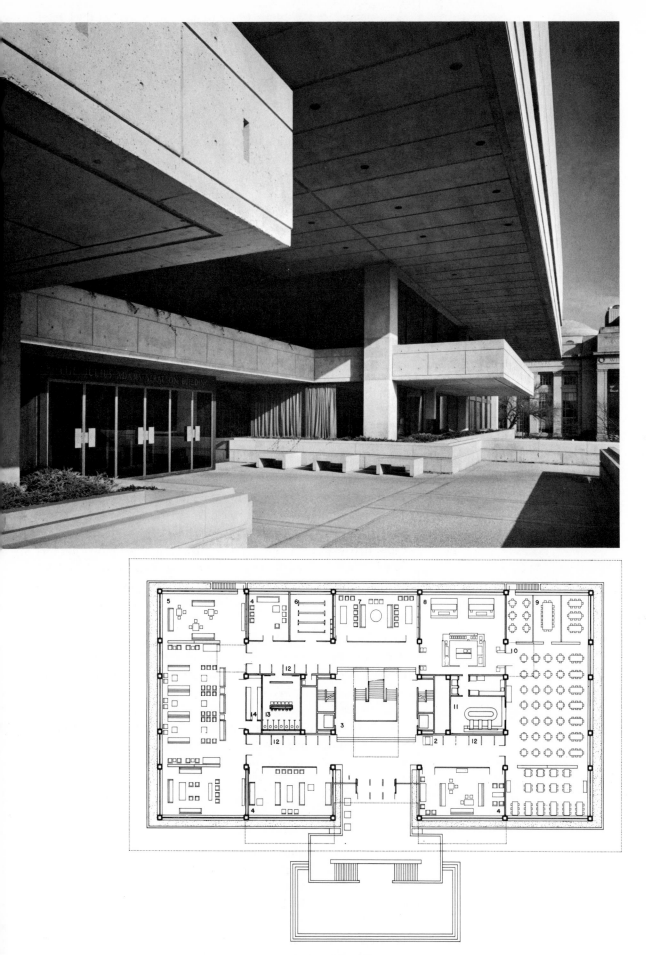

Student Center at M.I.T., Cambridge, Massachusetts.

As a member of the international design committee for the United Nations building in New York, it is acknowledged that Le Corbusier was responsible for its overall concept. However, the Carpenter Center for the Visual Arts at Harvard University, completed in 1962, is the only structure designed entirely by Le Corbusier to be built in this country—a commission secured for him at the urging of José Luis Sert.

Le Corbusier's buildings and writings have profoundly influenced the development of modern architecture from Europe, India and Japan, to the Americas. When he died in 1965, one of architecture's grand masters, in ours or in any time, one to whom only Mies and Wright can be compared, had gone. Like them he remained absolutely dedicated to his principles and ideals, and went beyond the exploitation of a natural talent to use intellect and instinct to transcend the measurable.

Whereas Mies has refined an architectonic language of steel and glass to achieve the maximum with an elegant minimum, Le Corbusier has shown the plastic potential of reinforced concrete to resolve individually responsive forms into a single mass. His continual awareness of the historic significance of surface interest and the architectural play of light and shadow, has been particularly persuasive and inspiring to those American architects with an increasing interest in reinforced concrete. Above all, Le Corbusier has shown the indestructible unity of artistic values in accord with theory; a poetic fusion of art, science, machine, nature, and life—probing the tangible reality and opportunity of our circumstance. His was an apocalyptic vision.

Architecture, like art, is an insight into the reality of a period; the architect, like the artist, seeks to give expression to its true forces. Not to be modern for its own sake, but to formulate concepts that express a society, a culture, and an origin—concepts in which an epoch can see itself reflected. The work of Wright, Mies and Le Corbusier is profoundly different in interpretation, yet their visions are parallel in one vital sense: the creation of a better environment for twentieth century man.

In particular, Le Corbusier's synthesis produced intellectually derived forms of poetic intensity that begin to project an image of what our twentieth century urban environment might be. Mies has narrowed in, possibly arriving at more unified answers, whereas Le Corbusier, in expanding a vocabulary, has possibly posed the more disturbing questions. His versatility as architect, sculptor, painter and poet inevitably engaged him in a manifold study of the shaping of space, and all its psychological implications.

Although Le Corbusier advocated his principles firmly and articulated them lucidly, he was flexible in their application; the mind of the great artist, at once refining an idea, and grappling with a new idea. His general theory was an anchor in his approach to the specific. Ronchamp is a good example: it deviates from many of his expressed beliefs and yet is still essentially Le Corbusier; a specific building for a specific purpose that, moreover, responds to a higher order. Le Corbusier's synthesis is difficult to effect. Without ignoring complexities, it simplified them into a cogent, unified statement; one that enabled him to approach the specific without forgetting universal principles. It is the type of synthesis that we seem to be struggling with in our transitional period, thus establishing Le Corbusier as a polemical figure. In *Space, Time and Architecture,* Giedion wrote: "A transition period may affect two observers in very different ways. One may see only the chaos of contradictory traits and mutually destructive principles; the other may see beneath all this confusion those elements which are working together to open the way for new solutions."

The five principles for modern architecture that Le Corbusier stressed in the 1920's are present in the Visual Arts Center: the free-standing column, freeing the ground level; the external and internal wall independent of the structural skeleton; the open plan allowing flexibility in the organization of space; the free facade, resulting from these former considerations; and the roof garden, positively utilizing all aspects of a building.

Set askew on the site, the building's mass is basically a square penetrated by two interlocking, banjo-shaped studio areas. A diagonal ramp through the center of the building links the streets on either side of the site, and rises to the third floor level with the main entrance to the building at its volumetric center. The building is a response to a supposedly rather nebulous functional program, and even Le Corbusier's most ardent admirers could not claim it to be in harmony with the quiet, brick atmosphere of its urban context. Clearly a vibrant inner force, authoritative rather than respectful of environmental continuity, has dictated its form. It challenges reaction and engagement, and shocks the complacent. At a time when the need for continuity in the urban context is being emphasized, it represents change.

Like the Guggenheim Museum it is a dynamic, sculptural statement. Walking around and through the building's fragmented overall form, one can see its surfaces in constant modulation. Le Corbusier wrote: "Architecture is the masterly, correct and magnificent play of masses brought together in light." Here, light and shadow become a part of the architecture, as they emphasize solid and void. It is a tour de force that has stimulated much controversy and, particularly in comparison to Mies's less assertive buildings, emphasizes our polemical situation.

There is a most regrettable tendency in our society for life to become somewhat bland; to minimize or negate the natural instinct of the individual to exert his intellectual and creative potential, to destroy his will to *do*—without which it is difficult to conceive of a sense of achievement and fulfillment in life. It is important that the occasional voice be raised to inspire the desire for a more complete life; to give the spirit opportunity to exist. As the caption of an engraving by William Blake says: "Teach their souls to fly."

Carpenter Center for the Visual Arts at Harvard University, Cambridge, Massachusetts.

JOSÉ LUIS SERT

The social promise of the modern movement in architecture has been the abiding interest and concern of José Luis Sert. He believes in urbanity, architecture as an expression of life, and the advantages of machines—including the much-maligned automobile. He is pragmatic about the means and idealistic about the ends. Sert was born in Barcelona, Spain, in 1902. The Catalans "were always in disagreement with everything on principle," he says. "This made one feel from the beginning that he was in revolt against existing conditions in life"—including arts and architecture. Painting was his great interest and has always influenced the way in which he regards a building. The bright colors of his friends Miró and Léger are frequent accents to his buildings.

As an architecture student in Barcelona, he took a trip to Paris and found a new stimulus: *L'Urbanism* and *Towards a New Architecture* by Le Corbusier. "The books got us thinking about many things we already suspected. The whole thing was in the air and materialized when we were able to see many of the ideas we had been discussing take definite shape in those books," says Sert. On a visit to Spain, Le Corbusier was asked to lecture in Barcelona. He invited Sert to work with him, and upon his graduation in 1929, Sert spent a year in his Paris office. It was the beginning of a long friendship and association, and for Sert, a continuing awareness of Le Corbusier's example—particularly of the idea that architectural form is derived from embracing and expressing the many aspects of daily life.

After a year with Le Corbusier, Sert returned to open his own office in Barcelona. In 1931, when the Spanish Republic came into being, a group had been formed to discuss the arts and social conditions in general. "From the very beginning we were deeply interested in the social implications of a new architecture, and we believed absolutely that architecture and changes in the structure of the country were very closely tied." The response from the government and the people to the group's activities and ideas was encouraging. Exhibitions were held of the work of the painters, sculptors and architects (Picasso and Miró were becoming well known), and a magazine was formed to publish the group's work. Between 1933 and 1935 a master plan for Barcelona was prepared in collaboration with Le Corbusier. It showed buildings as part of larger complexes, as elements of a new city, indicating how better cities could be developed. Housing and the improvement of urban conditions were a primary concern, and three of the group's studies, although small in scale, were built.

In 1937 Sert was asked to design the Spanish Pavilion at the Paris World's Fair in association with Luis Lacasa. Here he pursued another lifelong interest—the close collaboration between the architect and those in the visual arts. The Pavilion exhibited works by Miró and Calder, and Picasso's contribution was one of the great paintings of this century, "Guernica."

Sert came to America in 1939 and soon published *Can Our Cities Survive*. This book, whose cover showed a sardine can as a symbol of the congestion and poor conditions of the city, presented the views of C.I.A.M. (Congrès Internationaux d'Architecture Moderne) which Sert had become a member of in 1929, through Le Corbusier. The emphasis was on architecture and planning, with human problems and issues as the basic influences on the form of the city.

From 1945 to 1956, in partnership with Paul Lester Wiener, Sert prepared some dozen master plans for new cities and the renewal of old ones in Latin America, including Chimbote, Lima, Bogotá (with Le Corbusier) and Havana. Here, Sert's philosophy was confronted by the realities of a different hemisphere: "In our C.I.A.M. projects we had discussed high-rise buildings, how to group them, and at the same time separate them from shopping and other facilities. Our attitude was that everything had to be defined by a particular function, and be carefully separated from anything that was to be used for a different function." In Latin America, people lived above their shops and Sert found that facilities could not be simply classified and separated. A different climate, primitive building techniques and very limited financial means were further problems. Services could not be overextended since there was barely enough money to install and maintain those that were absolutely essential. In the United States, at that time, there was a preference for the individual house and garden, which extended roads and utilities and led to a dispersed, land-consuming planning. But in Latin America, economics necessitated higher densities, yet technology and living customs limited high-rise structures.

Sert's transitional solution was the court or patio house, where high densities and good living conditions are compatible. Sert's own one-story house in Cambridge—intimate, yet surprisingly large when its exterior spaces combine with the interior for large gatherings—although it stands alone, is a persuasive prototype for a repeatable house that is economical, while creating a gracious

Spanish Pavilion, Paris World's Fair.

living environment. Such a house would occupy and use actively all the space of a standard 50-foot by 100-foot lot. He says: "The service streets in these developments should look like country lanes defined by garden walls and fences, the garage doors providing breaks and accents. The trees, high over each fence, would dominate it and behind it everybody would be free to build what he preferred—a Cape Cod cottage or a modern glass house."

"The frustrating thing about planning work," Sert says, "is that a city takes much longer to develop than a building, and controls are very difficult; some elements of the plan are used, others misused, and many things are changed." But even if a small proportion of the basic elements are respected and developed, he might have added, the positive effect on the city can be significant, even fundamental.

In 1953 Sert replaced former Dean Hudnut, and Chairman Walter Gropius, at the Graduate School of Design at Harvard. He continues to bring the same emphasis on principles germane to his work to the recent generation of graduates. His private practice is in his Cambridge office of Sert, Jackson and Associates.

"When one considers a building as part of a city, one cannot avoid being interested in the larger issues and context. Residential buildings constitute the largest part of any city, and in C.I.A.M., we were always interested in houses for the greater numbers. Today, no architect is really worth very much unless he is interested in the larger issues, and this great challenge. Unfortunately, we are not given the opportunity to do very much about it.

"I am very worried about the attitude of many young architects who seem unaware that the improvement of living conditions for the greater number of people remains the ultimate problem. This does not mean only an interest in residential architecture. The house does not finish at the front door; it goes far beyond to in-

Sert House, Cambridge, Massachusetts.

clude facilities for community life, education, recreation, health services, and so on. And beyond these, it involves circulation, and the subsequent conditions under which people live.

"The tremendous number of automobiles on the road (approaching 80 million) presents a difficult and rather discouraging problem for the architect. A reorganization of life, such as the staggering of working hours would help and will probably happen. The trouble with expressways is that they are designed to handle rush-hour traffic, but are half-empty at other times. The main problem however, is not the moving, but the idle, parked car that occupies much more space than its driver does in a building. This will have to be solved by several methods; mass transportation, a greater use of automobiles that are continuously moving, and the redesigning of automobiles. We also should not forget the great advantage of mobility—a blessing in our times—so we have to allow for the automobile, or whatever replaces it, in our designs.

"The element of time, and how we allocate it to different activities during a day, is most important in the city. The trend is toward the shorter work week, permitting more leisure time for one's own activities, probably to be pursued nearer one's home. For centuries the business district has been the center of a city, now it may be living its last days. People should have the freedom to choose their place of work while also being able to preserve their ties with the area in which they live. Generally, people are interested in moving only during a certain period in their lives, or for a specific reason. When families are settled, and have attachments for people they know and like to live near, many are obliged to move against their will, because they have to work in a different place and must live within commuting distance. I envision a totally different pattern developing between metropolitan areas, deriving from the distinction between where people live and where they work. Rapid systems of communication have made it possible to conceive of a lineal development of working facilities, which people could get to and from very fast. Then, near their homes would be the facilities for shopping, recreation, entertainment, and the places where they work for pleasure, interest, research and discovery of new things.

"The government could establish, financed with a rotating fund, cultural facilities and services that really do not pay and that private initiative will never develop, to serve as a seed or a nucleus for the development of housing and shopping. With government seed money as encouragement, communities would gradually develop around new cores. Having reached a certain phase of development, which means that land is valued at much more than it was initially, government money could then be withdrawn to be used for a new seed elsewhere. People could choose their place of work, thus obviating the premise that cities are built around a central business district. What would give the idea validity would be the additional time that people would have for their own interests and family life. (This principle is contrary to efforts to animate and renew a central core which planners generally are trying to encourage at the moment.)

"I have been trying for years to animate the business core but find, especially in this country and which in the future will accelerate, that the business core is a place where people rush to and from. As we continue to shorten the working day, where one works becomes less important than the place where one spends most hours. The business core of the city is now a black spot at night.

American Embassy, Baghdad, Iraq.

Museum of the Fondation Maeght, St. Paul de Vence, France.

With this other solution the core would be made up of new and more significant elements, the more lively elements of the city that would be pulled together, and would stay alive until the early hours of the morning. I believe this will happen; and it will give impetus for a new shape or form for the city.

"In terms of clusters of buildings, on the scale in which we are going to build in the near future, sequence, size, and relationship will change, in terms of color, texture, and scale, when we think of things seen from a moving car or as a pedestrian. Generally, there are the parts of a building close to the ground, related to pedestrians, cars and trees; the in-between area; and finally, the part that meets the sky.

"The lower floors may be open, on stilts or pilotis. Free movement under buildings helps link spaces, but the pilotis solution does not limit and define spaces between buildings; openness at ground level, if used indiscriminantly as a principle, becomes boring and creates dead spaces. Diverse elements of animation and movement, such as shops, gathering places, building entrances, etc., are irreplaceable in making an urban environment lively. A mixture of uses contributes to animation at the ground level. There is no one, or best universal formula.

"In the middle sections of any building, one can see that the principle of repeating the best 'cell,' for such a 'monster' as the average man is usually accepted. It results in a uniform fenestration, which may be suitable for some buildings, but when applied to every building, is deadly. The window is a good example to show how variety can derive naturally in a building. Windows in the past had a triple function: to see, to light, and to ventilate. Today they can be picture windows, appropriate when scaled to the space inside and the view outside; diffuser windows that just filter and diffuse light; or opaque ventilator windows (Le Corbusier's *aérateurs*), meant only to ventilate. Thus we have a broad range and freedom of choice of possible combinations. The moment one starts to explore solutions, instead of accepting the uniform and the average, then one gets a variety of expression that might become an honest reflection of what really happens in a building, which in the majority of cases is more interesting than expressing structure.

"Where a building terminates against the sky there are often penthouses and mechanical spaces. One universal formula is simply to extend the curtain wall, pretending a constant treatment. This is not bad but one loses an opportunity of doing better —there are a variety of elements and desirable amenities, and the means to do interesting things are certainly not lacking.

"I am not against the present divergence of approaches and ideas, because our challenge is not in building isolated buildings but whole cities and new communities—which allows for this variety. The ideas we all stood for in the C.I.A.M. years were sound in many ways, but it has perhaps been advantageous that the cities we conceived of then have not materialized. Although we might have achieved interesting experiments, they would have been rather dull. We were operating with a very limited vocabulary and rigid principles. The great advantage of the postwar years has been the development of a much more flexible vocabulary in architecture, and the awareness of many of the younger generation that we are part of a larger plan, which hopefully will enable us to build more interesting and lively cities."

Sert has tried always to stress the total potential aspects of a project, to do as much as possible with whatever is available. In the American Embassy in Baghdad, Iraq, he proposed a group of buildings, relating to a series of outdoor spaces whose functional role they defined. In contrast, intimate courts in the center of the buildings provided sheltered spaces. The form of the buildings, and consequently their cogency, was very much influenced by needed sun-control devices. For example, in the three-story Embassy office building, the lower floors are stepped back, with the upper level supported by slab piers that act as vertical sunbreakers. An irrigation canal was essential, so the inclusion of the various pools fed from it became the unifying landscape theme.

One of Sert's most recent buildings is the Museum of the Fondation Maeght in Saint Paul de Vence, near Nice, France. It was built to show the collection of Paris art dealer Aimé Maeght, and is distinguished by the close relationship and variety of its roofed and open spaces. Four of the general exhibition galleries are specifically designed to show the works of Miró, Calder, Kandinsky and Braque. Windowless, with reflected lighting from curved shell roofs above, they are linked by glazed anterooms that look out on courtyards that are bordered by sculptures. Over the main gallery for temporary exhibits are two inverted shells—the most visually dominant curves in the complex.

Although both of these projects indicate Sert's aesthetic preferences, his university work in the Cambridge area most completely expresses his concept of living. A university is something of a micro-city and affords the opportunity to test urban ideas at a more manipulative scale. With the Holyoke Center and the recently completed Married Student Housing for Harvard Univer-

Holyoke Center, Harvard University, Cambridge, Massachusetts.

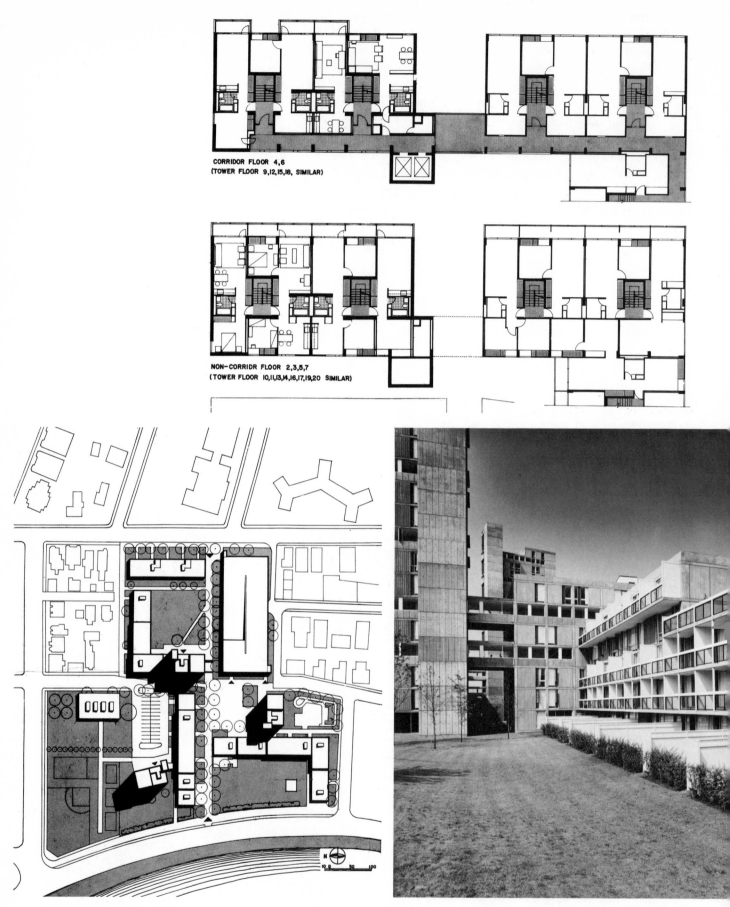

CORRIDOR FLOOR 4,6
(TOWER FLOOR 9,12,15,18, SIMILAR)

NON-CORRIDR FLOOR 2,3,5,7
(TOWER FLOOR 10,11,13,14,16,17,19,20 SIMILAR)

Married Student Housing, Harvard University,
Cambridge, Massachusetts.

sity, Sert was faced with the familiar urban problems of traffic congestion, insufficient parking space and lack of land. Land values are high in the vicinity of the campus, and since university land and buildings are tax free, the city is loath to see the university expand on land it would otherwise draw tax from. Hence low-density developments are discouraged. After studying the Charles River Basin onto which Harvard, M.I.T. and Boston Universities face, Sert decided that building heights of about 200 feet would not destroy the scale of nearby spaces and buildings and, on the wide river, were actually desirable.

The first "T" of what will be the "H-shaped" block of the Holyoke Center was completed in 1962. The spine of the scheme is the cross bar of the "H," an animated pedestrian arcade from which shops, offices, and the health services for Harvard and Radcliffe College are approached. Parking facilities are reached via ramps that pass beneath the arcade, thus separating pedestrians and automobiles. An interesting feature of the building is the use of a special obscured glass that admits filtered light while cutting down heat penetration and loss, in conjunction with transparent glass where views are desirable. It introduces a facade element, similar in impression to Japanese paper screens, that allows the distinction between the functions of seeing and lighting while also providing a visual link between solid and opaque walls.

Although the elements of diversity in this one-block complex are something Sert believes strongly in, it is the Married Students Housing, although at a limited scale again, that most represents what he has always been moving towards: A demonstration that it is possible and desirable to live at high densities in cities. It is an important architectural statement: a powerful statement of Sert's deep convictions. The complex has five hundred apartments, with parking facilities for 352 cars, and a density of 248 persons per acre. Sert stresses that if surrounding roads and services are adequate, good conditions can be provided for high-density living, providing space is well-allocated, and amenities and buildings well-planned. Density, for him, is an end result: a figure one discovers after a project is designed. He is adamantly at odds with the inverse procedure.

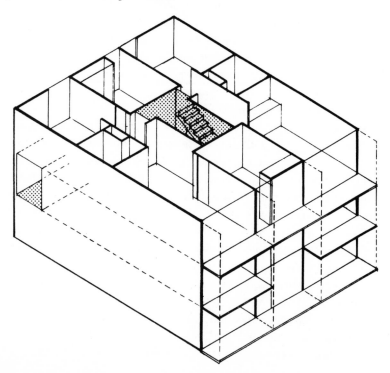

One of Sert's great strengths is the rare ability to design from the general, in, and from the particular, out: working from total aspects, the bigger picture and more general aims, while simultaneously scrutinizing the small, individual requirements of a project. The basic organizing element, of which all the buildings are multiples, which enabled economy, directness and speed of construction, is a structural unit three bays wide and three stories high, with a stair in its center bay. The vertical and horizontal massing of these units was carefully designed to create a sequence of varying exterior spaces.

A constant and vexing problem in modern architecture has been the relationship between high and low elements. Here the transition is well conceived. Rising from the edges, where it respects the low height of the surrounding residential neighborhood, to the center, three-, five- and seven-story horizontal volumes step-up to meet, and are linked by bridges to, the twenty-two-story vertical volumes of the three central towers.

The "slender" high units (usually more apartments per floor would be necessary) and "tall" low units (seven story walk-ups are impractical) were made economically feasible by the elevator system: Elevators in the towers stop at every third level, and residents walk either up or down one floor; the elevators also serve the fourth and sixth levels of the low buildings by providing access across the bridges. This arrangement also permitted apartments to extend through the full width of the slabs, thereby enjoying a least two views and having cross-ventilation. Many, but not all, of the apartments have private balconies off their living areas—presumably cost was the deterring factor. Facades vary in response to different exposures, sun conditions and views. This is in contrast, for example, to Mies's more formal approach, typified by the uniform envelope of the Lake Shore Drive Apartments.

Sert has reacted against elevating amenities on platforms, believing the ground, the level of trees, to be the best level for activities and buildings. Here the sequence of spaces is defined and enclosed in the tradition and scale reminiscent to that of the Harvard quadrangle. The spaces are linked by a tree-lined, brick promenade that bisects the new complex, connecting the community at its rear to the river at its front. This interpenetration is achieved without infringing upon the necessary privacy of the new residents. A grass common, defined on one side by the garage, opens down two steps into a brick plaza also flanked by the garage, so that after parking, people automatically enter the central, vital area of the scheme. Related to this space is a community center with public meeting and seminar rooms, drug store, dry cleaners, laundry and nurseries (with adjacent visitors' parking and children's playground). Finally, a "U-shaped" grass space, like those in nearby Harvard "houses," faces on the river, merging into the riverfront promenade. Sert sought to create alive spaces on the roofs also, where there are coin-operated laundries and drying areas, and sunbathing terraces sheltered by the stepping down of the low blocks.

There is a rare visual rapport in this group of buildings that derives from the careful measuring and subtle shaping of space, and the careful and appropriate relationship of building volumes to this. Sert has created a very distinguished complex of buildings, that, above all, is a concept of living that is realistically born of a sensitivity toward human needs.

Sert has also been active recently across the Charles River on the campus of Boston University. Again faced with a high-density situation, here on an awkward sliver of land, he has created pedestrian spaces, while sensibly reorienting the campus; his new buildings relate to the river instead of the avenue behind them. There is a definite tension and structural relationship between the old campus and the new buildings, neither of which "could stand alone," he says.

This, of course, is precisely his approach, and it is clearly evident in the Married Students Housing too. Sert does not create a structural frame within which the elements of a building are resolved, but rather he relates the functional elements loosely—elements that have derived from function and are also based on an appropriate structural principle—thus creating a greater flexibility and, in turn, a more plastic, animated architecture. He is more interested in the expression and nature of the elements; their differences; their liveliness. In fragmenting his forms and their surface treatment, Sert risks the loss of formal clarity and coherence. He does this to explore other equally important factors that formal directness is inclined to ignore. Consequently, he is at times accused of picturesque tendencies (although he would take exception to this since he believes architecture belongs to the spirit and technology of its time) by those who seek greater clarity in architecture. Always with continuity and the larger picture in mind, he has forsaken an *a priori* theoretical approach.

For almost four decades Sert has been close to some of the most important developments in the modern movement. When he has found the "rules" too academic, and it is well to remember that he was active in forming many of them in his C.I.A.M. years, he has broken them. To him, our approach today is "a healthy spirit of revolt." He emphasizes the visual approach, which after all is the artist's domain, but only insofar as it is a natural outgrowth of the uses and life of essential elements.

Plaza Plan, Boston City Hall, Boston, Massachusetts.

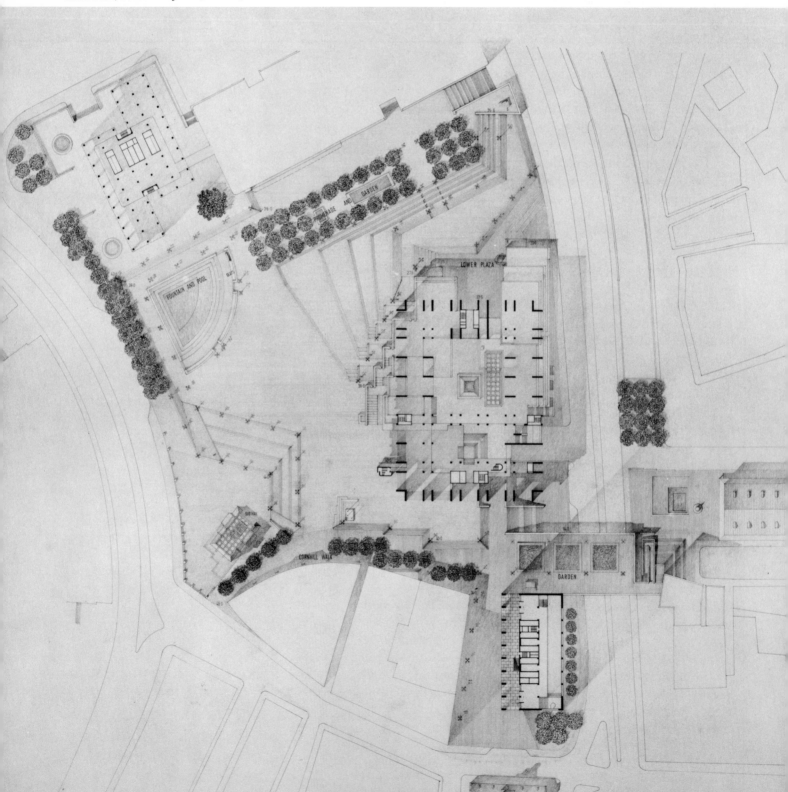

KALLMANN, McKINNELL and KNOWLES

In selecting an architect for a significant commission the client's expectations rest principally on the previous work of the chosen architect; selection is almost by brand name. But in an open architectural competition, an architect is chosen on the superior merits of his specific design submission, evaluated by a critical and independent jury. The choice is by product, rather than by brand name. For their City Hall, in 1961, Boston's city fathers resorted to an open competition; the last one in the United States for a major public building had been San Francisco's City Hall in 1909.

The site for the new City Hall is in Boston's historic, but deteriorated, central area, where it would become an important element in the new Government Center. A master plan for the area was prepared by I. M. Pei & Associates, defining traffic circulation and the location of open spaces and buildings; it somewhat predetermined the general form of City Hall and its urban context. The City Hall was to be a building 100 feet to 130 feet high and some 275 feet square, within an urban plaza of monumental scale where it would become the focus, both visually and symbolically. The general form and dimensions of other buildings in the immediate vicinity were equally clearly prescribed. The specific functional needs of the City Hall itself were outlined precisely in the well-detailed program.

Any winning design will obviously have a dissenting faction; a wise precaution was taken to appropriate funds for construction in advance of the competition, to prevent delay or even abandonment. Delgating three of the city's most important businessmen to serve on the jury helped to maintain the essential support of the local community. The appointment of jurors Wurster, Netsch, Rapson and Belluschi assured competitors that the assessment and recommendation of the jury would be just. The interest and excitement generated by the competition was reflected in the 256 entries, many from established firms by no means short of work. The eight entries selected to advance into a second and final developmental stage were all by younger, unestablished architects,

First Concept Sketch.

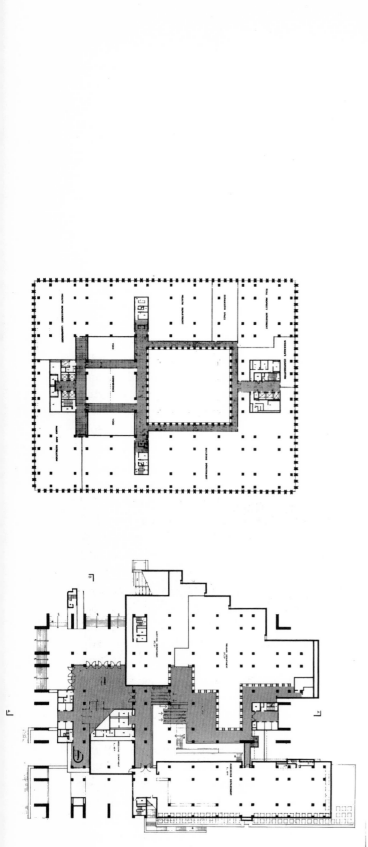

Eighth and Third floor plans.

finding a rare chance to acquire a significant commission on the merits of ability. The winning design was by Kallmann, McKinnell & Knowles. Of it the jury said, "At a distance the building achieves great monumentality, drama, and unity; and in detail the contrasting textures, the play of light and shade, the richness of forms and spaces, culminate in a series of dramatic terraces which provide a strong focus for the symbol of city government. It is a daring yet classical architectural statement, contained within a vigorous unified form."

All three architects were design critics at Columbia University when they won the competition. Since then, Kallmann and Mc-Kinnell have established an office in Boston to carry the design into the working drawing and construction stages; Knowles remains in New York, and is involved in the development stages only in a consulting capacity. Gerhard Kallmann was born in Berlin in 1915, and received his achitectural training at the Architectural Association in London. He left England to come to America in 1948, and since then has worked in several New York offices and been visiting critic at a number of American universities. Noel Michael McKinnell was born in Manchester, England, in 1935, and graduated from the local university in 1958. After teaching there for a year, he came to Columbia University for postgraduate studies.

Their winning design is a bold and powerful architectural statement. It represents an approach counter to the neoclassic tendency to resolve the many diverse functions of a building within one absolute envelope or pristine pavilion. Kallmann has written that this tendency manifests "the absolute dominion of the individual whole-form, self-enclosed and raised to universal significance." Kallmann and McKinnell think it necessary to approach each architectural problem without the application of a preconceived formal concept. With an "unpremeditated image" based on the existing situation, they seek an architecture of "continuous relatedness."

Their springboard for the initial design stages was a threefold analysis: the specific location with its particular regional, historical and societal implications; the program, attending to both the spiritual and functional requirements of the building; and the construction, with structure and materials to be determined by the former considerations. In concentrating on the major problems of site, program, and structure and method of construction, they focused on the cardinal concerns of modern architecture.

Their design has evoked sweeping praise and damning criticism. The main contentions of the skeptics can be expressed in two broad categories: the building's "brutal" and forbidding appearance that comes from a somewhat ponderous structure built of "raw" materials; and sculptural indulgences that might be considered an exaggerated, arbitrary exercise, not relative to the functional dictates of the building.

The structural system is modular, with alternating 15-foot and 30-foot concrete columns, poured in place, which contrast with the smooth surfaces of precast concrete floor trusses. Throughout the building, structure and methods of formwork are left exposed, and the jointing of precast elements is visually expressed. The internal and external walls of the building's base structure are of the same red brick as the plaza surface, creating a oneness, a sense of their having evolved simultaneously. This "rough object" is not tampered with; the structural skeleton and functional enclosures *are* the total expression. Although there will be no great maintenance costs, the extent to which this "as-found" approach recognizes technological advances, and responds to human needs, is quite controversial within the profession.

The City Hall is horizontally organized into three distinct components, each articulated from one another; the lower structure forms the base, the administrative offices the top, with the ceremonial elements in between. The lower structure, or "mound," containing large public lobbies, allows easy and direct access to those departments receiving the heaviest volume of public traffic. The administrative space, in the quietest zone, is shaped as a disciplined, rectangular doughnut. The offices are arranged in ascending tiers, stepped back from an inner court and, correspondingly, stepped outwards on the plaza facades. Supported free of the mound by columns and girders, this component gives a powerful definition to the building in silhouette. Suspended between this and the mound are the areas of ceremonial importance—the Mayor's department, Council Chamber and offices, and a Municipal library. These are clearly expressed by their shading hoods that cast deep shadows onto the windows. A glazed entrance lobby houses the stairs and elevators, and is skylighted through tall shafts from the roof. It connects all three parts of the building, and from it the visitor can see, at least partially, all the major elements of the building. As the administrative offices are raised clear of the mound, a series of sheltered, open-air terraces are

Competition Model.

South Lobby.

directly accessible from the plaza and the enclosed entrance lobby. This inner court is a gathering place for visitors, and encourages the free access and flow of pedestrians.

From the mound these red brick terraces radiate gently down into those of the plaza, so that there is no distinct separation. Moving from level to level, and looking across the plaza, through the building, and down into Dock Square and old Boston will make this a walk of great excitement. The discipline of the upper structure, in contrast to the variety of planes and fascination of shape at the pedestrian level, has been described as "a brilliant demonstration of the principle of order in the sky and tumult on the ground." The design license occurs within an orderly structure that accommodates not only the varied forms and attendant voids of the building's ceremonial elements, but also the flexible open area of the upper office structure. Personalized space and general space have been juxtaposed, with structure as the catalyst.

Heyer: "To what extent does the Boston City Hall reflect your design philosophy and to what degree is its expression symptomatic of your process in resolving the architectural problem?"

McKinnell: "Our design philosophy has found its most complete expression in this project. It also reflects the way we work—from the specific to the general rather than the other way."

Kallmann: "We distrust and have reacted against an architecture that is absolute, uninvolved and abstract. We have moved towards an architecture that is specific and concrete, involving itself with the social and geographic context, the program, and methods of construction, in order to produce a building that exists strongly and irrevocably, rather than an uncommitted abstract structure that could be any place and, therefore, like modern man—without identity or presence."

Heyer: "What were the important considerations and evaluations made in the initial stages?"

Kallmann: "Locality; function; monumentality, arrived at in a meaningful way through the intensification of the function, which is different from that of the usual office."

McKinnell: "A case of making the process of government so

meaningful that it becomes monumental, involving everybody; the people going to City Hall as visitors and tourists, and those who worked there—all involved and aware. It became monumental because it was meaningful."

Kallmann: "We thought the involvement of the people with their government would be the main theme and would give us the clue to the volumetrics of the building. This encouraged the interpenetration. Our first sketches show, from Beacon Hill, the access moving right into the building and through, in a flow of visitors and users. From this we derived the basic positioning of elements, always with an awareness of where and what they were. The idea of the mound structure evolved from the possibility of people walking into the upper courtyard and through it down into Dock Square, being aware of the process of government but not impeding it. This led to differentiating the massive public access of the lower mound structure, from the more remote access of the administrative offices—with the ceremonial elements of government hung in between them, visible and strongly expressed."

Heyer: "To what extent was the function of the building a generator of form, and how did it lead you to this sense of involvement, this presence?"

Inner Court.

McKinnell: "In the City Hall we have a series of people performing certain tasks. We feel strongly about their particular function, which may be no different from that in a normal office building, but demands a different form."

Kallmann: "From the differentiation or hierarchy of function we hope our design will gain a hierarchy of spaces which have meaning. We are not interested in abstract space exercises or spatial sensation, but in establishing a space and identity for the human being who works in this particular context. There is a stepping up of intensity in this case because we are trying to dignify the process."

Heyer: "Was the particular expression of the ceremonial elements a desire to initiate a plastic relationship of forms in space? How do these solids and interpenetrations correspond to functional dictates?"

McKinnell: "Our motivation is much less formal. We always said the City Hall would be the most conservative building that we had ever designed."

Kallmann: "There is good reason for this: government is a very conserving activity, and we felt the building needed staying power. It cannot be iconoclastic if it is concerned with these particular values. There is a certain vigor of government that we wanted to express. Maybe this was influenced by the Kennedy Administration at the time, when there was more optimism about the usefulness of government. In retrospect we may not have thought of this consciously, but it seems to have half come through. We had to make these elements of government exist with a very strong but not authoritarian presence. This was more important to us than the precise plastic form that they would be, and is sensed in the way we lead stairs and levels up close to them. They have the intimacy from this closeness which is necessary in a democratic government, as well as the dignity necessary to allow the people who govern to be dignified."

Heyer: "To what extent were you concerned with integrating the building directly with the patterns of circulation through the immediate area?"

McKinnell: "The plaza has been criticized by many people who see it in rather classical terms. It is not a conventional plaza in the sense of forming a culmination to something. We have always regarded the plaza as a place of passage; not as a point to which people come, but, rather, a point through which many paths pass. This is very important to the understanding of the building—to have a sense of the plaza passing through it. The whole lower concourse building is really the plaza hollowed out at this point. It is also the transition where the drop in the site, which is 20 feet, is taken up inside the building. By this manner the whole organization of the lower concourse building is a passage from north to south, so we get access to the building on many levels. On the lower part, the building is like a cliff which can stand up to the strain and proximity of cars; here the building joins modern times, standing right down in the traffic stream on the same level as Dock Square. In the master plan, made before the competition, the building was on top of a platform, rather removed, and was indicated as a rather classical doughnut shape. Ours, by a strange coincidence, is also hollowed out in the upper part. The court below is not so much a court as the top of the lower building, a place for one to pause and then pass on."

Kallmann: "The key to the lower building, and its floor plan, is that passage. A descending street through a galleria type of space—this is where the street life of the building will take place."

Heyer: "There is an almost Auguste Perret-like classical sense of structure to the building that is somewhat overlooked when people see the more evident variation of form and sequence of spaces in the design model. How does an essentially inflexible structural arrangement retain its logic while accommodating such diversity of elements and spaces?"

Kallmann: "Certainly the objective was not to make a clear demonstration of a crystalline structure, but there is a strong sense of structuring in the fabric which gives unity to the whole. We strongly believe in architecture as constructed space. You could take one piece of the building, and in it have the sense that runs right through the whole building. This will hold together the dichotomy of the lower brick structure and the upper concrete one, which ascend and descend—they are sort of serrated into each other. We don't mind if structure appears in the form of a short or long column in the same space—as when the terrain dips down and reveals a column 90 feet high, whereas next to it may be a column only eight feet six inches high—we really just let the chips fall that way. The more important program requirements determine volumes and the manner in which they ascend and descend. Through the whole building you will sense this very aggressive ceiling and column structure, which will give unity."

Heyer: "You were interested in maintaining a viable sense within the building, avoiding the neatly-defined, preserving the feeling of possible growth. Is this to recognize continuity and change both within the building and its relation to the city without?"

McKinnell: "We don't see this, I think, as a finished, complete, final building. The thing that draws us together as designers is that we are concerned with non-finished, non-Platonic volumes. There are certain aspects about City Hall that reflect our attitude towards cities and buildings. That is the idea of embedding in the matrix of a city structure yet another form: It is not inappropriate that a symbol of government should become a significant microcosmic element of the city as a whole."

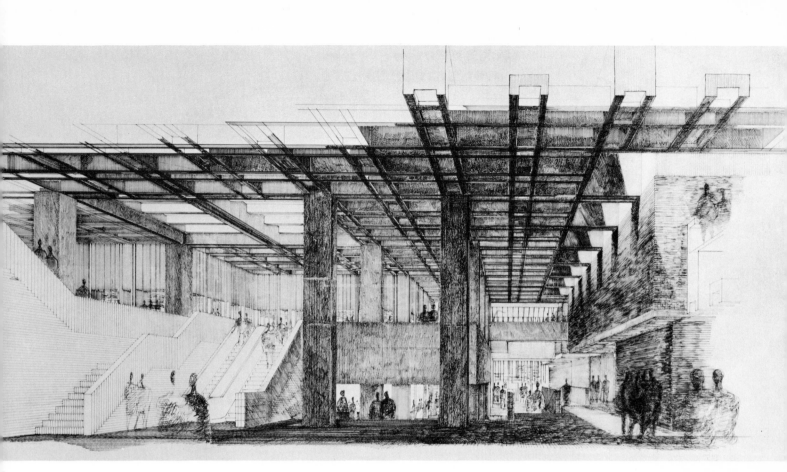

North Lobby.

Kallmann: "There is a dialogue in this building: what we call the conserving element, in concert with the vitality in stretching and breaking out—linkage to the rest of the city. The whole mound building is very much involved with the plaza and the comings and goings of people; the upper part, where the internal workings go on, is more aloof. The building was described as a miniature city, as it has the building materials of the rest of the city. We consciously chose the Boston brick that people find in the poorer quarters of the city; here it is shown in more august spaces, but it is still the same material."

McKinnell: "We think it's a robust and strong image. We don't fear for it, but feel that it can fend for itself."

"We must know better the here and now of 'our own' life in its Time and Place. In all we must learn to see ourselves as we are, as 'modern' man—and this be our true culture." In many ways these words of Wright apply to the Boston City Hall—a direct look at the reality of our time. Life is not really standardized, static and acceptable, but individual, fluctuating and rather perturbing. The design not only manifests this, but seems to gain strength from it. If most architecture is great because it transcends the inconsistencies and contradictions of life, cannot some buildings also come alive by specifically embodying them?

The City Hall is a demonstrably anti-precious statement. An "open-ended" aesthetic that invites from the onlooker involvement and possibly even conclusion. It invites interpretation in the best constructive sense of Paul Valery's expression, "I write half the poem. The reader writes the other half." Kallmann and McKinnell, without being extremists, believe extremely in their ideals. Although they have clearly found strength in Le Corbusier's example, their design is more than a mere Le Corbusier apéritif. Nor is it vastly apart from the spirit of many younger American architects, as a look at the efforts in a few architectural schools—certainly those on the East Coast—will show.

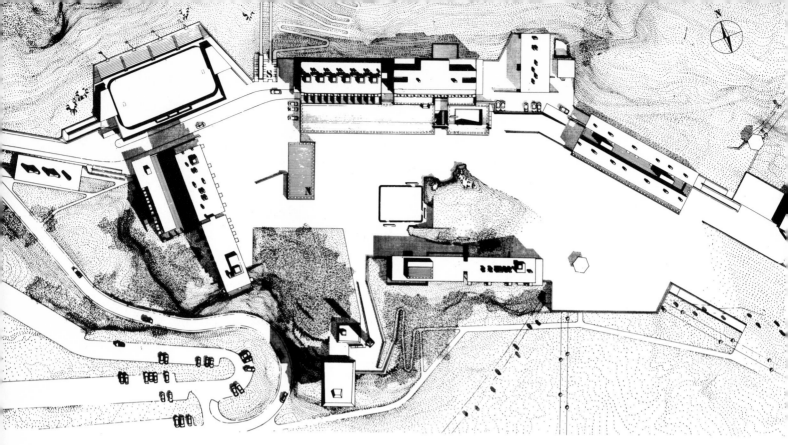

Resort Town Flaine, Haute Savoie, France.

Cesna Chair.

Marcel Breuer (signature)

MARCEL BREUER

Unity and excellence were easier to attain in earlier, more homogeneous epochs, where there was agreement on standards in themselves high. The lack of a central discipline is particularly evident today when two modern architects build adjacently. Economic expansion, technological advance, and new problems that we do not fully understand have to a large extent invalidated traditional disciplines; our present disciplines derive primarily from these very factors—and personal restraints—rather than cultural values. However, new disciplines will probably emerge as we pursue the task of making our buildings more than usable, our cities more than livable, and increasingly search the realities of our own circumstance.

In the Bauhaus, in 1923, Breuer said: "Hard as I try, I see no chaos in our time. Just because a few painters do not know whether they should paint realistically or in the abstract, or whether they should paint at all, does not mean chaos. Our needs seem clear—the possibilities limited only by us. The main thing is that we act whenever a need appears and use our strength to find an economic and coherent solution." Breuer still holds this opinion, in common with many of his contemporaries.

Breuer believes in diversity, which to him is symbolized in the form taken by a drop of water: "The front is broad while the back is tapered. If architects try to narrow architecture, they are already at the tail end. If they are broadening it, they are moving forward."

Breuer sees one of the dominant impulses of the modern movement as a striving for clarity: "To us clarity means the definite expression of the purpose of a building and a sincere expression of its structure. One can regard this sincerity as a sort of moral duty, but I feel that for the designer it is above all a trial of strength that sets the seal of success on his achievement; and the sense of achievement is a very basic instinct." The spirit in which he pursues his architecture is that of the artist working on the

Wassily Chair.

highest level of feeling and the technician working on the highest level of logic. "One needs no technical knowledge to conceive an idea," he says, "but one does need technical ability and knowledge to develop it." Breuer believes that the ability to approach a problem immediately, objectively and without preconception is basic to architecture. "There is the main concept, and there is the conception of details: between those two the design of a building just grows. Common sense, experience, taste and work carry it to completion. But no common sense, experience, taste or work is good enough without those first basic concepts."

Marcel Breuer was born in Hungary in 1902. At eighteen, he had gone to Vienna to attend the Academy of Art, and had started working for an architect-furniture designer; there he read of the Bauhaus program and departed to enroll in its second entering class. By 1924 he was in charge of the carpentry shop with the title of Bauhaus Master. A year later, apparently inspired by the handlebars of his bicycle, he designed his first tubular steel chair. "I already had the concept of spanning the seat with fabric in tension as a substitute for thick upholstery," he said. "I also wanted a frame that would be resilient and elastic. The combination of elasticity and of members in tension would give comfort without bulkiness. I also wanted to achieve transparency of forms to attain both visual and physical lightness. Mass production and standardization had already made me interested in polished metal, in shiny and impeccable lines in space, as new components for our interiors. I considered such polished and curved lines not only symbolic of our modern technology, but actually to be technology."

Apart from Gropius's own office there was little architectural instruction in the Bauhaus, and finding the industrial design emphasis too narrow for his own interest Breuer resigned in 1928, the same year as Gropius, to start his own practice in Berlin. He then designed his most famous chair—one continuous tubular steel frame, acting as a simple cantilever, with a cane seat and back in a black bentwood frame. "The component parts are different. The most up-to-date material—chrome steel—contrasts with the oldest material—cane seating and wood." This type of juxtaposition and catholic attitude have remained with Breuer. "I never had the feeling that certain materials were acceptable and others were not. For instance, polished granite for a table top is nearly perfect: the granite is old; what is new is the high polish. What I always aimed for was freedom in exploring materials, new and old, and freedom in exploring technological disciplines."

Breuer's great talent was unmistakable in his first two architectural commissions: the Harnischmacher House, in Wiesbaden, in 1932, and two years later in Zurich, the Doldertal Apartments, designed with Alfred and Emil Roth, for Siegfried Giedion. The house remains one of the best early modern ones in Europe. Its porches extended the interior space outwards, and a roof terrace screened by a glass wall employed steel cables as wind bracing support. It had a lightness and precision that was typical of his furniture and interior projects of that period. The apartments were two buildings, each with two apartments occupying a whole floor and two penthouse apartments. A latter-day criticism of the early modern buildings in Europe is their lack of provision for such problems as sun protection—which Breuer overcame here by using wooden roll awnings.

Harnischmacher House, Wiesbaden, Germany.

Doldertal Apartments, Zurich, Switzerland.

Gane's Exhibition Pavilion, Bristol, England.

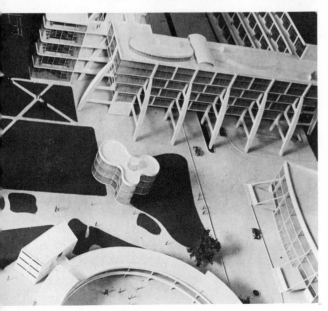

Project for the Civic Center of the Future.

Breuer spoke for the whole early European spirit—which Wright was extremely critical of because he thought it to be inorganic—when he said, "The art of architectural composition lies in assembling simple, elemental forms to arrive at basic solutions. The space bounded by such elements can be free and fluent, connected both vertically and horizontally, but the components encompassing it will be crystallic and man-made—forms that differ from other natural forms, though they are part of the same composition—wood against metal, space against void, a cube against a tree."

With unrest in Germany, Breuer moved his practice to England in 1935 and formed a partnership with F. R. S. Yorke. Their Ganes Exhibition Pavilion in Bristol, in 1936, marked a new direction in Breuer's architecture. Rather than slender, lineal structural parts, he emphasized mass by contrasting solid planes to large glass areas. In using stone masonry for the walls he may have foreseen another criticism of the white structures of the 1920's, whose surfaces tended to suffer rapid deterioration and discoloration from uneven weathering. Breuer, however, had precise ideas on the correct expression for this age-old material: "When stone is used in a wall, the aim is not to evoke some notion of rock, but to build a clear-cut slab—made of stone because stone is a good and durable and texturally-pleasant material. It should be clear that this is a wall built by a mason, executing drawings with dimensions and a given geometry; it is not a grotto or part of a romantic anachronism."

Another 1936 project received with great interest in England was the "Civic Center of the Future." Many spontaneous ideas in this model were prophetic of Breuer's future, such as the Y-shaped office building with a maximum of naturally lighted peripheral offices around a circulation core placed at the building's widest girth. This concept was to reappear over two decades later in such projects as the UNESCO and IBM office buildings.

In 1937 Gropius invited Breuer to teach at Harvard. In Cambridge

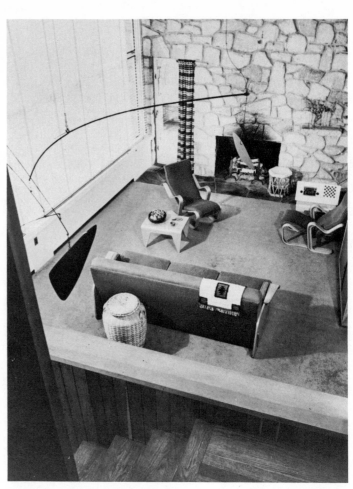

Breuer House, Lincoln, Massachusetts.

Breuer spent four years associated with Gropius, and a subsequent five years on his own, designing many fine houses that proved to be a great influence on American residential architecture. His own house in Lincoln, Massachusetts, which he designed in 1939, was planned on three open, interrelated levels, and singularly influenced his students.

Breuer has two favorite approaches to his house plans. His "long house," in New Canaan (the second of four that he has built for himself in America) and the Robinson House, "a bi-neuclear house," in Williamstown, Massachusetts, both in 1947, typify these approaches.

The "long houses" have living areas at one end, kitchen and utilities in the center, and a series of bedrooms opening off a corridor at the other end. In Breuer's own house, the timber structure is braced by diagonal boards and cantilevered in all four directions from a whitewashed concrete base. The "bi-neuclear houses" separate activities into distinct functional areas for sleeping versus living, children versus adults, and noise versus quiet. The Robinson house is an H-plan with living, dining, kitchen and music room in one leg and bedrooms in the other, linked by the entrance that is flanked by two small private courts. The wings have an inward sloping "butterfly roof," a favorite device of Breuer's. "One of the houses I like best," he said. "Often a house with an ample budget tends to become overcomplicated by the client's requirements. This was not the case here. The building program was kept simple and the concept generous. Consequently, the house does not seem overdesigned or cluttered with fussy details. The glass walls are especially appropriate, since the hills are behind them. Visually, the landscape provides the 'walls,' thus the true limits of the interior space." In all respects, Breuer's houses are sensitively related to their sites, yet distinct from them.

The treatment of fireplaces and staircases is of great interest to Breuer, as can be seen, for example, in the granite fireplace in the Robinson house, and the concrete stair treads between a field-stone retaining wall and steel truss railing in the 1954 Gagarin House, in Litchfield, Connecticut.

By 1946, Breuer had moved his practice to New York, where even when involved with larger problems, he still likes to have one or two houses under design in his office of twenty-five people. The importance of his residential buildings and his Harvard teaching in those first years in America is well known. One would no more deny Gropius's tremendous impact as an educator, than Breuer's as a "bridge" to a new generation. Many of today's outstanding architects in America—including Johnson, Rudolph, Pei, Barnes, Johansen—have been Breuer's students.

"I tried to approach my Harvard teaching in a broad way. I did not want the students to imitate me or work in my vernacular; whether I achieved that or not, is another question. Everybody realizes that a younger man is somewhat influenced by the teacher. Yet as far as direct teaching was concerned, I emphasized the importance of the student making his own decisions. I very seldom drew on their drawings, adding my correction, or showed them how to do it. I discussed principles of construction, solutions of function, what a window does, effects of daylight or sunlight, what is good or bad in a solution, and so on. This was the criticism —not showing how a building should look.

"I wanted to encourage individual search and research by my teaching; as against Mies, who showed his students: 'This is the corner solution, the brick solution, do it.' With all respect for Mies—who knows very well what he does and wants, but is much too narrow—my philosophy was not, and is not, to develop a definite style. If you do, you have already killed it. I am much more interested in the points of style that need further research and development. The development is the significant thing as it becomes itself the style of that moment.

"The students from that Harvard period, like myself, have pursued divergent paths. This is absolutely natural and I am happy about it. But you have to be critical of these divergent lines, as some result from new discovery and further development, some from ambition, demands of clients, and publicity—a mixed thing, not always good; but the fact of divergence is good.

"A great many tendencies are emphasized today: inventiveness, structure, plastic modulation, preoccupation with scale, and re-grettably, the all-is-permissible-to-the-genius tendency. This is due partly to the original emphasis of modern architecture on freedom from traditional precedents. The initial liberating process still has an active momentum; a fact we should welcome in view of the tendency of many 'successful' modern architects to codify and formalize architecture into a rather tyrannical discipline that is less related to true progress, to visual and human needs.

"I am sure that some very capable architects feel that today's architecture needs a shot in the arm, and that the glass wall is much overrated as a universal enclosure of space. Yet I do not want to abandon some of my own children: the transparency of architecture; the interior space connected with the exterior one, at least visually; the flow of space through a structure and be-

Chamberlain House, Wayland, Massachusetts.

tween its walls; the language of structural forces; the physical and aesthetic sensations of the material which promotes these various phenomena—glass. There are many possibilities in architecture provided it is not straight-jacketed into narrow rules. There are also many human needs that our glass wall does not fulfill. We need a broader aspect of aesthetics. We have materials to use other than just metal and glass. And we have needs other than just floating in space. I feel that the vocabulary of architecture has to be enlarged considerably.

"It should not worry us that on occasion the current scene seems chaotic in some quarters; architecture has its own, built-in correctives. Forty years ago, when I heard my first lecture on a not-yet-born modern architecture and an already-born modern art, I heard that word chaos, and I have heard it a hundred times since. I am sure that art critics of ancient Greece talked about chaos when their sculptors began to separate the arms of a figure from the torso. Nothing is easier to discover than chaos everywhere, and to have a bit of 'Weltschmerz' about it. It is part of the cosmos; Genesis is a continuous process.

"Architecture progresses by attacking on all fronts. I would like to see individual expression, whether the result of the analytical and functional approach or the result of imagination and rebellion, lead to more valid expressions of form and function in our architecture. To be valid, they will have to follow the main current of architecture. But I would welcome these individual adventures as laboratory experiments—visual, technical, or social ones—for a better architecture which moves forward; this is the point where individualism and discipline are one and the same thing. They are complementing traits, perhaps evident in the same personality and work. Only a synthesis of individuality and discipline allows us to move forward in balance.

"Yet it makes good sense to find similar solutions for similar problems: there is certainly not a great deal of difference between the problems of one 1961 New York office building and another 1961 office building, or between those of one 1961 eight-room house and another 1961 eight-room house of the same income group. There are variations, there are nuances, there are differences in character of owners and users, sites and local technology; but there is also a dominant general denominator in the solutions for each problem. The individuality inherent in similar problems is, roughly speaking, non-existent. Architecture has to create forms which stand repetition.

"What do we mean by individuality? Do we mean the individuality of the architect? Probably his personality and not that of the user is the one which strives for individual expression. A significant aspect of the individual search of the designer is his experimentation with a seemingly-solved problem. As far as I am concerned, this experimentation is, or should be, the controlling factor in the most disciplined work. The result may be commonplace, but in the process of conception it was at least attempted. The creative architect acts where a need is neglected, either physical or emotional. His endless testing of the possible new solutions is a key factor in the progress of architecture. Architecture can affect people in such a way that this opportunity should not be missed. If it is, then it will be like taking colors away from our life. Architecture, with all its discipline, and utilitarian and structural considerations, goes beyond use. This idea has always engaged me deeply and I have tried to achieve it in various ways. For

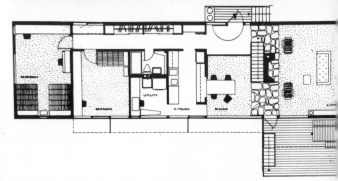

Breuer House, New Canaan, Connecticut.

example, the exhibition pavilion in England, although very simple, was obviously intended for formal or sculptural effect. Architecture is where structure, function, and abstract or pure form, are developed to the same degree. When one is developed at the expense of the other, there is a decadence or carelessness that I call vanity. Further development requires this balance. Pure architectural form is texture, with inventiveness of structure, use, and relation to surroundings contributing the tension in the work. Form is also subject to fashions, changes and convictions. It cannot be absolutely defined because it is elusive—but it is as important as function or structure, and should be there.

"Diversity is an advantage. The younger architects are more critical, less sure of themselves. As architecture is not formal or narrow, let us work on its every aspect."

Breuer's dormitory for Vassar College in Poughkeepsie, New York, in 1950, follows his "bi-neuclear" concept: the communal rooms are in a wing that connects directly, through an entrance lobby, to the dormitory wing on the second level, with an open bicycle-storage area at ground level. Soon after he completed this steel frame building, Breuer became interested in the facade as a sculptural element of texture and depth, and the use of concrete as both structural means and finished material.

European engineers have had as marked a preference for reinforced concrete, as Americans for skeleton steel structures. However, with the steel shortage of the Korean War, American engineers were forced to examine the possibilities of reinforced concrete. For Breuer this was welcome; he had already collaborated with Catalano on the design of concrete hyperbolic paraboloid structures. He saw concrete as "the completely plastic medium," that made it possible to design a structure as "sculpture with a function." To him, structure itself is art. "I like to see structure, to emphasize it, and to develop it—not just as a means to a solution. It is also a principle and a passion."

Robinson House, Williamstown, Massachusetts.

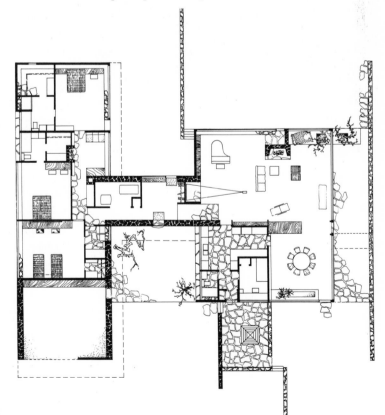

Gagarin House, Litchfield, Connecticut.

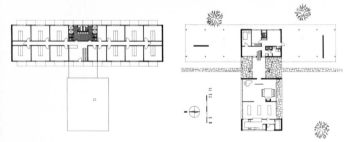

Ferry House, Vassar College, Poughkeepsie, New York.

Breuer's great opportunity to work at a large scale came in 1953, when he was selected to design UNESCO's new headquarters in Paris in collaboration with Bernard Zehrfuss of France, and Pier Luigi Nervi of Italy. The project had an international advisory panel of Gropius, Costa, Le Corbusier (who Zehrfuss later said "was as active as ten commissions"), Markelius, Rogers; and a direct consultant, Eero Saarinen.

The complex has two principal structures: the eight story, Y-shaped Secretariat building, with its top level for social functions, restaurants and terraces; and a trapezoid-shaped conference building. The two structures are connected by a lobby that functions as an informal meeting place.

Sun penetration has always concerned Breuer, and in the Secretariat, he shielded the predominantly glass facade with three systems, each applied according to the degree of exposure; vertical cantilevered slabs, horizontal louvers, and grey solar glass. The latter is free of the facade, supported on light metal projections to filter solar heat and glare, be cooled by circulating air to prevent heat radiation to the interior, and be cleaned by the rain. While functional in derivation, Breuer hoped that the combination of sun-screens would create an overall pattern, crystalline and shimmering in depth, that would enliven the whole facade.

The conference building encloses a dramatic, column-free, main assembly space, with an exposed folded plate structure that forms the roof and turns down to form the end walls. Concrete, in the roof and turns down to form the end walls. Concrete, in the "Civic Center of the Future" still essentially slab and column, was used here in a new, integral manner. Breuer shaped the walls and roof as one continuous structure, housing services in the shapes formed to give structural strength. This direct expression of a structural system, retaining the impression of its form work, is "principle and passion," and was to be further developed in the IBM building.

In a later tribute to his colleague, Breuer cited Nervi's mastery in projecting structural stresses into geometric form, his "razor-sharp analysis of the stresses working upon the structure and meeting these stresses face to face in a corresponding structural system—an organic system. Now, 'organic' is not meant as a catchword, nor in a metaphysical or nebulous sense, nor as an excuse. 'Organic' means a flow as real as the continuous strain starting at the shoulder, moving through the upper and lower arm, into the grip of the hand, fingers, and thumb. This is the real world of Nervi, the continuous stresses, branching out from support to girders, dividing into ribs and into the very fibers of the structure, only to combine again into ribs and columns." This, too, is clearly Breuer's philosophy.

The complex had commissioned for it art works by Miró, Calder, Picasso, and a Moore sculpture for the main entrance plaza. These are objects quite independent of the architecture. As Breuer says, "Art and architecture complementing each other, rather than parts of the same. Art is not necessary to make a good building, this is not a time like the Gothic period. But I welcome art as an addition to the architecture, the same way that I welcome people, flowers, books—signs of living and usage for which the space is the container."

Breuer often refers to the monolithic slab, either a horizontal or vertical cantilever, as uniquely capable of symbolizing the achievements of our epoch. This somewhat motivated his lecture hall for the New York University Heights campus in 1961, to be raised

Lecture Hall, New York University Bronx Campus,
New York, N.Y.

UNESCO, Paris, France.

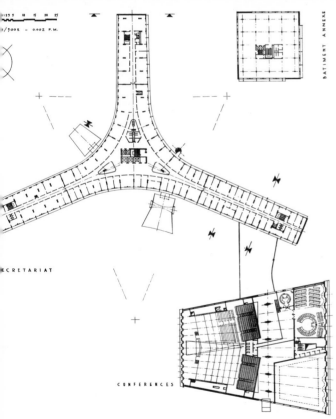

St. John's Abbey Church, Collegeville, Minnesota.

above the ground between heavily-textured, cantilevered side walls. But the "banner" for the 1963 Abbey Church of St. John's for the Benedictine monastery in Collegeville, Minnesota, is Breuer's most dramatic realization of this symbol. The "banner" is a slender, concrete cantilevered slab, pierced by two openings that contain a cross and bells. It is a sculptural gesture that announces the church while indicating its entrance beneath a parabolic arch. Its strength and majesty become a sign of assurance to the abbots, perhaps an inspiration of faith and hope. It is also the symbol that Breuer knew lay in our technology, "a spiritual expression of the possibility of what we can build." The silhouette of the banner is visible, from afar, above green trees and a rolling landscape. It prepares you for an occasion. Above all it is memorable, like Le Corbusier's gesture of the open hand raised in brotherhood at Chandigarh, or the silhouette of a town remembered as a place visited, remembered as a place liked.

Abbot Baldwin's introductory letter to Breuer set the note for an optimistic, rather than somber, design for the church: "The Benedictine tradition at its best challenges us to think boldly and to cast our ideals in forms which will be valid for centuries to come, shaping them with all the genius of present-day materials and techniques . . ." It gave Breuer sympathetic license for a direct, unadorned, visual statement in concrete within the architectural dignity and solemnity of a generous space. One enters the church beneath the banner, then through the low-ceilinged baptistry, beneath a balcony, coming suddenly into the main volume. Breuer placed the altar, with the Abbot's throne behind it, toward the center of the church, emphasized by a suspended baldachin. Around the altar is a semi-circle of choir stalls, facing pews for seventeen hundred on both the ground level and in the cantilevered balcony which is independent of the main structure: a scheme which seats the congregation close to the altar.

The church is a wedge-shaped space, within a folded concrete slab of wall and roof that is structurally continuous, and visually dominates both the exterior and the interior. The continuous slab helps to diffuse sound in the interior, while the ridges in the roof section contain the equipment needed to illuminate and ventilate the church. To increase the sense of space within the church, the folded plate construction is raised and supported on an edge beam, in which are concealed up-lights that illuminate the interior walls and roof at night. The edge beam transmits loads to buttress piers, thus visually extending the interior space between these piers to flanking cloister gardens. The interior is lighted naturally through these glass areas, and also by the banner reflecting southern sunlight through the north wall of glazed concrete hexagons.

Breuer has prepared a master plan for the monastery that will eventually replace most of its twenty-two existing buildings. A recently completed library building there has a 200 foot by 120 foot space where two central columns spread, tree-like, to support the waffle roof slab. The structure will be braced laterally by a system of peripheral piers.

Breuer employed a similar column system in the IBM laboratory building in La Gaude, France, in 1962, here, to minimize intrusion on the natural terrain, rather than obstruction in an internal space. Paris probably represents France to the Frenchman even more than London represents England to the Englishman. In an effort to decentralize the commercial and industrial concentration a-

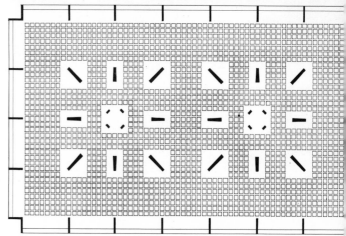

St. John's Abbey Library, model of columns, and reflected ceiling plan.

round Paris, President de Gaulle had issued regulations designed to discourage, if not prohibit expansion. IBM was obliged, therefore, to move away from the capital, and thereby risk losing most of its research staff, while placing itself at a disadvantage in attracting new personnel from all over the Continent for its expanding research program. Breuer chose a site near Nice, on a plateau in the dramatically beautiful rocky region just inland from the more intimate beauty of the Côte d'Azur. A measure of Breuer's achievement was that IBM was able to attract eighty-five percent of its original staff to its new headquarters.

Breuer adopted a double Y-plan to give each room an outside window and unobstructed panoramic views. As IBM did not want elevators, and Breuer thought a tall building would have intruded on this particular landscape, the new building was limited to three stories. His solution was to have two similar laboratory and office levels raised above the landscape on columns, so that the natural ground cover of scrub pine could run without interruption beneath the building.

He again used "branched" columns, reducing the depth of beams because branches go more directly to necessary points of support. But, more important, it minimized the number of columns, necessary because the uneven rock shelf, barely below the sand cover, had to be blasted to accommodate foundations for columns. Moreover, the uneven terrain could be equalized simply by maintaining a continuous floor level and varying the length of the columns.

The concrete columns were poured in place, while the structural wall units above were precast. Their 3-foot-deep facets shelter windows against the Mediterranean sun, while developing in their folded depth sufficient strength for an interior clear span of 40 feet from one exterior wall to the other. Their sloping planes create, in combination with ceiling spaces, negative spaces for the horizontal and vertical distribution of services to laboratories.

Breuer has prepared a master plan for a new mountain resort town called Flaine, for an eventual population of six thousand, in the Haute Savoie, near Geneva. Now under construction, all structures are to be composed of precast concrete elements and, with the exception of shops and public buildings, will be raised on columns to provide parking areas and avoid the problems of snowdrifts.

Research Center for IBM, La Gaude, France.

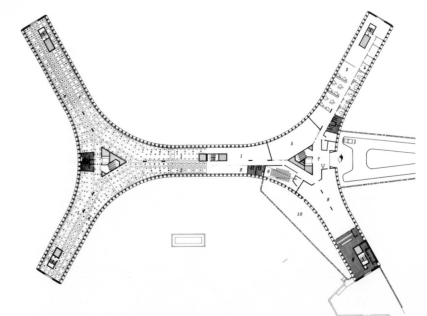

Breuer's selection as one of the architects for the UNESCO commission proved most fortuitous for him in that it brought him back to the attention of Europe, where, with his experience of American building methods and technology, he has secured several interesting commissions. Combined with an increasing number of challenging opportunities in America, Breuer has launched on the most productive decade of his career—a career that seems almost a measured progression, in the best sense of the Bauhaus, from the design of a chair to the design of a city.

One of the criticisms of his UNESCO building, and others, is a lack of integration of the various elements. Breuer's buildings are usually a complex of different elements, which he tries to resolve in the particular and then bring into a unified composition. As most architects know this is an extremely difficult thing to do. Breuer says: "If architecture is to reflect and help life, it will have to concern itself with differences—differences caused by conflicting requirements, contrasts in scale, conditions, personalities. The combination of contrasting forms into single unity seems a task of the highest order."

Breuer is very concerned with the need for economic yet enduring architecture. "Economical is not identical with cheap but relates to the ratio between effort and effect; between means and result. Architecture is not the materialization of a mood. Its objective is general usefulness, including its visual impact. It should not be a mere self-portrait of the architect or the client, though it must contain personal elements of both. It should serve generations, and while man comes and goes, buildings and ideas endure."

Resort Town Flaine, Haute Savoie, France.

PHILIP JOHNSON

"The painters have every advantage over us today," says Philip Johnson. "Besides being able to tear up their failures—we never can seem to grow ivy fast enough—their materials cost them nothing. They have no committees of laymen telling them what to do. They have no deadlines, no budgets. We are all sickeningly familiar with the final cuts to our plans at the last moment. Why not take out the landscaping, the retaining walls, the colonnades? The building would be just as useful and much cheaper. True, an architect leads a hard life—for an artist."

Beauty is the only thing of any importance, Johnson has often stated. Like "art for art's sake," his position appears to be capricious to those whose tenets are based on a moral foundation of formal, technical and social ideas. He has made what seem like digs at these ideas: "Comfort is not a function of beauty... purpose is not necessary to make a building beautiful... sooner or later we will fit our buildings so that they can be used... where form comes from I don't know, but it has nothing at all to do with the functional or sociological aspects of our architecture." This is the basic schism between those who still see such ideas as the moral basis of architecture, and architects like Johnson who regard them, and the narrowness with which they have been interpreted, as having led to the "sterility," or "Academy" of the modern movement.

Johnson has written: "Structural honesty seems to me one of the bugaboos that we should free ourselves from very quickly. The Greeks with their marble columns imitating wood, and covering up the roofs inside! The Gothic designers with their wooden roofs above to protect their delicate vaulting. And Michelangelo, the greatest architect in history, with his Mannerist column! There is only one absolute today and that is change. There are no rules, surely no certainties in any of the arts. There is only the feeling of a wonderful freedom, of endless possibilities to investigate, of endless past years of historically great buildings to enjoy."

Johnson's attitude towards architecture, what he calls restoring it to a "level of common sense," has an affinity to that of post-war American art: a disregard of the old artistic restraints and rules, a new way of looking at ordinary things for their own merit, and a pragmatic contact with real life. Personal feelings and preferences have ruled. But the vitality in a work of art comes when these are expressed within a proper discipline, are presented in a proper form. For Johnson, idea and feeling are the result of an

Johnson House, "Glass House," New Canaan, Connecticut.

abstract, complex problem-solving, accompanied by a taste that Vincent Scully, Jr. has aptly called "the most ruthlessly aristocratic, highly-studied taste of anyone practicing in America today." If one talks of quality, excellence, even taste (although this word is much misunderstood), Johnson has few peers. Of proper form, Johnson says: "I think of every building in history that has been similar in purpose. Then I think of the functional program—that's a major part of the study. At the same time, forms and processionalism are floating around in my head—how you get from one place to another, the relationships and effects of spaces as you move about in them."

Whereas the architects of the 1920's denounced history vehemently as an influence on design, Johnson has done as much as any modern architect to restate its importance: "We cannot *not* know history." Because of his respect for history, with also a slight dig at the functionalist tradition, he has said, "Form follows form, not function." Seeing the present as a more relaxed period, he purposely cites historical precedents for his own buildings. These are often so slight or completely rephrased that at times he seems overly generous to history. Jazz borrows fragments of familiar themes to veer off to bluer skies; nobody seems to mind that Sophocles and Aeschylus wrote about the same family; as Johnson said, "A good architect will always do original work."

Philip Johnson was born in Cleveland, Ohio, in 1906. While studying Greek and philosophy at Harvard, a few book and article references to Gropius, Le Corbusier, Mies and the De Stijl group made him suddenly aware of architecture; it was, as he puts it, a Saul-Paul conversion—"nothing existed but architecture." In 1930, Johnson traveled Europe with historian-critic Henry Russell Hitchcock, looking at modern architecture and preparing their book, *The International Style*, published in 1932.

It was a significant moment for Johnson because he was immediately attracted to Mies's approach rather than that of Gropius or Le Corbusier. Mies's classic approach and his use of elegant, beautiful materials in an architecture that appeared to be created for generations, has had a lasting impression on Johnson: "I have kept these throughout my divergence from Mies."

Well-educated, energetic and articulate, with a great interest in history and art, with his new-found love of architecture Johnson seemed an excellent choice to found the Department of Architecture and Design at the Museum of Modern Art in New York. Indeed, his years as critic and protagonist for the new modern architecture were eventful ones. It was under his direction that the Museum's landmark 1932 exhibition introduced the new architecture of Europe to America—the very architecture his book had presented.

In 1939 Johnson returned to Harvard to study architecture. Although this was the start of the "Gropius years," Johnson disclaims any influence. "I was just the purest possible Miesian that you can imagine." While a student Johnson had the advantage of being able to build his thesis project in Cambridge: a house designed as a walled court where the rectangular living volume opened onto a paved court through a glass wall—the possibilities of which Mies had studied but had not been able to build. After Harvard, he returned again to the Museum, and in 1947 published his book, *Mies van der Rohe*.

During the many long talks with Mies in preparing the book, they discussed the idea of a wholly glazed building. "I pointed

Johnson House, Cambridge, Massachusetts.

out to him that it was impossible because you had to have rooms, and that meant solid walls up against the glass, which ruined the whole point," said Johnson. "Mies said, 'I think it can be done.' It made me so angry that he thought it could be done when I did not see how, that I worked on the idea at the same time he did." The results were Mies's Farnsworth House, and Johnson's own "Glass House," in New Canaan, Connecticut, in 1949. Although Mies's was designed first, Johnson built his first, but with Mies's in mind. Both architects succeeded elegantly in achieving the domestic prism, almost a century after Paxton's Crystal Palace, while incidentally designing two of America's most famous houses. "Mies hates this house," said Johnson, "and that is quite all right. You never like what people try to do that's like you, but slightly different."

And differences there are. Johnson's house is more classic—as in its tendency towards symmetry, where four doors are centrally placed in each glass wall; or the brick plinth which raises the living space slightly above the ground while firmly anchoring it visually; and the living volume, sharply defined by the black-painted steel structure. This is unlike Mies's house where the asymmetrical living volume with its contiguous terrace, and lower terrace, are raised above the ground level, "floating," between white-painted steel columns. In Johnson's house the entire living space, to all corners, is more visible; and because it is broader—an area 32 feet by 56 feet with a $10^{1}/_{2}$-foot ceiling—it has a more centered feeling, a space where you have a greater sense of "coming to rest." In other words, where Mies's is dynamic in feeling, Johnson's is more static.

Johnson's Glass House is essentially one space with a few impeccably grouped elements establishing functional areas within it: a soft, white wool rug, on the highly-polished red brick floor of a herringbone pattern; a seating area graced by Barcelona chairs; a dining group; a veneered, buffet kitchen and bar, low in height; a taller wardrobe cabinet that suggests the bedroom area. The most dominant element, and the only internal one that cuts through the ceiling plane, is a 10-foot in diameter brick cylinder housing a leather-tiled bathroom, and a built-in fireplace for the living areas.

There are secondary points of interest too: a shaggy, bright-green potted plant contrasted to angular steel and glass; the seemingly chatting Elie Nadelman ladies, later to reappear as a duet, in duet, in the Lincoln Center; a romantic, Poussin land-scape in a banner-like, standing frame. Everything has been selected carefully and related with consummate skill—even to the small Giacometti "thin man" on the coffee table; and now adjacent to it, somewhat as a sign of the times, and perhaps tempting it, is the substantial, bursting banana-split by the Pop-artist, Oldenburg.

The site is fabulous, and the house enjoys it. The floor of the house appears to extend to the low concrete rail so that volume, from inside, is defined only by the boundary of the ample terrace; the view extends beyond this to trees and rolling landscape, or downward to the lake, with its idyllic, miniature Keatsian gazebo —perfect for snacks, swims, and snoozes. On its grassy shelf the house is always changing with nature: you look into it, through it, and see the landscape reflected in it. "With the lights out and the snow falling," says Johnson, "it is almost like a celestial elevator." Living in the house one is in a controlled, slightly detached communion with nature—an observer rather than participant. It also considers the human animal adaptable; if the house is hot in summer, one simply steps outside.

This was a great tour de force for Johnson, and in 1953 he embarked on a career of full-time practice, opening his own office—now in the Seagram Building with a staff of about twenty-five.

In 1953, the Wiley House, also in New Canaan, was another transparent glass box. Here is contrasted a lofty living space that contains the family quarters, resting, almost delicately, upon a rugged field stone base. A still finer variation on this idea was the Leonhardt House on Long Island, New York, in 1956, where Johnson followed closely a 1934 Mies sketch for a hillside house. Here the glass living area is clear of the ground or any substructure, cantilevered dramatically between its steel truss structure. It contrasts with the brick-enclosed, land-based parts of the house that contain the sleeping and dining areas.

Wiley House, New Canaan, Connecticut.

The Boissonnas House in New Canaan, in 1956, which he regards as representative of his best effort, culminates Johnson's early residential work. He has always shown a preference for the articulated, defined sense of space, and in this house he realized the contained, processional relationship of space that has distinguished all his subsequent buildings. Rather than the interpenetration of space, interior space is echoed in the outdoors: the double height of the living area is repeated on the adjacent terrace to make an outdoor living area, and the brick piers of the pergola echo the structural piers of the house while also defining a similar space. Such outdoor spatial suggestions in turn extend the physical sense of the house, moving it towards a larger complex and a grander expression. This, too, was significant, as his later work has shown.

The completion of the Seagram Building in 1958 marked the divergence from the Miesian discipline of Johnson and many of his contemporaries. Johnson, as Mies's associate architect for the building, was directly responsible for designing the extremely elegant interior of the building's Four Seasons restaurant. Shortly before, in a talk at Harvard, Johnson said, "Never in history was the tradition so clearly demarked, never were the great so great, never could we learn so much from them and go our own way, without feeling constricted by any style . . . in that sense I am a traditionalist."

Leonhardt House, Lloyd's Neck, Long Island, New York.

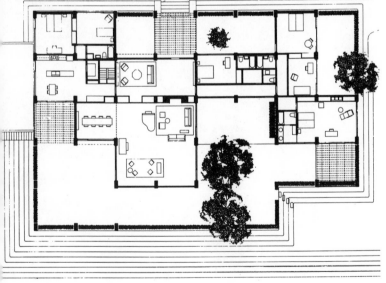

Boissonnas House, New Canaan, Connecticut.

Johnson's first large public building, the 1956 Kneses Tifereth Israel Synagogue in Port Chester, New York, appears to be from sources closer to the romantic, neoclassic work of Sir John Soane than that of Mies. The rectangular sanctuary is again defined by the crisp, black steel frame, but it is enclosed by white precast concrete panels, staggered to contain narrow, slit windows of colored glass. The interior, however, is illuminated principally through skylights that are concealed by a suspended, undulating canopy that doubles as ceiling. The even more dramatic variant from Mies is the synagogue's domed, oval vestibule.

Johnson followed this with several structures that had a central dominant space. In 1957, the Munson-Williams-Proctor Institute, in Utica, New York, was planned axially, with a gallery around the two-story center court space. It is a monumentally powerful granite-faced box that seems to hang—an effect emphasized by the glazed base of the building that faces onto a moat-like sunken area—between an external exposed reinforced concrete structure sheathed in bronze.

The antithesis of this enclosed volume is the Roofless Church in New Harmony, Indiana, built in 1960. It is a brick-walled space, open to the sky, with a shingled, high domed structure acting as a focal point and canopy for a Lipchitz bronze sculpture. Like the outdoor terracing he has designed for the Museum of Modern Art in New York, Johnson conceived and designed this space as an outdoor room.

The 1961 Nuclear Reactor, at Rehovot, Israel, is, like the Roofless Church, a low mass designed as a foil to a distinctive architectural form. From the exterior the building, with battered concrete walls, is powerful and rugged, but once within it opens to a glazed courtyard, protected from the sun by a projecting slab supported by tapered columns. The reactor itself is a faceted structure of hyperbolic paraboloids, facing first in and then out, thus creating an interesting graduated pattern of sun and shadow. It is a further indication of Johnson's increasing tendency to shape things, but unlike Saarinen's TWA Terminal, for example, in a very restrained way. The Israelis say this shape came from Egypt; Johnson says, smiling, "It might even be original, God forbid. But I do not think so because I do not think there is such a thing as originality."

Another of Johnson's museums is the Sheldon Art Gallery, designed for the University of Nebraska in 1963. A two-story space with surrounding galleries, it has a very delicately-shaped, columned structure, which at night is emphasized by upward illumination. Just as Johnson selects certain design expressions for a considered aesthetic effect, the structure here is shaped as it is, principally because he likes it that way. To those who believe in structural honesty, this is completely alien to the technological aesthetics of modern architecture.

"The best thing a person could approach architecture with in the 1930's, in America, was a knowledge of Mies. One felt that one could grasp his direction, and he intends it that way. It is Mies's conviction that architecture is teachable, and that the essence of architecture is building; if you build cleanly, you will arrive at architecture by a sort of hierarchy of attempts—which is, of course, completely wrong. Mies, like most architects, is under the delusion that he does what he says—but it is very fortunate that he does not. He pays no more attention to structural clarity and functional judgments than any other architect. His approach

Kneses Tifereth Israel Synagogue, Port Chester, New York.

is his passion for 'form,' which he would deny because he does not like the word. To him it brings recollections of neoclassic, Beaux Arts buildings, and he thinks that buildings just grow by internal stresses.

"The form sense of Le Corbusier and Mies has left its mark on this country. I say 'this country,' advisedly, because the architectural leadership, which the French and the English have admitted is here, did pass, with the advent of war, from Europe to America. The leadership has been Mies's. However, Le Corbusier's influence has been just as great because his form sense is so much richer, so much more changeable, and sculptural—although I hate the word. I am so Miesian that to me architecture is *bauen*, not plastic. It is made with sticks and stones and bricks and pieces of marble; it is built up. Le Corbusier's idea is a sculptural one: the Visual Arts Center is not *bauen*—Mies would not like that building. I love it but I have no intention of doing anything like it. To me it is death; architecture is a more serious business. I grant Le Corbusier his ability to do it, but that is not the way I see architecture.

Munson-Williams-Proctor Institute, Utica, New York.

"My eyes are set by the Miesian tradition, and like him, I still believe that God lies in the details—in contrast to Kahn and Rudolph who have no details. I do not know any period of great architecture that paid no attention to details. The continuity with my Miesian approach also shows through in my classicism. Mies is a great admirer of Schinkel, and I have learned more from Schinkel than I have from Mies; and more from Soane, who was a greater architect, than from Schinkel, which I dare not say in Mies's presence. Mies and I share the same belief in the clarity of the early nineteenth century over that of the eighteenth century, and Ledoux would, of course, be the precursor of this.

"In 1952, about the same time that my whole generation did, I became very restless. Pei and Saarinen were Miesian; Rudolph once told me that in his Florida work, he was a poor man's Mies. It was the only thing we could grasp—the only basis for architecture. In the last decade there has been such a violent switch that it is almost embarrassing. But it isn't a switch, so much as a centrifugal splintering of architecture, to a degree that I don't think has been seen in the past few hundred years. Perfectly responsible architects build, even in one year, buildings

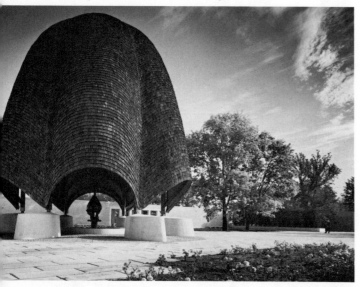

Roofless Church, New Harmony, Indiana.

Nuclear Reactor, Rehovot, Israel.

that you cannot believe are done by the same person. The classic example is Saarinen: building the skating rink at the same time he was doing the neo-Middle Ages dormitory, both at Yale, and the Bell Telephone glass box in New Jersey. Nobody could perceive that those three buildings could be by the same architect because they represent such violently different attitudes. History will somehow have to unravel it.

"In my office right now I am myself working on a neoclassic house in Washington; an upside-down building (I mean of course a La Tourette, that takes the base of a building and puts it on top and the columns dangle—brilliant idea), for Brown University; and an underground building very fitting for the way we are all building prematurely under the earth now. I don't know why . . . atom bombs, maybe. Who is to say what these influences are on form?

"When you sit down to design a building you do not go through a rational process of building up a conception—it just sort of drifts into your mind and drifts out again. Kahn can talk all he wants to, but there is actually no way of telling where he came by the Richards Medical Center. It is easy enough to point out that it came from San Gimignano—but why? I have no idea why all of this has occurred now, and I think that anyone who says he has, is crazy. It is easy enough to say that it is a revolt against the shackles of the International Style, but that is a negative point. Other styles did not pass that way. The neoclassic eighteenth century went into a nineteenth century version of itself: the row house of the eighteenth century looks like the early nineteenth century row house. Whereas today there is a violent departure from a style that is very definite and easy to work

within. We still overlap the International Style a little bit, because Mies still works within it.

"Do we lack convictions? Do we just flit around in all directions like butterflies as we are accused of doing by the people who are still with the International Style? The English, being articulate critics, say that we are all crazy here, and that the functionalist tradition of the Bauhaus, as continued by the likes of Stirling, is the only answer. Well it may be, but it certainly isn't evident in the way things are getting built.

"There is no common direction that you can say is a new movement. For instance, there is the romanticist Goff, or the neoclassicist Johnson, or a neo-romantic (about castles) Kahn, or a Rudolph who melts Le Corbusier and Wright together into concrete—it is awfully hard to put us all in one basket. This is, of course, myopic. History has ways of pointing out the similarities that we simply do not see. Nevertheless it remains a curiosity, and somewhat a matter of shame to contemporary architects. I remember Saarinen being a little worried about that. Rudolph and I were discussing it just recently, and I said: 'Paul, why do you make all your buildings different?' He was quite worried for the moment, not pointing out that I do, too. So that leaves us sounding like convictionless weaklings who pick styles superficially. Historically I suppose there is a continuity in architecture, but the architects do not notice it.

"Le Corbusier was violently influenced by his trip to Istanbul in 1911, but he never mentioned it because his generation was never ready to credit history. I caught Wright once. I was looking at one of his designs at Taliesin: he said, 'Philip, the Mayans could not have done it better.' I said, 'Oh! Mr. Wright, that is interesting. You can credit them with this idea.' He was very angry with himself for the slip. Publicly he could not admit that he was doing what the Mayans or the Japanese had done—but why not? I think our generation has that sensitivity. Rudolph copies the Larkin Building for the Arts and Architecture Building, and I copy an eighteenth century theater for Lincoln Center. My point is that everybody does; I am the only one who admits it.

"My big job now is the New York University campus, with its square blocks and rectangular street pattern, in the middle of New York City. How does one approach that problem? Only a few years ago we would have said: eliminate the roads, make superblocks, and build point buildings—the suburbanization of urban living. My instinct is violently against this; I believe in the nineteenth century street pattern. It has an absolutely superb clarity of principle that goes back to Peking and Greece. Its clarity far outweighs its boredom. Of course the accents then become very important. We have an accent already in Washington Square, around which the University clusters.

Sheldon Art Gallery, University of Nebraska, Lincoln, Nebraska.

"I interpret my problem this way. It is to re-establish the urban pattern of nineteenth century New York—now *that* is a historical way of putting it. I am sick of point buildings and I want streets, is a forward way of putting the same thing—but it is also a backward glance. The street evolved as a natural pattern of certain human needs, but was totally denied by the International Style. The superblock comes from Le Corbusier, not Americans sitting down and reforming their cities. When Le Corbusier sited his Unité in Marseille, he was so angry with the street, and so anxious to break the rhythm of any street as a centripetal force, that he put the building at a thirty-degree angle.

"The Bauhaus was an even more diagrammatic, theoretical way of living. I disliked much of it then, and I feel that my ideas are even more opposed now. The streets are the campuses of our lives. Is that a romantic revolt—is Jane Jacobs a romantic revolt? I do not see why—it is simply progress. The last generation's idea of the city was way off. But it is easy to say: 'Johnson, aren't you being a nineteenth century romantic?'—maybe, but if you stop worrying about the words and start thinking about the feelings as you walk down the street, then you do not have to worry.

"I never really had an interest in structure, and neither has Mies, inside him. It always amused me that he started to design the Seagram Building with a perfectly rational bay system of 27 feet 9 inches, derived from the lot size and the office divisibility module. Then, we arrived at the design of the big double-height rooms in the back (the Four Seasons Restaurant now) and we needed to double the size of the bay. All right, but what happens about the column that would have been in the middle of the bay—well, take it out. We had to double the span without deepening the beam, wrenching the cost and also the logic. If you start with a bay, you have a repeatable and economic beam. If you take out a column, just like that, you quadruple every-thing; and yet we had to keep beams within the same depth as the 27 foot 9 inch span because the building had to read the same on every floor. That is what I mean when I say that Mies does not pay attention to what he says.

"He took the column out for what purpose? To create space. There you come back to the theme that goes through all archi-tecture: to make spaces, to make interior spaces—all architecture is interior spaces. The Seagram is interior space because it is on

Sculpture Garden, Museum of Modern Art, New York, N.Y.

Four Seasons Restaurant, Seagram Building, New York, N.Y.

one side of a plaza. It is not a facade because the plaza is the feeling that you get and that, in a funny way, is interior space. Of course the skyscraper as such has no interior spaces other than the entrance. The skyscraper is death to architecture—no interest at all, just a beehive. The only space we did create within the Seagram Building is the Four Seasons. This brings us right back to what Mies is trying to do. His best room is his own school (Crown Hall) where he denied all the functions of a school; you cannot have a secretary there, keep the draughts out, interview anybody, or have separate classes—it is death. It is no way to build a building, no function at all; but the overriding thing with him was to make the great room. And that is all architecture is: the creation of great rooms. Mendelsohn once said that architects will be remembered for their one-room buildings. Wright will be remembered for the Guggenheim Museum; it is totally impossible, it does not work—but what a room! Well, all right, he missed the function but he got the room. Every architect has the right to commit every crime in the world in doing a one-room building: that is why churches and theaters are so important. The creation of a room is what we are on earth for.

"Every age has had a different means of entering a building. The Parthenon was, of course, approached in a most masterly way, up through the propylaeum and around; you experienced everything before you even got to the entrance. Or Bernini: the entrance to St. Peter's in Rome probably cost more than the church. You know where the church is, even though it is entered through a very second-class facade. Bernini's colonnade is so grand that you know you are going somewhere terribly important. These are the great experiences that remain with me.

"Processionalism—how you approach a building, how you get into it, and how you feel when you are there—has carried right through, as a main concern in my work, from Mies to today. The Guggenheim is one way: no entrance really, you pop into the great space, which is quite a kick. It is the opposite of Mies, where in the Seagram Building you approach grandly and go right into the middle of the building: you cannot miss the space, the clarity of the entrance, or the experience as you go in. Mies's approach is mine too; that is why a great many of my buildings are symmetrical, with the straight, grand experience of the entrance. In my theater, it is the trace of the feet as you get to the grand foyer above the promenade that is the main experience—escalators and elevators are against the principle of the sequence of space—it is how easily you make the turns and whether you make them inevitably. I wanted to make the theater a good experience, a sequential development of stairways, and turns, that ends in a lovely room. You cannot read that from a plan and you cannot see it in a photograph.

"I admit, as some critics have suggested, that the paired columns on my theater come from Perrault's facade at the back of the Louvre. I wanted to reduce the nine bays on the front of the Philharmonic Hall opposite, to three enormous bays divided by four double-clustered columns, all for the sake of clarity. I do not really object to the nine bays but I wanted my entrance to be so obvious—one door going only one way. The contrast with Philharmonic Hall is obvious.

"At S.O.M.'s Chase Manhattan Bank, the plaza is marvellous, but actually the main entrance is on the other side on the floor

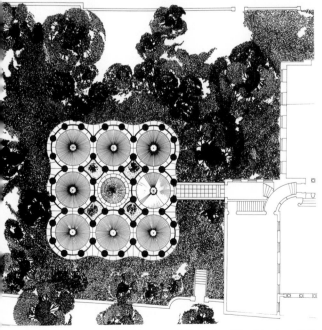

Dumbarton Oaks, wing, Washington, D.C.

below; you can get into the building from the Plaza, but it is not inevitable. You cannot have two entrance levels; somehow you have to get around that if you are a Miesian. Although they keep the grammar, they do not keep the spirit. I change the grammar all around but I try to keep the fundamentals of Mies's spirit, which is more important. There is no entrance in Rudolph's Art and Architecture Building. He says, too, 'I like to get lost and wander around in spaces.' In Saarinen's Gothic dormitories, the little 'Spanish walk' that goes between the buildings ends up on the other side—like Le Corbusier's ramp in the Visual Arts Center. To me when you have a path like that you end up in the building. The way you walk into a building is more important than any other part of that building. What I always liked about Mies's attitude was: if it is not inevitable enough, do not build it. That is the sign of great architecture that is going to last.

"I do not think we are in a great age of form innovation. The good architecture of this period no doubt has many features of Le Corbusier, Mies, and of other periods, because we are in a consolidating as well as a centrifugal period. I quote Mies again: 'I do not want to be original, I want to be good.' The search is for expression now, rather than for function. This is a much healthier period than the 1920's—they were so convinced of their own virtue that they said if you were not a functionalist you were not good. That is not true. I am a functionalist in the sense that I think the use of a building should influence its design. I know this sounds very reactionary, but I also think that if you pay too much attention to functionalism you get miserable buildings. Again, to design a very expressionistic building, where a loft space is called for, is a contradiction of our age. This is why Kahn really should design churches, where there is a freedom of expression that is not deleterious to the design.

"The direction of architecture in the future will be with the person who keeps a serious eye on the use of a building, and the creation of the most exciting space that best fits that use."

Johnson's most recently completed projects continue to show his neoclassic predilections for formal, elegant spaces. His jewel-like museum wing for pre-Columbian Art, at Dumbarton Oaks, Washington, D. C., shows the artifacts in a rich environment of glass, teak, marble and bronze, making for a total aesthetic experience. Eight 25-foot-diameter pavilions with curved glass walls are centered, in a square, on a court of the same diameter. The court is open to the sky, and contains a small pool and fountain. In the four spaces created where the circles come together, potted plants stand on a bed of gray Japanese pebbles.

Opened in 1964, the New York State Theater at Lincoln Center is Johnson's largest executed commission to date. Of the Center's five theaters, it is one of three grouped around a plaza with the fourth side open to the city. Six steps raise the plaza above the street level so that automobiles are not too obtrusive in this pleasant place. The architects, Harrison and Abramovitz, Belluschi, Bunshaft of S.O.M., Saarinen and Johnson were jointly responsible for the over-all site planning and relationship of their individual structures. Timing problems in phasing construction, and the difficulties of concord on a completely integrated scheme finally forced each of the architects to proceed, more or less as individuals. There was basic agreement upon a module—

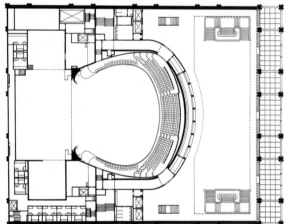

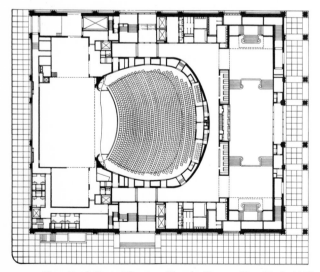

New York State Theater, Lincoln Center, New York, N.Y.

"which no one really believed in," said Johnson—and the use of travertine marble. However, most of the architects agree that a great opportunity for a unified statement was missed.

But not all was lost. Inside, the "great room" is finally the real theatrical experience with power to prepare and move an audience, the space for anticipation, and for Johnson, of course, elegance. Here he created two "rooms": a foyer or grand promenade, and the auditorium.

Johnson's two hundred-foot-long promenade, rising through four balcony levels with people silhouetted on each one, is an elegant anticipation space. Pedestrian circulation is so comfortably and excitingly planned that the walk to the balconies—processionalism—is far more appealing than using the elevator. The Nadelman sculptures that appear to supervise this space show Johnson's agile sense of humor.

The auditorium seats 2,729 persons—three-quarters of them within a hundred feet of the stage. Johnson has achieved this intimacy despite such a large seating capacity, by wrapping four balcony levels around the orchestra level. He has also adopted the continental seating arrangement, with each row of seats a comfortable forty inches apart, to be entered only from side aisles. The interior derives from the horseshoe-shaped, Baroque theater that achieved both greater intimacy and a festive community feeling where playgoers had good views of the stage and each other.

Johnson has been criticized for building such a classical theater; some architects feel it is almost too authentic. "Some shapes have been perfected, and I use that word advisedly," says Johnson. "How can you improve on the shape of the Georgian spoon? And a horseshoe or lyre shape with its curved corners is best fitted for the stage and the people looking at it." The theater has no boxes. It is, says Johnson, "the first modern Volkstheater—a large theater for the masses, a non-aristocratic house, with elegance." With its red plush, gold leaf, and the glitter of crystal, it is referred to by some architects as one of New York's most elegant, exciting new spaces, while others view it as a lapse of taste in a man distinguished by impeccable taste.

Our culture has not yet created a building comparable to the great public spaces of history. Consider the churches of the Middle Ages—is it religion, or the emotional impact of the great space that moves us? Or the railroad stations of a century ago, where arrival in a great space breathed anticipation of the city. One thinks of city halls but the vicarious thrill from their spaces has gone. Perhaps the theater, the grand room of cultural gathering, comes closest today. Johnson's theater shows the potential in two such spaces that have the ability to evoke an audience's response. It also most clearly states Johnson's aims in architecture: the universal appeal of elegance, of beauty and of an architecture that will endure for generations. . . . "I like the thought that what we are to do on this earth is to embellish it for its greater beauty, so that oncoming generations can look back to the shapes we leave here and get the same thrill that I in turn get in looking back—at the Parthenon, at Chartres Cathedral. . ."

Art and Architecture Building, Yale University, New Haven, Connecticut.

PAUL RUDOLPH

"Things are quite chaotic. We are faced with a vast change of scale, new building forms which have not really been investigated, and the compulsions of the automobile. When faced with the truly new, the serious architect must search for solutions equally dynamic." So says Paul Rudolph, an architect of great aesthetic skill and virtuosity who, like Johnson, but for a different reason, is accused of art for art's sake. Rudolph's individual, vigorous expressionism has taken a direction that could become one of the most influential forces on the contemporary American scene.

While architecture is clearly an art for Rudolph, he just as clearly thinks of it as a civic art. His references are primarily within the greater urban context where architecture becomes the city, essentially the concern of the minority but with implications for the majority. "Just as the nineteenth century architects showed so little regard for construction, we twentieth century architects tend to disregard our role in the cityscape."

Rudolph sees the city as a burgeoning force where we have barely begun to adjust to the reality of accretion and the time element; the fact that mobility—the rhythm and speed of movement—can itself produce cohesive design systems on a comprehensible scale for the city. In the design of a building Rudolph also sees the need to be cognizant of the growth concept: The crystalline form is static, incapable of growth; the tree however is organic, a growing, changing form, that has a hierarchy of scaled relationships from root, to trunk, to branch, to leaf, while its basic upward direction of growth contains the principle of divergence, controlled and interrelated.

The principal criticism of Rudolph's architecture is that function appears more of a result than a motivation for architectural form. "Many of our difficulties stem from the concept of functionalism as the only determinant of form," says Rudolph. "We can't pretend that we solve our problems without precedent in form." He is often accused of fuzzy structural systems, and that structure is employed obtusely to create what to Rudolph is the more important architectural delineation of space. He replies: "One becomes conscious that there are many ways to organize a building; that structure is not an end, nor a beginning, but a means to an end—and that end is to create space that is an appropriate psychological environment. Perhaps the greatest chapel of this century, Ronchamp, has a most impure structure—sprayed concrete covers everything. It does not resort to the crutches of geometry and pattern-making, but creates breathing, dynamic spaces appropriate to human use." To the charge that in an age of technology his finishes are "arty", and details, since they come from the very complex interior spatial configurations that must "read" on the exterior, not standardized, Rudolph answers: "We continue to ignore the particular. Each material has its own potential, and one seeks the most eloquent expression for it."

Paul Rudolph was born in Elkton, Kentucky, in 1918. He studied architecture at Alabama Polytechnic Institute, before going to the Harvard Graduate School of Design in 1940. A naval officer during the war, he was in charge of ship construction at the Brooklyn Navy Yard. He returned to Harvard, completing his Master of Architecture degree in 1947. For the next five years he practiced from Sarasota, Florida, in partnership with R. S. Twitchell, with a year traveling in Europe on a Wheelwright Fellowship. Like most architects, Rudolph's first efforts expressed various ideas he had been exposed to in school—in his case "this was the International Style, as Gropius saw it." He attempted to carry out these precepts in small structures such as guest houses, "because the main house would quite often be given to another architect." He now considers invaluable the experience gained in complete control of such small projects. "My first projects were in a sense much more pure, because they were based on a fairly understandable formula, with the various functional and structural elements clearly articulated." Rudolph experimented with several structural systems, "often exhibitionist in character": post and lintel timber construction was soon succeeded by the bending of plywood to make vaults, which in turn led to investigating steel in tension.

The Healy guest house in Sarasota, Florida, in 1950, was the most publicized of his early buildings. It had a weathertight

Healy Guest House, Sarasota, Florida.

plastic roof on fiberboard, supported by steel bars suspended in their catenary curve, a structural system that Rudolph now says was inaptly mannered for such a small, 22-foot span. "I was so impatient, I couldn't wait," he said. "The appropriateness of a structural system was quite often sacrificed in my early buildings to magnify structure to the point where it dominated." But clarity was there, and structure was the basic ordering device.

Rudolph's ability was soon recognized. In 1954 he received the "Outstanding Young Architect's Award" at the São Paulo Bienal. In 1958, having served as a visiting critic at several schools, he was appointed Chairman of the Department of Architecture at Yale University. The same year he received the Brunner Prize from the American Academy of Arts and Letters, awarded to the man "who shows promise of widening the horizons of architecture as an art."

Larger commissions were soon forthcoming, such as the Mary Cooper Jewett Arts Center for Wellesley College in Massachusetts, in 1958. Unfortunately, it coincided "with the desire to find myself, in a more specific way," he says. "I was completely unprepared for it. Not only was it in a different climate for me, but a different area and atmosphere, and of a new scale and magnitude." Rudolph, who has called the building "a disaster," attempted to work with the College's pseudo-Gothic character in a twentieth century manner. He followed the campus tradition of setting buildings on high terrain, grouped to form large courtyards. The Arts Center was based on a repetitive 15-foot module, with vertical emphasis, small-scaled detailing, and elaborate silhouettes. "One of modern architecture's greatest failings has been its lack of interest in the relationship of the building to the sky," says Rudolph. "One doubts that a poem was ever written to a flat-roofed building silhouetted against the setting sun. All of this probably led to a kind of movie set effect, or a new eclecticism, which robbed the building of its own dynamics."

For an addition to the Sarasota High School, in 1959, Rudolph sought a closer integration and expression of structural and mechanical systems. Columns were capped by concrete ducts that contained mechanical services while creating a lively silhouette and rhythm for the roof line. This design emphasis came from his awareness that large buildings *do* need to be considered from many viewpoints and at various distances. It led to a flat-planed rather than linear design: his earlier post and lintel construction systems that tended to reduce members to their smallest dimension, gave way to an arrangement of solids and voids based on light and shadow, with infilling glass walls protected from the sun.

Mary Cooper Jewett Center, Wellesley College, Wellesley, Massachusetts.

Sarasota High School, Sarasota, Florida.

Chapel for Tuskegee Institute, Tuskegee, Alabama.

Blue Cross–Blue Shield Office Building, Boston, Massachusetts.

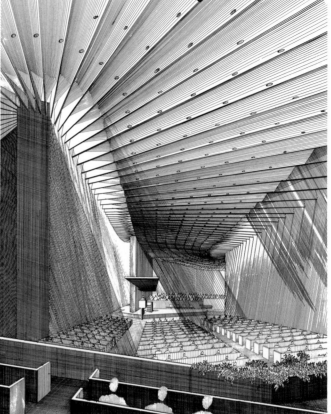

Married Student Housing, Yale University, New Haven, Connecticut.

In a transitional period in the early 1960's, Rudolph explored various design ideas in a series of buildings. In the Blue Cross-Blue Shield office building in Boston, vertical concrete columns, incorporating air-conditioning ducts, are carried on Y-shaped columns at the ground level with intermediate non-structural columns, between structural ones, serving as additional ducts. Rudolph has been severely criticized for the lack of structural clarity here. The chapel for Tuskegee Institute in Alabama is a rough concrete sculptural design "based on acoustical requirements," that pays lip service to Ronchamp. The Married Student Housing, for Yale, is a tight complex of fifty units on a sloping site only 250 feet square; it is approached through narrow pedestrian alleys, each unit having its own private terrace or garden, either on the ground or on the roof of an adjoining unit. Due to budget limitations, the original scheme was not built, and a vastly inferior one was actually constructed. The parking garage in New Haven was more successful architecturally, and captured the sense of the new urban scale that interests Rudolph. Here, pairs of columns joined by arches and based on the parking module of ten feet become the vigorous sculptural form of a two-block-long building that spans a street and parks fifteen hundred cars on twelve split-parking levels.

Parking Garage, New Haven, Connecticut.

Milam House, Jacksonville, Florida.

The Milam House in Florida was the catalyst for exploring a spatial idea that was subsequently to be more powerfully and engagingly expressed in Rudolph's Art and Architecture Building. Mies achieves spatial continuity and clarity by carefully locating free-standing planes in an open complete volume so that there is always a sense of the space beyond, over and around the planes. Rudolph, however, strives for continuity of space—where the recognition of complexity becomes the dominant theme—by projecting defined smaller volumes of space into loosely defined larger ones, which the smaller volumes, of course, partly define.

The Milam House has seven interconnected volumes, consisting of a series of bent planes that form one continuous plane of floor, walls and ceiling. The extensions of these bent planes dominate the exterior while also shading it from the sun. Yet his motivation was a spatial idea—still very impure here, but increasingly present in his work—rather than the arbitrary sculptured sun-screen of which his critics often accuse him.

Similarly, in the Art and Architecture Building for Yale University, completed in 1963, the uniformity and clarity of structure as an organizational method are replaced by that of location and character of spaces, at the expense of the simplicity and economy of the statement. Rectangular volumes of space, with ceiling heights ranging from 7 to 28 feet for varying psychological effects, interpenetrate vertically and horizontally; they are brought together in a vaguely rectangular envelope, modified by alcoves of space at each corner and service cores separate from the main volume, with extremely animated surfaces. These interlocking volumes find a powerful exterior expression in the fragmented mass of the total composition. Whereas Kahn would have the geometry of a clear structure lead to a more coherent organization of spaces, Rudolph, while he admires Kahn, abhors any tendency towards "pattern making" and feels that twentieth century architecture suffers from over-emphasis on the formal.

The dramatic entrance to the building is up a narrow flight of steps that penetrate deeply into the mass of the main volume, between it and the main vertical circulation tower. Future extension of the building will simply connect to this. The strong vertical striations of the corduroy-textured surfaces are obtained by pouring concrete into vertically-ribbed wood forms, that are then stripped away, and concrete edges hand-hammered to expose the aggregate. This has become Rudolph's favorite treatment for exposed concrete surfaces, because, apart from being an interesting surface, it controls staining and minimizes the effect of discoloration inherent in concrete. Art works, restrained use of lively colors—mainly orange—and cleverly built-in furnishings enhance the architecture, which is intended "to excite and challenge the occupants," says Rudolph.

Thirty-seven changes of level accommodate functional and circulation areas, and since walls are de-emphasized these levels are defined principally by floor and ceiling planes. Rudolph, like Kahn, is concerned with the method and drama of natural lighting. This has clearly been an important factor in the design of the building, as it contributes to the changing character and psychological implication of space.

Internally the building is organized around a central core space defined by four large concrete slab columns that, similar to the external towers, are hollow to accommodate mechanical services. On two sunken levels, sculpture and basic design studios encircle a central auditorium, the approach to which is rather tortuous and obscure. At street level, the library occupies a single story but with two double-height reading areas on the street entrance side. Above this, with the possibility of looking down into the reading area, is a two-story central exhibition hall, with administrative offices on its mezzanine, and a central, sunken jury pit. Starting at the fourth level is the most dramatic space: an architectural zone on five levels, each connected by a few steps, an element in yet a part of the greater space, above which run two parallel mezzanines spanned by a channel-shaped bridge. Between the four central piers two skylights rise as giant clerestories, intensifying natural light in the center of the space that receives it on all four sides through peripheral glazing. Painting and graphic art studios are on the top two levels, with an open terrace for sketching. Finally, there is a penthouse apartment for guest critics, that also has its own terrace.

Rudolph has been criticized for the serious functional shortcomings of the building: that he put the areas he cared least about in the basement; that the painters are very disturbed by south light; that the sculptors are in the low-ceiling "caves"; that the best spaces are reserved for architectural activity. Functionally, Rudolph's building is a studied, politically architectural statement. Architecturally, it tends to extend beyond its own boundaries to influence and generate further relationships in its urban context. It cleverly establishes a general urban scale and a particular internal scale, both compatibly and expressively related.

"Since the building is on a corner," says Rudolph, "its role in the cityscape is to turn that corner. A pinwheel scheme has therefore been adopted." This seems to be his favorite plan formation, probably because it is a dynamic and moving form, that even suggests expansion in its geometry. The bold paired columns and horizontal floor slabs of the interweaving interior platforms express the pinwheel configuration in the exterior mass. The building is actually much larger than it appears because of the two stories below street level so that the lower horizontal mass of the building lines up with Kahn's gallery, its highest vertical point with Bingham Hall, two blocks away. The streets at the corner form an obtuse angle which the building's projections carefully follow.

The Art and Architecture Building raises the question of foreground as against background buildings. Rudolph has expressed the need for a hierarchy of building types in the environment, and he has well stated that we tend to treat each one as if it were dominant. He obviously prefers to design foreground buildings, but admits that it is more difficult to design background ones. His Art and Architecture Building is an important educational facility on a corner site, announcing itself to the central green of New Haven two blocks away; as such one can argue that it deserves to be (particularly if you are an architect) a foreground building. Just as future structures near it cannot help but be influenced by its design, so, too, will it probably dominate them. Rudolph's parking garage in New Haven is also a foreground building, but with less reason: "It is the dominant building only because the other architects wouldn't dominate it. It's all according to which key you are playing in. If they would let me do the other buildings, I would certainly dominate that parking garage," he says.

In the Art and Architecture Building, the complex functional program required seven distinct design phases, each reviewed by the Yale authorities. As a result, Rudolph initially had a major role in defining the sequence of personally phrased spaces that he sought. A vastly different problem, designed at the same time,

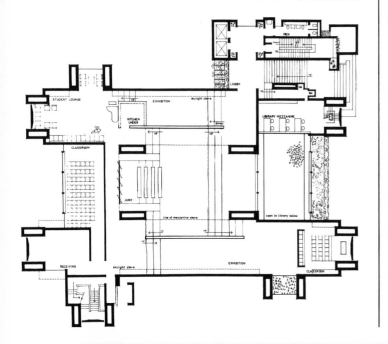

Art and Architecture Building, Yale University, New Haven, Connecticut.

was the Endo Pharmaceutical Laboratory in Garden City, Long Island, New York. It, also, is far from a "package" solution. The early promise of such fine industrial structures as the Van Nelle factory in Rotterdam seemed a vision long-faded; Rudolph's building is a restatement that there is always something to be contributed in any building type. He succeeded in translating a complex set of functional requirements into a compact architectural statement. The laboratory processes required highly-specialized spaces of specific dimensions that had to be interrelated vertically and horizontally to accommodate gravitational production lines. The production areas form a simple rectangular base for the more exuberant administration and research areas and roof garden above. A double, curving staircase, reminiscent of the Baroque period, rises to an entrance lobby, and from there another one ascends to the administrative levels. The staff cafeteria is a glass-enclosed pavilion, with views of the roof garden. The strongly expressed curved elements are "turrets" that form skylit alcoves in offices and laboratories. Methods of natural lighting throughout the building determine its configurations to a considerable extent.

The many challenging commissions now offered to Rudolph, coupled with his disenchantment with the approach to the teaching of architecture in general, prompted him to resign from Yale in 1965, to have more time to concentrate on his practice, and the purely theoretical. He does not believe in architecture in the Gropius teamwork sense, and because of his intense personal involvement with each project, limits his staff to about twenty-five. Energetic, dedicated, a highly talented draftsman, he still occupies a drawing position along with the rest of his staff.

"A small office cannot take on more than about seven million dollars worth of work a year, or its leader becomes nothing more than a critic of his draftsmen. Architecture is a personal effort, and the fewer people coming between you and your work the better. This keeps some people from practicing architecture, like the sculptor Nivola, who says 'I cannot stand anybody coming between me and my work.' This is a very real problem, and you can only stretch one man so far. The heart can fall right out of a building during the production of working drawings, and sometimes you would not even recognize your own building unless you followed it through. If an architect cares enough, and practices architecture as an art, then he must initiate design; he must create rather than make judgments. The judgment of the artist is rather poor, as he is so personally involved he cannot objectively disassociate himself from the thing he is criticizing. So the critic, again, requires a certain type of mentality.

"I have always been interested in the specific, and drawing from it whatever generalizations one might find. The universal space concept is a denial of the richness and complexity of life that architecture must celebrate. I want to accentuate the differences in our life, not nullify them. It is important, though, that universal spaces such as offices, manufacturing and commercial buildings read as such.

"I am fascinated by the relationship between what is large, and what is small, not only in terms of building but also of organization. In America there are many good house architects who cannot deal successfully with the large concept. This is somewhat due to the precepts of modern architecture, which tended not to deal very much with the problem of urban design. Revolutionary movements dictate destruction of the existing order; but most cities evolve with the element of time and the efforts of many. The complexities of our time suggest that buildings should not be thought of as complete within themselves—they should have an open end, and should change. However, we tend to build boxes and call them buildings. I am firmly convinced that you cannot put up boxes scaled merely by the owner's pocketbook, and call them a city. You must be able to join one building to another, to make transition from one scale to another, and to define the space in between in various ways and by various heights. The box cannot always do this; it requires several different types of building. The streamlining of all the parts into a box is currently fashionable, but it does not permit graduations of scale.

"The notion of urban design was largely omitted from the educational process at Harvard, and planning substituted. The whole relationship of the new to the old, and the small to the large, was not really very clear. In my day in school it was felt that the planners would take care of the overall environment while the responsibility of the architect was to make individual buildings. Urban design in the early part of the twentieth century was rather negated: Wright wanted an acre for every man—and certainly wanted to design every building; Le Corbusier proposed tearing down part of Paris and building skyscrapers; Mies made very few proposals in terms of urban design, contenting himself with the individual building; Gropius produced diagrams indicating density relationship and sun charts, which of course do not culminate in design.

"Making the entire environment of the city a more habitable and indeed a more beautiful and significant place, is our real problem. Neither the architects nor the planners, at least in this country, have had very much to say about improving the visual image of the city let alone the environment. The planners, from a legal and popular viewpoint, have the power now. But it is noteworthy that no matter how many two-dimensional maps and reports are made, the physical environment does not really improve very much. New Haven has been a so-called leader in planning in this country, and in the limited scope of the planners' concern, they are very successful. But the City of New Haven has improved very little since the planners were actually in charge. The architect has abdicated from his traditional role as civic designer, and tends to be concerned only with his individual building and site. Large scale, three-dimensional design, as an integral part of what has gone before and what is likely to come must be the province of somebody. I would call him an architect. More recently we have examples of buildings grouped in blocks, such as Lincoln Center, but even then a problem remains: there is no comprehensible way for surrounding buildings to grow out of the fixed, static, and complete quality of the central complex. It is as if a great fence had been built around this group of buildings.

"The rules governing larger structures are different from those governing the small. An ant is designed differently from an elephant. It is the continuity of any urban complex that primarily interests me; the appropriateness and role that any building plays in the cityscape as a whole. Some buildings are more important than others so there must be a hierarchy of building types. The role that a building plays in relationship to others,

whether it is the focal point, turns the corner, or is a flanking building, must be clearly defined. This is always the point of departure which any building must work from (a cliché of modern architecture) to give cohesion to an environment.

"I have built on several campuses that vary in scale, feeling and materials; each a different and a defined entity. I do not see how you could build the same kind of building on each of them. Designing on an isolated site is easy, where the configurations of nature, the qualities of light and the psychology of the users are the only fundamental determinants. As we do not have a comprehensive theory allowing today's architects to work simultaneously on a group of buildings, it is easier to relate the new to the old—a glass wall reflecting old buildings; if you have one glass wall reflecting another, the whole thing looks like an enlarged barbershop.

"To grasp the spirit of the times is the real task. Our prime need is to build in such a way that we make coherent cities. The Renaissance had definite rules. We need to have rules, but appropriate to our own time. Our order may come from systems and means of communication that we have not yet defined or delineated to the point where they can react on our building forms. For example, inherent in the automobile are all sorts of organizational possibilities on a larger scale. Our environment needs to recognize that the automobile provides a scale for our cities that they never could have had before. Those forms that the automobile dictates should be brought together with forms for human inhabitance, rather than always fighting this. The automobile is, in a sense, our greatest problem, but it is also the greatest organizing element that we have in our cities."

Rudolph's most important commission to date is as coordinating architect for the Boston Government Service Center, and designer of two of its three buildings. To be situated on an irregularly-shaped, sloping site related to the hill of the Massachusetts State Capitol Building, the complicated program involves three buildings for the Division of Employment Security Department, the Health, Welfare, and Education Departments, and a Mental Health Hospital.

The architects agreed that the buildings should be a unified group, paralleling the periphery of the property in accord with the existing street pattern, but with setbacks to create small plazas of the type that gave Boston its character, where streets form three acute angles. Heights of five to seven stories were determined, relating to the old scale of the area. The complex was to be entered from a central pedestrian plaza, marked by a high building which would identify the Center from a distance, making its silhouette count in the cityscape.

Urban scale was Rudolph's prime consideration. There is an effort to recognize the scale of the automobile at the perimeter, the pedestrians within the plaza, and generally the heightened sense of scale of a monumental scheme.

Rudolph's concept is the reverse of that of the new Boston City Hall two blocks away. Whereas the City Hall is set within a plaza defined by the surrounding buildings, in the Center the plaza itself is the focal element defined by the buildings. The comparatively small mass of the Boston City Hall—a building Rudolph considers one of the best of this decade—will dominate its surrounding structures principally because of its plastic, exuberant expression. Rudolph has created a similar heightened sense of scale by emphasizing disparate elements. Fixed functions such as stairs, toilets and elevators are housed in a series of solid towers, distinct elements free from the regular structure and irregular in shape, juxtaposed to flexible, open office spaces, and augmented by an auditorium and the hospital. Expressed as curved towers, the fixed elements are used visually to turn irregular corners (except for the Social Security building, which follows Rudolph's theme but was not directly designed by him). Thus the entire complex will be animated by light reflected by the various surfaces, and the bold juxtaposition of solid to void magnified by shadow. "Sunshading is probably more elaborate than it should be for such a climate," admits Rudolph. The

Boston Government Service Center, Boston, Massachusetts.

sculptural impression of the Center is further accentuated by its shape that derives from the irregular street pattern cut back at the corners to create small plazas, and is dramatized by the large central plaza. "I think every curve and line has to have real meaning; it cannot be arbitrary," says Rudolph. "The Government Center perhaps looks arbitrary and complicated, but I think I could defend the configurations up to a point. Then it finally comes down to the way you happen to see things, and handle a problem."

The design has a structural system, monumental in scale, expressed around the periphery of the Center, related to the scale of the automobile. In the central plaza there is a more intimate scale, where each floor level is emphasized by setbacks forming terraces that shape the plaza like a faceted bowl—the negative of the hill. The plaza will be variegated by the irregularity of the increment of setbacks. From some vantage points the impression will be horizontal, from others, almost vertical; the plaza will thus appear structurally clear yet visually elaborate. Although points of entry to it are evident from the articulation of the exterior building facades, the plaza itself remains somewhat secretive, a place of expectation. A great series of stairs link its various levels, which Rudolph explains "are not there because that many people will be going between levels, probably a quarter of the stairs would suffice, but in order to connect the three levels of the plaza." The plaza is not a podium on which the buildings sit but a clearly-articulated series of platforms, not connected to buildings in an attempt to express that the plaza is hollow beneath. The plaza paving touches the buildings at their three points of entry, and buildings will probably appear to grow in terraced layers out of the levels of the plaza.

The twenty-eight story tower contains office space similar to the lower buildings and is a visual pivot for them and the plaza. Office levels had to be large enough to be economical (7,700 square feet per level is still small) yet the tower had to be slender enough visually to act as a pivot. The corners of the tower, as in the low buildings, are treated as separate structures housing services, but, in some places, office space too. Accepting the tower on visual terms, it is most skillfully related to the lower mass. Despite the questions it raises, and Rudolph raises most of them himself, they do not obscure a bold and imaginative stride forward into an area we know very little about—the relationship of the small to the large. Whereas Lincoln Center, conceptually, represents a fragmented, backward glance, Rudolph's Boston Government Service Center searches for a new, relative and cohesive urban scale.

Mies has narrowed in, continually refining an approach for the last three decades. In contrast, Rudolph is always moving on, experimenting and expanding his vocabulary. In what is an older man's profession, Rudolph, in his forties, is a young architect; where his path will lead and how valid it will have been, only time will tell. It is certain that he will follow that path with sustained energy and enormous imagination. The best work of an architect of Rudolph's position and creative temperament usually lies ahead. Kahn phrases it wonderfully, certainly encouragingly: "Those who have the sense of knowing what to do are the poets, and they must write the books that are not yet good before they are able to write the ones that are completely indestructible."

I. M. PEI

Everson Museum of Art, Syracuse, New York.

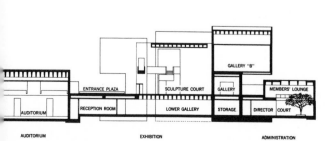

"To understand an epoch means to understand its essence and not everything that you see," says Mies. And in this vein he builds—the clear idea, the essential, grand single statement. Rudolph, on the other hand, wants to preserve, react to and express all the inputs, however minor compared to the essential purpose. I. M. Pei tries to embrace the best of both approaches. Where a building type repeats similar elements he will make the general statement without fearing monotony; where a building type is naturally composed of varying elements he will express them. Pei's buildings have a formal coherence, a quiet unity and harmony in the spirit of Mies's universalism, which he successfully combines with a sensitive response to specific needs. His rigorous analytical approach to resolving the complexities of a building, while it produces a highly-disciplined and simple geometric order, clarifies the complexities without negating them.

Pei has been aptly described as combining a classical sense of form with a contemporary mastery of method. He would be sympathetic to Mies's statement, "I would rather be good than original." Pei considers architecture and planning as one; the design of buildings and spaces as an entity. His emphasis on total planning and the restrained, rather formal, refined statement related to it, is timely in view of the great need for a sense of unity, direction and purpose in our cities.

Ieoh Ming Pei was born in Canton, China, in 1917. He came to the United States in 1935 and enrolled at the Massachusetts Institute of Technology. Five years later he received a Bachelor of Architecture degree, and travelled on an M.I.T. Fellowship. Pei then worked for an engineering firm, and the National Defense Research Committee at Princeton, before entering Harvard in 1945 to receive a Master of Architecture degree a year later. He remained to join the faculty, while also working for Hugh Stubbins. From 1948, until he opened his own office in 1955, Pei was Director of Architectural Research for Webb and Knapp, one of America's largest real estate companies. He was awarded the Harvard Wheelwright Fellowship in 1951, and in 1961, the Arnold Brunner Award of the National Institute of Arts and Letters given for excellence in the field of architecture.

Pei's association with William Zeckendorf, the dynamic and imaginative president of Webb and Knapp, gave Pei the opportunity to mature his ideas on major comprehensive planning, redevelopment, and architectural schemes, for what he terms "investment architecture." Where Johnson, Rudolph, Barnes and Johansen worked from small personal commissions towards the design of larger prestige buildings, Pei is receiving these commissions after a very different experience. As a result, he seems relaxed and facile in coordinating the various talents required to resolve large, complex problems.

Pei's office is reminiscent of the late Eero Saarinen's, with a hint of S.O.M. He has three partners and five associates and a staff of a hundred persons. The office is organized for comprehensive teamwork, and Pei supervises all projects, each of which is managed by an associate. There are planning, architectural, interior, graphic, and model-making departments, yet with a flexibility, Pei says:" where we sacrifice organization for individualism."

The Denver Mile High Center, in Colorado, in 1955 was the first important commission of I. M. Pei and Associates from Webb and Knapp. A twenty-three-story speculative office building, it occupies less than twenty-five percent of a pleasantly landscaped site. In 1958 the May-D & F department store was added, one block away on Denver's busiest shopping street. It is a four-story 266-foot-square building, approached across a landscaped plaza with a sunken area used for skating in the winter and as an open-air restaurant in the summer. The predominantly enclosed main volume is entered through a hyperbolic paraboloid shell structure whose huge triangular glass walls create a dramatic display area. The store connects directly by elevators to an underground parking garage for one thousand one hundred and sixty cars. As a part of the complex, the Denver Hilton hotel was opened two years later. It too connects directly to the parking garage, and from its lobby, is linked by a clear plastic-enclosed bridge above the street, to the department store.

The earlier steel and glass office tower, with its unprotected curtain walls, had experienced problems with sun penetration. These were solved in the hotel by recessing the glass 16 inches behind reinforced concrete curtain walls that cover the guest rooms in a grid 2 feet wide by 8 feet high. This pattern is varied slightly at the second level to indicate the principal space of the main 22-foot entrance lobby. The heavily-textured facade is more attuned to the rugged mountain landscape than was that of the office tower, with its warm reddish-brown granite excavated from the site, and crushed as aggregate for the concrete. The experience of making this interdependent group of buildings with direct physical links led to one of the most successful speculative urban developments of recent years, the Place Ville Marie, three

Mile High Center, Denver, Colorado.

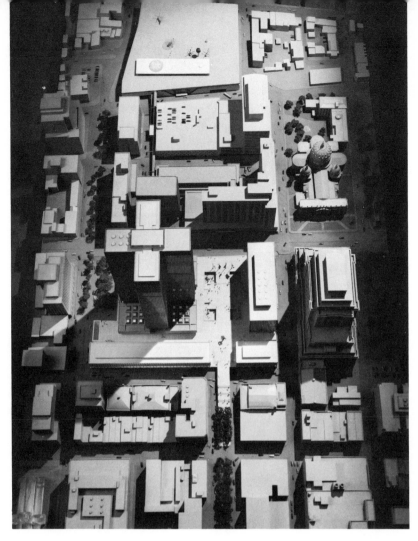

Place Ville Marie, Montreal, Canada.

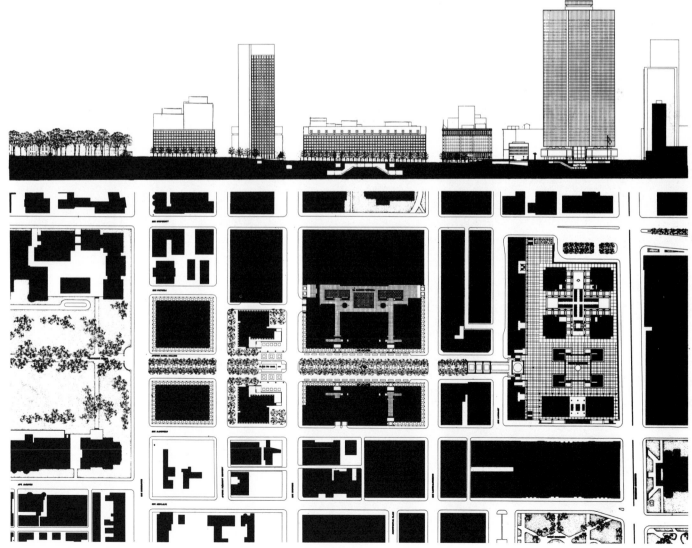

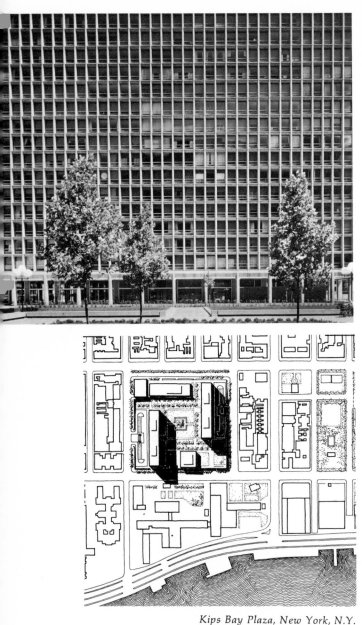

years in design and three years under construction, completed in 1961, in Montreal, Canada.

The usual urban development is an incoherent, lot-by-lot happenstance that does not attempt to generate broader area relationships or study the general problems of its physical context. Not Place Ville Marie. It endeavored to anticipate, for example, the traffic and parking problems that it would generate, and resolve these in relation to existing problems on a city-wide scale. A broader sequence of pedestrian spaces was also considered, with a widened, tree-lined avenue proposed to link the site to the campus of McGill University. Then a master plan was prepared to study the physical interrelation between three contiguous city blocks owned by Canadian National Railways. Finally, Pei and his partner H. N. Cobb prepared detailed designs for one, seven-and-a-half acres in extent, to be called Place Ville Marie. It was a combined attempt to create a project, financially sound for its investors and economically and socially beneficial to the city. Place Ville Marie has underground parking for fifteen hundred automobiles, beneath an enclosed shopping promenade that is cleverly connected by four sunken courtyards to a pedestrian plaza at ground level. From this plaza rises a forty-story office tower, sheathed in glass and aluminum, and cruciform in shape to create large, daylighted continuous floor areas. The second and third levels are banking areas that visually form a square base for the tower, and are skylighted from above in the four angles of the cruciform. The plaza is framed on two sides by low rectangular buildings, for shops with office space above.

Place Ville Marie attracts sixty thousand visitors a day; the tower alone has a working population of one-sixth of that. Sensibly, in view of the severe winter months, its many and varied uses are accessible from enclosed malls. The project is a model of restraint from landscaping to buildings to commercial signs. As a stimulating focus, it has played an important role in rejuvenating the central area, and has shown how a commercial venture can be combined with civic responsibility.

I. M. Pei and Associates have designed urban-renewal housing

Kips Bay Plaza, New York, N.Y.

New York University Village Towers, New York, N.Y.

Washington Square East, Society Hill, Philadelphia, Pennsylvania.

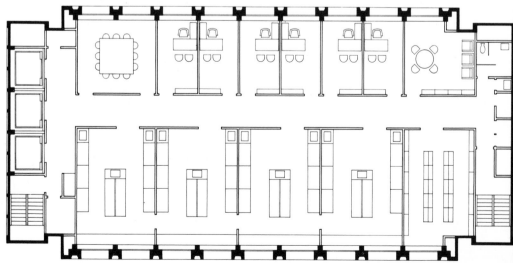

Cecil and Ida Green Building, Center for the Earth Sciences, M.I.T., Cambridge, Massachusetts.

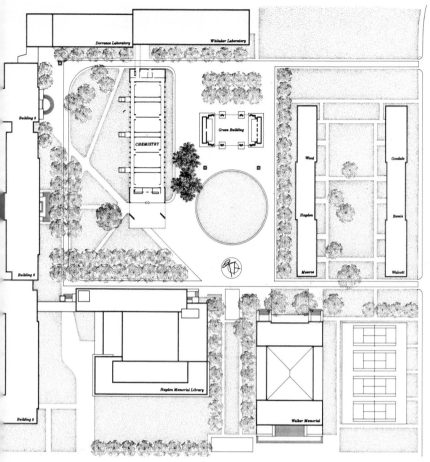

Cecil and Ida Green Building, M.I.T.

projects for Webb and Knapp in Chicago, Washington, New York and Philadelphia. Construction costs for this building type, even for middle-income apartments, become a real challenge. Where costs of up to thirty dollars per square foot are acceptable in speculative office buildings, for apartments twelve to fifteen dollars per square foot seem to be the maximum; the quality of finishes, fixtures, etc., inevitably suffers. In an effort to contain costs, speed-up construction time and produce a more refined residential expression as an alternative to the characterless mediocrity of most apartment buildings today, Pei developed a basic system of load-bearing, reinforced concrete screen walls that serve both as structure and, with glass infilling, as facade.

The twin, twenty-one-story apartment buildings for Kips Bay Plaza in New York, the first of which was finished in 1960, were the prototype for this system. The structural frame and its careful proportioning is the architectural expression, and it is accentuated by the strong shadow lines on the recessed glass plane. Pei is very sensitive to the charge that he is an "expensive architect." As Kips Bay cost less than twelve dollars per square foot, it proved, said Pei, "that architecture can compete with non-architecture economically."

The Society Hill project, completed in 1964, is part of a comprehensive urban renewal of the area adjoining Independence Hall in Philadelphia. Many old houses have been retained and rehabilitated; in harmony and scale with these, Pei added a series of new town houses planned around courtyards. The focus of his scheme is a cluster of three, thirty-story towers, whose handsome, well-proportioned structure is a refinement on Kips Bay Plaza. However, the spatial experience of the schemes is very different, and provides an interesting comparison in the psychological im-

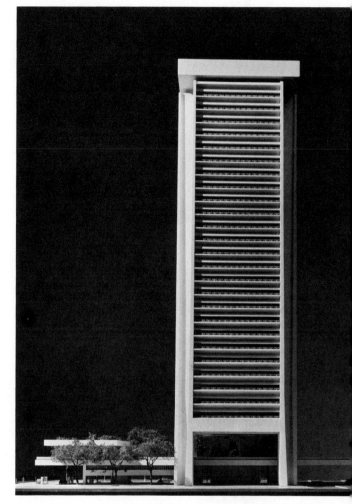

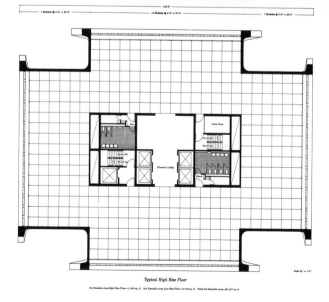

Typical High Rise Floor

Pan Pacific Center, Honolulu, Hawaii.

315

pression of urban space. At Kips Bay the parallel 400-foot long slabs tend to create a static sense of confined space between them and a predictable silhouette, although they are staggered and 300 feet apart.

At Society Hill the three towers never contain; there is a fluid sense of space despite the grouping of the towers around a space only 180 feet across. And although the buildings are of similar height as at Kips Bay, their silhouette is more variable as they combine to compose a more interesting profile. There is a subtlety in the way Pei turned the long axis of one of the towers against that of the other two: Mies made a similar distinction when he opposed the axes of his twin towers on Chicago's Lake Shore Drive.

Another comparison is with Sert's Married Students Housing at Harvard, where the four facades of a building vary according to view and sun. Pei's towers, similar to Mies's, show the neo-classic tendency towards a uniform treatment for all facades. This leads to a more unified building envelope, but raises the question as to whether the various elevations of a building should not respond more to the variances of exposure and view.

"In buildings designed for urban situations, generally I prefer a somewhat more unified building envelope expression. I see no need to express an arbitrary variety on the facade of an apartment house or an office building designed for a multiple and transient tenancy.

"The complexity of the requirements of urban life and the need to accommodate change demand flexibility. The highly articulated design is an inflexible design, hence in my view inappropriate. Kips Bay is Miesian in its inspiration. It was designed around 1955 when we were deeply involved in slum clearance projects, and urban housing was (still is) our greatest challenge. I admired immensely Mies's Lake Shore Drive apartments but the steel frame, and metal and glass skin were too expensive a solution. We decided to take one step forward by making the structure also the facade, thereby eliminating the skin-bone relationship in the building. Since then the same approach has been used in the design of several projects, the most recently completed being the New York University Married Students Housing. These attempts in urban housing required considerable research into the use of reinforced concrete which is a significant fact itself, for I have been concerned for some time about the tyrannical limitation upon form imposed by structural steel as an architectural material. We now see the plastic possibilities of reinforced concrete which has, in my opinion, contributed much to the present highly expressionistic trend which some call the 'new Baroque.'

"I see no danger in this provided, of course, we exercise a degree of self-restraint. This discipline of restraint is all the more important today when we are confronted with the enormously difficult task of remaking our cities. As artist-architects the temptation is to give self-expression to every building we design. We tend to forget our greater responsibility to the whole—which is the street, the square or the city itself.

"We are increasingly building for a transient society. The majority of buildings in our communities are impersonal in nature and should in my opinion be so expressed. This is not to say that a church, a museum, or a city hall should all look alike. On the contrary, this uniqueness of design called for by their uniqueness

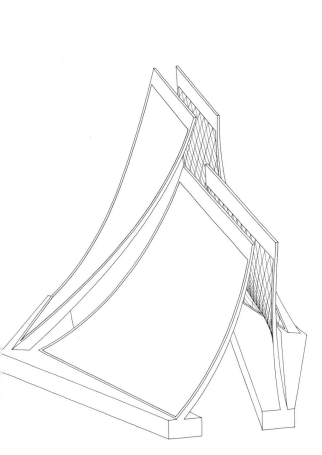

The Luce Chapel, Tunghai University, Taichung, Taiwan.

of function is made all the more significant when not competing with unique apartment houses, unique office buildings, unique garages, and unique buildings everywhere. A city of prima donna buildings is a chaotic city aesthetically! This was brought about, I believe, when we lost the traditional hierarchy of values in our cities. In the Middle Ages the focus was the cathedral; one hundred years ago, the city hall; today, anything and everything!"

In the 1960's Pei's all-round professionalism and rational approach have brought him many commissions apart from the Zeckendorf patronage.

The twenty-one story Earth Sciences Center for M.I.T. continues Pei's interest in a clearly-expressed and refined reinforced concrete frame, as a pragmatic aesthetic for tower structures. Each floor is a column-free space, 48 feet by 93 feet, with the "bearing wall" along the long sides, between service and circulation cores at either end. Solar-bronze plate glass windows are fitted directly into the poured concrete frame, that contains a limestone aggregate to produce a color and texture similar to that of the existing buildings. It breaks with the M.I.T. tradition of continuously linked five-story buildings, to create "a focus for a pivotal space on the campus," says Pei, "and to concentrate floor space to allow the development of a major open space." Since it would be a very visible landmark, Pei also wanted to restate the classical theme of the campus that had been earlier expressed in M.I.T.'s symbolic dome, but at a new scale and as a product of our technology.

The Pan Pacific Center for Honolulu, for which the preliminary design stages are now completed, further refines the structural idea of the M.I.T. tower. Here, solid bearing walls at the four corners of the tower, increasing in their thickness towards the base, will support beams that clear-span the distance between them, visible on the exterior. From these, secondary beams span to the central core.

A different expression are the two pairs of concrete shells, separated by narrow bands of glass, that enclose the intimate soaring space of the Luce Memorial Chapel at Formosa's Tunghai University. The exterior form is clad with gold-colored glazed tiles. On the interior the concrete is exposed and the stresses, which increase towards the base of each shell, are reflected in the diamond-shaped rib pattern that increases in dimension from top to bottom.

An earlier "universal space" building was Pei's own weekend house, built in New York's Westchester County in 1952. There, a simple post-and-beam timber structure is clearly articulated and visible throughout the one skylighted living space (all partitions are glass-topped to preserve the continuity of space) that extends outwards through clear or translucent glass sliding screens to a broad, surrounding screened porch. A variation on this at the vast scale necessary to handle masses of people in transit is Pei's 600-foot-long and 30-foot-high universal space, won in a limited competition held by the Port of New York Authority in 1960 for its new terminal building at Kennedy Airport. The space, within which various activities are symmetrically organized, is covered by a space frame of steel tetrahedrons supported on massive perimeter concrete pylons, outside the glass enclosing walls.

The use of an appropriate structural system and its direct expres-

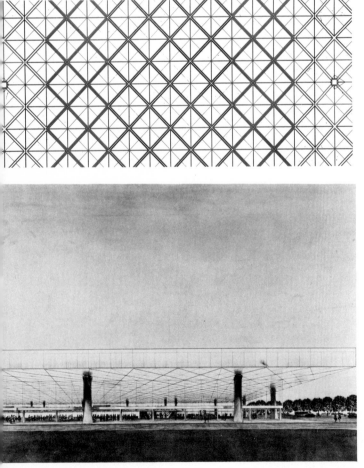

National Airlines Terminal, Kennedy Airport, New York, N.Y.

Pei House, Katonah, New York.

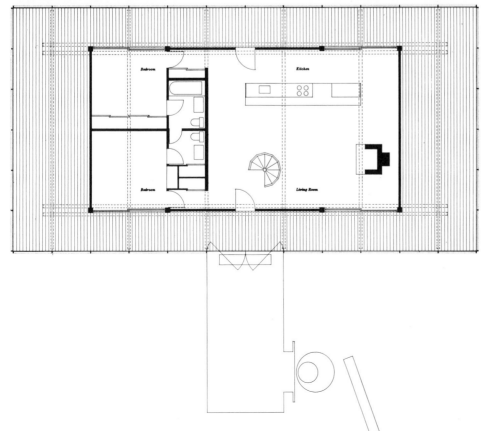

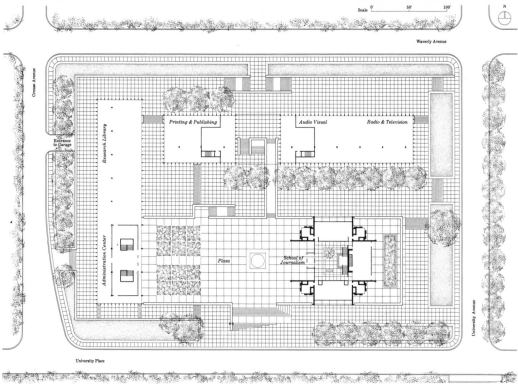

sion to define and shelter a simple space is elemental to the two towers, church, house, and terminal building. As his commissions have become more monumental and complex in function, and more personal in purpose, Pei has tried to express this architecturally. He has increasingly chosen to emphasize the variation and relationship of spaces, an approach he would explain as deriving from the changed nature of his commissions.

The School of Journalism in Syracuse, New York, completed in 1964, is the first and focal element of a three-building complex to be called the Newhouse Communications Center. The other buildings, eight- and five-story slab blocks, will be devoted to research and instruction in television, radio and other electronic communication developments. The three buildings "will emerge sculpturally from a podium that is the unifying element," says Pei. The podium, while giving the buildings a prominent setting, will contain photography studios and heavy mechanical equipment areas that do not require natural lighting, plus common usage classrooms and lecture halls. Structural piers, symmetrically placed at the four corners of the square three-story structure, are of the same pink granite, exposed aggregate concrete as the plaza, giving the building a monolithic effect that is further emphasized by the pier's buttress-like shape where they meet the plaza. At the plaza, and beneath the heavily-expressed, concrete roof line, glass areas are deeply recessed, heightening the sculptural impression of the building.

In contrast to the formal, cruciform plan of the Journalism building are the informally-grouped, sculptural concrete masses of the Everson Museum of Art, also at Syracuse, completed in 1965. A basic design problem was how to prevent the comparatively small building from being overpowered by its neighbors; and to create—which the Museum's Director thought appropriate for the scale of the city—small exhibition spaces that had an intimacy and individuality, rather than flexible, universal space. Pei's solution was four major exhibition galleries, cantilevered out from a podium that contains minor gallery spaces, studios, administrative, working and storage areas. The major galleries, connected by four bridges at the corners of a court, are grouped around a two-story central sculpture court, the interior focal point. Completing the group, while forming an entrance plaza and additional area for the exhibition of sculpture on either side of the interconnected gallery spaces, are the raised elements of the auditorium, and the members' lounge and board room that are part of the podium. Of all his designs, this is Pei's favorite.

The National Center for Atmospheric Research on a small plateau at the foot of the Rocky Mountains, near Boulder, Colorado, is presently under construction. Whereas S.O.M., in the Air Force Academy, met the tremendous scale of nature with a shimmering, reflective expanse of glass, Pei has returned to the elemental forms of sheer walls of unfinished concrete of a dark reddish-brown aggregate to match the color of the mountains. Research facilities for five hundred scientists, adjoining common-use facilities across a terraced plaza, are grouped in towers of offices and laboratories to ensure a degree of privacy for individual research groups.

Criticism of Pei's work is rare, and invariably refers to some of his projects as appearing too monotonous or too intellectual. With the earlier residential projects, usually connected with slum clearance programs, time is needed for them to mellow into the context of freshly landscaped settings. It is Pei's nature to rationalize the approach to a problem. He wisely selects new commissions to maintain the control and quality of his work, rather than make the mistake of spreading his ability too thin. Although it is far from profitable, most successful architects still like to have one house under design within their office; Pei's choice is one urban renewal project, although he says: "My least successful buildings are those in dense urban situations, and they demand ten times the effort."

Pei's commissions now, however, are mostly for prestige designs that are naturally leading him into a more individual design phase. In 1964 he was selected from a short list that included Mies, Kahn, Bunshaft of S.O.M., Rudolph, Johnson and Warnecke to design the Kennedy Memorial Library at Harvard. Breuer echoed many sentiments in saying, "He was a wonderful choice."

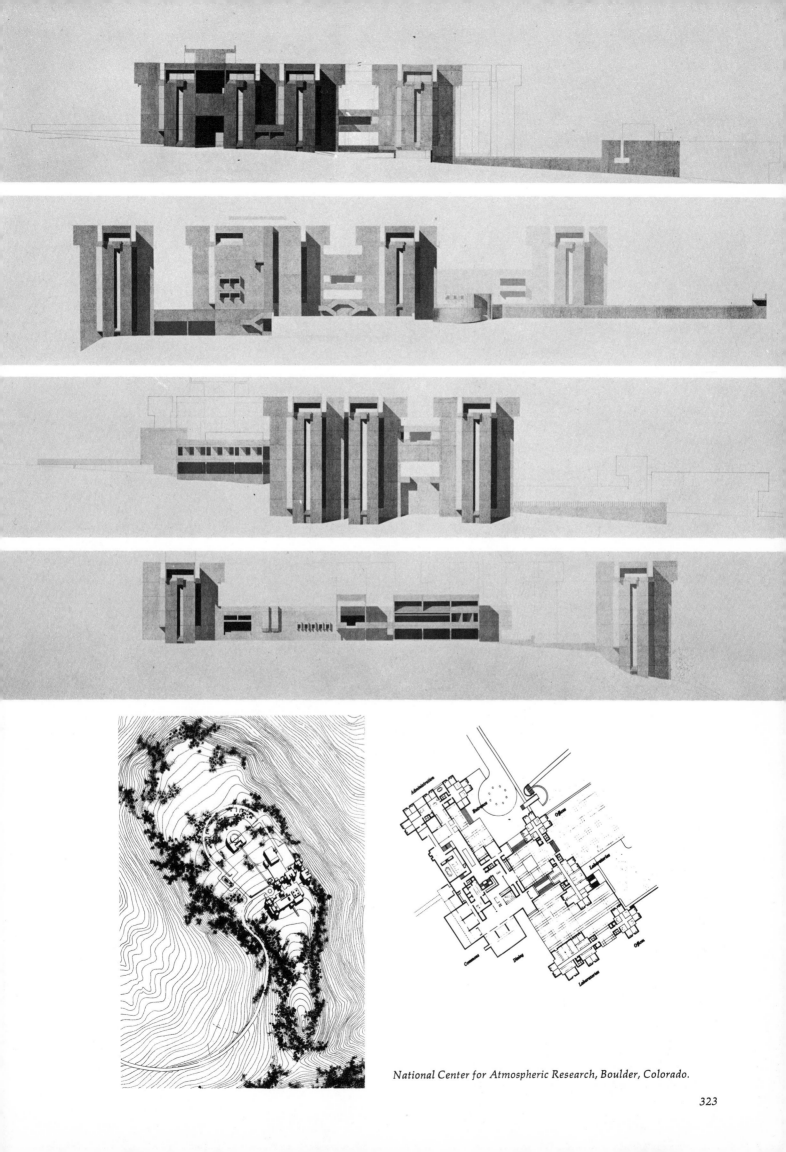

National Center for Atmospheric Research, Boulder, Colorado.

323

Edward L. Barnes

EDWARD LARRABEE BARNES

Every building is the product of a hierarchy of ideas: social, functional, formal, structural, environmental. With each new problem the priority of these ideas changes, as they generate an architectural statement. For Edward Barnes this statement is a spatial concept, related to human activity, in which form and function are inseparable. "Because," as Barnes says, "a purely formal approach ignores the *use* of the building—be it static or dynamic—and becomes at best, sculpture not architecture."

Edward Barnes was born in Chicago, in 1915. He studied the history of architecture at Harvard, and taught English and Fine Arts at Milton Academy, before returning to the Graduate School of Design in 1940, to study architecture. After graduation he worked first in the office of Gropius and Breuer; then, during the war, as a naval architect in San Francisco. In 1948, he opened his own office in New York where he maintains a personal practice, and in addition, he is visiting critic and lecturer at several universities.

Many architects, including Barnes, treat a problem as part of an episode in the exploration of an architectural idea. This does not mean that a specific problem becomes merely a means to a predetermined end, but rather that the architect is developing a series of approaches to a central idea. The work of Wright and Le Corbusier, for example, falls naturally into such episodic divisions where ideas are often pursued until every aspect has been carefully explored. "You can never get everything in one building," says Barnes.

Osborn House, Salisbury, Connecticut.

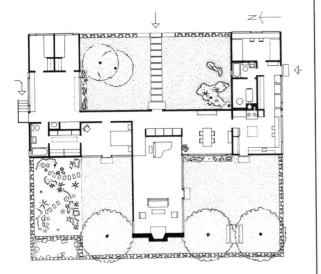

The earliest clearly-defined episodes in Barnes's work have to do with platform houses—good examples of which are his own house in Mount Kisco, New York, and the Osborn house in Salisbury, Connecticut. The central idea is to separate the house from the natural landscape by building it on a generous platform, which then becomes a highly-developed extension of the house; a formal living space where flowers, ground cover and trees can be planted and carefully tended without destroying the natural character of the site. Thus the often awkward or amorphous relationship between the modern house and its landscape is gracefully solved, while both the platform gardens and wild surroundings are enhanced.

The second group of designs evolving from a central idea includes the several camps for the Herald Tribune Fresh Air Fund, and culminates in the Straus house in Pound Ridge, New York, built in 1959. In this period Barnes was interested in developing a sympathetic design vocabulary for woodland buildings. He used natural materials in a simple post and lintel construction, crisply detailed to harmonize with the heavily-wooded camp sites.

The Straus house is a restrained, meticulously detailed and precise statement of this approach. Its informal living areas, nestling among trees on the edge of a quiet pond, are supported on wooden piles above the ferns and moss-covered rock ledges. The house has four principle volumes: the children's bedrooms and play area; the master and guest bedrooms; the kitchen, dining room and servant's rooms with an extension for a garage, and a screened porch that projects over the pond; and finally a large living room, whose high-pitched roof dominates the complex. These volumes are clustered to form small, carefully-landscaped formal courts, and are connected by glazed galleries. Here, it is interesting to see how far Barnes has moved from the Harvard emphasis, while still being firm about geometry. The Straus house is a sensitive, romantic expression of site and mood, which still does not take the direction of an organic approach such as Wright's.

"At Harvard, Le Corbusier was the hero; but he was one step removed, and we saw the International Style at first hand through Breuer's work. His own house in Lincoln was a revelation of a new world of light and space; a two-story living room, a bedroom on a balcony, and a dining room a few steps down. I had never seen such fresh details and materials. I admired the sureness of his touch—his ability to combine totally dissimilar elements and

Hidden Valley Camp, Fishkill, New York.

Straus House, Pound Ridge, New York.

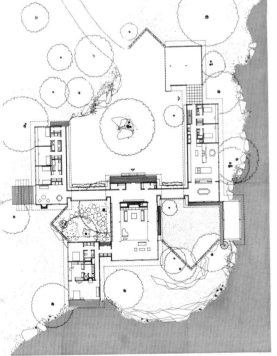

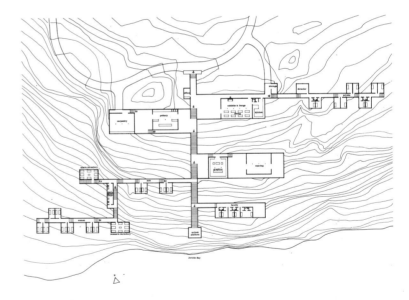

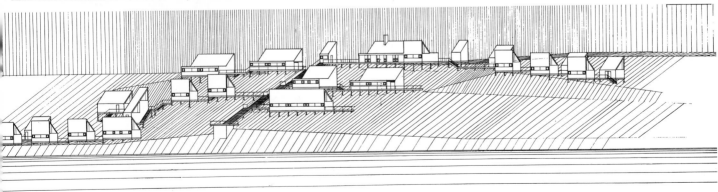

Haystack School, Deer Isle, Maine.

St. Paul's School, Concord, New Hampshire.

Farm, Wayzata, Minnesota.

materials and yet not crowd the space. To me, his architecture was like a Klee painting in which disparate objects floated in space—an arrow, a moon, a flower, a glass—all unrelated, yet held together by a tension, by their exact placement. This quality of tension and contrast seemed to be a true expression of our lives at that time.

"The Harvard training with its strong functional base, later ridiculed for being too narrow, was actually a good approach—a good discipline in combination with vital aesthetic and formal considerations. I have never been able or willing to reject it. Rudolph, Johnson and other people were actually irritated by functionalism—for me it always seemed a valid approach. I felt that the use, the life and the activity of a building, were terribly important; and that if one broadened the meaning of 'functional' to include psychological needs, one might in effect create *expressionist* architecture, with its roots firmly planted in functionalism.

"Kahn recognizes that the real activity of a building, what it 'wants to be,' is regulated by its use. This does not contradict a more doctrinaire functional approach. I react against buildings that seem to be approached as pure form. Philosophically, the difference between architecture and sculpture has to do with use, with its relation to an activity of man. However, just as a monument, or a pyramid, is something in between art and architecture, so there are bound to be buildings in between. These 'in between' buildings are pure examples of expressionist architecture.

"A building must have a strong idea that is architectural rather than sculptural or painterly—one that is related to the activity in the building. The idea should be something that can be drawn on a napkin or an envelope. When one architect says to another: 'What kind of a building are you doing?' one should immediately be able to draw an abstraction, or a diagram of the architectural idea.

"I believe that every human activity can be reduced on analysis to an organic form. This does not mean that the form cannot be elaborate, with many tentacles and variations, but simply that there is essentially a oneness about every job. In the best solutions there is a strong central idea involving activity; it may be static or mobile, but it has to do with the human being in space.

"Can one apply these design ideas to City Planning? Can we see our changing cities as total organisms rather than a disparate collection of unrelated problems? In New Haven, where I am a planning consultant to Yale University, I have had a chance to observe the Yale community interacting with a growing city plan. The pattern is typical of many cities; express roads and boulevards are defining neighborhoods. Now, I know that the highway engineer is often ruthless, and that Robert Moses is a villain. I know that Jane Jacobs and others fight expressways, and that Scully argues for a sort of ostrich do-nothing approach where the 'mess' continues to 'happen.' However, I submit that by intelligently concentrating traffic, we also make it possible to return whole neighborhoods to the pedestrian. This is what we hope will happen at Yale—that when a ring road is built, it will be possible to close streets within the campus. And surely this concept of the protected neighborhood merging almost as a single building, surely this organic separation of traffic from community life points to city plans where the total form is a more comprehensible expression.

"Fly over our cities at night and you will see that the gridiron disappears and the meaningless 'city beautiful' vistas vanish. What is etched in light are the rivers and streams of major traffic, circling and defining quiet dark neighborhoods. It is easy to talk nostalgically of the market squares and plazas of Europe, but what is needed is a firm architectural concept for the major arteries, the true city entrances, and centers, and most important, the individual neighborhood communities.

"One of the things that one always hopes to find in architecture is mood, a sense of atmosphere. This is present in Wright's and Mies's work, and perhaps in the best of one's own. One feels this in a certain contact with nature—a kind of wood, or a kind of day—it is within one's power as an architect to establish a mood, or destroy it. Thinking about a specific problem deeply enough, it suggests a mood that may be somber, cheerful, fresh or serious, but it is a true reflection of the architect's own personality. So when I say that an architect must retain a kind of mood, I mean that he must be responsive to himself.

"In the buildings of Le Corbusier and Wright there is always mood and self expression. I can also see personal expression in the architecture of a few of my contemporaries, yet critics rarely search out the particular point of view of the architect.

"There comes a moment in every project when you have the illusion that you have found the truth and are actually coming to grips with it. That is the real break-through point in any design even though, in fact, you may only have released something within yourself."

Breuer's strength, and perhaps his weakness too, is an ability to combine disparate objects, materials and textures and relate them in space. Barnes found an alternate, simple and direct solution to the problem of unity in space: suppress multiplicity. His suc-

cess is not that he did a subtraction of the Breuer world, but that he went beyond elimination to emphasize what had been injected. "For me," says Barnes, "continuity means the use of fewer materials, the elimination of expressed articulation, as little tampering with the land as possible, and emphasis on what is alike rather than different. It means designing with respect for nearby buildings—their scale and color, and mood. It means considering the space between the buildings, bearing in mind that it can be more important than the buildings themselves."

On a visit in 1960 to the Middle East and the islands off Greece, Barnes was deeply impressed by the strong unity between villages and their natural environment—particularly the simplicity and continuity of white Mykonos. Society, rather than the individual, was the decisive unit, and each building was conditioned by its context and by what had preceded it—the feeling of harmony and serenity was overwhelming. Barnes's move toward greater simplicity dates from this visit. He entered a third and very fruitful phase.

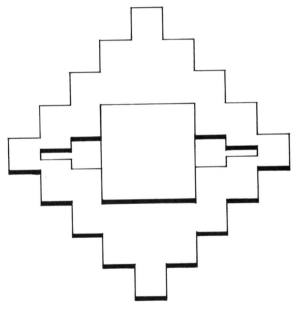

Nieman-Marcus Shopping Center, Fort Worth, Texas.

Among the first projects were Hidden Valley Camp in Fishkill, New York, and Haystack School on Deer Isle, Maine, both opened in 1963. Each is based on a "village" prototype of closely huddled, distinctive, yet related buildings. The walls and roofs of the crisp volumes are clad in cedar shingles that give a continuity of surface and emphasis on volume, which are echoed in the interior. At Hidden Valley the buildings are regulated by a 12-foot by 18-foot structural bay, a consistent floor-to-eave dimension, and a uniform roof slope that runs north-south in contrast to the east-west direction of the flat-roofed connective structures. Although equally quiet architecturally, the Haystack School is more dramatic because of Barnes's clear organizational idea that takes full advantage of a beautiful, precipitous slope overlooking the ocean: a wide central spine of wooden stairs, leading directly down the slope to a lookout platform at the water's edge, from which secondary wooden walkways branch in either direction and at right angles to the stairway, providing access to the small dormitory buildings, the workshops and the studios. Twenty-three peaked roofs create a lively, sharp silhouette, sometimes paralleling the steep tree-covered slope, sometimes opposing it, in what is one of Barnes's most impressive designs to date.

The buildings on Mykonos merge with the landscape, in a plastic way; Frank Lloyd Wright's buildings grow romantically out of the landscape but in a *bauen* manner. Both approaches can be called organic. Although Barnes creates a romantic mood at Haystack, he never breaks the clear angularity of volumes, never allows the walkways to meander. Sharp geometry is the evident discipline throughout. The walks and platforms follow the conformation of the site, but leave it undisturbed.

The village idea, which began with the Hidden Valley Camp, is further explored in the dormitories at St. Paul's School, Concord, New Hampshire, built in 1963. The walls, corridor floors, terraces and walks are red brick with dark mortar. The flat roofs of the boys' dormitories, surfaced with a red brick gravel, contrast with the copper-clad pitched roofs of the masters' houses, common rooms and penthouses. Each student room has a vertical window, while tilted square windows illuminate the masters' spaces. The single-story student buildings, hugging the terrain and punctuated by the higher, masters' elements, continue the scale and reinforce the old street line of adjacent Victorian buildings, thus creating a more defined spatial sequence for the campus.

Another variation on the village theme is the farm in Wayzata, Minnesota, built in the same year. The farm is a cluster of white buildings around a court. Living room, master bedroom, playroom, servants' quarters, guest house and barn, separately roofed with steep gables and raking studio roofs, are linked by continuous flat roofs and low walls. There is unity in the all-white forms, and diversity in the separate expression of the parts. In all the peaked roofs, huge skylights bathe the rooms with a light which has some of the luminous quality of Mykonos.

A second all-white complex, built also in 1963, was the Nieman-Marcus shopping center in Fort Worth, Texas. Fourteen tenant shops, each separately-expressed, step up the sloping site and surround the central, two-story top-lit store which is approached through small entrance courts flanked by the shops. The only surface material used, including all the sculptured lettering, is rough white stucco. Thus the merchandise is set off against a continuous background, and the white-on-white forms are defined only by light and shadow.

Two weekend houses, one at Fisher's Island, New York, and the other at Blue Mountain Lake in the Adirondacks, further explore the episode of monolithic, continuous surfaces. The continuity of wall and roof is particularly striking in the Fisher's Island house where the wedge-shaped form flares in plan toward the sea and in section toward the land. A long fence defines the entrance court and visually relates the guest area to the house. In the Adirondack house one enters through the roof plane into a wedge-shaped volume. The surface materials emphasize the continuous skin; the exterior is entirely shingled and the interior is completely sheathed in spruce.

The Princeton University Administration Building is a clear ex-

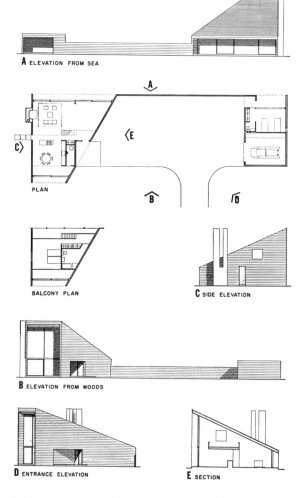

A ELEVATION FROM SEA

PLAN

BALCONY PLAN

C SIDE ELEVATION

B ELEVATION FROM WOODS

D ENTRANCE ELEVATION

E SECTION

Weekend House, Fisher's Island, New York.

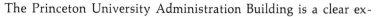

Weekend House, Blue Mountain Lake, New York.

Administration Building, Princeton University, Princeton, New Jersey.

ample of Barnes's approach to volume. Here, the short square tower with a central elevator core has an exposed concrete frame with dark glass windows. Unlike the Miesian system, where the expression is *bauen* and mullion stiffeners are applied outside the volume, the volume itself gives the impression that it has been carved away to form the deep, window reveals. The wide, "Chicago style" windows are recessed four feet so that the facade is deeply shadowed. In contrast to Rudolph's technique, the concrete is poured against smooth plastic forms so that the outer volume is accurately defined and expressed. "The result," Barnes says, "is a more plastic architecture, yet one that is still precise and disciplined."

As he undertakes larger commissions, perhaps Barnes is entering a new period. Yet the feeling for volume and continuous material remains. He has designed a forty-story steel frame office building for Boston's new Government Center. The exterior material is dark red granite with tinted glass. A special feature is the asymmetrical column spacing that accommodates a great banking hall along one side and a high arcade along the other. The bottom of the building, which rises from a sloping pavement, and the stepped top with a restaurant and roof garden create a bold base and crown for the building.

Barnes's architecture is distinguished by the thoroughness and logic with which he defines his design premise and executes it. Motivating the approach to each of his designs is a single clear idea. The strength of his architecture is not in elaboration, but rather in the directness and simplicity with which he gives expression to each new problem.

Office Building, Government Center, Boston, Massachusetts.

Taylor House, Westport, Connecticut.

John M Johansen [signature]

JOHN M. JOHANSEN

"Some architects in the United States are searching for beauty," says John Johansen, "but I am not one of them." His search is for character. As character is never formed, but always being formed, so his buildings intentionally lack a sense of completeness. "If forms are alive and growing and evolve naturally in honest performance, then I find them to be true and to have character if not beauty."

Office buildings, residential and industrial developments are all building types of universal space or repetitive units of space, where certain principles or design coefficients are established and limits defined; houses, institutional and public buildings have more personal spaces, permitting stronger and more varied expressions of function, allowing an architect a more personal involvement and identification. This latter category is Johansen's interest.

With a small staff of ten, he is very much the originator rather than the critic, deeply involved in all aspects of the creative process. In the arts the view is often expressed that the amount of work and technical knowledge required to create a building, plus the supposedly less controllable factors of client, program and budget, come between the architect and his work. Johansen, who is also a serious painter, and possibly as much a pure artist as an architect can be and still produce a significant amount of work, does not think that this is necessarily so.

The first precautions are the careful selection of the commission and client, with a reciprocal understanding and acceptance by the client. "Very often the opinion of clients must be disregarded in their own interest," says Johansen. "An architect has to lead, but in a direction mutually agreed upon. There has to be a coming together of minds in the search for a design. The program must be met to the client's satisfaction: the architect must consider the program, the client and his needs, and then find an idea that is applicable. An architect may be capable of several valid ideas; however, he must be sensitive to the client's reaction, and not push or force him; often he may have to come back with another idea that is more appropriate to specific conditions. He will succeed, if he can develop an idea all the way, and the client is with him. As one client said to me: 'Are you getting as much out of

Warner House, New Canaan, Connecticut.

Maid 12'6" x 14'6"

Kitchen 12'8" x 25'3" pantry

Entrance

Dining 26'6" x 17'6" bar / music

Living 26'6" x 29'6"

Bedroom 12'9" x 9'8"

Bedroom 12'9" x 9'8"

Bedroom 12'8" x 10'10"

balcony

balcony

walled patio

Guest Study 14'1" x 12'8"

court

Bath-Dressing

Bedroom 14'6" x 20'6" TV

storage

storage

this idea as you can, and are you fulfilling yourself? Because if you win, then we win.' It is never a compromise but a correct selection from ideas, any one of which might be valid to the architect."

If an established architect is to have any significant working capacity, he must have assistants—again, a question of mutual compatibility. It was a common practice in the past, even for artists, to work with assistants; the "master" was freed from some of the more routine operations, to devote his energies to purely creative work while the "apprentice" had the opporunity to mature while acquiring valuable experience. Anyway, it is a unique animal that cannot benefit, at some level, from discussion with others. Johansen avoids collaboration, but believes in carefully-built teams as effective extensions of himself as an individual artist.

John Johansen was born, to parents who both were painters, in New York in 1916. After receiving a Bachelor of Science Degree from Harvard College, he went on to the Graduate School of Design, receiving his architectural degree in 1941. He worked for Breuer and S.O.M. before starting his own practice in 1948. Since then he has been a visiting critic and lecturer at a number of universities.

His early work had a "disciplined, rational approach—it looked very much like Gropius and Breuer's work with some Miesian influence also," he says. In the 1950's his work developed in two particular directions. In retrospect, most of the Gropius-trained men are critical of the lack of emphasis on the historical influences on design. When Johansen became interested in historical influences, he produced several neo-Palladian houses that were well-disciplined, but always romantic. The Warner House in New Canaan in 1958 is just such an example: the main living space is a bridge that spans a stream, with a triple-arched ceiling, flanked by four strong masonry enclosures at the corner positions.

The other direction was organic in the extreme. Modern building techniques have made it possible to disregard the expressive forms of shelter, but Johansen believes that there are basic needs of man's nature that must also be satisfied; deep rooted primitive experiences, common to all people in all times—what Freud and Jung referred to as the "Collective Unconscious." Johansen feels that one such need is the experience of shelter. The result was a series of extreme statements in sprayed concrete, where the primitive idea of the cave and the enclosure was restated in forms developed from a re-evaluation of both human and construction processes.

Johansen overcame the limitations of rectangular wooden formwork by spraying concrete directly on to a structure of reinforcing wire mesh that was attached to steel form ribs; a system of construction in a way as primitive as applying mud to a bamboo frame. Thin curving shells, their shape not determined by formwork, no longer made the conventional distinction between floors, walls and roof. Separate curving forms, with the edges of the thin planes crimped for greater strength, had openings between them sealed against the weather by clear plastic inserts. The fusion of enclosure and structure in flowing shapes made it possible to accommodate function within a greater variety of form; it also created an immediate sense of "continuous construction," and the potentially more expressive quality which Johansen calls "Functional Expressionism."

Based on this principle, he designed a project house for himself of simple and compound curves that had it been built, would have been a "sculpture big enough to live in—it was a great release for me," he says. Frederick Kiesler had previously experimented with this method of construction, and Soleri's earth houses are a more recent variation. One of Johansen's sprayed concrete designs actually was built—a pavilion for the 1956 Trade Fair in Yugoslavia.

His main conclusion from these studies was that "function is really the life force of a building—to forget this for the sake of

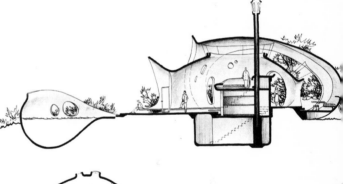

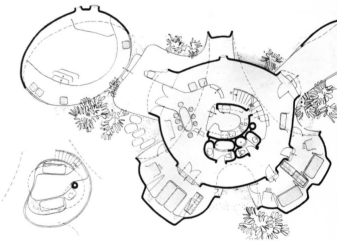

Spray Form House.

form alone is wholly false; true architectural expression can only evolve from human and technical processes. I found this in the sprayed concrete house and have hung on to it ever since; this makes a building true to me. I would rather be true enough to be good, than too good to be true."

The neo-Palladian houses and the sprayed concrete structures represent opposite approaches. Since then, Johansen has apparently moved to a middle ground, merging the discipline of the former and the freedom of the latter, in his search for an expressive and personal architecture.

"I am not a functionalist, as I started out under Bauhaus training, but a 'functional expressionist,' never losing hold of what I first learned but expressing it more dramatically. So I am not fighting function as have so many who turned against the Bauhaus toward formalism. I am interested in a return to basic fundamental experiences and processes—not caring whether they are modern or not. They are always with us. I am interested in the collective unconscious, which we must return to and find a place for in our conscious lives. Regardless of how modern we are, we must attempt what Jean Cocteau called the 'eternal return' to recurrent experiences and needs, based on biologic and psychic processes which are unaffected by changing building technique. If you speak of house, there is always an essence of house; therefore, I am against the deceptions of outside as inside and inside as outside. We do not have to imitate the troglodyte caves, but we do have to start with human processes and find out what their essence really is; and similarly, we must find the essence of school, office building—spaces that are specific spaces, rather than the universal space of Mies.

"I feel close to the pure arts, so that it is not unnatural for me to approach architecture rather directly as a pure art, or for my buildings to have a strong sense of sculpture. However, I find

Taylor House, Westport, Connecticut.

myself correcting people who say that my buildings are very sculptural, that I must have started from a formalist position and worked back, and made it fit the functions. It is quite the opposite. My design begins with an analysis of functions, and it grows; and if there is an order to the life and its accommodation in a building, it will result nearly always in workable organization, which is not in itself a work of art, but must be stated with artistic expression. So architecture, to me, is a poetic statement of the structural and functional condition. This then distinguishes it from planning, regardless of scale.

"Like the artist, the architect's search must be made alone. We can talk about collaboration with other men, planners, researchers, men of specialized technical knowledge, but ultimately the architect must make the balanced decisions and judgments. Again it is the dialogue between an artist and his work. Kahn says that at a certain stage of development, your work speaks back to you; I am very conscious of this—and of Kahn's awareness of the 'insistence will' of a building being what it wants to be.

"The position of the creative architect is a lonely one, for to originate means to have made the creative venture first, and alone. You have to have been everywhere, and first. The architect is also a philosopher in the sense that he has to have lived fully, have aware acute perceptions, and find an order and a meaning in life, which he then must state in such an essential and clear way that others may understand. He must be interested in the physical and psychic human processes that are to take place in his buildings, because it is a precise accommodation of these processes that makes a building come alive; his architectural forms can only derive from a correct understanding of these processes. He tries to pre-live all the possible experiences that others may enjoy them in the building's use; he pre-lives life so that others may see in his buildings a way of life. It is a huge responsibility, and a very gratifying task to fulfill.

"We can learn much from nature, but we do not explore it very much today. There is a right place, for example, for the heart and other organs in the body. In a building you like to feel that things are also in the right place, that there is something true about the relationship and disposition of spaces and forms, as well as

U.S. Embassy, Dublin, Ireland.

341

equipment. There is a lot of confusion and falseness in American architecture currently, and we would do well to seek for essential qualities in our buildings. I am not against extreme statements, but they must evolve from something, be well-founded, and have a basic truth.

"Perhaps *process* is the most important word, as it explains more of what I am doing than anything else. I have great faith that through the emerging idea I will arrive at a successful form. It is fear that makes many architects seize upon the form first, instead of having faith in their own creative process. It is dangerous to rush into a preconceived idea of form, be it neoclassical or brutalist. I make mistakes, but I am no longer afraid.

"The creative architect should not read too much or be too aware of the work of others, but certainly he should be aware of his own derivations and sources. I am interested in the conditions and the environment of primitive forms of life, human and sub-human, and also in more primitive and prehistoric structures such as African, and early Greek. I am interested in the process by which the product evolved rather than the finally perfected form. I am more interested, for example, in the clumsy search at Paiesdon than the perfection of the Parthenon. It seems to me that when a building has been perfected, the architect has killed it. And I am more interested in life.

"If there is any philosophy alive today, it is Existentialism. Does it affect our professional thinking? Perhaps. We cannot determine ahead of time how conditions and circumstances will be and we do not know all the answers; things change constantly and we simply make the best decisions we can—on the basis of being involved, actively committed—and accept the consequences. We also feel ourselves not apart from nature, but a part of nature. So our architecture must be less rational, eloquent, complacent, finite, complete, and specific. Unlike a clean and perfect neoclassicism, we must design buildings that are improvisations, that allow for further growth and adjustment without destroying the idea."

The house for Dr. and Mrs. Howard Taylor, in Westport, Connecticut, in 1962, is on an exposed site on the edge of Long Island Sound. It is probably the clearest statement of Johansen's beliefs, demonstrating what, after function, are his two central concerns. First, the return to essential, protective and somewhat primitive forms of shelter, with basic space sequences following psychological aspects of life within a shelter: the idea of the cave, the tunnel, the path, the tower, the bridge, and the labyrinth—repeated experiences in the collective unconscious—and perhaps, too, something of a protest against oversophistication in the machine world. And second, in an effort to overcome the prevalent alienation from nature, an analogy to simpler forms of plant and animal life: in this case the shell, or the cluster of shells, in a sense an accretion of forms in the process of living together and of growth. The varying wall height and the vertical formwork suggest actual construction processes.

The idea was to create a strong structure as a bulwark against the elements, which suggested a masonry enclosing wall system. The wall became the dominant design element, structurally, functionally and sculpturally; each wall encloses a function, and wall clusters enclose a group of related functions. "The intention" says Johansen, "was to have the forms not only fit the functions, but to suggest, on sight, what particular functions they housed. The curved walls grew directly from a diagram of function, disposition, and circulation paths. The final plan remains the 'conceptual sketch,' merely more disciplined and clarified."

The house consists of four dominant shell groupings: a central one, surrounding the hearth and extending upward to form a tower library above, with the living room, dining room and entrance hall grouped below; the master suite, including bedroom, study, dressing and bathrooms; a service area containing kitchen-breakfast room, rear hall, servants quarters and garage; finally, the fourth grouping is a detached but linked guest area. Concave surfaces suggest enclosure, and contain specific elements of the plan. Convex surfaces create more fluid spaces that have a sense of movement, and are used for the circulation areas and the active space of the living room. Thus the curved planes suggest two types of space, each clearly related to its function.

The outer, convex surfaces of the poured-in-place concrete walls have strong vertical striations produced by the random width, rough-sawn, oak framework against which it was poured. Inner, concave surfaces have a smooth plaster finish, or are covered with soft, smooth fabric—colorful in contrast to the rough-textured concrete, and a specialized finish appropriate to its particular location. Johansen likens these curved walls to shells, whose shape is determined by an organism and its function: a sea shell whose protective outer surface is coarse and sea-worn, the ectoderm; and whose inner surface, the endoderm, the part in direct contact with the organism, is smooth, shiny, or soft and colored. An analogy that must have been very convincing to a doctor.

As a protection against rising tides, the floor platforms are suspended above the ground between the curving walls. From the roof, the labyrinthine character of the entire plan is visible: the

Charles Center, Baltimore, Maryland.

parapet walls, extensions of the curving walls, form protected areas for sitting and sun-bathing. A staircase, at the side of the tower room, leads to a higher lookout terrace with its own outdoor fireplace, from where there is a superb view of Long Island Sound.

"You start," said Johansen, "with an analysis of function, giving the appropriate expressions to the functions of living, then end up with a sculpture. A free, improvised treatment, but basically a practical solution. I tried to unify or reconcile form and human life within, which in nature is complete in one organism."

Johansen's recent commissions have been for larger structures. For the United States Embassy in Dublin, completed in 1964, he chose a finite shape. "The circular form is prominent in all early Celtic-Christian design. It is found in the early round towers of the fifth century, and much later, in the defensive towers of Napoleonic times," Johansen points out. Practically, it proved a good solution for its awkward corner site, a thin wedge-shape; it provided a handsome and friendly facade in all directions and also preserved most of the existing trees.

It is a four-story building—three above grade, and the fourth a basement surrounded by a 20-foot garden moat that pleasantly provides a sense of privacy. Over the moat two bridges give pedestrian access. The structure of the building is two circular facades of precast concrete with a reconstructed limestone finish; one, a 100 feet in diameter, the other, a 50-foot ring enclosing a central three-story, glass-covered rotunda. Precast concrete floor slabs span between the structural cylinders, containing offices that are entered from circular galleries overlooking the reception area in the rotunda. Three concrete towers on the periphery of the rotunda house the vertical transportation facilities. The building's salient feature, both on the facade and in the rotunda, is the sinewy, sculptural expression of the structure. The Embassy is a direct and simple solution to a difficult problem, the monumental yet not ponderous building, symbolizing government.

Probably more compatible with his personal approach to architecture, and more representative of his "touch", are the Clowes Memorial Hall designed for Butler University in Indianapolis, with Evans Woollen, associated architect, opened in 1963; and the theater block, a part of the Charles Center redevelopment project in Baltimore, completed in 1966.

The Clowes Memorial Hall is a multi-purpose facility to seat twenty-two hundred people attending symphony concerts, opera, dance, drama, lecture, choral presentations, cinema, and a student workshop. In a time of highly-specialized design for each of the performing arts, Johansen questions attempting all this in one building. However, many cities need a modern cultural facility, yet cannot support a Lincoln Center.

The primary design determinants were: the acoustical requirements for symphony, a "shoe-box-shaped" hall with parallel sidewalls, high volume, and hard surfaces; for opera and drama, a proximity to the stage (here, only 113 feet separate the stage from the last orchestra row); and a continental seating arrangement (eliminating aisles and providing more comfortable, wider-spaced rows), for which the fire codes require side exits not more than 15 feet apart. These determinants led to the development of 15-foot sidewall elements, parallel for acoustical considerations, arranged to allow seating to "belly out" into a more curved shape for proximity to the stage, and staggered to form semi-concealed

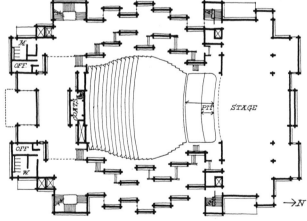

Clowes Memorial Hall, Butler University, Indianapolis, Indiana.

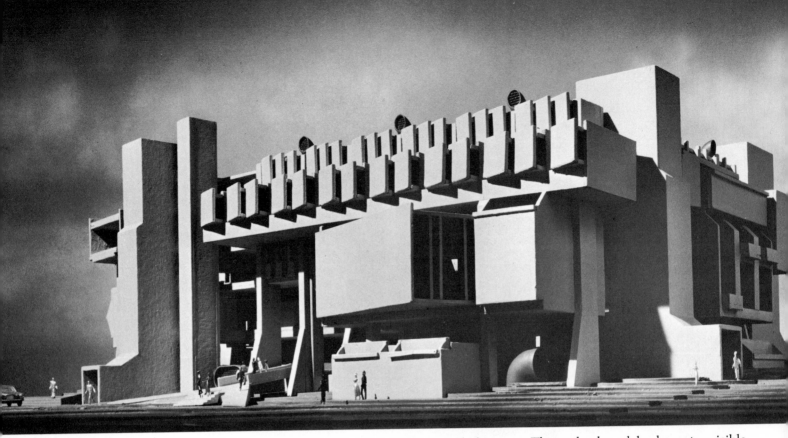

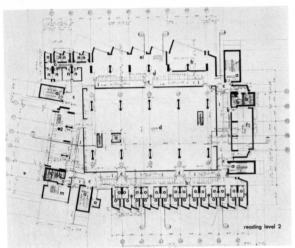

reading level 2

exits and vestibule areas. These slender, slab elements, visible on the exterior, become the unifying motif of the design, while also forming large corner stair towers. Tapering upwards, they create a lively silhouette and facade.

In the main hall the surfaces of the staggered sidewalls are white plaster, used dramatically to reflect light into the interior, and separated by walnut panels. The balconies, stepping down toward the stage, are silhouetted against them. A pattern of suspended plywood panels covers the ceiling and conceals the electrical services. Acoustics, most critics agree, are splendid. Colors are those of the classic European concert hall—red, gold, and white. Entering the building between the narrow slab walls into a multilevel, 60-foot-high grand foyer, then into the irregular, secretive side vestibules, and finally emerging on the main hall, the audience is itself involved in the pageant and drama of theater.

In the Charles Center project, economics necessitated the development of a city block where diverse uses find a mutually-advantageous location: two levels of parking for two hundred cars in a basement, and a complete floor of 50,000 square feet at street level for shops and restaurant, forming a platform for the theater above. The tight finances required that the inner form of the theater, determined from the seating arrangement and the acoustics, become in turn the outer form. The result is a fan-shaped structure, held aloft by concrete piers, flaring outward as it rises, expressing grouped segments of seats, over the lobbies, lounges, and circulation areas.

For Clark University in Worcester, Massachusetts, Johansen has designed a library of reinforced concrete with brick infill panels, to be consistent with the existing and proposed buildings of the campus. The building, raised one story above the ground, will straddle the major pathways of the campus. Around a central three-story "box of books" is a random arrangement, a free assemblage of reading spaces supported by a separate system of concrete piers. This outer structure is a loosely-connected cluster of enclosures to accommodate an intricate program for specialized study.

The building itself expresses the several stages of the design process, says Johansen, and in seeing the final form one will feel as though one has come upon the various parts of the building in process of assembly or attachment. The faculty lounge propped on one lofty pier, "is a shameless afterthought," he says. "I did not 'design.' Rather, I presided and guided the structure as it developed itself, letting it exercise its 'insistence will,' and assert its purpose. This building does not attempt, then, to be architecture, a work of fine art, a thing of good taste or beauty, but is a search for the essential nature or quality of Library. It is simply performing a job, representing the processes of human life within; I hope that by truly accommodating these processes, the building too may come to life." The Library shows his continuing and intensifying search for an unpretentious yet impressive, honest yet dramatic, expression of purpose.

In a way, Johansen seems typical of the creative individual: aware that an artist's life and work are at times bound to fail, but persisting in the belief that in the struggle against failure exists the drama and reward of life itself. Giacometti dramatically expressed it "I sculpt because I am curious to know why I fail." An artist's work is never finished. The creative life is one of action. It is through what he has already achieved that the architect measures imperfection and so transcends his own accomplishments. It is the search beyond the visible toward the invisible, beyond the conditional toward the absolute.

Goddard Library, Clark University, Worcester, Massachusetts.

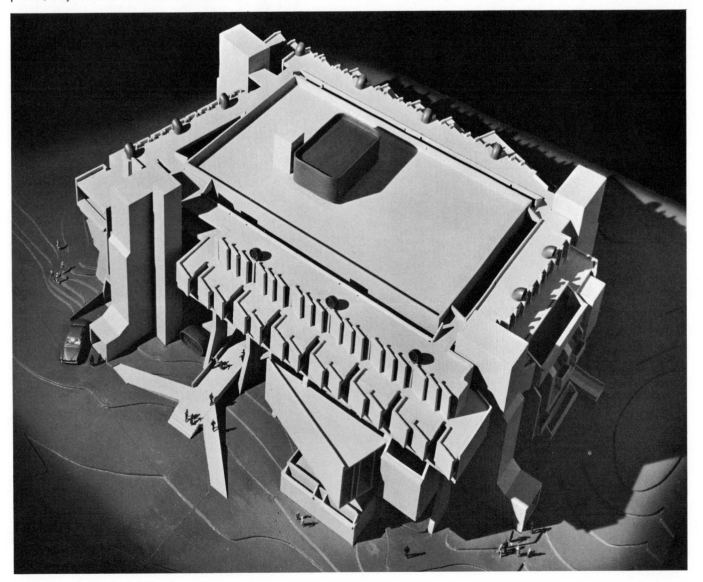

Morse and Stiles Colleges, Yale University,
New Haven, Connecticut.

Deere Building, Moline, Illinois.

General Motors Technical Center, Warren, Michigan.

EERO SAARINEN

An architect's convictions, tested and matured by experience, generally direct his approach to architecture. Mies's convictions have led him to formulate a set of rules that he adheres strictly to in every project, allowing him increasingly to refine a particular architectural approach. The perfection attained in Greek architecture was the result of an expression meticulously studied to an ever-increasing degree. However, many creative people believe that to perfect something is to kill it; and that if an approach is too narrow there is a danger of inflexibility towards the differences in problems. Another view is that the creative energy of a great talent should be used in the pursuit of new forms and expressions—which need not necessarily imply that one is without conviction—exploring and expanding rather than perfecting a vocabulary.

This latter course was that of the late Eero Saarinen (1910-1961), making his career one of the most interesting of the second-generation modern American architects. His approach to each problem as the specific, an individual insight evolving and developing within each problem and carried through with strength, resourcefulness and originality, marked him as a remarkably rigorous creative force. When he died at the height of his creative powers, there was no hint of a consistent direction in his work. Oscar Wilde's observation that "consistency is the last resort of the unimaginative" would be a fitting epitaph for Saarinen.

Eero Saarinen was born in Finland. His father, Eliel, himself a well-known architect, won second prize in the Chicago Tribune Tower Competition, and used the prize money to bring his family to America in 1923. At Cranbrook Academy in Michigan, the elder Saarinen brought Eero into contact with such student talents as Eames, Weese, Rapson, the sculptor Bertoia, and the present Director of the Philadelphia City Planning Commission, Edmund Bacon. After studying sculpture in Paris for a year, and architecture at Yale, Eero became an instructor at Cranbrook. In 1937 he went into partnership with his father, upon whose death in 1951 Eero took over the practice and embarked on the design of the hundred million dollar General Motors complex in Detroit. The Saarinen office soon expanded to its present size of about a hundred, with forty active designers.

TWA Terminal, Kennedy Airport, New York, N.Y.

Joseph Lacy, project manager, John Dinkeloo, production chief and technologist, and Kevin Roche, chief designer, were the key members of Saarinen's staff recruited for the G. M. project. Roche, with whom Saarinen used to discuss design problems for long hours, worked directly with him on subsequent major design commissions. Kevin Roche was born in Dublin in 1922, studied at the National University of Ireland, and worked in Dublin and London, before coming to study at the Illinois Institute of Technology. He joined the Saarinen office in 1950.

After the design for General Motors, a unified campus-like setting carried through in the Miesian manner, Saarinen designed a series of buildings that constitute a representative collection of trends in American architecture in the 1950's. His work is probably the clearest example of the fracturing of approaches, and the nuances present in American architecture today.

Roche: "When the Kresge Auditorium was designed, immediately after G. M., there was little reinforced concrete work of any consequence in America, and practically no shell concrete construction. So, in a sense, the challenge was of building with concrete, and it had all the other old fascinations for Eero of building in a campus."

Heyer: "Was that the trigger for Saarinen's subsequent tendency towards the shaping of his structures—for example, the Yale hockey rink and the even more ambitious plastic forms of the TWA Terminal?"

Roche: "I think it was, because up to this point the discipline had been primarily a steel one, with Mies's vocabulary. This was a chance to try another material that would have another expression, while employing Mies's principle of the universal space (a shelter) in which a specific function (the auditorium) could take place. The shell was the universal space, not formed specifically for its contents—the two were just brought together, one inside the other, one not necessarily reflecting the other."

Heyer: "How successful did he find this approach?"

Roche: "He did not use it again. Although I suppose you could say that the Bell Telephone Laboratories were a similar thing—just an enormous piece of machinery covered with a glass skin. But, for instance, Dulles Airport is a very specific building in which the inside and outside are one; there is no shelter with a function inside it. In this respect I think it was the only attempt. The Auditorium was pivotal because with it Eero began to find his direction. It embraced all of the things he then considered constituted architecture: the functional problem; the exploitation of technology; the development of structure; and the expression of a simple form."

Heyer: "Yet this would probably be considered one of his least successful buildings."

Roche: "Probably he would not have said that, and I suppose that is what really matters. Success ought also to be measured by the amount a man grows in the process of doing something. Even though the building may not have been as successful as later ones, it had a great significance in his personal growth."

Heyer: "After the design of the Auditorium there was a period before his work reached a premise comparable to that of G. M. Was this due to his move away from the Miesian discipline, the search for a more flexible discipline? How did he come to his later strength?"

Roche: "It is important to consider this in the context of the 1950's, which was moving very fast in one sense, and hardly at all in another. People had accepted Mies's as the ultimate solution—all you had to do was build it, and suddenly you were realizing the golden age—and there did not seem to be any reason to do anything different. To act contrary to that and still have ambitions of being a serious architect was an extremely difficult thing to do; it was a soul-searching process. It does not seem so now because the whole scene has fractured so much, but then a trend had been established and it seemed that architecture had arrived.

Ingalls Skating Rink, Yale University,
New Haven, Connecticut.

"Eero had just completed what was the major project of that whole school, as G. M. came before the Seagram Building and the Chase Manhattan Bank. Here he was, an architect of the younger generation clearly established in the same mode, direction and philosophy as S.O.M. and Mies's other disciples, including Philip Johnson. Outside of the people who had never really been in the mainstream, like Goff—and this is no criticism—there was nobody with serious intentions breaking from the mold."

Heyer: "Do you know where Saarinen felt this approach fell short, or why he became disenchanted with it?"

Roche: "I do not think he really became disenchanted. Eero always regarded architecture as a very personal art and expression. He had a feeling that it had to be something more than it was at that particular moment, that it had to include some other things, and that it had a right to grow and develop. Of course he had the unique opportunity of being allowed to build a large group of buildings in a short period of time, at the very beginning of the establishment of this particular style or school. He was much less involved with it, having done it, than an architect who had not had that opportunity. For him this was something that was done and he wanted to move on, feeling that there was more that he could contribute. By nature he was very restless anyway; he always wanted to move, change, try. The process of his work was one of redoing, reconsidering, reworking, over and over again until the very last minute."

Heyer: "One of the principal criticisms of Saarinen was his changing attitudes and lack of a consistent approach to problems —the Bell Telephone Laboratories, the Yale Dormitories, and the TWA Terminal were all conceived in one short period."

Roche: "They belong to the same couple of years, and it seems completely logical to me that they are different. They were built in different places, for different clients, of different materials, and most of all their functions were completely different. They had no reason to be similar."

Heyer: "This would be consistent with the idea that each building demanded its particular solution."

Roche: "This, of course, was Eero's philosophy: the Sullivan one of the solution being in the problem, and a very particular thing. What you bring to it is your art, and it brings its reason; the two come together and the answer is, specifically, that building, of that moment, for particular purpose."

Heyer: "Saarinen seemed to bring the exploration of a particular idea to each problem; a positive expression of a strong central idea. And, apart from their great versatility, his projects show a tremendous interest in different structural and technological solutions."

For example, G.M. expressed the precision and mass production of machine technology, a smooth, shiny repetition more in scale with automobile than pedestrian movement. In contrast, the Yale Dormitories are a pedestrian-scaled complex of rugged texture, a conscious effort to relate to the neo-Gothic environment, and a desire to express individual and college, not anonymous and dormitory. Or the Yale hockey rink with its dramatized structural statement of a central, curved reinforced concrete spine from which steel cables, in their caternary curve, support the wooden roof; the oval shape on an open site naturally suggests an independent building. Then the flowing contours of the interlocking

Bell Telegraph Research Center, Holmdell, New Jersey.

352

vaults of the TWA Terminal symbolizing movement—a memorable prelude to the drama of flight. Again, in three of his last and most interesting buildings: the forceful directness of the steel-structured Deere building, like a piece of farm machinery, robust and dark in a tree-studded ravine; rising out of a sunken plaza, the free-standing reinforced concrete shaft of the C.B.S. tower, whose verticality is emphasized by the upward thrust of granite-clad triangular structural piers; and the cable-suspended, curved concrete roof of the Dulles Airport—the gateway to the Nation—and the product of an excellent synthesis of circulation and function.

Roche: "What he looked for was: What is there in this problem that is particular to it, and of its nature? He included all the factors he could: the site, structure, economics, function, the psychological needs of the people in the building, and the key question, 'Why do these people want to build this building?' The answer to that has to justify the building as a reality later on. An attitude-of-mind approach would characterize more of what Saarinen wanted to do than anything else; it was in his great ability to realize the building that he found the answers."

Heyer: "What are the values, the principles and experience that have remained with you, and helped Saarinen Associates in developing a new role?"

Roche: "Although Eero talked a considerable amount about his architectural beliefs, a philosophy was never stated in so many words. It was always understood that a problem was particular. I personally think that the preoccupation with self-expression is a healthy thing; Eero would not say that, although I think he believed it too. He would strongly defend the right for self-expression, but I do not think he operated from that position, although he did consider architecture as a personal art and expression. Our common ground was the attitude: What is this thing and why is it happening? This is a good base because it is not narrow and gives one a great deal of courage to move. There are in fact no rules when one proceeds from that point—only the challenge of answering the problem."

Heyer: "There are no preconceived notions."

Roche: "We like to feel that the solution comes right at the end of the process of design, but it is not quite like that. Normally it is a very slow process of building up, taking away, and reworking, in large study models. TWA resulted from a lot of detailed study and resolution of problems. What we have learned from Eero is, I hope, that same approach: that we start at the very beginning. For example, the solution to the Bell Telephone Laboratories revolved around two things: the communication of people (when you have six thousand people in one building, the ease of communication—not just picking up a telephone—is very necessary); and the problem of services that can become so extended and expensive. There, the building was again the product of need and situation, function and the human element, just at that particular moment."

Heyer: "Saarinen always emphasized the need for an awareness of the times."

Roche: "The overriding consideration in the later work was just that. It was very directly, seriously, carefully and responsibly the product of its particular time, availing itself of every conceivable aspect of the reality of that particular moment. I would

C.B.S. Headquarters Building, New York, N.Y.

also like to think that that is what architecture is supposed to be. "Into a building you put your own reason, artistry, competence and responsibility. As with all things that aspire to be creative, there is no necessary uniformity. What one wants to do is swim in the water, not stand up in it.

"In our complex society it is almost impossible to grasp the quality of our technology and our economic structure. Architects have tended to turn away from this problem and do the one thing that they can handle. This is not the function the architect should fulfill. Nature has a great way of providing the right people and opportunity at the right time. These people are necessary, because their investigations will ultimately contribute a great deal. The total result of twentieth century architecture is not going to be just this individual approach, or the avoidance of the total responsibility. If architects do not embrace our real problems somebody else will. They have to be tackled, and will be. Architects have already given up a large part of their responsibility. The whole city problem has drifted away—maybe the time has not been right to tackle it yet. Particularly in the evolution of technology, we are really going to get lost if we are not careful—we have to be in the forefront of that battle if we are to win it.

"We are part of a growth that is continuous. If we have a more open-end feeling about what we do then we can look forward with more hope that, because we have laid the proper foundations, somebody at some point will make more sense out of life than we did. This moment is not the last in history. If one looks at life from that point of view, it may perhaps temper a little what one does."

Dulles International Airport, Chantilly, Virginia.

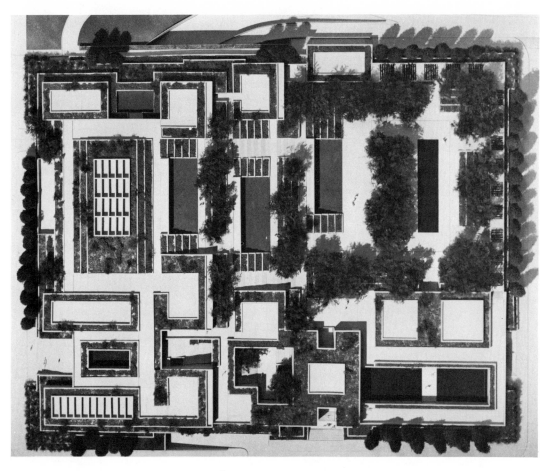

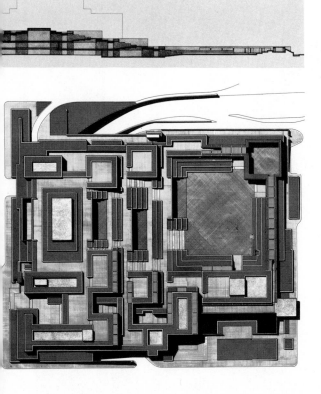

Oakland Museum, Oakland, California.

KEVIN ROCHE

Lacy, Dinkeloo and Roche form the core of Saarinen Associates, and the original staff remains fairly intact. They have not lost a client since Saarinen's death, have completed the projects in hand, and secured some challenging commissions of their own. With an approach to architecture similar to Saarinen's, they are developing their own strength and identity—"there would be no point in our existing if we were just trading on Saarinen's name," Roche says, sincerely and emphatically.

The first important commission secured by Saarinen Associates, over some forty other well-known firms, was for the design of the Oakland Museum, across the Bay from San Francisco. The design process began by clarifying the reason for building: "Otherwise you are building shells for a function that may not exist," said Roche, "and you are building a monument, not a living thing." The city had appropriated six million dollars to build what it regarded as the image of a museum. Roche crystallized that image. By interviewing people in the community, studying the history of the city's growth in that particular area, a series of city plans were developed. At the same time the basic concept was established—a total museum related to the California scene: showing how nature and the cultural heritage that derives from it, and the migration of people relate to all of man's efforts and the art he produces.

The museum will have three principal levels of bunker-like galleries, for art, history and natural science. Each has its individual identity yet forms a unified group, with the roof of one level

355

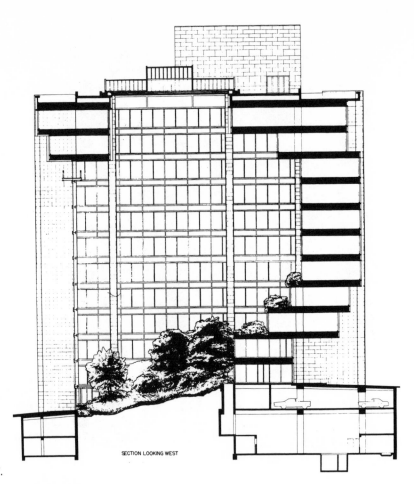

SECTION LOOKING WEST

Ford Foundation, New York, N.Y.

becoming the terrace of another. The museum spaces open to outdoor display areas and tiers of gardens, courts, plazas and stairways. An intricate sequence of garden and museum spaces that form a focal civic space, the museum will assert its physical presence as a living, vibrant element of the city.

Another imaginative resolution of a particular problem, and a concept that promises an especially exciting building, is the Ford Foundation headquarters, for a site near the United Nations in New York. The typical office building is primarily the product of real estate dictates, evolving as variations on a theme of a central service core with perimeter office space. This conventional approach, however, tends to isolate the individual where he experiences only the lobby, elevator, and corridor to his own office cubicle, affording him little sense of the community to which he belongs.

The Ford Foundation has some three hundred and fifty people from the academic world, with the enormous responsibility of allocating approximately three hundred million dollars annually. Roche's intention was to establish a sense of communication and awareness of the total endeavor, "a sense of the individual identifying with the aims and intentions of the group." The result is an L-shaped office volume looking onto a landscaped interior court, that is glazed on two facades and rises through the full twelve stories of the building to a large skylight. The court becomes a transitional space between office and street, and a community focus for the building. Ten floors of offices will have windows opening onto the park-like conservatory space, as will the top two floors of executive and dining areas that ring the court on all four sides visually defining its upper limits.

The group of people, the function, the location, the moment in history—the building reflects Roche's emphasis on a specific solution to a specific problem. It also accomplishes two things that should be basic to building in an urban location; it takes the best that the city has to give, and gives an equal measure in return. It takes, for its court, the existing view of the park and river, and by extending the best of the nature of the city, in a sense, gives back another park.

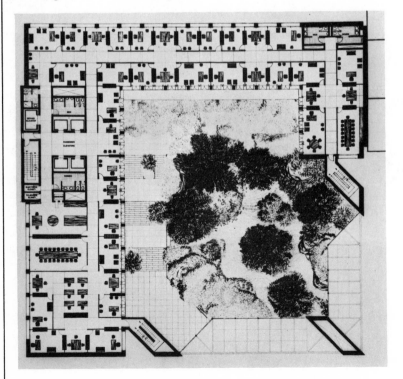

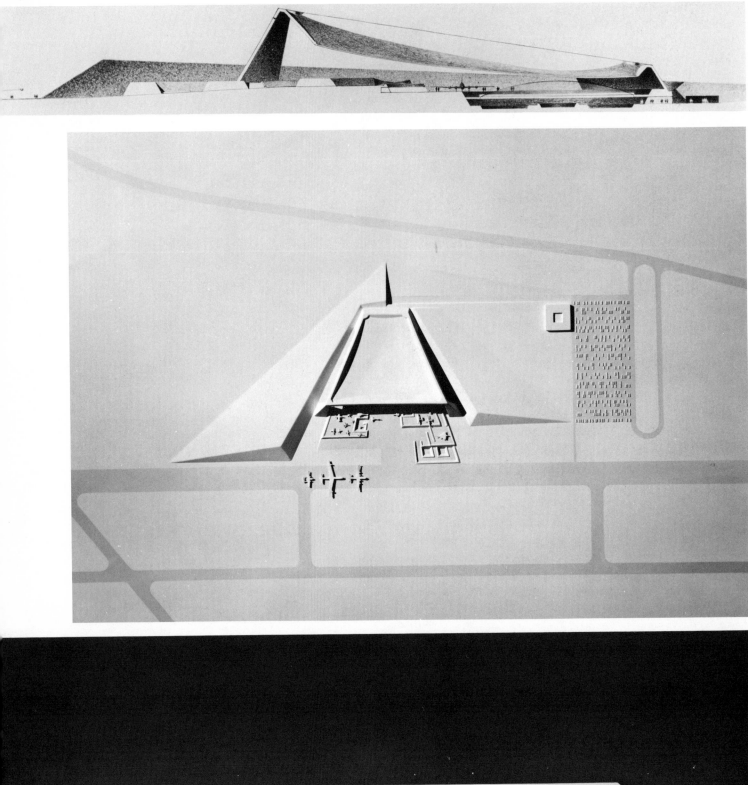

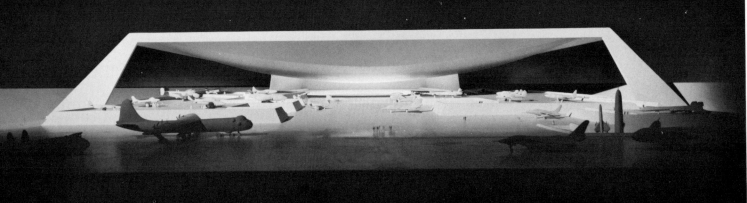

In the design for the Air Force Museum, for Wright-Patterson Air Force Base in Dayton, Ohio, Roche has tried to create an environment no less technologically-advanced than the artifacts it houses; a place "that would fill the visitor with a sense of awe and pride at man's achievement," while also being a monument to the spirit of the men of the Air Force. Hence, the first emphasis will be not on the building or the exhibits, but on the names of all the Air Force personnel from its inception, which will line the approach ramp from the parking lot, "deliberately located at some distance from the building so that the visitor can take this memorial walk and become properly prepared for the magnificent story which unfolds in the Museum."

The building itself is a shelter, wedge-shaped in plan and section, with a roof of steel cables covered by a steel deck, dramatically supported at four corner suspension points. Beneath this vast space, covering eight acres, will be a multi-leveled series of ramps and platforms, "so that as a visitor progresses from the starting point of Wright's flyer the progression is in a space which is ever-expanding outwards and growing higher, soaring up to the sky—the field of action for these men and this equipment." The shelter's immense 700 foot-wide by 130 foot-high opening to the airfield will frame against the sky the most modern aircraft and rockets so that they appear not as individual incidents but part of a total and continuing effort. The angular lines of the shelter, landscaping and runways have been carefully considered too, for their visual relationship as seen from the air.

The sense of nobility that Roche tried to emphasize in the Air Force Museum is also his concern in the New Haven High School. Since most of the sixteen hundred students will come from poor families, Roche wants them to be able to identify with a structure that generates an atmosphere of imposing dignity. Four individual "houses" containing general classroom areas will be linked at the upper level by peripheral corridors to the central library and toilets around which they are grouped. Beneath these "houses" will be specialized classrooms, workshops and other facilities. Whereas so many schools today seem to be "educational diagrams" to the point of becoming non-architectural, this school, with its compact and formal distribution of elements, is a refreshing, disciplined solution.

New Haven High School, New Haven, Connecticut.

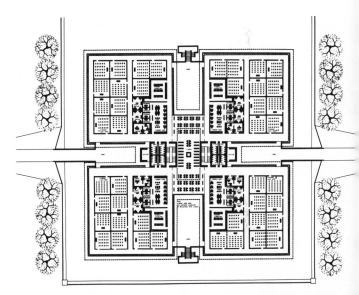

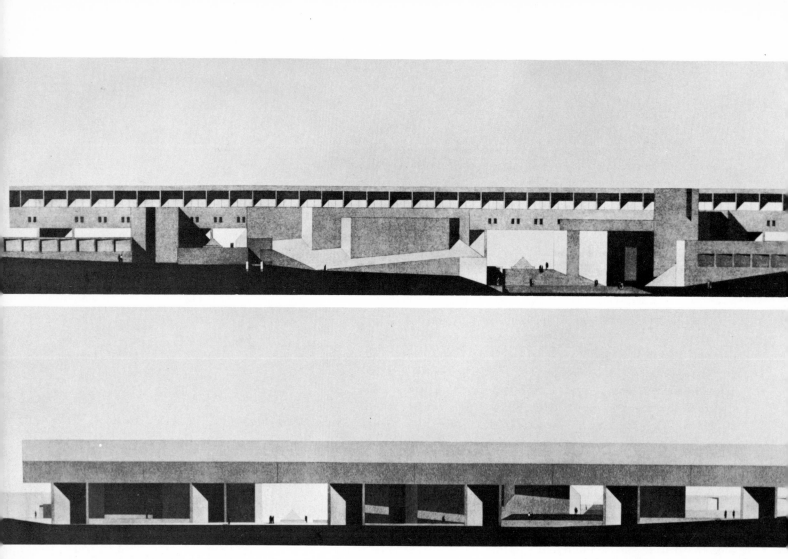

Fine Arts Center, University of Massachusetts, Amherst, Massachusetts.

The Fine Arts Center for the University of Massachusetts at Amherst is a building that will establish a gateway to the campus. The visually-forceful, long structure containing the art studios is raised up on a double row of bold concrete stilts to form the "cornice" for the complex. Beneath this are loosely strung a twenty-six hundred seat concert hall and a seven hundred seat theater, forming the imposing portal through which one enters the University, and facilities for the music and speech schools. Employing the art studios to create a powerful unifying element architecturally, Roche is then able to flexibly develop the form most appropriate to the particular function of the other elements: each of the elements will have "the freedom to grow properly, as it must as the problem develops."

By comparison, the proposed Knights of Columbus Building in New Haven is a more diagrammatic solution. Its twenty-six floors are supported entirely by four cylindrical corner towers, that will be clad in dark brick and will contain the stairs, toilets, and mechanical shafts. A central core will comprise only six elevators. The form of the building is derived in part from the method of construction, explains Roche. The four towers will be of concrete, continuously poured into slowly rising forms, between which will then be slung the main horizontal steel girders, 80 feet long, that in turn will support the steel floor structure. The glass is recessed 5 feet behind the face of the girders for sun protection.

In comparison to Saarinen's romantic tendencies, Roche is referred to as being more of a rational designer. Certainly there is the same preoccupying search for the strong generating idea, and its technical accomplishment. Clearly, as they should and must be, Saarinen Associates are an architectural force in their own right. Although their only completed building to date was the IBM Pavilion at the recent New York World's Fair designed in collaboration with Charles Eames, this is already apparent from their various projects.

Roche's situation and opportunity strikingly parallel Saarinen's own at the beginning of the 1950's. And today the future looks as promising and the effort as intense, as it undoubtedly must have, and was, when General Motors was on the boards and Saarinen's was well-known as the office always *en charette*.

Knights of Columbus Building, New Haven, Connecticut.

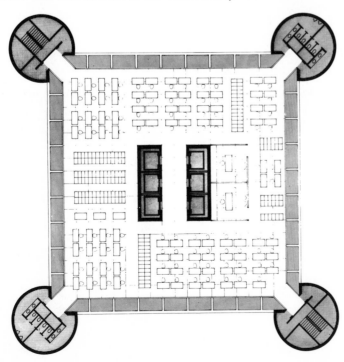

American Republic Insurance Company, Des Moines, Iowa.

SKIDMORE, OWINGS and MERRILL

The direct, thoughtful assembly of the physical elements of a building, and the use of quality materials that have been precisely detailed and well proportioned, can invoke an almost incredulous admiration for the ingenuity and commanding skill of the designer. The impression is persuasive because, to the smallest detail, there is the sense that the designer has always known his intention and exactly how to execute it. Such mastery can appear as art itself—almost. For, as every good architect knows, all the tangible, factual and technological inputs require that something extra to transpose them into a presence that is greater than simply an assembly of the reality of the facts could ever be. The genius of Le Corbusier was his grasp of the essence of architecture; we do not admire his accuracy and detail as we might that of Mies. Yet *means* and *ends* would be an erroneous over-simplification; would one want to describe the Gothic Period as only means? Clearly, Le Corbusier was as concerned for the means, as Mies is for the ends.

What has made Skidmore, Owings & Merrill one of the most successful large firms is its facility with the means; a seemingly instinctive grasp of the power of a technological culture, coupled with a "constant concern for form." And most important, an ability to establish the organization method (an American strength), a responsible professionalism proportionate to the scale of our complex urban problems. S.O.M. is of a structure and temperament that can utilize the specialist's know-how most advantageously; the secret of its success is the understanding to select him initially. An excellent example of this is S.O.M.'s superb choice of paintings and sculpture for its buildings, set in interiors and landscaping that are executed with an unerring awareness of the appropriate and the timely.

Lever House, New York, N.Y.

*Connecticut General Life Insurance Company,
Bloomfield, Connecticut.*

The essential seriousness and no-nonsense quality of S.O.M.'s buildings have brought it prestige commercial commissions. Since the firm understands corporate structure and has an appreciation of the hierarchy of specialized responsibility, it has a natural acceptance with its corporate clients. Commercial work, however, does not necessarily preclude its considering building as an art. It is sheer romanticism to assume that art thrives on poverty; one is tempted to conjecture that the richer the commerce of a society, the richer its art can be. With business replacing the Medicis as patrons of the arts in the 1950's, S.O.M. did much to show that good architecture could be good business. With the American emphasis on culture and education in the mid-1960's, S.O.M. continues to show the importance of good architecture. There are critics, however, who see the S.O.M. effort as the manifestation of the "air-conditioned nightmare." But, faced with the confusion and complexity of our time, there is surely a hint in S.O.M.'s effort that we may yet realize, in our lifetime, a real relationship between art and science; not just a technical aesthetic, but a new framework for urban living.

Louis Skidmore and Nathaniel Owings (presently Chairman of President Johnson's Pennsylvania Avenue Committee, in Washington) formed a partnership in 1936 in Chicago. By 1939, when John Merrill, Sr. joined them as a limited partner, they had already opened an office in New York. Ten years later five full partners were named—W. S. Brown, G. Bunshaft, R. W. Cutler, J. W. Severinghaus, and J. Merrill, Sr. Others have been added since then, and there are now eighteen active partners, with offices in Portland, Oregon, and San Francisco, totaling an office staff of around seven hundred persons. Skidmore died in 1962 and Merrill has retired. The titular design leaders and also partners are: Gordon Bunshaft (born in Buffalo, New York, in 1909, and studied at M.I.T. After travelling in Europe on the Rotch Travelling Fellowship, he worked briefly for Edward Stone before joining S.O.M. in 1937); Walter Netsch, Jr. (born in Chicago in 1920, studied at M.I.T., and joined S.O.M. in 1947); Bruce Graham (born in Colombia, South America, in 1925, studied at the University of Pennsylvania, and joined S.O.M. in 1951); Edward Bassett (born in Port Huron, Michigan, in 1921, and studied at the University of Michigan. He received his Master of Architecture degree from Cranbrook Academy of Fine Art in 1951, and had worked for Eero Saarinen for five years before joining S.O.M. in 1955); and Roy Allen (born in Sayre, Pennsylvania, in 1921, studied at Pennsylvania State University, and joined S.O.M. in 1946).

Many commissions for similar building types have enabled S.O.M. to carry over ideas from one project to another, to develop and refine a stage further, for which the firm is often accused of the stereotype solution. This is misleading because, although S.O.M. has designed many high-rise commercial structures, for which the firm has most successfully developed varying, imaginative solutions, the design criteria had to derive from practical considerations that are generally non-architectural and fairly constant—realistic forces that cannot be denied. "There was a survey by *Architectural Forum* of the largest architectural firms in the country, and the amount of work they were doing," says Bassett. "We were included, and found out, to our chagrin, that for our dollar volume of work we had approximately twice as many people as any other architect performing the same scale of services.

Chase Manhattan Bank, New York, N.Y.

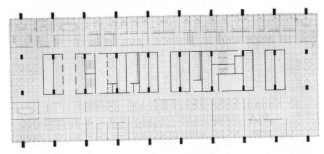

The probable reason is that all the main people in the firm, whether they have anything to do with the design process or not, are oriented towards doing the best architecture they can. The design process has always been uppermost in the hierarchy of the office function.''

The Lever House in New York, in 1952, was the firm's first tour de force. Unless one looks carefully, its merits have been somewhat obscured by new, lesser buildings that might not at first appear too dissimilar. The simple rectilinear slab, occupying only twenty-five percent of the air space, is sheathed in a curtain-wall of stainless steel and a blue-green, heat resistant glass. It seems to ''float'' above a lower, clearly articulated rectilinear volume that, in turn, is free of the slab and the ground, and has a roof garden for employees. This lower volume has an open center that allows a sudden dramatic view upwards of the slab from within the site. An aesthetic of reflection had replaced the play of light and shadow on mass. The last decade has shown us that the reflected image becomes important, and that glare and sun control, heat penetration and loss, were not really adequately handled by the curtain wall alone.

John Hancock Mutual Life Insurance Company, San Francisco, Calif

Pepsi-Cola Company, New York, N.Y.

Although its vernacular, and this is general to S.O.M.'s buildings, undoubtedly owed a lot to Mies's example, it conceptually derived from a different premise, which a comparison with Mies's neighboring Seagram Building reveals. Where the Seagram Building stands on a podium in a "classic" manner, the volumes of the Lever House, and they are opposed to each other to emphasize this, "float" dramatically. Where Mies's building "stands back", a withdrawn aristocrat approached formally across a plaza with flanking fountains, S.O.M.'s building allows the street, carefully defined by the lower volume, to penetrate quite informally within its plaza spaces. Lever House set a precedent in commercial structures; it heralded the decade of the curtain wall, and its plaza spaces encouraged others in opening up areas of the city once again to the pedestrian.

S.O.M.'s buildings are distinguished by the recognition of an environmental responsibility, as shown by many of its office towers which spring from well-landscaped pedestrian plazas.

Says Bassett, "We make it clear to a client from the outset that we expect a building to fulfill certain social obligations and make certain gestures towards its urban context."

The machined elegance was more crisply stated in the complex for the Connecticut General Life Insurance Company, in Hartford, in 1957. The complex consists of three elements; a three-story building 468 feet by 324 feet—perforated by four courtyards with planting and sculpture by Noguchi—that contain easily expandable clerical areas; a four-story wing for management; and a one-story cafeteria wing. The simple balanced forms, the clear formal statement and the masculine directness expressed here have remained basic to S.O.M's buildings.

The full measure of S.O.M.'s accomplishment can be seen in the Chase Manhattan Bank, New York, completed in 1961. The sixty-story tower rises from a spacious plaza, a welcome open space in the Wall Street district and a bold vision indicative of the spirit of a new scale of thinking. It is beautifully built, carefully considered to the smallest detail, handsomely furnished, and has excellent art works that seem effortlessly integrated— no single skimpy mural here, no token art. All forces seem to have been harnessed to create an efficient and totally considered environment—an assured statement of American process and production. Unlike the Lever House, columns are located outside the glass skin of the building, providing a flush inside surface for partitions that can divide space on the regular four-foot ten-inch window module. Interior columns are located within the central service core, preserving open spaces and allowing maximum flexibility.

John Hancock Mutual Life Insurance Company, New Orleans, Louisiana.

The variation of S.O.M.'s office buildings can be seen by comparing just three small structures from a distinguished list: the Pepsi Cola Building, New York, and the John Hancock Building, San Francisco, both in 1959, and the John Hancock Building, New Orleans, in 1961. The Pepsi Cola Building is an eleven-story steel structure on a corner site, visually separated from its neighbor by a black, recessed service core. On the exterior, the building is about the ultimate in reduction: floor spandrels and window mullions faced in aluminum, windows of a single sheet of glass nine feet high by thirteen feet wide, and thin white lines of vertical venetian blinds. In contrast to this, instead of a columned structure, the fourteen-story John Hancock Building in San Francisco returns to an external reinforced concrete-bearing wall, surfaced with polished granite that has delicate changes of plane, and with gray tinted glass windows set in bronze frames. Interior space is column-free back to a structural, centrally-located core. The arches and columns of the recessed base, and the roof parapet where the mechanical equipment floor is located, are of exposed concrete. The seven-story John Hancock Building in New Orleans has a similar column-free office space from the exterior bearing wall to the central core, but here the slender, closely-spaced upper columns, functioning like a bearing wall, are clear of the glass plane and provide both sun protection and space for window cleaning.

Ironically, the structural frame that made the high-rise building possible is now frequently dispensed with in preference to an exterior structure, similar to a bearing wall, of planes or closely spaced columns, and a central structural core with clear office floors in between.

S.O.M. has designed several buildings that are developments of

Banque Lambert, Brussels, Belgium.

this principle. In the Banque Lambert in Brussels, Belgium, completed in 1965, a grid of cross-shaped, precast concrete structural elements on a four-foot six-inch module are joined centrally between floor slabs by stainless steel pins, forming the external supporting wall elements that visually dominate the facade. As in the New Orleans building, a heavy reinforced concrete beam over the ground floor transfers the loads to recessed concrete columns.

For all of the buildings so far discussed, with the exception of the John Hancock Building in San Francisco by Bassett of the San Francisco office, Bunshaft of the New York office was the partner in charge of design. He frequently has been referred to as one of the most consistent American designers. Recently, however, he has explored approaches other than his earlier steel and glass vernacular, in such projects as the Banque Lambert and the Beinecke Rare Book and Manuscript Library at Yale, in 1964. The Beinecke building has an exhibition hall of books that is

approached from a gray-tinted, glass-enclosed entrance lobby at the plaza level, that also gives access to a below-grade research and office center, opening to a sunken court with sculpture designed by Noguchi. The shell of this monumental hall is constructed of four vierendeel trusses of prefabricated, tapered steel crosses, faced with granite aggregate similar to that used in the plaza, with $1\frac{1}{4}$-inch thick white marble octagonal infill panels. The shell gives the impression of being poised above the plaza, resting on four concrete corner columns and connected by steel pins. In the center of this shell are the rare books, climatically sealed by a bronze-framed curtain wall of glass and surrounded by an exhibition gallery. While outside, the building and its immediate landscaping are almost blinding white in the sunlight, the richness and warmth of the muted light, filtering through the thickness of the marble, create a memorable, somewhat ethereal interior.

Bunshaft says, "A bold idea, plus precision, care, and thought make a good building." The library achieves that, but there is controversy as to how good a building it is. Some critics view it as a too manneristic approach, an expensive dead end. A montage by a Yale student caricatured it as a surrealistic, "di Chirico-like" stage set—withdrawn and remote, yet exerting a strong presence. One thing its critics cannot deny Bunshaft: the ability to achieve his intention, an ability to put something together with an excellence few can equal. It is a tradition characteristic of the best eighteenth-century French architecture, characteristic of the work of McKim, Mead and White at the turn of this century, and characteristic of S.O.M. today. The firm's attention to detail has remained constant at a time when many architects, trying to stress *what* is said, often tend to neglect *how* it is said.

Netsch, of the Chicago office, has had the opportunity to work

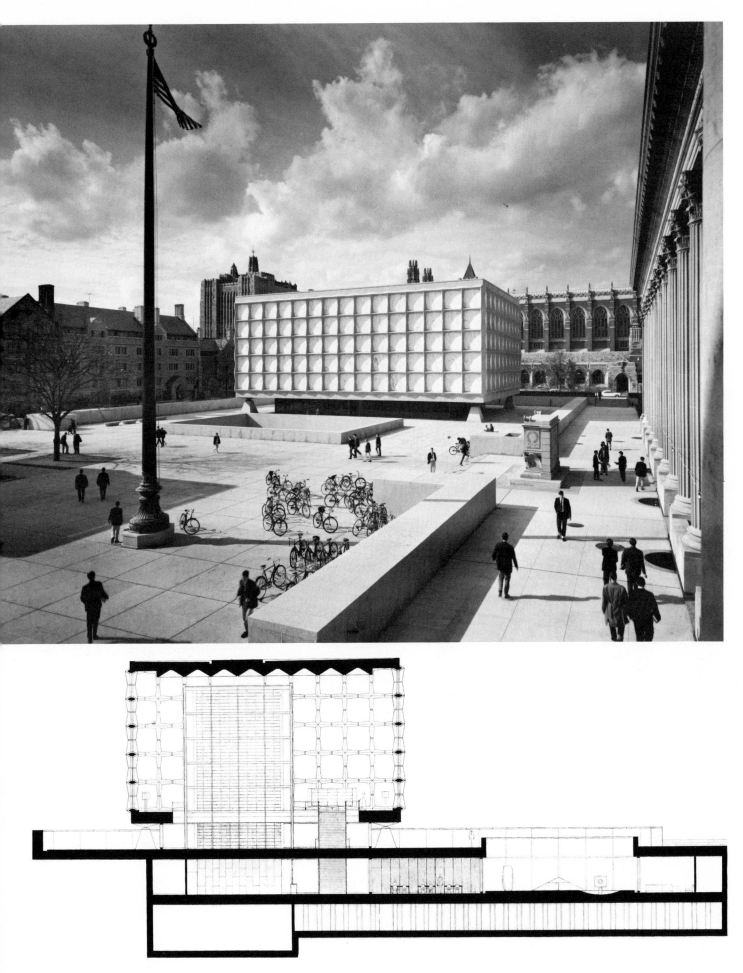

Beinecke Rare Book and Manuscript Library, Yale University, New Haven, Connecticut.

on larger building complexes. The first, a complex of five structures, was for the U.S. Naval Postgraduate School in Monterey, California, completed in 1955. But it is in the Air Force Academy at Colorado Springs in 1957 that he really showed the potential of technology to create an environment of a character and at a scale (at General Motors it is that of the moving automobile, at the Air Force Academy the marching step) for which there seems little historic precedent. For these reasons it is sometimes referred to as inhuman and relentlessly repetitious. Apparently funds have not been forthcoming for much of the landscaping that would have helped to alleviate this. The strength of its statement, however, comes from this unified singularity of purpose and grand scale; one thinks back to Thomas Jefferson's campus for the University of Virginia, the sweep of the crescents at Bath, Haussmann's boulevards for Paris—all, broad organizational statements.

The regular rectangular lines and bold horizontals of the buildings and the vast paved landscape areas, with long sweeping ramps and earth retaining walls, are attuned to and enhanced by the dramatic, awesome scale of the planes and the mountains. It is at the large organizational and ceremonial scale that the Academy has its public life, and stands as a national symbol. The 2600 cadets assemble, for example, to march to the dining hall which seats the whole Academy in one column-free space. Skillfully planned for their more private life are the cadets' living quarters, around more private open courts; the quarters are on two levels above and two below an open entrance level that is a man-made plateau on which the buildings are located. Here, the character of space is as important as the vernacular and detailing of the buildings themselves. The chapel, of aluminum-sheathed tetrahedrons, is the only building to vary the geometry. Says Netsch: "Its more complex order acknowledges that society has many orders of influence that should be reflected in architectural form and character."

Of a completely different character, but again with bold scale, is the Chicago Campus for the University of Illinois, where construction will cover a third of the 106-acre site, providing by 1969 for a total student enrollment of twenty thousand and parking for six thousand cars. High-rise buildings, containing offices and seminar rooms, will border the perimeter of the campus, related to larger open spaces and visually defining the limits of the campus. Lower, three and four-story walk-up buildings are grouped more compactly towards the center, accommodating classrooms and laboratories which generate peak mass movements of students between classes. Laboratories, requiring higher ceilings, will be separated from classrooms for their functional difference rather than the academic discipline they serve. This will encourage interdisciplinary contact, and create more flexible, interchangeable space that can more readily accommodate new teaching techniques.

Circulation within the entirely pedestrian campus will be by an elevated walk at second-floor level, providing split-level access to the buildings and a covered way at ground level. The walkway will connect directly to two multi-story parking lots at either end of the commuter campus, entered directly from expressways that border the campus, and a subway station. The academic core and focal point of all pedestrian circulation is an elevated, 450-foot by 300-foot Great Court that is the roof of the lecture hall

University of Illinois, Chicago, Illinois.

center. Twenty-one halls with varying capacities from forty-five to five hundred persons comprise the center; four large lecture halls are each expressed by an exedrae in the court, providing intimate seating areas there. At the center of the Court is an amphitheater that can seat twenty-five hundred persons.

The buildings are exposed reinforced concrete structures, with the same strength of concrete and amount of reinforcing steel used throughout. Where columns carry a greater load, they are larger. Netsch was seeking "the unsophisticated wonder of recognition, of why things are smaller or larger;" the opposite of this, as Bunshaft pointed out, is of course to make all the columns the same size and have everyone wonder how the structure was accomplished. In the twenty-eight-story staff and administration building, instead of increasing the size of columns, more are added diminishing the bay size and its proportionate end cantilever in the lower floors. Naturally, the transfer beams and columns to the ground are correspondingly larger. Netsch comments, "We are looking today for a more complex enriched order in which structure can participate."

This intensely developed campus is important as an example for our future urban educational facilities. The resolution of traffic and pedestrian circulation, the provision for orderly growth, the interrelation with the urban context, while creating an identity within generous and pleasant space, have been economically achieved.

Air Force Academy, Colorado Springs, Colorado.

Northwestern University, Evanston, Illinois.

Aluminum Company of America, San Francisco, California.

John Hancock Mutual Life Insurance Company, Chicago, Illinois.

Netsch has prepared master plans for M.I.T., and for Northwestern University, which is expanding onto filled land in Lake Michigan. The first building at Northwestern will be a complex of three, four-story research library pavilions, connected to each other and to the existing library. The complex will house books on the social and behavioral sciences, the humanities, and history. Seeking a more cohesive synthesis of reader and books, Netsch developed a radial, rather than lineal stacking system for bookshelves. A geometry was eventually established in which columns were not equally spaced, but still had a perceivable ordering. The result was a "squared-circle" that allowed more individual and specialized spaces for private study, quiet reading, and seminar rooms in contrast to the more public stacking areas.

Structure—and the firm is continually exploring this discipline—remains the basis and strength of S.O.M.'s architecture. It is one of the architect's most powerful means. The aesthetics of the high-rise office building, for example, usually derive from a structural condition; it is invariably the organizational and most obvious element, and naturally lends itself to the strongest expression.

The steel columns, diagonals and hangers, sheathed with bronze-colored anodized aluminum, that frame the exterior wall of the 25-story Alcoa office building in San Francisco, designed by Bassett, are, for instance, the aesthetic of the building. Some critics may consider the Alcoa building's accentuated structure overly dramatic, and its raking diagonals disconcerting from within the building, yet, with its structure projecting $3^{1}/_{2}$-feet beyond bronze-tinted glass that preserves the buildings monochromatic appearance, it will undoubtedly be dramatic in contrast to the more involved, less polished and less reflective masses of the Golden Gate housing scheme.

It is indicative of the dialogue that occurs in S.O.M. that the diagonally braced tower idea is carried to a new boldness in the John Hancock Building in Chicago, designed by Graham of the Chicago office, to be completed in 1968. His is a skin-and-bones approach to architecture where the elements of a building are invariably contained within a precise, modular structural cage. In what will be the tallest building in Chicago, designed to create as complete a community as possible within a single unified envelope, dissimilar functions are given a single expression: the tapering one-hundred-story tower will accommodate offices, apartments, parking for over eleven hundred cars, commercial and recreation facilities.

The early Lever House days and the refinement of a vernacular in the 1950's resulted in many outstanding buildings. The firm's search in the 1960's has been towards bolder concepts to problems of a more particular character, and an increasing interest in exploring the design potential of reinforced concrete.

The recently completed headquarters for the American Republic Insurance Company in Des Moines, Iowa, designed by Bunshaft, is a clever integration of structure and mechanical services. Two great structural walls of poured-in-place concrete, each resting on four pin-connectors support precast, prestressed "T" beams that span the full ninety feet between walls. The "T" beams are exposed as the finished ceiling on the interior, increasing its apparent height; suspended within its coffers are air conditioning ducts that also have an acoustic cover to absorb sound, and act as baffles for lighting fixtures.

American Republic Insurance Company, Des Moines, Iowa.

The new Mauna Kea Beach Hotel in Hawaii, designed by Bassett, is clearly conceived to develop a rapport and have a close integration with its lush surroundings. The staggered section creates an open garden court that runs the length of the building, protected from the sun, linking directly to the landscape through garden loggias at the open ground level.

A product of our present cultural emphasis is the proposed Symphony Hall for Pittsburgh designed by Bunshaft, an important element in the city's Cultural Center which is being developed in a beautiful park-like setting near the central, Golden Triangle area. The Symphony Hall and a restaurant are located on a massive podium, 1000-feet by 300-feet, that creates a level area on a steeply sloping site, provides garage space for twenty-four hundred automobiles, and visually forms a horizontal background for the existing Auditorium. Poised on eight columns above this podium, will be a light steel truss roof 400 feet by 200 feet. Beneath this umbrella and physically separated from it, and surrounded by a glass-enclosed promenade of monumental scale, is the Symphony Hall, which itself has an interesting plan. The orchestra is at one end of a long room, not separated from the 2240 audience by a proscenium, thus creating an intimacy similar to that of the music salon.

The Carlton Center in Johannesburg, South Africa, designed by Roy Allen, will be something of a catalyst for the renewal of the central business district that evolved on a street plan originally designed for a mining camp. The Center will consist of a 51-story office tower and a 32-story luxury hotel, two department stores and 150 shops, all opening to landscaped pedestrian malls. Environmentally, the Center will do two important things: its 3¹/₄ acres devoted to gardens will increase the public open space in the business district by more than a half; and it will provide parking for three thousand automobiles, nearly half the number that at present park on streets in the business district.

These projects all go beyond a facility in manipulating structural-technical means, and bring to the resolution of a problem an imaginative approach: the search for a powerful parti, a striking concept. There is, too, a fundamental sense of restraint—a sense of discipline.

If S.O.M.'s design leaders do not act as disciples of one another —Netsch, for example, seems interested in exploring different avenues, while Graham seems more concerned with the evolution and refinement of an approach—they do seem to have found the freedom in teamwork to concentrate their attentions appropriately. How S.O.M. operates and maintains such a quality in its architecture is something of an enigma—but there is a pointer: the firm is not pyramidal, with one leader, like the usual large organization, but comprises a group of professionals, similar to a medical fraternity, who practice together and complement and contribute to each other's effort—many interdependent pyramids. As our architectural problems continue to become inflated, and already we have the collaboration of several firms on larger commissions, S.O.M. may be only the forerunner of even larger organizations. The pace has been set.

Mauna Kea Beach Hotel, Kamuela, Hawaii.

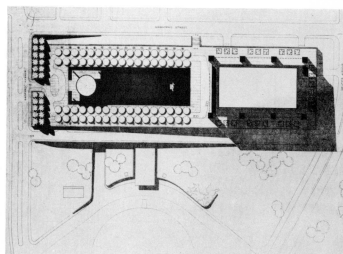

Pittsburgh Center for the Arts, Pittsburgh, Pennsylvania.

Carlton Centre, Johannesburg, South Africa.

Two mile Hemispherical Dome for New York City.

R. BUCKMINSTER FULLER

There can be few worthier claimants to the title of "Renaissance Man" than R. Buckminster Fuller. He has been variously described as scientific idealist, mathematician, chemist, engineer, philosopher, prophet—and even uncharitably, crank. Fuller describes himself as a "comprehensive designer," which he elaborates as, "an emerging synthesis of artist, inventor, mechanic, objective economist and evolutionary strategist."

Born on the Massachusetts coast in 1895, of a distinguished creative family, his intellectual environment gave him an early sense of the continuity and interdependence of life's many facets; his physical surroundings an early love of boats, and an impression that "boat building was the parent of technology." Two years in the Navy were profitably spent in the invention of a seaplane rescue mast and boom, and a "jet stilt" vertical take-off aircraft. It caused him to speculate: "What would happen if the real potential of modern industry were to be applied directly to serving man's needs, say in housing, instead of operating as a by-product of weaponry?" He was concerned by the time lag between numerous inventions and their industrial realization. In the radio world it was about two years, aircraft four, railroad an average of fifteen, but "in the world of building I found an enormous lag—approximately forty-two years."

A personal tragedy, the death of his daughter just before her fourth birthday—the victim of three diseases that were epidemic during the First World War, influenza, spinal meningitis, and infantile paralysis—led Fuller to write: "The fact that the housing we were in was very poor made me feel many times that the conditions we were operating under were in many ways responsible for our child's sickness."

The culmination of these forces led Fuller in 1927 to reject the conventional preoccupation with livelihood and embark on a personal period of research and development. He realized that this would entail a minimum of "twenty-five years of detached reconnaissance activity, before the individual might be able to bring into industrially useful economic harvest any of the kinds of initiations that he might undertake."

The idea of the potential effectiveness of the individual, coupled with the plurality of men constructively tapping the "progressively and regeneratively integrated information of man," paralleled Fuller's central concern with man's total environment. He was convinced that the understanding of the magnitude of man's scientific and technical capabilities would add "degrees of new advantage in respect to his ability to swiftly alter his—a priori—physical environment patterning." And this alteration would ensure the betterment of many "without the deprivation of any."

1927 was a pivotal year for Fuller; it comprehensively set the direction of his succeeding research and developments. He made a World Town plan with the accompanying idea of a ten-deck building of lightweight construction to be delivered and lowered into place by a zeppelin. He designed his first Dymaxion House (Dymaxion is derived from "dynamic" and "maximum," meaning maximum gain of advantage for minimal energy input). Five years of experience in the building industry had impressed on Fuller how inadequate traditional building techniques were to resolve present problems and anticipate future needs. The Dymaxion House demonstrated great technical advantages in the creation of a controlled environment. It had a double-glazed enclosed area containing a living room, two bedrooms and bathrooms, a study, and service room; and above an open relaxation area shaded by a roof. The ground level was an open, sheltered service space and parking area.

Structurally the house was supported by a radial system in which cables in tension extended from a central mast, similar in principle to the ten-deck building. The mast contained a centralized mechanical system for lighting, plumbing, and air conditioning. The many mechanized labor-saving devices in the house were visionary at that time.

World Town Plan.

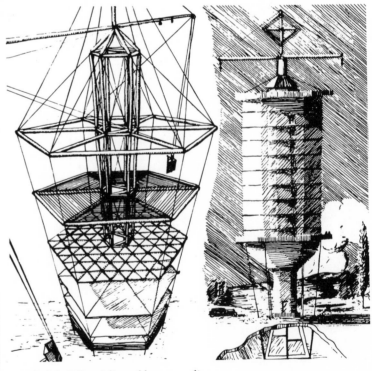

Ten-deck building delivered by a zeppelin.

Dymaxion House.

Dymaxion Car.

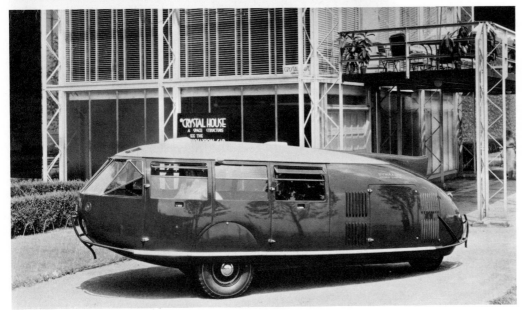

Fuller's technological criterion of "performance per pound" of material used, was evident. He found it lacking in such contemporary housing as the 1927 Deutscher Werkbund exhibition that Mies was directing. Fuller was harshly critical of such "fashion inoculation." Although his Dymaxion House was a prototype for industrialized production, it created a finished object, to be repeated, and not the elements of a house to be flexibly assembled as need and stuation dictated. As a universally applicable solution, it was bound to be treated with reserve.

In 1933 Fuller applied the Dymaxion principle again in the design of a car that, by comparison, would make the majority of Detroit's creations today seem vastly over-designed.

Fuller believed that there would be a lag of twenty-five years before the acceptance of his general idea and the development of technology would enable him to produce his first Dymaxion

House. But by 1946 he had designed and built a second in Wichita, Kansas. It had certain structural and skin refinements made possible by the advances in increased strength of metals. By limited mass production the house would have cost six thousand five hundred dollars—even less, as demand and production increased. Fuller received thirty-seven thousand unsolicited requests for reproductions of his prototype, but the postwar lack of either funds or a scientific installation and service industry to distribute the houses robbed Fuller of the chance to mass-produce his industrialized dwelling.

The Wichita House marked the end of an era for Fuller. He had discovered that the mass-produced dwelling involved the complete separation of the environment controlling shell from the contained mechanical service package—just as the aircraft industry had separated the air frame and power producing units. Fuller's realization that while the mechanical services solutions were in hand the structural solutions were not, embarked him on intensive research into geodesic (the shortest distance between points on a curved or spherical surface) structures. It enabled him to analyze further the nature of structure, another of his prime mathematical interests.

The invitation to conduct short courses at universities freed Fuller from the more restricting, pragmatic stipulations of industry, and gave him an opportunity to experiment and advance in great strides. A potential industrial breakthrough presented itself in 1953 when the Ford Motor Company commissioned a 93-foot-diameter dome for its Detroit plant. The size of clear area spanned, the lightness ($8^{1}/_{2}$ tons) and the speed of erection immediately demonstrated the inherent potential of Fuller's concept and brought him public recognition.

In 1954, the United States Marine Corps asked Fuller to advise on a mobile, flexible shelter system. The result was a series of solutions, from a 55-foot-diameter dome which could be delivered by helicopter, to a 15-foot-diameter disposable paperboard shelter for six men which was immediately referred to as the "Kleenex House." It was "one-third the weight of a tent, cost one-fifteenth as much, used less than ten dollars' worth of material, and packed into a small box."

The geodesic form, giving the maximum enclosed volume with the minimum enclosing surface, is now a standard part of the architectural vocabulary. The St. Louis Climatron, in 1960, is one of its most poetic demonstrations; the United States Pavilion in Moscow, in 1959, one of its most internationally convincing; the Plastic Radomes for the Arctic Dew Line area, withstanding subzero temperatures and two hundred mile per hour winds, yet permeable to radar beams, is its most challenging technically; and the dome for New York City, two miles in diameter, one of its most dramatic. This last comes the closest yet to realizing Fuller's concern for total environmental control.

As Fuller developed the geodesic domes he also worked on Tensegrity (tension integrity) structures, as a method of environmental enclosure. Here, wires in continuous tension are interspersed by struts in discontinuous compression, each employed to its maximum operational strength. Fuller has used the word "Synergy" to describe his structures; the "behavior of a whole system unpredicted by the behavior of its components or any subassembly of its components."

"The professions of architecture, engineering, and all the sciences

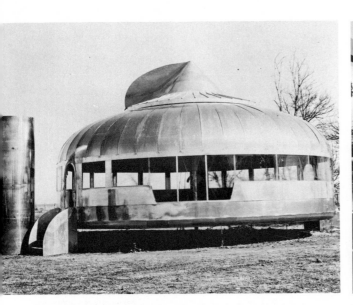

Wichita House.

are slave professions. There are two that are not—the medical, and the other which is semi-slave, the legal. Doctors are in immediate proximity with death, dealing with the reality of yes or no. The engineer and architect deal with death, but so indirectly that what they leave untended may kill people in due course, but nobody blames them for it. If the doctor is inattentive and his patient dies, he is a criminal. The doctors have the initiative; they want their new colleagues to have a good general education so that they really understand humanity. They educate their students to be anticipatory, knowing that if they get a case a little earlier they will have a better chance of solving it; if they can prevent people from falling ill it would be even better. The doctors are committed to the complete organism of man, yet they have to leave it to the architect to design their hospital, and they cannot do anything about the homes the architect creates that have corners to breed horrible little things that attack humanity.

"The profession of architecture, as practiced today, is a slave function, exercising good taste in purchasing and assembling industrially-available components, a superficial veil to cover the steel or concrete frames which are completely conventionalized and organized by the engineers. This slave profession only goes to work when it is hired and told what to do. The client says, 'I am going to build a building on such a corner; this is its purpose; this is what it is to cost; this is what it should look like; this is what the building codes and labor unions tell you you are going to do; I want my relative's equipment used.' The architect plays his game with those dominoes. Under such conditions all you can do is arrange a few beautifully-laid brick panels between the columns. That world of architecture is completely superficial and is going out. There are going to be individuals who do not assume a client knows what he wants or a society knows what it wants to do, but examine potential environmental controls, human needs, world resources and industry's capabilities.

"World indifference and ignorance have passed the responsibilities on to the politician, who is not a designer. He doesn't have the prerogative to undertake an extended design program; he can work only within his country and not on a world basis. Politics cannot resolve our problems. The only way they can be approached is by individuals with integrity who really see that there is a design revolution, not a political revolution, and who take the initiative, join forces, give up competition and set about making the world work through competence.

Ford Rotunda, Detroit, Michigan.

"The architect has to take the initiative, like the doctor. He must say that the client hasn't the slightest idea of his needs, that 'world man' doesn't know, politicians certainly don't know, and that he is going to make the world work by cooperation, using the resources, which are unevenly distributed, and the integrated knowledge of all men. Our failure is the failure of the sons of the Industrial Revolution to take the initiative. Only about one percent of our present profession can survive; this will be the segment that will aid the young people to make the eventual breakthrough.

"The student around the world is life at its first moment of freedom with a vast store of knowledge available. He is in the presence of an atom-powered submarine going under the polar ice, he sees a rocket going through the sky, and he asks: 'Why isn't the world working? Why are we putting all this stuff into armaments before we make the world work?' At the university students must acquire competence mathematically, chemically and economically, to understand industrialization and to use those tools to understand the world, man on earth, and man's ambitions. Students are beginning to realize that this is their task, and that to do it by design competence is the challenge; this is the world revolution.

"Industrialization is not a local craft, it only works as a world organism. Industrial tools cannot exist by themselves but they are all part of a great complex; we cannot make one industrial tool without using another. The larger the industrialization, the more people participating in it, the quicker we amortize one design generation and move on to a new one. All tools are externalizations of original integral functions of man. For example, a cupping of the hand to hold liquid—later on you make a ceramic cup. We have thus externalized the complex tools of our internal organism—we increase the limits of the capability in respect to the functions, where the functions were originally integrally solved. Industrialization means that we have greatly extended the limits of the capability of serving those functions, so we then have a completely externalized organism, which eventually is a world industrialization. It would be very easy to increase the performance per pound of overall machine efficiency in industrialization —now only about four percent, to about twelve percent. Thereby it is highly feasible to go from forty percent of humanity being served by our resources, upping performance per pound—which has only been done in weaponry and never in houses—and applying this to the world task of making the same metals take care of one hundred percent of humanity with a higher standard of living than man has ever known. That is the design challenge.

"Man in fear built his castle and made the walls thicker and thicker hoping this would give him security. Pirates, however, realized that a fortress would be much better if it floated because then they could move it to guard any place. They realized that it wouldn't last very long, but that they could always build another, and that it would have to be of wood, because stone wouldn't float. It had to span giant waves, take the crushing load of green waters heavier than an avalanche and turn nature's most hostile forces to actual advantage. They solved its problems by setting up a schedule of the functions to be served. By cutting down on weight they got there a little faster and outdid other pirates. How could they move a gun that would weigh less and shoot farther? Performance per pound became the essence of ship

Plastic Radomes, Mount Washington, New Hampshire.

Air Deliverable Theater, 140-foot diameter, Ford Motor Company, Detroit, Michigan.

building, and eventually led to the steel ship and the blast furnace to make it. From there the equation went into the sky and performance per pound became even more important. In the rocket we have the most exquisite high performance per pound in all weapon technology. On the land we don't ask how much a building weighs, let alone what its function per pound ratio may be. We are still on the old theory, whereby the bigger the castle the greater the security, and the architect is still carrying out decorations that belong to castles.

"The concept of performance per pound, which can only be realized through advanced industrialization, can make the world work. Once we achieve this there will be enough to go round; then there will be no more war. Everyone thought Malthus was right, there was not enough to go round, that is why we are on the defensive, why we have weapons. We do not talk about the Department of Offense, but the Department of Defense."

The constant goal of Fuller's research and work has been a means of harnessing all of man's resources to bring prosperity to the entire world family. A practical means of implementing this would be "allowing the architectural students around the world to invest a large part of their time in considering the relation between world resources and the needs of world man." In 1961 Fuller proposed a World Design Decade, from 1965 to 1975. To coordinate and stimulate the program's activity in sixty national centers, Fuller has established a center at Southern Illinois University, in Carbondale, where he has been research professor since 1959. Fuller's program has so far published two weighty documents, the first on "Human Trends and Needs," and the second, "The Design Initiative." They bear the overall title of "Inventory of World Resources," implying comprehensiveness—materials, total natural world resources, and the potential and capacity of world intellect—covering every environmental and social endeavor, directed towards ameliorating change. At a time when the whole question of architectural education is going through a period of flux and reevaluation, Fuller, if anyone, might be able to implement his idea. H. G. Wells stated the need for what he termed a "world brain" to correlate information and extrapolate it at a world scale; Fuller is already active.

Fuller believes that our problems should also be tackled by considering man's life as multi-dimensional in relation to the earth. Going beyond lines and area into volume and frequency modulation, adding the time factor plus velocity—not three dimensions, but a really dynamic fourth dimension. "You are in an airplane; the faster the plane the less seconds you will be in any one point and the less probability of running into something else. This is the principle employed by the Almighty in designing the universe, with atoms moving at thousands of miles a second having approximately no probability of running into each other. Frequency modulation is the velocity with which things get occupied. Our earth is moving through the heavens at a very high velocity—about one thousand miles per hour in rotation at the equator, let alone the orbital velocity of sixty-five thousand miles per hour. The amount of time you occupy a space if you are moving slowly, say on an ocean boat, is large. If you are going through a given point in a split second the chances of running into another passing body are very low. The higher the speed, the less probability of interference—this is the principle of frequency modulation."

Tensegrity Mast, 1959 Fuller Exhibition at the Museum of Modern Art, New York, N.Y.

Perhaps Fuller's own mobility is above average, but his is an increasingly common pattern. Our ecological pattern has changed so much and our mobility is so great that before we can accept our situation as world-man it may have to be changed to universe-man. An astronaut in eight days now covers more distance than the well-traveled Fuller has in a lifetime. As he says: "Thermonuclear reactor propulsion is the next breakthrough, the intelligence system says the Russians have brought it to a very advanced stage. With it man is going to be able to cruise through space. We are about to have an entirely new relationship to the universe."

Fuller believes that the problems of expanding urbanization and population centralization can be resolved in the evolving future city by a new scale of design and thinking. In 1953 a thirty-foot dome was flown and lowered by helicopter; in 1956 a fifty-five-foot dome; in 1960 a hundred and fourteen-foot dome; the curve is increasing. Within a few years Fuller hopes to be able to cover a whole city in a one-day series of air drops, controlling the environment and creating a potential all-season garden-living situation. He explains that "the bigger the environment controlled, the more stable the atmosphere."

A recent design idea of Fuller's has been that of constructing "structural clouds." A sphere one hundred feet in diameter would contain in weight twenty tons of air; Fuller can make a structure of one-and-a-half tons to contain this air. In doubling the size of the sphere the weight of the structure would increase about three times, but the volume of air contained increases by the third power, approximately eight times as much, to one hundred and sixty tons. As the size of the sphere increases, the ratio of the weight of the structure to the weight of the air becomes increasingly negligible. A rise in temperature of the air within the sphere of only one degree Fahrenheit would expand the air significantly. It would be allowed to escape to maintain the original pressure, and then the total assembly would weigh less than the air around it and would float.

Fuller believes that this could be a means of occupying space productively. The weight of one thousand human beings would, like the enclosing structure, be negligible in comparison to the

Tensegrity Structure, Bear Island, Maine.

"Climatron," Missouri Botanical Garden,
175-foot diameter, St. Louis, Missouri.

Yomiuri Inagamachi Golf Club Field House,
170-foot diameter, Star Tensegrity Dome, Tokyo, Japan.

weight of air. The height could be controlled by allowing the air out through the outer membrane when the sun warmed it during the day. The evening pressure of air trying to return would be so very mild that the membrane would easily resist it. Such "sky-balls" could, for example, become "food factories, as the sun impounded would be enormous, reflecting back the ultraviolet rays; with a chemical atmosphere and a small amount of moisture you would be able to grow enormous amounts of food." Fuller was talking fancifully of an idea that could become reality.

Says Fuller, "The control of man's environment will strengthen his health and physical fiber; man was born to be healthy. He is not born lazy, but becomes so from the frustration of being punished for his motions. We must design on behalf of our fellowman to ensure that he is not hurt and does not become lazy; that is a form of disease too." He continued, "The hypothetical approach leads to the practical. You need to involve others, thereby generating a capability beyond your own. I am not interested in the old world of architecture which is simply self-expression; the new architecture has the task of making man a success."

Not long after the success of his polio vaccine, Dr. Salk was sitting next to Fuller, to whom he turned and said, "I've always felt that those Dymaxion gadgets, cars, houses, maps, etc., were only incidental to what you really are interested in. Could you tell me what your work really is?" Fuller replied, "I've been engaged in what you might call comprehensive anticipatory design science." "That's very interesting," Dr. Salk said, "because that's a description of my work too."

As specialization advances, the man who can generalize knowledgeably and has the vision to comprehend the potential of our science and technology becomes increasingly valuable. In doing this, Fuller shows the way "... into that vast, unattended potential harvest."

Louis I Kahn (signature)

LOUIS I. KAHN

Years of patient search and dedication in the face of much indifference led to the 1950's when virtually overnight Louis I. Kahn became an architect of international stature and consequence. When Frank Lloyd Wright died in 1959, the titular leader of American architecture had gone. The strong and loyal group who find Kahn a rallying figure would suggest that he occupies this position today. In a profession where criticism abounds and is a life blood, Kahn's quiet manner, intense involvement and eagerness to communicate have won him wide respect and affection.

Born in 1901 on the Estonian isle of Osel, Kahn immigrated to Philadelphia in 1905 with his parents. Since then, that city has been the base for his activities and the vehicle for many of his planning theories. Asked to define the essence of a city Kahn said, "The city, the gathering of persons, each a singularity, their ways of living and their ways to express, is a place where a boy beginning his life can sense what he would become." As a boy he was gifted at both painting and music and could have had scholarships in either; but at sixteen, inspired by his high school art teacher, he chose architecture.

A beaux arts education at the University of Pennsylvania and a great drawing ability inevitably drew him to Europe for a year in 1928. The splendor of Greek and Roman antiquity impressed him. These images, combined with the new images Le Corbusier presented, fired his mind with the desire to express and set his direction. The creative man links what has been done in his field with his sense of the essence of his art. He breaks away from style because architecture—the spirit, knows no style. He senses what is true though it may appear unfamiliar to the eye. Le Corbusier was such a man. The images created by him touched in Kahn a sense of architecture.

In 1947, Kahn became Visiting Critic at Yale and was soon made a professor there. Five years later, he was given his first real opportunity: he designed an extension to the Yale Art Gallery, and in so doing created the University's first modern building. Since it was the first new University building in many years, various needs had accumulated causing the program to necessitate an essentially universal space—galleries, offices, drafting rooms, and work areas—easily adaptable to future requirements of area divisions and services. This led to the idea of a loft space on four levels, centrally divided on each level by the vertical connection of mechanical services, elevator and stairs. The 40-foot free

Laboratories, Salk Institute for Biological Research, La Jolla, California.

389

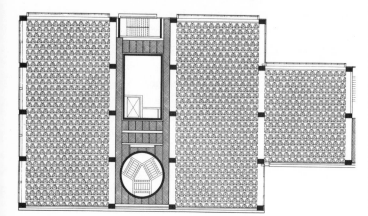

Yale Art Gallery, New Haven, Connecticut.

spaces, supported by columns at 20-foot intervals, are designed as trussed space slabs, about 3 feet in depth, which harbor the air conditioning, the electrical service and lighting, and break up the sound. These services are exposed but do not project below the ceiling plane, perspective and the solid planes of the trusses concealing them from view. Kahn applies "order" to this space slab because the integration of services and structure is in harmony with the nature of the space and desire for an uncluttered ceiling.

The exterior walls, clearly independent of the structural system, are brick on the street side in color sympathy with the existent building, and they define and repeat the scale of the street. At a break in the wall at right angles to the street is a narrow recessed glazed entrance, placed in this manner to avoid conflicts in scale with the openings of the existing Venetian Gothic building. The floor levels are punctuated on the blank walls by the introduction of watertables to shed rain at intervals. The planes facing the garden are glass.

Kahn said that as soon as the building was finished, he began to make sketches of how he would have designed it if his new realizations of "order" were before him. The order of the three-dimensional slab would have led him to a more comprehensive order—allowing a freer disposition of hollow triangulated columns in structural sympathy with the tetrahedral geometry of the slab—precluding the need for beams, incongruent with the continuity of services in the slab. The columns would have acted as vertical shafts of service, and even the stairway would have been a hollow column. The Gallery forecast Kahn's direction; however, he was still in a period of search towards its refinement.

Kahn returned to the University of Pennsylvania as a critic in 1957, and was invited to design its Richards-Medical Laboratories. One of the decade's most important and influential statements, either here or abroad, it established Kahn's reputation. The Medical Research Building is a powerful advocate for the realization of fundamental form, of characteristic and inseparable elements inspiring shapes and composition.

The realizations in the form "Laboratory" come from the need for uninterrupted space for changing area arrangements, spaces in light and in darkness, the separation of the air to breathe from the air to dispose of, the need for ready escape, and the accessibility of services. The square studio clusters are constructed to give natural light to the corners, with dark cross interiors; the towers for the supply of vertical services also act as direct air exhausts from each studio, to which a stair tower is also attached. The open vierendeel trusses give immediate access to the exposed, "to get to" services. The four towers bringing in fresh air to the air make-up machines on the central service tower's top floor were considered from the beginning.

The central service tower containing the animal rooms, storage rooms, elevators and a common service stairway played its part in the construction order as the first building cast-in-place, giving time for the three studio clusters to have their structural parts prefabricated. By the time the prefabricated parts arrived, the tower was built and served as the work and storage room for the utilities, piping and ducts for the laboratory towers at each corresponding level. The construction order was the realization of the inherent economy in designing for sequences of constructing

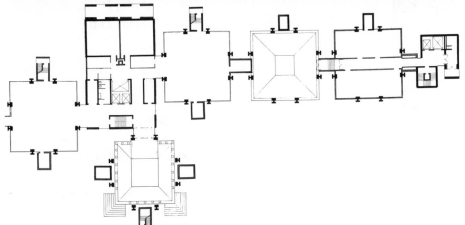

Richards Medical Research Building, Philadelphia, Pennsylvania.

in continuity.

The exterior reflects the composite order of concrete and brick. The gray-red rather purplish brick was chosen to harmonize with other campus buildings. The service towers rise high, two stories above the laboratory clusters, combining to give the impression of a lean, assertive structure.

The building has functional shortcomings: area programing proved inadequate as there is not enough space, and the result is crowding and overflowing of equipment in corridors. The sun control glass in the sensitively shaped cantilever beams, budgetarily calculated to counter the south and west sun conditions, proved inadequate. Nevertheless, the clarity of Kahn's thinking resulted in a building of strong presence and the quality of timelessness.

The catch-phrase "servant spaces and served spaces," coined to apply to the new hierarchy of spaces, was first realized in the Trenton Community Bath House. In the Richards Building it is expressed by the exhaust and stair towers, the central utility tower and the deep trusses as "servant spaces," and the laboratories as the "served spaces." The mechanical services to the major spaces of a building have become more numerous and complex today. To Kahn, these services must be made a part of the order of the structure, give shape and light to the "served spaces"; the "served spaces" themselves, the raison d'être of a building, must emerge gracefully.

Bath House for the Jewish Community Center, Trenton, New Jersey.

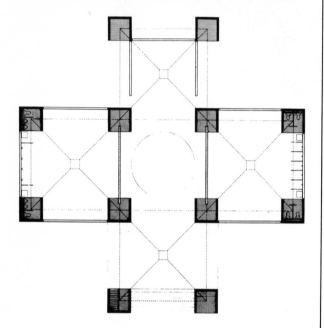

Project for a City Tower.

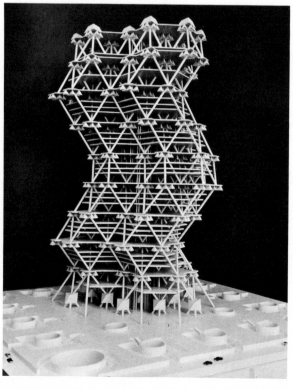

Some critics said that the expression of the "servant" areas was over-dramatized and disproportionately strong in relation to the "served" areas, and erroneously believed Kahn to be enamored of ducts, when it is quite the opposite. He says, "I hate them so thoroughly that I feel they have to be respected for their nature and given their place. If I just hated them and took no care, I think they would invade the building and completely mangle it." The Medical Towers are a strong architectural statement of a clear idea. The order is a realization of the nature of the spaces and their position in the hierarchy of spaces as they act to serve or be served. The order realization becomes the basis of design. Then, believes Kahn, if the order does not hold, one should generate a higher sense of order. He has written:

> Form is the realization of inseparable characteristics
>
> Form has no existence in material, shape or dimension
>
> To begin is the time of belief in Form
>
> When the work is completed the beginning must be felt
>
> A design is but a single spark out of Form
> It is of material and has shape and dimension
>
> The form "symphony" does not belong to the composer
> His design, his composition does.

Like Paul Klee, Kahn had gone back to that field of unimpaired vision, soon lost and almost never regained, where a simple question could be asked with the maturity of experience, yet with a child's innocence. As he said, "I once learned that a good question is better than the most brilliant answer"; or form conscious realizations even poorly expressed could have the qualities that lead to architecture.

In the late 1950's, Kahn made his important clarification between Form and Design. "Form is what, Design is how. Form is impersonal, but design belongs to the designer. Design is prescribed by circumstances—how much money there is available, the site, the client, the extent of skill and knowledge, and above all the individual's tendencies of expression. Form is free of conditions. In architecture, it is the realization of a harmony of spaces good for a certain activity of man." Kahn elaborates, "'House' stands for the abstract concept of spaces good to live in—where the institution of home is inspired. 'House' is thus a form in the mind, without shape or dimension. 'A house,' on the other hand, is a conditioned interpretation of living space. This is a design. In my opinion, the presence of an architect depends more on his power to realize that which is 'house' than on his ability to organize the specific space needs and costs of 'a house'—something prescribed by circumstances. 'A house' needs 'house' to belong to Architecture."

Kahn's references to Form are viewed with reserve in some circles, where they carry the old, decadent overtones of formalism, pattern-making, and preconception. Kahn uses the word Form in all innocence; to him it is a realization of appropriateness that brings conceptual strength and unity to his architecture. There is also, of course, a strong suggestion of classicism through his reference to the Greek and Roman, and his predilection for geometric balance, particularly in the early design stages of a project; but this invariably, and soon, becomes more directly expressive of Form as the art of making meaningful and expressive shapes. For Kahn, Form is the beginning strength when the area require-

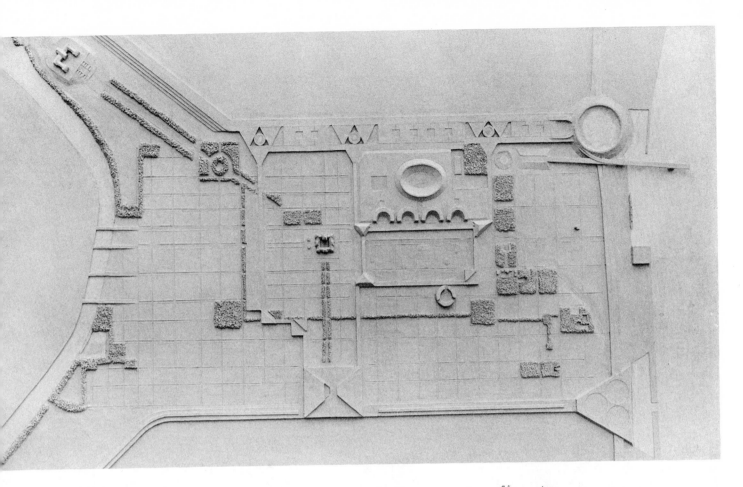

ments of a client's program are transformed into a realization of appropriate spaces.

Closely allied, and related to his method of working, is his idea that all works of architecture must start with the immeasurable, become measurable in the transitional period of design for the making, and after it is built again reflect the immeasurable; a quality that may reach the point where it is worthy as an offering to Architecture. Kahn's realizations in the immeasurable begin with the idea of the "belief" and its place in the Spirit of Architecture. A design problem set students at the University of Pennsylvania in 1964 particularly appealed to him: to find the architectural qualities of a symbol of freedom. The site was opposite Independence Hall in Philadelphia, where the Declaration of Independence was signed in 1776. Kahn was invited to attend services here for President Kennedy: The place felt so right—he went back to his class. Kahn liked the place because "without ordained function it was able to express a faith." In the problem, "Form follows function" was thus so transformed as to just "want to be" ideas—the symbolic expression of a belief.

In the late 1950's, Kahn explored ideas that showed his range of interests. One such study was for a city tower whose plan was a hexagonal shape which shifted its position as it rose at intervals of 33 feet, a combined tetrahedron and octahedron space frame. The 660-foot helical structure was designed to allow varying uses and positions to exist within its triangulated growth. In a sense the exercise tried to allow a building to design itself, stability against wind forces being inherent.

Kahn also turned his attentions at this time to an urban study for Philadelphia. Existing streets were redefined to accommodate a hierarchy of movement and, for example, separate car, bus and truck movement. Order of movement recognized places of stop-

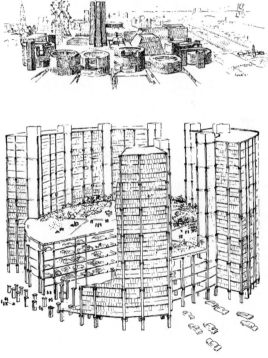

Project for a plan for Philadelphia, Pennsylvania.

393

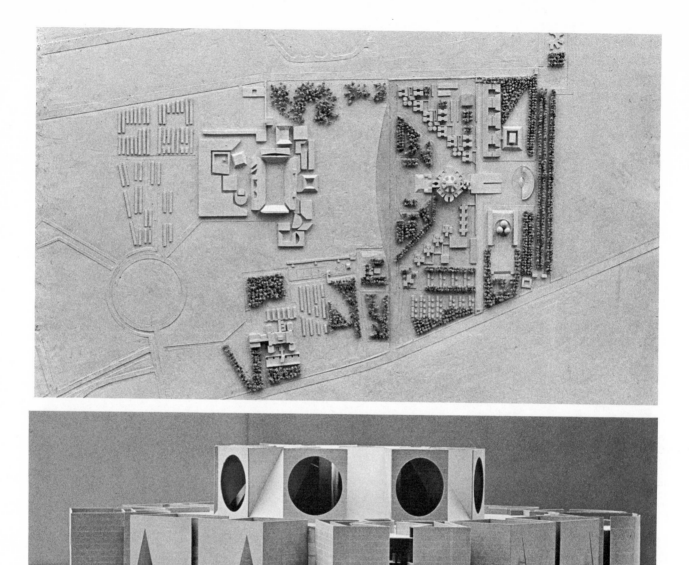

Second Capital, legislative, Dacca, Pakistan: Master plan and Assembly Building.

ping, for example, as belonging to the design of the street, their location corresponding to where important commercial building also wanted to be. Composite buildings were thought of for such locations, exploiting the periphery as a place of light for places to live and work; the interior, without light, being utilized for car storage. The street level, too important to be sacrificed to the demands of movement alone, became the place of continuity of commercial areas, interrupted only by the entrance to parking areas above and below.

In his Algiers Plan in the early 1930's Le Corbusier had proposed apartment buildings above and below a major highway. In his new town of Chandigarh, India, in the late 1950's, circulation was planned with a hierarchy of movement, from on wheels to on foot—the scale and growth of the city, and the rhythm and speed of movement itself suggesting cohesive design systems. Sadly enough—and how our cities testify to it—too few architects have brought this type of conceptual thinking to our urban problems. Such urban ideas of Kahn, though reasonable and promising a new urbanism, tend to fall into that no-man's land between the un-compromisingly visionary and the strictly pragmatic and are therefore vulnerable to misunderstanding; though only briefly stated in uncommissioned drawings these ideas are the constant subject of his lectures and seminar discussions with his students. Kahn contends that his statement of "servant and served" spaces applies to the city as well as to buildings. There is as definite an architecture, he says, to Water as there is to Wind, Light and Movement. Their integration with the Architecture of the Institutions of Man is roughly the total architecture of the city. And the services stay where they are no matter how the city grows. He explains, for example, that processed water is a precious commodity that needs to be distinguished from the water that washes down the streets or is used for air conditioning and fountains. The interchanges in the design of streets serving the "order of movement" could be integrated with the spaces serving the "order of water," bringing reservoirs into the body of the city. Other interchanges could be so designed that their residual areas could become the police stations, fire stations, maintenance headquarters and storage centers.

In his new commission to design Chandhinagar, the capital city of the State of Gujarat, the "architecture of water" of "wind, light and movement," and the "architecture of connection" will play a major role in the establishment of zoned estates, of housing, of work spaces, and of public spaces. These distinctions are made to search for "Form City," for the characteristics which distinguish the city of yesterday from the city today. He visualizes that the water towers—viaducts and aqueducts—are a valid framework of these estates which will be divided by streets that follow in their direction the benefits of wind, and that the architecture of light will be expressed as buildings within buildings, one to the sun and one to interior living. "How wonderful it would be to sense the realm of spaces that inspires an architecture expressive of the Institutions that arise but of a sense of a way of life," says Kahn.

"I know architecture as a spirit rising out of the presence of architecture. Greek architecture is foremost in my mind. In the beginning, architecture took hold because it was true to man. Once felt and expressed it always was to be.

"The psyche, a prevalence in all living things, is felt in man through inspirations: the inspiration to live, to learn, to question, to express—an in-touchness with the unmeasurable. I sense that there is the reality of belief and the reality of the means. One is intangible, the other tangible. Belief is inspired and is the constant motivator of the means.

"The reality of belief suggests the realization that every building serves an institution of man.

"The inspiration to learn motivated the institutions of learning. It is the key to the body of realizations which lead the spirit of its expression and the rules of its making.

"Everyone is a singularity. The city is a melting of singularities. In each is that which expresses a fundamental commonness. From others one learns about one's self. This atmosphere of human relations brings about new social needs of learning, of health, of art, of science, of government, of worship. A city is the place of the institutions. Their particular expressions by individuals and their environment in architecture, in the organization of

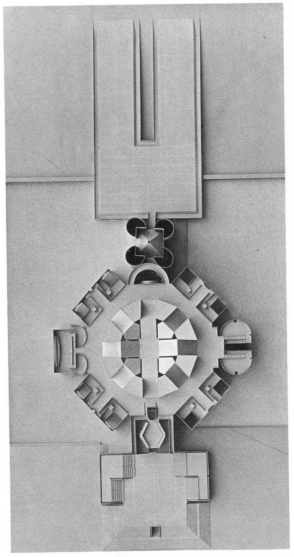

Assembly Building, Dacca, Pakistan.

connections, indoor and outdoor, combine to characterize one city from another.

"When the architect receives a program from a client, it contains nothing in the way of architecture. He must make areas into spaces, a lobby into a place of entrance, make galleries out of corridors. In so doing, he is serving that which is in the particular realm of spaces, that which belongs to the activity of man vested in the institutions: the establishment of an environment expressing the inspirations.

"All buildings do not belong to Architecture. A work of architecture is presented as an offering to Architecture and to its Treasury of spaces. The place of entrance, the galleries of movement and places of connection, the places of work, of learning, of meeting, and the places of privacy, once expressed, evoke the desire to live, to express. As a painting is made as an offering to the spirit Painting, which favors no period or style, so must a building dedicated to Architecture be nonconscious of style. The realms of Sculpture, Painting, Photography and Architecture are governed by psychic rules that lead art to the making of a life— a validity. Complete and immediate are Cartier-Bresson's realizations in photography when he says 'I look for the decisive moment.' The play of circumstances is unpredictable and continuous. Each iota of moment is already chained to the next. His sense of 'the moment' reveals a prerogative of the photographer, to choose, in the midst of the myriad of happenings. The art lies in the choice within which lies the incredible. In the psyche—natural flow—the incredible is the isolated though it belonged to the successive. The isolated, the choice, gives Gogol the frame of a story that combines the child, the mountain and the serpent. What man creates, nature without man cannot. What nature makes, man cannot. Nature makes through order. Man makes through art.

"How we were made is recorded in us. In everything that nature makes is contained the record of its making—be it rock, tree or man. The inspiration to learn we sense from the record of how we were made which involved all the laws of the Universe and fills us with a sense of wonder which in turn wants to play back the processes of order to learn to create our own instruments of expression; the reason to live is to express. The Inspirations to express are the motivations of Art.

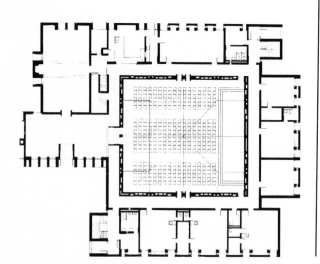

"We are born with a sense of what to do, but a sense of how to do it we are not born with. Experience primes the 'what and the how.' Le Corbusier was capable of many more works than he was asked to do. His remarkable sense of the spirit of architecture, were it expressed more continuously, could have rewarded the world even more with the wonders of architecture.

"Through his work, an artist comes to know himself. The work of an artist is always less than himself and inspires the next work. The works of an artist are but one work."

Presented with a program of need, Kahn seeks to sense the environment good for the spaces that reveal themselves to him. Areas of the program aspire to rise with yet unshaped "wanting to be" spirit. The realizations, yet without defined shapes, have in them the ingredients to give life to the space needs of what he understands to be the institution of man, which the program implies. Unprogrammed spaces, too, come to life to fulfill the desires of environment. He believes that architectural realizations, free of solution, free of method, preceding design, can direct the mind to a realm of appropriateness and lead design to a freedom of expression.

Kahn's thought of what a space "wants to be" is centered around the giving of continued life to spaces involving the activities of man; the space itself inspires the activity. In architecture, a space in which to learn should inspire learning.

To Kahn's realizations, there is no process: there is no sequence. What is within the experience may have to serve as beginning, but it cannot take the place of a constant feeling that a new moment carries with it new demands. In time, for him, if the desire to express the nature of an environment of spaces is not shaded by means in readiness, the form and its elements will present themselves as the departure in design.

"The art of making may be analagous to the way we were made, to aspire, to be man, to express—Aspiration—Form—Design."

Form, a nature of inseparable elements, is what Kahn was searching for when the numerous requirements of Dacca, the Second Capital of Pakistan, were presented to him. This can be illustrated by his discussion of his Master Plan.

"When I was asked to design the Second Capital, legislative, of Pakistan in Dacca (the First Capital is in Islamabad and is the executive capital), I was given an extensive program of buildings: the assembly, the supreme court, hostels, schools, a stadium, the diplomatic enclave, the living sector, market, all to be placed on a thousand acres of flat land subject to flood. I kept thinking of how these buildings may be grouped and what would cause them to take their place on the land. On the night of the third day, I fell out of bed with the idea which is still the prevailing idea of the plan. This came simply from the realization that assembly is of a transcendent nature. Men came to assemble to touch the spirit of commonness, and I thought that this must be expressible. Observing the way of religion in the living of the Pakistani, I thought that a mosque woven into the space fabric of the assembly would have such effect. I feared the presumption to assume this right, that is to know it to fit symbolically their way of life. But this assumption took possession as an anchor. Also the program required the design of a hotel for ministers, their secretaries, and the members of the assembly. But this requirement became in my mind a corollary to the assembly, and

Unitarian Church, Rochester, New York.

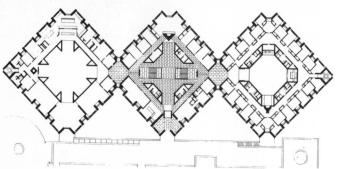

Dormitories for Bryn Mawr College, Bryn Mawr, Pennsylvania.

I thought immediately that they should be transformed from a hotel to studies in their gardens on a lake. The supreme court in my mind was the test of the acts of legislation against the philosophic nature of man. The three became inseparable in the thinking of the transcendent nature of assembly.

"I couldn't wait until morning in my anxiety to relate these thoughts to Kafiluddin Ahmad in charge of this project. In the morning I was there at 9 o'clock sharp and told him about the symbolic importance of the mosque; I got no immediate response, no reaction. But he got on the phone and talked to several ministers. After he had spoken for some while, he turned to me and said, 'Professor Kahn, I think you have something there.' I felt enormous confidence that the plan could have form. 'But,' he said, 'you will have a problem with the Chief Justice of the Supreme Court because he doesn't want the court next to the assembly.'

"We saw the Chief Justice the next day, and we were greeted with the usual tea and biscuits. He said: 'I know why you're here—the grapevine is very well developed in Pakistan. You're barking up the wrong tree, because I will not be a part of this assembly group. I will go to the provincial capital site near the provincial high court where the lawyers are, and I think I will feel much more at home there.' I turned to him and said, 'Mr. Chief Justice, is this your decision alone, or is it also the decision of the judges who will follow you? Let me explain to you what I intend to compose.' And I made my first sketch on paper of the assembly with the mosque on the lake. I added the hostels framing this lake. I told him how I felt about the transcendent meaning of assembly. After a moment's thought he took the pencil out of my hand and placed a mark representing the supreme court in a position where I would have placed it myself, on the other side of the mosque, and he said: 'The mosque is sufficient insulation from the men of the assembly.'

"I was very happy that the motivations of religious thought were communicable. It was not belief, not pattern, but the essence from which an institution could emerge, which changed his mind.

"The relationship of the assembly, mosque, court and hostels in their interplay psychologically is what expresses a nature. The Institution of Assembly could lose its strength if the sympathetic parts were dispersed. The inspirations of each would be left incompletely expressed.

"In the first sketch of the mosque I indicated four minarets. The meaning of the mosque with the assembly was then intuitively necessary and expressed in borrowed terms. Now the question of the nature 'Mosque' related to 'Assembly' has questioned the minarets, and at one time in design the mosque was a pyramid, the peak of which was a minaret. Now it graces as a detail the main entrance, but the question of its form still remains.

"Because this is delta country, buildings are placed on mounds to protect them from flood. The ground for the mounds comes from the digging of lakes and ponds. I employed the shape of the lake too as a discipline of location and boundary. The triangular lake was meant to encompass the hostels and the assembly and to act as a dimensional control.

"The assembly, hostels, and supreme court belong to the Citadel of the Assembly and their interrelated nature suggests a completeness causing other buildings to take their distance. Then because of the intellectual entity of the related buildings of the assembly, its meaning caused me to realize that the acts of assembly lead to the establishment of the institutions of man. That made me realize that the buildings of the program other than those related to the assembly belong to the Citadel of the Institutions which I placed on axis and facing the Citadel of the Assembly.

"It occurred to me in thinking about the meaning of institutions that the inspiration to live remains meekly unexpressed in the institutions of man. It is a building I hope to sense the form of, which could lead to its design. It would be a place of baths and place of exercise and meeting. It is the place where the athlete is honored and a man strives for physical perfection. The idea of such an institution is inspired by the Roman bath. I have in mind an environment of spaces far reaching considering the resources of today. The responsibility of a country to its people in regard to their physical well being is certainly as important as the culture of the mind and the regulation of commerce. This institution is expressed roughly as a building harboring a stadium as well as the rooms of meeting, bath, exercise and their gardens, and flanked by a school of science and a school of art. Also composed with these buildings is a block of satellite institutions and commercial services. This block is the anchor of the dwelling places which are being recomposed out of an old village with its mounds and depressions already established."

Unlike Frank Lloyd Wright, who was searching for a more plastic spatial expression, Kahn in his work reflects his early classical architectural training in which volumes were carefully delineated by their enclosure and developed a defined spatial sequence. Kahn's discipline in geometry has become increasingly strict, stemming from his own understanding of nature's laws and construction methods. For him geometry is always answerable to a continuum. Geometry is the link between measurement and space, and improvisation earns its right through order. The most tortuous shape must conform to mathematics, and the laws of nature are the instruction for its making. Kahn emphasizes that the aesthetic order of sculpture, of painting, and of architecture are not the same. Painting does not answer to the laws of gravity; sculpture does and so does architecture. "Chagall can paint a village upside down and paint the powers of dream. Architects wish for 'sky-hooks' but must use cranes."

Again one becomes aware of the classical training from which he learned that a column relates itself to the next by the nature of stone which sizes the lintel, defining the column and the lintel as inseparable elements of construction and the elements of plan, the portico and cella as inseparable space elements of the temple. His consciousness of the plan elements, disciplined by this strong sense of geometry, is increasingly evident and central to Kahn's architecture. The element is not a personal thing, he states, but part of the architectural vocabulary. He is giving it its own clear and distinct identity, not allowing it to "enter" the plan before he can sense it as a "poetic entity." Form is the inspiration for the design and choice of shape, but he is most careful to avoid confusing shapes with form.

In the Trenton Community Center (in which Kahn also explored the "servant-served" idea in a large, carefully articulated, moduled structure) the concern for the hierarchy of spaces was substantially explored for the first time. The servant and served elements used elementally give a sense of an aesthetic order coming out of architectural prerogatives in contrast, for example, to the pre-rogatives of hand-made sculpture.

Kahn's search for the nature of the element is well illustrated by a discussion of the light-giving element. His concern for the way in which light enters the interior, stems from his appreciation that the window thought of as an element takes on its own independent nature (possibly Kahn also recalled the shortcomings of the Medical Towers). He believes that one wants to get away from light, or at least its glare, without needing a curtain, and that side walls should modify the light contrast so that one can even sit in the window as if it were itself a room. "In buildings of old, walls were thick and the window existing by its grace had its side walls in light given to it by the wall's depth."

Kahn recognizes the window as having a nature of its own born out of the ancient wall. But as technology made the wall thin, it took the window along with it, the window losing its depth and its sensitive side walls. Overhangs, brise-soleil, are but correctives not essentially recognizing the window as an element with its own powers. In view of this, he is trying to restate the requirements of the window, or the light-giving element, in terms of present techniques. Weight is costly; we build thin walls today, but the window needs its own walls.

Kahn explains the development of the light-giving element for his Dacca plan. "Structure makes space. Choice of structure is choice in the character of light. Space between columns is the light of the interior. If one thinks of the thick Greek column made of much larger diameter permitting a light-well as its interior and the space between columns as interior areas, the concept of light-giving elements to the spaces in the heart of the plan in the Assembly Building may be understood. The eight light-wells are like those expanded columns, not columns any-more but walls enclosing a source of light; in the Dacca plan these wells are regularly spaced as a light-giving element. Thought of this way, it could have been of various shapes if the space served and its light demanded it. It is a court, the pierced walls of which light the spaces. Peculiarly enough, through my pre-occupation with the search for plan elements, these were first thought of as outside the plan to study them for their own nature, which gave them the potentiality of varying shapes. I was in-terested in using them in a freer more offering way to needs and in that way could have expressed them more poetically. Had I in the customary geometric arrangement considered them out-right as light-wells already incorporated, I would not have come to the realization of their elemental resourcefulness. Though finally this light-giving element in the Assembly Building is regular in dimensions, the consciousness of its potential freedom of shape added to my architectural vocabulary."

The problem of getting light in a centrally positioned space away from the enclosing walls of a building is present in two of Kahn's recent buildings. In the First Unitarian Church of Rochester, New York, the central space is a directly expressed concrete structure lighted by hooded rooflights at the four corners. Within this concrete encasement is defined the sanctuary chamber, which is an enclosure in block placed sufficiently away from the inde-pendent concrete walls to form an ambulatory. The rooms around the periphery have an independent brick wall-bearing structure. These are the classrooms, library, kitchen, and entrance lobby, grouped around the hall on two levels; the shape and projection

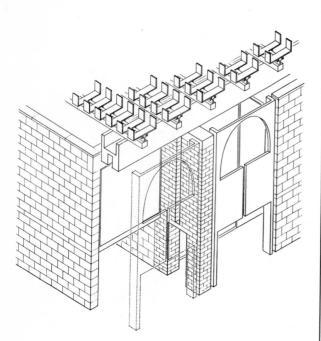

Project for the U.S. Consulate, Luanda, Angola.

of their spaces derive from their function. The rooms are lighted by vertical bands of glass, located between small window-seat bays. The four hoods create a powerful central massing to the building, which is further emphasized visually by the forceful articulation of the bays.

The dormitories at Bryn Mawr College, Bryn Mawr, Pennsylvania, are similar in concept. There also is the same problem: this time, three central areas, constructed of concrete as an independent order, are the means of getting clerestory light to the central areas; architecturally, this light is clearly different from the light obtained around the periphery. Rooms have window seats in bays and are grouped around these central communal spaces lighted from above. But, where a centralized concept for the church was subsequently modified and loosened up by functional dictates, the repetitive nature of the dormitory rooms led Kahn to the retention of a tighter, and what at first might appear a more mannered, geometric solution. The complex, in three squares connected at the corners, appears from the outside to be an undulating wall. Kahn's arrangement obviates the "institutional" corridor and creates smaller, more intimately structured social groupings. The communal space is exposed concrete, while the exterior has a precise tautness with the dark-gray slate walls defined by thin white trims of precast concrete.

These three examples involved clerestory light. In the project for the United States Consulate in Luanda, Angola, Kahn became aware of the importance of integrating the problems of glare with other problems of light from a window. He observed that strong light coming from a window contrasted violently with any wall against the light. When the walls against the light were also made to be in light by some secondary source, the glare disappeared. This gave him the idea of allowing full openings towards the light and introducing in front of these openings a garden wall which received natural light and itself had very large openings cut through it. This not only eliminated glare but gave better ventilation, avoiding the use of curtains or brise-soleil that he saw prevalently used throughout Luanda. In his studies for the "Meeting House" for Dr. Jonas Salk's Institute in La Jolla, California, this solution becomes even richer, more dramatic, and architecturally integral. Circular rooms are within square screening devices, and square rooms within circular ones.

The Salk Institute will comprise three major building groups: the "Meeting House," providing quarters for visiting scientists; the "Village," housing for unmarried resident scientists; and the Research Laboratories. The first stage, completed late in 1965, is the two parallel research laboratories, each 65 feet by 245 feet, flanking a plaza overlooking the Pacific. The reinforced concrete structures are clear-span, open spaces with a peripheral corridor beyond which are the supportive elements: along the outer sides of the laboratories is a series of service towers; facing the plaza is a series of scientists' study towers, angular in profile to catch the ocean breezes and connected by bridges to the laboratories; at one end are mechanical rooms, and at the other end are administrative offices facing the ocean.

Spaces are not only appropriate to function but, in their independence as entities, so are the building's structural systems. The laboratories are given eleven-foot ceilings, clear-span trusses creating a pipe loft space nine feet above and below the laboratories. This combines to create a monumentally impressive

Salk Institute for Biological Research, La Jolla, California: Master plan and Laboratories.

Project for a City Tower.

sense of scale, complemented by the boldly expressed elements that rhythmically encircle the laboratory space.

The established institutions express a way of life; Kahn felt that the purposes of the Salk Institute were to create an intellectual atmosphere of science and art where men like Picasso and Copland would at times be invited to be with the scientists. To him this indicated a new quality expressive of a new type of institution. Responsive to function, disciplined in structure, expressive in articulation and geometry, concerned with space and the nature of space, with light and the introduction of light—Kahn, whose reputation was initially gained on few buildings, is clearly in full stride. There is a sense of permanence and tough urbanity about his buildings, like those of Mies, that few modern architects have successfully achieved: continuity.

Yet for some critics there remains his concern for geometry that some imagine is the prerogative of the beaux arts. But Kahn has mentioned in several of his writings the possibility of composing a plan made of gigantic prefabricated elements designed as entities belonging technologically to the crane. He also sees the joint where these large elements come together as an episode of ornament. Design, as an act, must recognize technological potentiality. It must also be the initial inventor of new means. Here, always, geometry will play a part. The passing of the beaux arts does not preclude the use of geometry. As Kahn emphasizes, the spirit of Architecture has no style.

Kahn has that sense of dignity that distinguishes a powerful creative force of considerable consequence and integrity. He has remained true to himself and, consequently, true to his architecture—however difficult this might make life for his clients. His great strength is his ability to think conceptually, seemingly detached, and like Fuller controlling his own course entirely, from our frenetic world of action and of building. The lack of this ability, or the inability to create such a circumstance for themselves is limiting too many of America's other fine talents.

With all really important creative energies there is that honest endeavor to seek and see beyond self-expression to the true nature of art. It is a pursuit, never-ending. To realize consequence is to perceive the arts as prophetic, of social consequence related to the technologies of an epoch: it is to steer a steady course, amidst all diversions, to durable, human ends. It is the idea of the artist losing himself in his subject, becoming so imbued with his subject that he moves towards finding and understanding himself as an artist. For a building "lives" from the life an architect gives it: Significance —not gesture nor less.

As Jung said, "The work in process becomes the poet's fate and determines his psychic development. It is not Goethe who creates Faust, but Faust which creates Goethe."

Indian Institute of Management, Ahmedabad, India.

BIBLIOGRAPHY

Banham, Reyner/*Theory and Design in the First Machine Age.*
    The Architectural Press, London, 1960.
Blake, Peter/*The Master Builders,*
    Alfred A. Knopf, New York, 1961.
Bush-Brown, Albert/*Louis Sullivan,*
    George Braziller, Inc., New York, 1960.
Giedion, Sigfried/*Space, Time and Architecture,*
    Harvard University Press, Cambridge, Mass., 1947.
Jones, Cranston/*Architecture Today & Tomorrow,*
    McGraw-Hill Book Co., Inc., New York, 1961.
Mumford, Lewis/*Roots of Contemporary American Architecture,*
    Reinhold Publishing Corporation, New York, 1952,
    Grove Press Inc., New York, 1959.
Scully, Vincent, Jr./*Modern Architecture,*
    George Braziller, Inc., New York, 1961.
Szarkowski, John/*The Idea of Louis Sullivan,*
    University of Minnesota Press, Minneapolis, 1956.

•

Carter, Peter/"Mies van der Rohe,"
    Architectural Design, March, 1961.
Carter, Peter/"Mies,"
    20th Century Magazine, Spring, 1964.
Johnson, Philip/*Mies van der Rohe,* 2d ed.,
    Museum of Modern Art, New York, 1953.
Kuh, Katharine/"Mies van der Rohe: Modern Classicist,"
    Saturday Review, January 23, 1965.
Mies van der Rohe/*An Address to the American Institute of Architects on the
    Occasion of Receiving Its Gold Medal,* April 1, 1960.
Persicz, Alexandre, and Valeix, Darielle/"L'Oeuvre de Mies van der Rohe,"
    Editions de L'Architecture d'Aujourd'hui, Paris, France, 1958.

•

Goldberg, Bertrand/*The City Within A City,*
    An Address to the Design Conference at Aspen, Colorado
    on "Environment," June 28, 1962.

•

Scully, Vincent, Jr./*Frank Lloyd Wright,*
    George Braziller, Inc., New York, 1960.
Wright, Frank Lloyd/*Writings and Buildings,*
    Meridian Books, Inc., New York, 1960.

•

"The Architecture of Bruce Goff," introduced by Ben Allan Park,
    Architectural Design, May, 1957.

•

Blake, Peter/"The Fantastic World of Paolo Soleri,"
    Architectural Forum, February and March, 1961.
Soleri, Paolo/*Tentative Plan for the Cosanti Foundation,* 1963.

•

McCoy, Esther/*Five California Architects,*
    Reinhold Publishing Corporation, New York, 1960.
Temko, Allan/"Buildings in the Vernacular,"
    Saturday Review, January 23, 1965.

•

Temko, Allan/"Planned Chaos on the Piazza,"
    Architectural Forum, October, 1961.
DeMars, Vernon/*The Urban Environment,* Lecture from the People's
    Architects Series at Rice University, Semicentennial Publications.

•

Esherick, Joseph/"Theory and Practice,"
    Western Architect and Engineer, December, 1961.
"Form Is What Things Are,"
    Progressive Architecture, May, 1964.

•

Kump, Ernest J./*A New Architecture for Man,*
    The National Press, Palo Alto, California, 1957.

•

Temko, Allan/"Humanist Architecture of John Carl Warnecke,"
    Architectural Forum, December, 1960.

•

McCoy, Esther/*Modern California Houses,*
    Reinhold Publishing Corporation, New York, 1962.

•

McCoy, Esther/*Richard Neutra,*
    George Braziller, Inc., New York, 1960.

•

Jones, A. Quincy, and Emmons, Frederick E./*Builders' Homes For Better
    Living,* Reinhold Publishing Corporation, New York, 1957.

Atcheson, Richard/"Edward D. Stone: Maker of Monuments,"
     Show, March, 1964.
"Directions in Modern Architecture, A Conversation with Edward D. Stone,"
     Gentlemen's Quarterly, April, 1959.
Stone, Edward Durell/*The Evolution of an Architect*,
     Horizon Press, New York, 1962.
Stone, Edward D./"What Architecture Should Be,"
     Show, March, 1964.

•

Yamasaki, Minoru/*A Humanist Architecture for America and Its Relation to
     the Traditional Architecture of Japan*, Marley Lecture,
     Royal Institute of British Architects, London, November, 1960.

•

Fitch, James Marston/"Three Levers of Walter Gropius,"
     Architectural Forum, May, 1960.
Giedion, Sigfried/*Walter Gropius, Work and Teamwork*,
     Reinhold Publishing Corporation, New York, 1954.
Gropius, Walter/"Architect in Society," *Lecture at Columbia University*,
     New York City, Spring program, 1961.
Gropius, Walter/"Continuity and Change in Modern Architecture,"
     Connection, Visual Arts at Harvard, May, 1964.
Gropius, Walter/*Scope of Total Architecture*,
     Collier Books, New York, 1962.
"Walter Gropius et Son Ecole,"
     L'Architecture d'aujourd'hui, February, 1950.

•

Belluschi, Pietro/*Architecture as an Art of Our Time*,
     Lecture from the People's Architects Series at Rice University,
     Semicentennial Publications
Belluschi, Pietro/"The Meaning of Regionalism in Architecture,"
     Architectural Record, December, 1955.

•

Sert, José Luis/*Changing Views on the Urban Environment*,
     The Annual Discourse at the Royal Institute of British Architects,
     London, February, 1963.
Sert, José Luis/*The Urban Crisis*,
     A Lecture to the Harvard Club of New York, May, 1965.

•

Breuer, Marcel/*Marcel Breuer Buildings and Projects 1921-1961*,
     Thames & Hudson, London, 1962.

•

Jacobus, John M. Jr./*Philip Johnson*,
     George Braziller, Inc., New York, 1962.
Johnson, Philip/*Commencement Address*,
     Pratt Institute, New York, 1963.

•

Rudolph, Paul/Paper Delivered at the International Design Conference,
     Aspen, Colorado, 1964.
Rudolph, Paul/"The Six Determinants of Architectural Form,"
     Architectural Record, October, 1956.

•

Temko, Allan/*Eero Saarinen*,
     George Braziller, Inc., New York, 1962.

•

Architecture of Skidmore Owings & Merrill, 1950-1962,
     Introduced by Henry-Russell Hitchcock, Frederick A. Praeger, Inc.,
     New York, 1963.

•

Banham, Reyner/"The Dymaxicrat,"
     Arts Magazine, October, 1963.
"Centre of Gravity for UIA 1965,"
     Architectural Design, February, 1964.
Fuller, R. Buckminster/The Annual Discourse at the Royal Institute of
     British Architects, London, June, 1958.
Fuller, R. Buckminster/"Universal Requirements Check List,"
     Architectural Design, March, 1960.
McHale, John/*R. Buckminster Fuller*,
     George Braziller, Inc., New York, 1962.
Kahn, Louis I./"Form and Design,"
     Architectural Design, April, 1961.
Scully, Vincent Jr./*Louis I. Kahn*,
     George Braziller, Inc., New York, 1962.
Wurman, Richard and Feldman, Eugene/*The Notebooks and Drawings of
     Louis I. Kahn*, The Falcon Press, Philadelphia, 1962.

•

In addition to the specific books and magazine articles listed here, the author
is indebted to *Architectural Forum*, *Architectural Record* and *Progressive
Architecture* as a general source of reference.

GENERAL INDEX

PHOTO CREDITS

THE DEVELOPMENT OF MODERN ARCHITECTURE
page 19 / The Crystal Palace
   courtesy of the Royal Institute of British Architects
page 19 / Marshall Field Store
   photo by Chicago Architectural Photographing Co.
   courtesy of the Museum of Modern Art, New York
page 20 / Auditorium Building
   courtesy of the Museum of Modern Art, New York
page 21 / Home Insurance Building
   courtesy of the Museum of Modern Art, New York
page 22 / Wainwright Building
   courtesy of the Museum of Modern Art, New York
page 23 / Reliance Building
   Chicago Architectural Photographing Co.
page 23 / Guaranty Building
   courtesy of the Museum of Modern Art, New York
page 25 / Carson, Pirie Scott
   photo by Chicago Architectural Photographing Co.
   courtesy of the Museum of Modern Art, New York

LUDWIG MIES VAN DER ROHE
page 26 / Crown Hall / Balthazar Korab
page 28 / brick country house
   courtesy of the Museum of Modern Art, New York
page 28 / glass skyscraper
   courtesy of the Museum of Modern Art, New York
page 29 / glass and concrete office building / Williams and Meyer
page 29 / apartment house
   courtesy of the Museum of Modern Art, New York
page 30 / Barcelona Pavilion / plan—Williams and Meyer
   exterior—courtesy of the Museum of Modern Art, New York
   interior—courtesy of the Museum of Modern Art, New York
page 30 / group of court houses
   courtesy of the Museum of Modern Art, New York
page 31 / Tugendhat House
   courtesy of the Museum of Modern Art, New York
page 31 / Illinois Institute of Technology
   courtesy of the Museum of Modern Art, New York
page 31 / Crown Hall / exterior—Balthazar Korab
   plan—courtesy of the Museum of Modern Art, New York
page 32 / Farnsworth House / exterior—George H. Steuer
   plan—courtesy of the Museum of Modern Art, New York
page 34 / Lake Shore Drive / Hedrich-Blessing
page 34 / Convention Hall
   courtesy of the Museum of Modern Art, New York
page 35 / Seagram Building / Jane Doggett and Malcolm Smith
page 36 / Gallery of the Twentieth Century / Hedrich-Blessing

JACQUES BROWNSON
page 37 / Geneva House / Richard Nickel
page 38 / Continental Insurance Co.
   detail—Richard Nickel / overall view—Hedrich-Blessing
page 39 / Chicago Civic Center
   top—Richard Nickel / bottom—Hedrich-Blessing
page 40 / Chicago Civic Center / Hedrich-Blessing

HARRY WEESE
page 41 / Eugenie Lane Apartments / Balthazar Korab
page 42 / Walton Apartments / exterior view—Hedrich-Blessing
page 44 / Eugenie Lane Apartments / Hedrich-Blessing
page 44 / La Salle redevelopment / sketch by H. Weese
page 45 / Milwaukee Center / interior—sketch by H. Weese
page 46 / Arena Stage / exterior—Balthazar Korab
   interior—Balthazar Korab / plan—Hedrich-Blessing
page 47 / Elvehjem Art Center / sketches by H. Weese

BERTRAND GOLDBERG
page 48 / Marina City / Hedrich-Blessing
page 51 / Astor Tower / Orlando R. Cabanban
page 53 / Public Housing / photo of model—Mart Studios
page 54 / Project Office Building / Hedrich-Blessing

RALPH RAPSON
page 55 / Tyrone Guthrie Theater
   interior—Bob Jacobson / exterior—Eric Southerland
page 56 / U.S. Staff Apartments / Paul Cade
page 57 / Chateau Dining Club / Ralph Rapson
page 57 / Pillsbury House
   interior—Ralph Rapson / exterior—K. M. Lockhart
page 58 / State Capitol Credit Union
   exterior—K. M. Lockhart / interior—Warren Reynolds

FRANK LLOYD WRIGHT
page 60 / Kaufmann House / Hedrich-Blessing
page 61 / Taliesin West / Paul Heyer
page 61 / Taliesin West / Paul Heyer
page 62 / Larkin Building
   courtesy of the Museum of Modern Art, New York
page 63 / Unity Church
   photo by George Barrows
   courtesy of the Museum of Modern Art, New York
page 63 / Robie House
   courtesy of the Museum of Modern Art, New York
page 64 / Taliesin East
   courtesy of the Museum of Modern Art, New York
page 64 / Midway Gardens
   courtesy of the Museum of Modern Art, New York
page 64 / Imperial Hotel
   courtesy of the Museum of Modern Art, New York
page 64 / Millard House
   courtesy of the Museum of Modern Art, New York
page 65 / St. Marks Tower
   courtesy of the Museum of Modern Art, New York
page 65 / Taliesin West
   courtesy of the Museum of Modern Art, New York
page 65 / Johnson Wax Building / courtesy Johnson Wax
page 66 / Guggenheim Museum
   courtesy Solomon R. Guggenheim Museum

BRUCE GOFF
page 67 / Triaero House
   courtesy *Courier-Journal and Louisville Times*
page 67 / Crystal Chapel / Ulric Meisel
page 68 / Ford House / exterior—Wayne Williams
page 69 / Bavinger House / Gene Bavinger
page 70 / Bachelor's House / Joe D. Price
page 71 / Phi Kappa Tau / drawing by Richard Britz

HERBERT GREENE
page 72 / Greene House / Julius Shulman
page 74 / Greene House / Julius Shulman
page 75 / Joyce House / Julius Shulman
page 76 / Anne Frank / montage by H. Greene
page 76 / Cunningham House / Julius Shulman
page 77 / Cunningham House / Julius Shulman

PAOLO SOLERI
page 78 / Cosanti Foundation / Edward Beaty
page 80 / Earth House / Stuart Weiner
page 80 / Ceramics Workshop / Dan Pavillard
page 81 / Cantilever bridge / Edward Beaty
page 81 / Tubular bridge / Edward Beaty
page 81 / Dam model / Edward Beaty
page 82 / Mesa City / drawing by P. Soleri
page 82 / Higher learning center / Stuart Weiner
page 83 / Mesa City / Stuart Weiner

THE GROWTH OF MODERN ARCHITECTURE IN CALIFORNIA
page 85 / Christian Science Church
   photo by Mock
   courtesy of the Museum of Modern Art, New York
page 85 / Gamble House / Wayne Andrews
page 86 / Scripps House
   courtesy of the Museum of Modern Art, New York
page 87 / Lovell House
   courtesy of the Museum of Modern Art, New York
page 87 / Rodakiewicz House
   photo by Woodcock
   courtesy of the Museum of Modern Art, New York

WILLIAM WILSON WURSTER
page 89 / Bernardi House / Ernest Braun
page 90 / Behavioral Sciences / Morley Baer
page 90 / Yerba Buena Club / Roger Sturtevant
page 91 / Pope House / Roger Sturtevant
page 91 / Coleman House / Roger Sturtevant
page 92 / First Unitarian Church / Roger Sturtevant
page 93 / Golden Gateway / photo of model—Gerald Ratto
   overall view—Roger Sturtevant

VERNON DeMARS
page 94 / DeMars House / Roy Flamm
page 96 / Farm Workers' Housing / Dorothea Lange
page 96 / Eastgate Apartments / Ezra Stoller
page 97 / Easter Hill Village / Roger Sturtevant